THE BIG EMPTY

The Modern American West
Richard W. Etulain and David M. Wrobel, Editors

Carl Abbott
The Metropolitan Frontier: Cities in the Modern American West

Richard W. Etulain
Re-imagining the Modern American West:
A Century of Fiction, History, and Art

Gerald D. Nash
The Federal Landscape: An Economic History
of the Twentieth-Century West

Ferenc Morton Szasz
Religion in the Modern American West

Oscar J. Martínez
Mexican-Origin People in the United States: A Topical History

Duane A. Smith
Rocky Mountain Heartland: Colorado, Montana, and Wyoming
in the Twentieth Century

William G. Robbins and Katrine Barber
Nature's Northwest: The North Pacific Slope in the Twentieth Century

R. Douglas Hurt
The Big Empty: The Great Plains in the Twentieth Century

The Big Empty

The Great Plains
in the Twentieth Century

R. Douglas Hurt

The University of Arizona Press   Tucson

The University of Arizona Press
© 2011 The Arizona Board of Regents
All rights reserved

www.uapress.arizona.edu

Library of Congress Cataloging-in-Publication Data
Hurt, R. Douglas.
 The Big Empty : the Great Plains in the twentieth century / R. Douglas Hurt.
  p. cm — (The modern American West)
 Includes bibliographical references and index.
 ISBN 978-0-8165-2970-4 (hard cover : alk. paper) —
 ISBN 978-0-8165-2972-8 (pbk. : alk. paper)
 1. Great Plains—Politics and government—20th century. 2. Great Plains—
Social conditions—20th century. 3. Social change—Great Plains—History—
20th century. 4. Ethnicity—Great Plains—History—20th century. 5. Cul-
tural pluralism—Great Plains—History—20th century. 6. Agriculture—Great
Plains—History—20th century. 7. Great Plains—Economic conditions—20th
century. 8. Great Plains—Environmental conditions. I. Title.
F595.H94 2011
978'.033—dc22   2011010715

For
Mary Ellen, Adlai, and Austin

Contents

List of Illustrations   ix

Preface   xi

1 The Age of Optimism   1

2 The Ethnic and Racial Divide   32

3 The Age of Uncertainty   64

4 The Anxious Years   91

5 The Age of Certainty   125

6 The Perils of Agriculture   166

7 The Inevitability of Change   195

8 The Politics of Race and Agriculture   216

   Epilogue   242

   Notes   261

   Selected Bibliography   293

   Illustration Credits   307

   Index   309

Illustrations

The Great Plains   xvi

Published versions of the extent of the Great Plains   xvii

Tar-paper house and homesteaders   5

Election Day in Meadow, South Dakota   15

Mexican railroad workers   36

Ku Klux Klan rally   54

Arthur C. Townley speaking to a crowd   75

Farm foreclosure auction   83

Dust Bowl map   92

Black blizzard   95

Work relief street project   98

Federally funded sewing center   99

Oklahoma oil held   101

The Shelterbelt Zone   107

Bomber assembly line   129

Lunch counter sit-in demonstration   141

Extent of Ogallala Aquifer   189

Center-pivot irrigation   190

Coal mining   210

Map of Republican votes in presidential elections   238

Mount Rushmore nearing completion   247

Preface

This is a small book about a big country. It is about the environmental, social, economic, and political history of a region that is amorphous. Almost everyone who knows anything about the Great Plains can tell you when they see it, something akin to art being in the eye of the beholder. Natives will tell you that visitors are "in" or "on" the Great Plains but that *they* are "of" it. This is no fine point of semantics or rhetoric but a deeply held cultural belief that often transcends into the negative "They don't understand us." All definitions of the Great Plains, of course, are arbitrary, and one is usually as good as another. Some find it beginning on the east at the ninety-eighth or hundredth meridian. Step across the line and you are there. Others complicate matters by defining the eastern boundary using annual precipitation lines, soil composition, or the shading of the grasses from bluestems to buffalo, that is, from tall- to short-grass country. In 1936, the Great Plains Committee used all of these definitions when it surveyed the drought-laden, dust-blown region in an attempt to figure out what should be done about it. Ultimately, the committee identified 399 counties in the region to give some system and order to its study and recommendations for improvement. In time, other scholars followed, particularly sociologists, with their own tally of sample counties that they used to gain intellectual control over approximately fifteen hundred miles from Canada to the Gulf of Mexico and covering between two hundred and nearly a thousand miles from east to west, depending on the varying geographical definitions and how you count.[1]

My definition for the Great Plains is as arbitrary as others — perhaps even more so, because I add the complexity of politics. Many of the larger towns and cities, including state capitals, lie outside some Great Plains boundaries and definitions of the region, but politics and policies made in Oklahoma City, Topeka, Lincoln, Pierre, and Bismarck and events in Denver, Tulsa, Dallas–Fort Worth, Cheyenne, and Billings, among other cities and towns, have made a difference in the historical canvas of the Great Plains during the twentieth century. Given that, my definition of the Great Plains for this study includes the ten Great Plains states with the eastern border following the political boundary of North and South Dakota, Nebraska, Kansas, and Oklahoma before angling downward to Dallas and San Antonio, then stretching northward through Roswell, New Mexico, to Albuquerque and then along the foothills of the Rocky Mountains through Denver, Colorado, Cheyenne, Wyoming, and Billings and Great Falls, Montana. The southern and westward boundaries are imprecise, too, but these are the general parameters for my study.

Most scholars and travelers know when they get to the Great Plains. In this sense, the Great Plains depends on perception, that is, it is a state of mind, a mental landscape. It is the horizontal yellow of historian Dan Flores; it is the grasslands of South Dakota where writer and poet Linda Hasselstrom notes that ranchers "stick" because they know how to do it, and they do it very well; it is a land where culture makes a difference, as geographer James Shortridge has observed, where people identify themselves as coming from "western Kansas," the "Sand Hills," and the "panhandle" or the "West River" or "Big Sky" country, because those terms mean something to them. It is their sense of place.

The Great Plains also is a land where most of the cities skirt the fringe of the region and distance betrays time. It is a region of isolated inland communities so far removed from the East and West Coasts that people had to learn to think for themselves, often to fend off outside economic and political dictates and intrusions—a land of self-reliant and wary people. It is a land where insiders and outsiders argue about the nature of the agricultural economy, with some charging that capitalists ruined the country and others contending that the region needs more of them. It is a region of hard-nosed religion where people fear God and pray for rain but fear running out of water more than the Almighty. It is a region where windmills spinning in the hot south wind remain symbols of enduring hope against grim odds.[2]

More scholars have tried to save the Great Plains, usually from itself, than any other region, except the South. Their solutions for improvement have ranged from the sensible though difficult, even impossible, to the uninformed and impracticable, even impossible, though some would argue intellectually suggestible. In sorting out the contested history of the Great Plains during the twentieth century, I have tried to synthesize the scholarly literature and have added my own primary research to give narrative form to the region's history.

The Great Plains remained a vast, low-populated, seemingly vacant land during the twentieth century. Yet it was as much a land of promise and opportunity for some at the end of the century as it was for others when the century began. But not for all. The Great Plains is not only a region with a harsh climate but also a land with a hard social, economic, and political environment. It is a diverse geographical region that includes at least three mountain ranges: the Wichitas in Oklahoma, the Black Hills in South Dakota, and the Turtle Mountains in North Dakota. It is a region where race colors everything in red, white, and black. It is a region where cynics say that water runs uphill—toward money, often the meatpackers.

At the turn of the twentieth century, the Great Plains was a region of promise and hope as well as disappointment and despair. It remained so when the century ended. Outsiders often wondered why anyone lived there at all and contended that people with talent came from the Great Plains, they did not go there. Transferees hoped for the best, and they and many natives left as soon as possible. With few exceptions, however, the population of the region increased during the twentieth century, although it shifted considerably from farm to town, that is, from rural to urban. At the end of the twentieth century, most residents lived in the towns and cities. In this context, the Great Plains is an urban region.

To trace even a rudimentary history of this vast, sprawling land over the course of the twentieth century, I have provided a loose chronological story. The chapters, however, do not begin and close at precise decennial marks or even with the closure of major events, although that is sometimes the case. Life is not bound by the arbitrary calculations of time. One thing blends into another across time and space. The participants might change, but the issues of the day frequently remain. As a result, I chose to emphasize the environment, race, politics, and agriculture of the Great Plains, although I also touch on other matters such as economic change, ethnicity, and daily life. I deal with these subjects cross-sectionally, that is, at the same time over roughly twenty- to forty-year periods. My goal in writing this book has been to present sufficient detail to permit meaningful generalizations for the region, knowing full well that diversity (that is, cultural and physical heterogeneity, not homogeneity) gives form and substance to the history of the Great Plains.

My intent is to show how the people of the Great Plains attempted to control the environment during the early twentieth century but later settled for just trying to conserve and preserve it — that is, sustain it — which proved difficult enough. They knew by the late twentieth century, as they had not known a century earlier, that the environment set the parameters for their lives, and they used it based on cultural influences and practices as well as technological and scientific change. In this essentially white region, racism against African Americans, Hispanics, and Indians remained endemic and easy to practice or ignore. Whereas politicians once thought of the common good, interest groups came to control much of the political agenda, which they designed to meet the needs of their members, that is, individuals. It is a region where the political landscape has seen Oklahoma socialists championing the right of private landownership, individualistic North Dakotans demanding state ownership of grain elevators and banks, and the Kansas State Board of Education giving the stamp of scientific legitimacy to the teaching of creationism in the public schools. It is a region where voters in general tended toward fiscal conservatism and social responsibility. Democrats could be conservatives in the twentieth-century Great Plains and Republicans liberals on some social issues. Agriculture still shaped much of the economy of the region with its multiplier effect, but it had a form far different at the end than at the beginning of the twentieth century. Moreover, the agricultural industry along with the extractive industries of oil, natural gas, and coal depend on outside markets and prices that farmers, miners, and others cannot control. Outside capital financed manufacturing and industry. In many ways, the economy of the Great Plains during the twentieth century remained at least superficially colonial. Other substantive matters could be included in this history, but the parameters of the book required hard choices, and these are mine. I hope that anyone wanting an overview of the Great Plains in the twentieth century will find this book a useful place to begin.

Knowing something about the history of the Great Plains in the twentieth century, I sense that it remains a region still in the process of becoming after a tumultuous century of change for both good and ill. If so, then what Willa Cather said of Nebraska during the early twentieth century can be applied to the Great Plains at the turn of the twenty-first millennium. It was, she wrote, "not a country at all, but the material out of which countries are made."[3]

Acknowledgments

The research for this book was supported by a Plains Humanities Alliance Fellowship from the University of Nebraska and a travel grant from the American Heritage Center at the University of Wyoming. A Big XII Faculty Fellowship further aided my research, as did support from Purdue University. The staff and collections at the Carl Albert Center and the Western History Collections at the University of Oklahoma, the Southwest Collection at Texas Tech University, the Kansas State Historical Society, and the Nebraska State Historical Society as well as the libraries at the University of Nebraska and Purdue University made this study possible. At Purdue University, Larry Mykytiuk, history and microtext librarian, and Bert Chapman, government information and political science librarian, provided essential expertise. The staff in the Interlibrary Loan Office as always proved efficient and professional. Terrance D. Bolden at the University of Nebraska Press aided with the maps. Linda Hein at the Nebraska State Historical Society, James Kroll at the Denver Public Library, Matthew Reitzel at the South Dakota Historical Society, Sharon A. Silengo at the State Historical Society of North Dakota, Kristie Stanley at the Kansas State Historical Society, Terry Zinn at the Oklahoma Historical Society, and Jeff Laudin at Valmont Industries provided invaluable assistance for the selection of the photographs. I am grateful for their generous support.

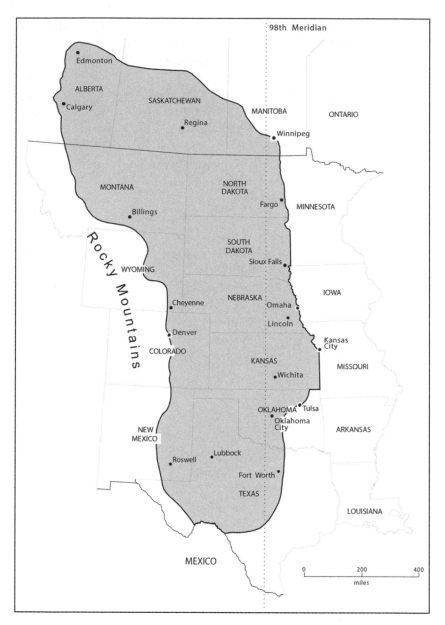

The boundaries of the Great Plains are imprecise and depend on individual and disciplinary definitions. This map shows a useable and reliable regional location.

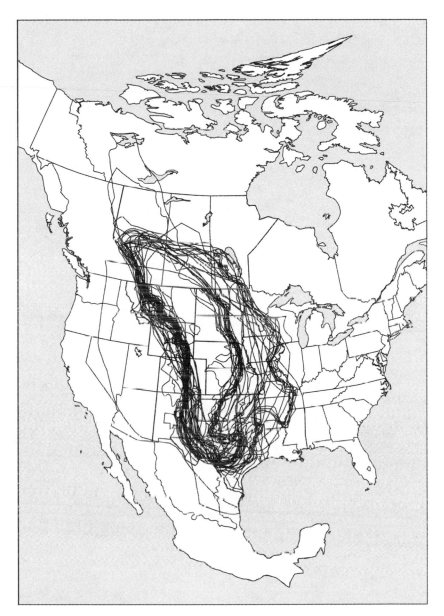

At least fifty versions of the Great Plains regional boundary have been published. This map shows the complexity and variety of the scholarly definitions of the region.

THE BIG EMPTY

CHAPTER ONE

The Age of Optimism

January 1, 1900, dawned with a customary chill that seemed ordinary across the length and breadth of the Great Plains. Few people cared whether the new year marked the last of the nineteenth century or the beginning of a new millennium, but they anticipated the promise of a better life firmly linked to the land, as they had for nearly a half century. Much had changed since settlers occupied the eastern fringes of the Great Plains following the Civil War. The Indians had been confined to reservations, railroads crossed the region, and towns were scattered about the countryside. In 1896, the Populists had blown themselves out in a storm of rhetoric, and all that remained of the party were a few cranks, whom most people ignored. Yet grievances still festered among rural men and women against railroads, corporations, and banks that they believed denied them fair and equitable treatment.

One aspect of the past remained — the pull of free land for homesteading and with it the last opportunity to participate in the great drama of western expansion. As in the past, the land proved a siren song that many could not resist, and they followed it by the thousands. Between 1900 and World War I, more than 100,000 people settled west of the Missouri River in South Dakota, while some 250,000 men and women claimed land in North Dakota between 1898 and 1915. As late as 1910, two-thirds of North Dakota's population had been born outside the state. In northeastern Colorado, nearly 75 percent of the settlers filed claims after 1900, and homesteading did not peak until 1910. They came to conquer the land, change the environment to meet their needs, and establish flourishing farms and towns.[1]

1

But these homesteaders were different. They often came by train, not wagons, and communicated by telegraph and sometimes telephone with family and friends in the towns and cities left behind. Many soon hired custom plowmen with powerful steam-traction engines to break the native sod instead of using horses and sulky or walking plows. Yet, like their predecessors, they knew little about the harsh environment. If they had heard that extreme heat and cold, little precipitation, a propensity for drought, and nearly incessant winds, which blew from the south during the summer and the north during the winter, characterized the Great Plains, they ignored these environmental realities, which often became limitations. Those who came to the Great Plains in the early twentieth century and stayed (like those who came before them) became a "wait-and-see" and a "next-year" people as well as a defensive people with a keen eye for outsiders who might not understand but would instead denigrate their stoicism, self-denial, and sense of place, that is, their lives in the Great Plains.

In the West River Country of South Dakota, the federal government opened unallotted Indian lands to homesteaders through a lottery process designed to prevent the chaos and fraud of the land rushes in Oklahoma during the late nineteenth century. Applicants began registering for the land lottery on July 5, 1904. Soon thereafter, federal officials supervised a drawing for the names of the lucky homestead winners. More than 106,000 men and women registered for claims, but these lands were not free, as had originally been provided by the Homestead Act of 1862. Land prices ranged from $4 to $2.50 per acre depending on the quality of the land and the time of settlement. Homesteaders could still "commute," that is, pay for their reservation lands and gain title after fourteen months of residency, or pay by installments.[2]

The railroads brought these settlers far closer to their new lands than the homesteaders who had sought farms with map in hand a generation earlier. In 1905, the Chicago and North Western and the Chicago, Milwaukee, and St. Paul raced to extend their lines from Pierre to Rapid City to transport people into the region and agricultural commodities out, while the Northern Pacific brought homesteaders to St. Paul and Minneapolis, where they bought wagons and supplies and headed west to locate their claims in North Dakota. Many of these men and women showed more exuberance than those who had homesteaded in the late nineteenth century. Some observers believed it the equivalent of greed. In 1907, for example, Edith Kohl, a homesteader in Lyman County, South Dakota, reflected on the opening of the Lower Brulé Reservation: "We who had grown accustomed to the sight of the empty prairies, to whom the arrival of the stage from

Pierre was an event, were overwhelmed by the confusion, the avalanche of people, shouting, pushing, asking questions, moving steadily across the trackless plains toward the reservation." A year later, a half dozen trains arrived in Pierre daily, bringing as many as eight hundred passengers by nightfall who sought homesteads on the Rosebud Reservation. Most would be disappointed, but for those who acquired land in an area that many considered the last frontier, optimism prevailed. One eastern journalist caught the spirit of the time when he wrote that "the best that was our fathers . . . is with us yet."[3]

To the south, by 1903, settlers had claimed all the homestead land in Oklahoma's Cherokee Outlet, pushing the ranchers who used it to the open range country in New Mexico, by fencing farmlands to keep cattle from wandering across newly planted fields. Many of these Oklahoma homesteaders had relocated from Kansas and other midwestern states, but a considerable number of German Russians also arrived. Soon towns, schools, and churches rose from the plains as the population grew, and communities went about the business of governance, including approving bond levies for local improvements. Most "strippers" considered their achievements progress that boded well for a new century. They also accepted the seizure of Indian lands as their prerogative and resented anyone who was not Caucasian in their communities.[4]

The Santa Fe railroad brought settlers to the Texas Panhandle. Santa Fe officials ran special immigrant trains at reduced rates and promised quick wealth from "primeval soils." By 1910, the population of the Texas Panhandle had increased 400 percent, from 21,284 in 1900 to 89,285 people. Homesteaders also took up public lands in eastern New Mexico. Hispanic and Indian peoples had used those lands for grazing. Without adequate water for irrigation or enough land to support profitable cattle raising, most of these homesteaders remained only until they "proved up," that is, met the requirements for residency and improvements to gain title. Then they sold out to nearby livestock raisers. One woman rancher recalled, "Because of our friendly attitude, the homesteaders always offered their property to us first." Other New Mexico ranchers, like those across the Great Plains, disliked the homesteaders for denying them the free use of the public domain.[5]

By the turn of the twentieth century, Amarillo had come to serve as a railroad and cattle shipping center for the Texas Panhandle. Large ranches surrounded the town of 1,442 people, but soon settlers arrived by the score, stepped down from the train, and went about the business of acquiring land. Under the Plemons Four Section Act, which the Texas legislature approved in 1895, a settler could claim 2,560 acres. This legislation permitted an individual to purchase one section (640 acres) of agricultural land for two dollars per acre and three sections of grazing land for one dollar per acre, with only eighty dollars down and four years to pay the remaining obligation. Buyers had to live on the land for three years and make improvements, such as building a house and digging a well. The farmer-stockman rather than the ranchers benefited. Many of these settlers migrated from other parts of Texas and the Midwest.[6]

By 1910, the number of farms in the Texas Panhandle had nearly doubled and the population quadrupled since the turn of the century. West Texas settlers primarily raised cattle, but they broke native sod for oats and for grain sorghum to feed livestock. Some farmers planted winter wheat, and in 1912, the Santa Fe railroad shipped 2.8 million bushels from the Texas Panhandle. Some ranchers purchased 100,000 to 250,000 acres from the XIT Ranch to fend off homesteaders and remain in business with enough land to graze cattle. Other large-scale ranchers began leasing land to the newcomers because it proved more profitable than raising cattle. These settlers bought land, supplies, and equipment, stayed in hotels, and ate at local restaurants. Farm equipment dealers, particularly those who sold windmills, made a fortune. Panhandle land that brought two dollars per acre in 1900 sold for thirty dollars per acre in 1912. Land companies and real estate offices announced with great anticipation, "People are coming."[7]

As services increased for farmer-stockmen, Amarillo businesses grew and residents built more schools and churches on town lots, all within hearing distance of the cattle in the stockyards awaiting shipment to Fort Worth. Literary, library, and women's suffrage clubs softened Amarillo's cow-town roughness. Women, primarily middle-aged, white, upper-class Protestants, took an active role in civic affairs (similar to that of women in the towns and cities across the Great Plains), and they provided leadership and support for many Progressive Era reforms.[8]

Like their predecessors, many of these twentieth-century homesteaders built sod houses, if the soil and grasses permitted that construction, but the railroads brought cheap lumber to the small towns that soon lined the tracks, and settlers often preferred to erect a ten- by twelve-foot residence (as required by the government) from wood and cover the inside and outside with tar paper, thereby earning the sobriquet "tar-paper homesteaders." When one woman first gazed on her tar-paper shack, which broke the desolate plains landscape, she recalled, "This was not the West as I had dreamed of it." Another twenty-three-year-old woman, while not unhappy that her husband had taken her to a homestead in South Dakota, wrote that she felt "900 miles from nowhere."[9]

The homesteaders in the northern Great Plains often built wooden shacks, which they lined inside and out with tar paper to help keep out the wind, rain, and snow. By the early twentieth century, homesteaders had gained access to lumber and tar paper via nearby towns and railroads, and they avoided building the sod houses that had been customary of the late-nineteenth-century homesteaders. In 1908, this tar-paper house was located in Meade County, South Dakota. The glass windows indicate a modest level of affluence.

Homesteading in the Great Plains could be forlorn and lonely, at least temporarily. Often settlers traveled miles and hours to attend dinners, parties, and dances. But in 1905, a girl homesteading with her family in North Dakota observed, "The meadowlarks sing beautifully and all together it is fine and dandy." Even so, many of these twentieth-century settlers had acquired homesteads for speculative purposes rather than to make a permanent home in the Great Plains, as had been the case with the previous generation. Moreover, homesteading offered an irresistible opportunity for thousands of women. After 1900, women constituted approximately 20 percent of the homesteaders in North Dakota, where 40 percent of these women lived on their claim for the required five years to "prove up" and receive title to their lands. In April 1909, a woman homesteader, who taught school and hired a man to farm the land, wrote that she would soon "make proof" at the land office in Hugo, where she had an appointment with the receiver. She admitted dealing with "futures" in her mind, hoping for forty bushels of wheat per acre. Without rain, she anticipated twenty bushels and at least fifty cents per bushel. Many women used their homesteads as investments and moved on, while others stayed and struggled to conquer the land. Some regretted their role in changing the environment. One woman recalled, "That first summer there I grew to love the prairie in its natural wild, untamed state and I felt a bit sad now it would be cut up, plowed up, used and trampled over by the feet of men, many caring only for the money it would bring."[10]

Yet networks of family, friends, and neighbors as well as jobs as teachers, nurses, and seamstresses gave women homesteaders contact with the "outside" world. At the same time, they practiced gendered work patterns. Although most managed their own lands, they generally conducted housework while men labored in the fields. Still, ethnicity, circumstance, and choice determined whether women worked outside the home and farmyard. The German Russians, for example, expected women to labor in the fields as well as the household. Anglo-American and Scandinavian women conducted less fieldwork, but necessity and choice also determined whether they worked in the fields. For women homesteaders, necessity knew no law.[11]

Women homesteaders also proved up their claims and received title to their lands as often as men. In Sheridan County, North Dakota, for example, 72 percent of the male and 76 percent of the female homesteaders gained title, while in McIntosh County the success rates were 71 percent and 68 percent, respectively. Similarly, in Colorado and Wyoming, women constituted approximately 12 percent and 18 percent of the homesteaders, respectively. Ultimately, 42 percent and in some areas 60 percent of these women gained title, compared to 37 percent of the men, but while women might have considered themselves isolated or exiled, they had homesteaded on their own free will. Some women (like men) failed or endured a loneliness compounded by the barren, nearly treeless plains, but no one had forced them to take a claim in the Great Plains. They had accepted the challenge of the land.[12]

Certainly, women homesteaders considered a quarter section (160 acres) of land nothing less than the promise of independence, freedom, and security. They homesteaded first for their own economic gain and second to enhance family land holdings. By so doing, they stood in sharp contrast to Utah women, who homesteaded exclusively for the benefit of their families. In North Dakota, many women homesteaders came from Europe or were descended from foreign-born parents. In Colorado, women homesteaders tended to be native-born whites. Many women homesteaders already lived in the Great Plains and did not considered homesteading an unusual challenge. Still, the Great Plains could be daunting, even for women who lived and worked in the region. In 1908, Ada Kelsy homesteaded near Alexander in McKenzie County, North Dakota. Her father staked the claim, and her sister agreed to stay and help. At Granville, they boarded the Great Northern Railway, which carried them to Williston, where they took a stage to Alexander, then traveled by wagon to their claim. An eight-foot by ten-foot clapboard shack and a pile of coal, left by their father, greeted them. Ada reflected, "For a moment we just sat there on the buckboard and quietly stared. I think even the horses wanted to go back."[13]

In the early twentieth century, most women homesteaders in the northern Great Plains were young and unmarried women who desired land in their own name, but older single women, many of whom had been widowed or divorced, also filed claims for 160 acres. In North Dakota, women between twenty-one and twenty-five years of age constituted 53 percent of the female homesteaders, women between the ages of twenty-six and thirty constituted 17 percent, and 13 percent ranged between the ages of thirty one and forty. Most of these women homesteaders were single (83 percent), but 15 percent were widows. All women homesteaders, like men, had to be twenty-one years of age and considered the head of a household. Most had Anglo-American or Scandinavian roots, 65 percent were American born, but only 8 percent were natives of North Dakota. Most women homesteaders in North Dakota came from Minnesota (35 percent), while Norway provided the largest number of foreign-born homesteaders (65 percent). By 1907, at least five African American women had filed claims.

In North Dakota, approximately 60 percent of women homesteaders remained on the land little longer than the six months required for commutation, that is, to qualify for purchase at full price. Approximately 32 percent consolidated their homesteads with their husbands after marriage. Other women rented their acres for income and took employment in nearby towns. Even so, many women homesteaders developed strong bonds with the land, would not sell it, and kept their land in the family. Addie Linsley staked her claim in North Dakota but returned to Minnesota discouraged by the isolation and endless work. Yet homesteading had changed her. "The prairies had got such a hold on me," she wrote, "that I had to come back when I had been gone but a year. While I was gone, I thought only of the prairie with its unadulterated sunshine, its endless green and wonderful sunsets." Sara Elizabeth Toipe of Providence, Rhode Island, reflected (as women settlers had observed a generation earlier), "I loved the rolling prairies and the waving grass reminded me of the ocean." Women who failed to prove up and gain title to their claims, later lost them to banks for unpaid mortgages, or sold their homesteads often regretted their loss. Homesteading became a life-defining experience for these women. One daughter recalled, "After Mother came west, she never rode side-saddle, she always rode astride."[14]

In Texas, few women homesteaders held land, because the state constitution of 1870 prohibited single women from filing a claim on the public lands of Texas. The Homestead Act did not apply to Texas, because the state retained its public lands upon admission to the Union. Moreover, by the turn of the twentieth century, Texas no longer had unclaimed land suitable for homesteading. Even so, the proportion of women homesteaders increased across the Great Plains during the early twentieth century. Homesteading strengthened the influence of women in their families, and it expanded their work roles in the home and community. Homesteading reinforced the ability of women to act independently as self-determining people who took responsibility for their lives. By homesteading, single women gained access to property, managed their land, controlled their resources, and decided how to spend their money.[15]

By 1910, settlers had claimed all but the most arid portions of the Great Plains. Where precipitation rates averaged less than eighteen inches annually, a new technique called "dry farming" became popular. During the first decade of the new century, Hardy Webster Campbell, a South Dakota farmer, promoted dry farming as a scientific way to ensure profitable agriculture in a risky environment. Dry farming essentially meant deep plowing in the fall and spring so the soil could absorb and retain moisture, a dust mulch of several inches prepared by harrowing the surface, and the use of a "subsoiler" (an implement with a series of iron wheels that packed the soil when pulled across a plowed field) to compact it and prevent percolation of moisture. Dry farming also involved summer fallowing, that is, the practice of leaving a field unplanted for a year between crops to regain soil moisture, but with periodic plowing to keep the weeds from absorbing the moisture and to create a spongelike residue that absorbed moisture. Dry farming also meant agriculture without the aid of irrigation. This agricultural technique seemingly provided a way to use science and technology to control the environment, and dry farming extended agriculture to areas where it could not be practiced successfully otherwise.[16]

Between 1907 and 1916, railroads, bankers, real estate agents, and merchants, among others, sponsored a host of dry-farming congresses across the Great Plains. These congresses proved popular among the farmers who attended to hear agricultural experts and politicians proclaim the possibilities of this new farming technique for the Great Plains. In 1909, a Montana resident who attended the congress meeting in Billings contended, "We believe the dry lands of Montana offer the homesteader the best returns, the best living and the easiest way to make a living of any place in the United States today." Railroad magnates quickly saw the importance of dry farming for settlement along their lines and, with it, trade. Soon railroad companies located demonstration farms along their main routes and publicized the benefits of dry farming as well as their lands, which they hoped to sell. During the first decade of the twentieth century, however, much of the Great Plains received above-normal precipitation, and settlers acquired land in the semiarid areas where success seemed guaranteed even without dry-farming techniques. When drought returned, however, dry-farming practices could not save crops, and many farmers necessarily returned their plowed fields to grass or abandoned their farms.[17]

By the early twentieth century, agricultural experts and Great Plains politicians had come to recognize that farmers could not earn an adequate living on 160-acre homesteads in this semiarid region without irrigation. As a result, in 1904, Moses P. Kinkaid, congressman from Nebraska, introduced a bill that became the Kinkaid Act. This legislation provided 640-acre homesteads in the western two-thirds of Nebraska for settlers who lived on the land for five years and made improvements. Cattlemen were the ones who primarily benefited from the Kinkaid Act, because the U.S. Congress intended them to use the legislation to establish small-scale grazing homesteads. Eventually, however, large-scale ranchers profited the most by purchasing these homesteads from the settlers who could not raise sufficient crops to support livestock raising. Most settlers who hoped to begin a mixed agricultural operation of crops and cattle on a 640-acre homestead in Nebraska usually failed because of inadequate acreage, insufficient capital, and the harsh environment.

In 1909, Congress attempted to meet the needs of settlers in the West by providing more land for homesteaders. Under the Enlarged Homestead Act, a settler could claim 320 acres of nonirrigable and nonmineral land by living on the land and cultivating it for five years; Congress, to prevent speculators from quickly purchasing the acreage of discouraged homesteaders, prohibited commutation. Many settlers claimed land in the Great Plains under the Enlarged Homestead Act, but 320-acre farms beyond the hundredth meridian proved too small for profitable — that is, commercial — agriculture. Moreover, the best lands had been claimed. As a result, many of these homesteads soon became consolidated under a single owner. By this time, the terms *drought* and *dry* had become so negative that South

Dakota officials declined to participate in the distribution of federal lands under the Enlarged Homestead Act until 1915, because they believed that settlers would consider South Dakota a dry state.[18]

Although a homesteading frontier remained, most of the Great Plains had been settled and farmed since the late nineteenth century. New varieties of wheat and corn resisted disease and harmonized with the climate from the relatively mild southern to the harsh northern plains. Agricultural experiment stations provided useful advice for farmers, and by 1906, steam tractors could plow thirty-five to forty acres per day, compared to farmers who used horses and a two-bottom moldboard plow to turn five to seven acres per day. Soon, however, gasoline tractors began replacing steam-powered engines for plowing, planting, and threshing on the large-scale farms in the wheat country. Specialized, single-crop agriculture required high capitalization to pay for machinery, labor, and land, the latter of which substantially increased in value as commodity prices climbed. Most farmers cut their small grains, particularly wheat, with binders, although large-scale operators used headers to save the labor costs of shocking. Even so, wheat farmers needed considerable labor at threshing time.

In the Great Plains, the largest wheat farms, known as "bonanza" farms, particularly in North Dakota, often totaled thousands of acres, employed hundreds of unskilled workers at harvest time, and made great investments in machinery. Most farms on the Great Plains were not large operations, however, but their owners needed workers, particularly for the wheat harvest. Although an independent contractor usually owned the steam engine and threshing machine, farmers hired unskilled local and itinerant workers to haul the sheaves by wagon to the threshing machine, pitch the bundles into the thresher, sack the grain, and haul it to a warehouse or grain elevator for storage, sale, and shipment. A moderate-size wheat farm might employ a dozen or more men at harvest time. In 1912, Kansas farmers employed 85 percent of their harvest labor from outside the state. In both Kansas and Oklahoma, more than 50 percent of the wheat harvest workforce moved from county to county following the ripening grain and farmers' needs for laborers. Nebraska and South Dakota farmers planted more corn, but they still seeded about half of their cropland to wheat, thereby also requiring harvest and threshing labor.

The itinerant workers who followed the harvest generally were unmarried, white men in their twenties and thirties. Plains residents called them "bindle stiffs" or "harvest stiffs." Most came from Kansas and Oklahoma and other states to the immediate east of the Great Plains, although Colorado and Montana farmers and miners often sought harvest work in Kansas, Nebraska, and North Dakota. Approximately two-thirds of the migrant farmworkers were unskilled and worked a variety of jobs in urban areas. Virtually all migrant workers saw the wheat harvest as an opportunity to increase their income in a relatively brief time, either weeks or months, depending on how far they traveled following the ripening grain. Newspaper advertisements, acquaintances, and their own sense of timing told them where and when to seek harvest jobs, which they usually reached by railroad. Yet long days, poor living conditions, and low pay (often as little as $1.50 per day), as well as the usual desire of local communities for these workers to depart as soon as the wheat harvest ended, caused many migrant farmworkers to consider the value of an agricultural union.[19]

They did not need to think long or hard about a solution for their grievances. By 1906, the Industrial Workers of the World (IWW), some of whose members (known as Wobblies) migrated from the Far West during harvest time, had begun organizing the union in the Great Plains, with three locals in Oklahoma Territory and two in Indian Territory. Farmers and other employees on the Great Plains feared the IWW, a labor organization born amidst the labor strife in the hard-rock mining camps and eastern factories, because the organization rejected the ballot box and espoused sabotage to achieve reform (which alienated the Socialist Party in Oklahoma). The IWW advocated direct action via strikes and free speech demonstrations, which usually brought violence instead of industrial unionism. By 1910, thousands of Wobblies were following the North Dakota wheat harvest, but their recruitment efforts through free speech, fights (Minot had one of the bloodiest in IWW history, and Aberdeen, South Dakota, also experienced a violent demonstration) with local authorities, and efforts to link with nonagricultural workers usually failed. In 1914, IWW organizers sought a wage increase from $2.50 to $3.00 for a ten-hour day, but they encountered hostility and threats of violence. Ultimately, they achieved little other than to frighten Great Plains residents whenever IWW activity occurred.[20]

While Wobblies advocated direct action in the form of work slowdowns or strikes, business leaders considered the IWW an organization that used violence and the destruction of property to achieve its goals. Upon statehood in 1907, seasonal and unskilled workers constituted nearly all of the labor force in Oklahoma, especially in agriculture, the construction industries, and the newly emerging petroleum industry. Among these workers, IWW organizers circulated as evangelists, advocating an organization and sense of class solidarity among the working class, including the large number of tenant farmers in the cotton area. IWW organizers, however, received violent treatment in the oil-boom towns, zinc- and lead-mining communities, and wheat areas. By World War I, IWW efforts to create an industrial union in the Great Plains had failed, but it had committed to recruiting "floaters," that is, migrant agricultural and oil-field workers, rather than settled workers. IWW radicalism portended more violence in the coming years.[21]

By the turn of the twentieth century, the People's Party and Democrats who followed Nebraska's William Jennings Bryan had faded from political power; only the sharp, vocal edge of a few party members, by then considered political cranks, remained. W. D. Vincent, long a traveler on the political left and within the agrarian reform movement in Kansas, hoped that the "better class of Republicans" (not those controlled by the trusts and corporations) would join the People's Party and work for political victory in 1904, particularly because the Democratic Party seemed poised to abandon its principles. He hoped that "honest Democrats" also would join the Populists in the organization of a new party. Few Great Plains Democrats and Republicans paid attention to his rationale, but they recognized his verbal bite as an increasingly common tool of Great Plains politicians.[22]

With the assassination of President William McKinley, however, many Great Plains Republicans favored the reform ideas of Theodore Roosevelt, particularly regarding government responsibility and service for the public good. Between 1900 and World War I, a Progressive movement swept the Great Plains. Progressive politicians emerged in the Republican and Democratic parties in response to public dissatisfaction with the increasing disparity of wealth, concentration of business control among a few financiers, low wages, and discontent among farmers over the practices of grain terminals, railroads, and banks or other credit institutions. Great Plains Progressives understood that cheap railroad rates, lower interest rates, and government regulation of the grain trade would increase farm income and the welfare of those who depended on agricultural prosperity, particularly small-scale businesses.[23]

Overall, politics in the Great Plains centered on agrarian issues, with the exception of Prohibition and women's suffrage, although both had rural influences. Few advocated the nationalization of the railroads in the Populist spirit, but a pervasive hostile attitude remained against the railroads resulting from excessive rates. Grievances against the railroads caused an organized rebellion in the Republican Party that contributed to the Progressive movement in the Great Plains. In December 1903, Coe I. Crawford, a former Republican state attorney general and soon to be governor, charged that party leadership in South Dakota worked with the railroads, Standard

Oil, and insurance companies (among other businesses) for personal and corporate gain rather than the best interests of the people. Crawford urged the state legislature to enact the political reforms that would be necessary to "shake off from the state the incubus of corporate dominion and to wrest [it from] the control of the party bosses."[24]

Although the Republican Party remained entrenched in most Great Plains states, those who supported political and economic reform, particularly in relation to agriculture, expressed varying degrees of liberalism. Reformers particularly sought a direct primary election law to break the control of party bosses in the state legislatures, thereby gaining for themselves the sobriquet of "insurgents." In 1906 when Crawford won the governorship in South Dakota and Progressive Republicans were elected to the congressional seats, a new political age seemed to be dawning. Indeed, in the 1907 legislative session, South Dakota Progressives in the legislature enacted direct primary legislation, passed an antilobbying law, and prohibited corporations from making campaign or personal contributions for political purposes, while the public used the referendum to permit Sunday "[moving] picture shows." The legislature also set maximum passenger railroad rates, created food and drug and telephone commissions, provided free textbooks for public schools, and prohibited railroads from giving free passes to politicians.[25]

Progressive legislators in other Great Plains states pursued many of the same reforms. In 1907, the Nebraska state legislature also enacted direct primary legislation and urged Congress to support a constitutional amendment for the direct election of senators and, in 1912, approved legislation providing for the initiative and referendum to keep government close and responsive to the people through the democratic process. On the national level, Congressman George Norris joined other Progressive Republicans and Democrats as insurgents who fought the traditional power structure. Norris and his Progressive colleagues supported tariff reform, railroad regulation, and antitrust legislation as well as a parcel post system. Later a senator, he advocated federal regulation of the utility companies, as well as the federal generation of electric power at Wilson Dam at Muscle Shoals, Alabama. Hydroelectric power generated by the federal government would serve as a yardstick to help government officials determine the fairness of rates set by the private utility companies for electric power. In Nebraska, Norris challenged the business practices of the Nebraska Power Company (in Omaha), which produced about 60 percent of the electricity for the state. Pietistic Protestants, however, used the referendum to place statewide Prohibition on the ballot and, in the primary, championed select candidates who supported it, proving that reform is in the eye of the beholder. Prohibition also caused divisions between Democratic Party "wets" and Republican Party "drys."[26]

In Montana, Progressives in the state legislature attempted to curb the power of the Amalgamated Copper Mining Company; provided regulations to protect workers in the mines; passed legislation providing for workman's compensation, railroad regulation, pure food and drug restrictions, and milk and meat inspection; created a state board of health; and expanded participation in government with the initiative, referendum, and direct primary. In 1904, the Montana State Federation of Women's Clubs, the Women's Christian Temperance Union, and the Montana Federation of Labor campaigned against child labor and gained approval of a constitutional amendment that prohibited employment in the mines of children under sixteen years of age.[27]

Similarly, in Kansas, the liberal or Progressive Republicans became known as "Boss Busters" in their fight against conservative party leadership, and they too sought a primary election law, railroad regulation, equitable taxes, child labor regulation, a juvenile court system, regulated work hours for railroad employees, a maximum freight-rate law, a tax commission to assess railroads, an anti-pass law to prevent free transportation for politicians and reciprocal favors, workman's compensation, a commission to regulate public utilities, state inspection of meatpacking plants, and the regulation of the sale of stocks and bonds — all legislation that had its intellectual roots in the late nineteenth-century agrarian reform movement, including tariff reform that led to the Payne-Aldrich Tariff of 1909. The old Populist agenda seemed alive and well throughout the northern and central Great Plains.[28]

Kansas also adopted a state constitutional amendment that gave women the right to vote after years of a controversial running fight with voting males that had begun with the Wyandot Constitutional Convention in 1859. Many Kansas women held jobs at that time and made substantial contributions to suffrage associations that hired speakers to canvas the state. Some wealthy, property-owning women, including the wife of Governor Walter Stubbs, also became suffragettes. To avoid criticism that the national office controlled their actions, Kansas suffragettes rejected recruiting outside speakers. By stressing the importance of the ballot for humanitarian reform, the Kansas suffragettes distanced themselves from those who advocated using it to influence Republican Party politics.

During the 1911–12 campaign, the Republican, Democratic, and Progressive parties in Kansas did not want the old-guard politicians to gain

ELECTION DAY.
MEADOW S D. Nov.8ᵀᴴ 1910

The small towns in the Great Plains served as local service centers, including providing residents a place to vote. On November 8, 1910, Meadows, South Dakota, prepared for Election Day. The businesses on both sides of Main Street indicate growing prosperity and promise of success.

credit if the amendment passed, and each party supported the suffragettes as a matter of necessity. Moreover, most voters at the time believed in the justness of this Progressive reform. Although the suffragettes fought among themselves over policy issues, they practiced savvy political maneuvering. One woman warned her Kansas sisters, "Do not allow any woman speaker to abuse any man, even if he is the veriest blackguard in existence. You are asking something of them, and while it is gall and wormwood to be compelled to ask some of the specimens whose only claim to manhood is that they wear trousers, yet remember always, that they have the vote." They even used sex appeal to champion their cause when one suffragette invited Governor Stubbs's wife and Lucy Johnston, president of the Kansas Equal Suffrage Association, to a district convention in Wichita and urged the governor's wife to have her stenographer write a publicity statement complimentary of the attractiveness of these two women to draw a larger crowd. In the end, one Kansas suffragette reflected, "We did *not fight* for suffrage, we *worked* for it. Therein lies a great secret."[29]

Jeannette Rankin led the movement in Montana. As a tough-minded, skillful grassroots organizer, she urged solidarity among the state's women, saying, "We want to vote" to help improve the public health and welfare as well as ensure honest politics. In 1914 after a close election, voters approved the suffrage amendment to the state constitution. In North Dakota, however, the woman suffrage bill met defeat in 1914, due to opposition from the foreign born (particularly Germans), the liquor interests, railroads, and the Republican political machine. Woman suffrage would not come to North Dakota until 1917, when the Nonpartisan League captured the state legislature and gave them the right to vote in local and presidential elections; South Dakota women were not enfranchised until a year later. In Nebraska, suffrage reform often centered on ethnic loyalties and religious belief. German males usually thought that women should focus on domestic responsibilities, not politics. One German-language newspaper editor warned his male readers to "hold on to your pants tightly so they are not stolen by the suffragettes." Nebraska women would not receive the right to vote until 1919, when the state ratified the Nineteenth Amendment. By 1920, when the federal government mandated woman suffrage, Oklahoma and Texas had not yet approved this Progressive reform.[30]

In June 1913, William Allen White reflected on the Progressive years, saying that Kansas City, Kansas, had voted to construct a municipal electric plant, while the federal circuit court approved municipal ownership of the city's streetcar system and the attorney general ruled that the manufacture of ice was a public utility. With tongue in cheek and pen in hand, White wrote, "The Socialists are getting too conservative for this country. They will have to get a move on themselves or they will be without an issue in 1916. For the Bull Moosers have stolen the Socialist thunder, and the progressive Republicans declare they are just as progressive as the Bull Moosers, and the Democrats say they are more progressive than the Progressives." White contended, "Unless the Republicans and Democrats are lying about how progressive they are . . . the Socialists might as well go out of business, for all the great parties will be swiping the Socialist planks." White's musing had considerable substance as state governments gave more regulatory attention to the general welfare in the Great Plains.[31]

In North Dakota, Progressives sought more than regulatory reform. They advocated a state-owned terminal grain elevator and helped pass a federal grain grading law to prevent farmers from being cheated when they sold their grain. Although many Republican reformers were lawyers, businessmen, and educators, often with conservative records, and had opposed the People's Party, they preferred to champion a progressive agenda to maintain party domination over the Democrats. In North Dakota, Republican

Progressives received their strongest support from the Norwegians, while the German Russians supported the old guard. Wheat dominated the agricultural economy and created common enemies, which North Dakota Progressives attacked through the political process.[32]

Overall, Progressives or reformers in the Great Plains worked for stronger business regulations, greater consumer protections, expanded labor benefits and rights, and electoral reform, among other issues. Between 1905 and 1919, however, they often became mired in the fight over Prohibition. Social regulation often proved different in reality than in theory; in 1908, Kansas governor Edward Hoch was content with the state's Prohibition law being "fairly well enforced," as it was in 80 percent of the 105 counties. State budgets limited enforcement, and counties with large immigrant populations ignored the law, as did the old cow towns, such as Wichita. Even so, Kansas earned the reputation as the Prohibition leader in the Great Plains. In 1912, Governor Stubbs proclaimed Kansas the "driest state in the Union," while Topeka, the capital city, enjoyed its reputation of being "very wet." Until passage of the Eighteenth Amendment, its governors continued to proclaim, as did Governor Arthur Capper in 1915, that Prohibition was an "unqualified success from every standpoint in Kansas." In that same year, the Wichita police chief was arrested for selling confiscated whiskey in city hall, proving once again that the long-standing messianic morality of some Kansans could not divert bootleggers, who met a consistent demand from those who refused to abide by self-appointed guardians of the state's moral order. Most Kansans who did not drink abstained for personal beliefs, not because of legal proscriptions. In North Dakota, although a state Prohibition statue of 1889 remained poorly enforced, the Women's Christian Temperance Union (mostly Methodists, Scandinavians, and Lutherans) supported it, in part to keep harvest-time hands and other farmworkers from drinking.[33]

As the twentieth century dawned, however, no farm organization with a strong political agenda existed in the southern Great Plains. But this state of affairs did not last for long. In 1902, Newt Gresham in Point, Texas, founded the Farmers Educational and Cooperative Union of America, soon commonly known as the Farmers Union (FU). The FU endorsed the collective marketing principles of the Southern Farmers Alliance; many of the FU members had gained organizational experience in the Alliance and dabbled on the fringes of politics until the 1890s, when the People's Party drew away its more radical members and the Farmers Alliance collapsed.

Alliance men and women had gained experience campaigning for economic and institutional change for the benefit of society. The Farmers

Union advocated a withholding action to force commodity prices higher, particularly for cattle and wheat. By withholding crops and also marketing and shipping through the members' own cooperatives and clearinghouses, the FU believed it could break the hold of banks and furnishing merchants who kept them in a state of indebtedness, poverty, and near peonage. These plans abruptly ended with the Panic of 1907. Without credit, FU members could not keep cotton from market until they received their desired fifteen cents per pound. Yet FU members, some 70,000 strong, constituted a significant voting block in Oklahoma upon statehood. Farmers Union members were disgruntled, politically skilled, and organizationally sophisticated. In 1908, many of these farmers drifted to the Socialist Party because neither the Democrats nor the Republicans offered reforms that would meet their needs.[34]

In Oklahoma, farm tenancy increased in the cotton area, and decades of single-crop agriculture and soil erosion reduced production to as little as one-half bale per acre. One cotton tenant lamented, "There has been too many butchers of the soil here." Texas and Oklahoma bankers charged usurious interest rates of 10 percent or more, and with local merchants charging even higher rates, farmers could not afford to borrow money for improvements, whether to buildings, crops, or livestock, and they believed that cotton ginners, who often owned the land, cheated them with inaccurate scales. Most tenant farmers and sharecroppers hoped to earn ten cents per pound of cotton and waited for better days that never came. By World War I, they were living lives of desperation and want. Some looked west to California.[35]

Many of these farmers had been Populists and Democrats, but upon the founding of the Oklahoma Socialist Party in 1900, they quickly created their own identity by proclaiming in the party platform, "No person may own real estate. Every acre is owned by [the] whole people through the national government—taxes are simply rent." The Socialists wanted the state to rent its lands to tenants at a reasonable rate and desired an "orderly transfer of banks and public utilities, natural resources and key industries to social ownership and democratic management," that is, the government. By advocating such fundamental changes as publicly owned cooperatives and state credit for farmers, they gained considerable public support. In 1910, the Oklahoma Socialist Party had more members than in any other state. Oklahoma Socialists gave Eugene V. Debs more than 42,000 votes (16.6 percent) in the presidential election of 1912. By the outbreak of World War I, the Socialist vote had doubled in every election since statehood in 1907, primarily because of attacks on the Democratic Party as an organization of the economic elites (whom Socialists characterized as "parasites in the electric light towns"), whose policies impoverished the common people. In November 1914, 20 percent of the voters cast their ballots for Socialist candidates for state, county, and local offices, particularly in the southern counties.[36]

A rural, farmer-based Socialist Party, however, did not develop quickly in Oklahoma. Although Oklahoma tenant farmers and sharecroppers were isolated from political power but not its effects, the Socialist (that is, Marxian) call for the nationalization of land did not appeal to farmers, who considered property ownership in the form of land the guarantee of economic freedom and financial security. Moreover, leaders in the Oklahoma Socialist Party did not acknowledge the dominance of farmers in the organization until 1909. Finally, in 1912, caught between Socialist principles to collectivize the land and the poverty of Oklahoma farmers and recognizing the need to gain more votes, the Socialists adopted a party platform that supported the distribution of privately held land to the landless, that is, tenant farmers, not the collectivization or nationalization of land under government control. Indeed, the Socialist Party endorsed a new definition of the proletariat: "The working class of Oklahoma is largely made up of agricultural workers."[37]

In 1912, this philosophical change of course influenced the National Socialist Party of America to include farmworkers, that is, tenants and sharecroppers, in its platform by pledging "to support the tillers of the fields as well as those in the shops, factories and mines of the nation in their struggle for economic justice." Even so, Socialist Party officials refused to accept reforms for the capitalist system that included collective marketing and cooperative buying, thereby losing the support of FU members who remained unhappy in the Democratic Party but had no political alternative. By equating tenant farmers with wage workers, who were at the "mercy of the employers," the Oklahoma Socialists joined Jefferson and Marx. Only landownership guaranteed freedom and equality. By so contending, the Oklahoma Socialist Party remarkably and creatively advocated the collectivization of land for its redistribution to small-scale farmers. The land would be distributed not to the state but to autonomous farmers who would own it, hence the blending of Marxism and Jeffersonianism for political power that would provide a viable alternative to the Democratic and Republican parties. By advocating the redistribution of land "from possession of the landlords into the hands of the actual tillers of the soil," Oklahoma Socialists would create a strong yeoman class. Socialism in Oklahoma, then, emerged from traditional republican values about equality and the independence of small-scale producers rather than from ideas about the inevitability of a class-divided society.

The Democratic Party, however, did not forfeit political power. Instead, the party flexed its muscle in the statehouse to gain legislation for a literacy test to qualify people for the right to vote, as well as the grandfather clause to keep sympathetic African Americans from voting Socialist. (Most black Oklahomans nevertheless continued to support the Republican Party instead of switching their allegiance to Socialist candidates.) In 1912, Socialist gains in county and local elections fostered considerable optimism for success, with organizational work intensifying in advance of the election in 1914. In the November election, 175 Socialist candidates gained county and local offices and six state legislative seats. Quickly, the party looked ahead to the presidential election two years later.

The arrest of the Socialist Party's gubernatorial candidate for supplying weapons to striking miners at McAlester and the inability of the Socialist legislators to achieve significant reform, together with Democratic control of the election process, however, spelled doom for the party. Although the Socialists had organized optimistically, after 1916 they lost influence to the Democratic Party amid charges of treason for not supporting the war effort. Socialism as a political party would not regain its voice in the southern Great Plains during the twentieth century. Still, the Oklahoma Socialists made a remarkable contribution to the political discourse in the Great Plains by arguing that those who worked the land (that is, farmed it despite a lack of ownership) were legitimate members of the working class. As such, land redistribution to tenants and sharecroppers became a democratic reform rather than corporate collectivization by the State.

For a brief time, the Oklahoma Socialists welded Marxism and Jeffersonian-republicanism on the anvil of the agrarian experience, thereby uniquely contradicting the general American belief that socialism ran counter to the republican principles of the American Revolution. They also argued that their brand of agrarian socialism was a legitimate alternative to the Democratic and Republican parties. Few could argue against the desire, even the right, of a farmer to own the land that he worked. In this context, socialism in Oklahoma was American, not foreign, born. When socialism next emerged in the Great Plains, it would resound from the north, but the matter of land redistribution would not be part of it.[38]

The significance of the environment is as clearly understood by all men and women who live on the Great Plains today as it was by those who settled the region during the late nineteenth century. Drought, searing sun, blizzards, and subzero temperatures, as well as hailstorms with high winds at harvest time, continued to make life in the region a matter of perseverance and adaptation. Although the term *environment* is well known, the concept of environmentalism is relatively new; in the context of conservation, that is, the protection of nature, those who have lived on the Great Plains have been environmentalists in other ways throughout the history of the region. In little more than a century, the residents of the plains have used the concepts of the change, control, and preservation of nature to govern their relationships with the environment and, by so doing, make both settlement and agriculture possible in the Great Plains.

The men and women who settled the Great Plains during the late nineteenth century confronted a harsh, semiarid environment far different from the subhumid eastern United States. With precipitation sparse and the native grasses short, these settlers attempted to remake the environment based on the best empirical evidence available. Both scientists and settlers assumed that the Great Plains environment could be altered to increase precipitation and improve their chances for agricultural success, because they believed that trees caused rainfall. Trees would draw moisture from deep beneath the surface of the earth, which would then evaporate from the leaves. After the moisture passed from the subsoil to the atmosphere through the intermediary of the trees, it was expected to condense and fall to the earth as rain. Consequently, the planting of trees in the Great Plains would alter the environment. The environment of the Great Plains, however, proved more difficult to change in reality than in theory. Although settlers planted trees, rainfall did not increase; without irrigation from a nearby stream, the trees died by the score.

Although plains residents failed to change the environment by planting trees and cultivating the soil, not everyone believed defeat to be inevitable. In 1891, after persistent urging from Charles Edwin Bessey, a botanist at the University of Nebraska, the Division of Forestry of the United States Department of Agriculture (USDA) began an experimental tree planting project in the Nebraska Sand Hills, an area occupying approximately twenty thousand square miles north of the Platte River, about one-fourth of the land area of the state. Primarily located west of the hundredth meridian, the Sand Hills receive less than twenty-two inches of precipitation annually. With its moist spring weather, Bessey believed that the area was well suited for coniferous trees. The USDA had resisted Bessey's requests to establish a forest in the Sand Hills during the 1880s: agency officials did not believe that tree planting in western Nebraska would succeed, and ranchers opposed Bessey's idea because they wanted continued use of those federal lands for grazing, while farmers saw possibilities for homesteading in the area. Indeed, ranchers and farmers as well as local politicians were belligerent at best about Bessey's recommendation.[39]

In 1890, however, Bernhard E. Fernow, head of the Division of Forestry in the USDA, visited Nebraska and told the state board of agriculture, "I believe that forest planting is one of the necessary requisites to permanently reclaiming this vast domain; I believe that reforesting this large area, deforested by fire, buffalo, and consequent desiccation is not impossible." This change in the federal view resulted from the newly created division's need to make its mark, and Fernow hoped to do so by using trees to help *control* the environment of Nebraska rather than to perpetuate any lingering belief that trees could *change* nature in the Great Plains. Fernow preferred for the federal government to direct any forestry project in Nebraska, but he believed that the state could also provide leadership. For Fernow, government direction was essential because "success [could] be forced only by cooperation, by a well-conducted army, attacking the enemy under a comprehensive plan, systematically and methodically carried out by generalship, commanding knowledge, men, and power, such as government alone, be it State or General government, can command."[40]

Bessey and Fernow discussed the possibility of planting trees in the Sand Hills and scheduled an experimental project for the spring of 1891. The Division of Forestry would provide the trees and planting instructions, but Bessey had to furnish the land. Fortunately, Edgar G. Brunner, a colleague of Bessey's, owned land with his brothers in southwestern Holt County. Their property included Sand Hills land, and they agreed to provide four one-acre plots for experimental purposes. Although Bessey and the Brunner brothers prepared the land and planted ponderosa or western yellow pine along with jack and Scotch pine and Douglas fir trees according to the instructions of the Division of Forestry, enthusiasm for the project soon waned, because many of the trees died by the end of the year. As a result, the Brunner brothers and the foresters began giving their attention to other matters. Although Bessey continued to believe in the viability of forestry in the Sand Hills, the trees were abandoned and the project was almost immediately forgotten.[41]

A decade later, Gifford Pinchot, chief of the Bureau of Forestry, sent a group of foresters to investigate the potential for tree planting in the Sand Hills, primarily because the USDA had recently upgraded forestry from division to bureau status but also to help foil the bureau's transfer to the Department of the Interior, which he considered corrupt. He also needed to show that the bureau could make an important contribution to the growing conservation movement in the nation and gain congressional support for government tree planting in a region that had a history of favoring this government-sponsored activity. To their amazement, the group found pine trees growing twenty feet tall on the old experimental plots, and a dense thicket with forest conditions was established on the site. When William Hall, who led the group, reported its findings, he recommended the renewal of the experimental plantings.[42]

Hall's report encouraged Pinchot to pursue the matter further, and he sent another reconnaissance team to the Nebraska Sand Hills in July to make a thorough survey regarding tree planting. This Sand Hills Reconnaissance Survey team reported to Pinchot late in 1901, recommending the creation of two forest reserves in the Nebraska Sand Hills. Pinchot and President Theodore Roosevelt agreed that the creation of a forest would not only instrumentally improve the environment by conserving the soil but also help control the environment by serving as a nursery for farmers who needed trees for windbreaks to protect their fields, livestock, and homes from the nearly constant winds that scorched their fields in the summer and piled the snow in drifts during the winter. In time, the forest would improve soil humus so that extensive agriculture would be possible. Moreover, a forest would help the Sand Hills store water for irrigation, hold the sand, and prevent the movement of sand dunes eastward. Pinchot and Roosevelt also believed that the creation of a forest in the Nebraska Sand Hills would "ameliorate the dryness of the atmosphere" so that the agricultural land to the east would receive a greater amount of precipitation.[43]

Accordingly, on April 16, 1902, Roosevelt, by executive order, created the Dismal River Forest Reserve between the Middle Loup and Dismal rivers west of Halsey in Thomas County and the Niobrara Forest Reserve between the Niobrara and Snake rivers south of Nenzel in Cherry County. Beginning in 1903, foresters with the Bureau of Forestry (renamed the Forest Service within the USDA in 1905) planted nearly 30,000 acres primarily with native red cedar and ponderosa pine to control the environment by holding the soil to stabilize grazing lands. In 1907, these reserves became collectively known as the Nebraska National Forest. It was a national forest of 208,902 acres, mostly without trees.[44]

The task of planting a forest required both time and resources, particularly seedlings. Although the Forest Service had much of the former, it had little of the latter, but it quickly went about clearing forty acres for a nursery near the Dismal River Reserve headquarters in Halsey. Forest Service employees also acquired about 70,000 jack pine seedlings from Minnesota and approximately 30,000 ponderosa pine seedlings from the Black Hills, which they planted during the spring of 1903. By 1906, the foresters had learned by trial and error that the one- or two-year-old seedlings raised at the nursery proved hardier and more adaptable to transplanting than trees acquired from other areas. Thereafter, no plantings were made from field collections. The foresters also quickly learned that the native red cedar would be an important species for any forestation of the Sand Hills.[45]

The Forest Service soon discovered that prairie fires as well as the semi-arid environment proved major obstacles to creating a planted forest in the Great Plains, but foresters believed that with the control of fire the forestation of the Sand Hills could be easily accomplished. In 1910, however, they could not contain a prairie fire that began sixty-five miles west of Halsey and swept eastward with such speed and ferocity that it could not be stopped before reaching the forest. After it passed, only one hundred acres of trees remained. It was a devastating setback for the project, but the Forest Service began replanting from its nursery, which produced 1 million seedlings annually at the time.

By 1913, the Forest Service could hail the Nebraska National Forest as a major conservation success that benefited both the land and ranchers. Before the foresters had stabilized the Sand Hills, the service reported, cattlemen had damaged the land by excessive grazing, primarily because they had overstocked the public range to make up for low returns that averaged only about fifty cents per acre. In time, the service contended, forestry in the Sand Hills would enable a higher return on the land, because trees would protect cropland from wind erosion and add humus to the soil. The Forest Service also championed the concept of multiple use (meaning that the national forests should be used for many economic and recreational purposes) and contended that the Nebraska National Forest also would provide a local timber supply, particularly for rough lumber and fence posts.[46]

In the meantime, stock raisers and farmers continued to object to the removal of so much public domain from grazing or settlement, and Congress agreed to adjust the boundaries of the Nebraska National Forest by opening the North Platte Division to entry. In 1908, this area consisted of 347,170 acres that had been added to the national forest. Congress made this revision in the land laws under the Kinkaid Act, which reduced the forest to 208,902 acres on October 1, 1913. This removal reduced the area of the Nebraska National Forest to approximately 2 percent of the Sand Hills.[47]

Stock raisers, however, had begun to admit that fenced land in the Nebraska National Forest, which the service had opened to grazing by permit, helped them improve breeding practices by keeping out unwanted bulls.

Moreover, controlled grazing permitted a better stand of grass and heavier cattle. In addition, many local residents, who had maintained a hostile attitude toward the project in the beginning, had become friends of the Forest Service by 1914, because the agency provided seasonal employment for approximately one hundred men. As a result, the Society of American Foresters proclaimed the Nebraska National Forest an "unqualified success" and noted that "if fires are kept out, [only] exceptional conditions . . . can bring disaster."[48]

Buoyed by the potential for tree planting to control the environment with the creation of the Nebraska National Forest, Theodore Roosevelt also set aside 30,000 acres of sand hills south of the Arkansas River on July 25, 1905, for the Garden City Forest Reserve. There, the Forest Service planned to create the Kansas National Forest based on the Nebraska project, with the intention of controlling the environment, providing timber for fence and telegraph posts, and encouraging settlers to practice timber culture in this essentially treeless region.[49]

Assistant Forester Royal S. Kellogg also contended that no one had proved that tree planting and cultivation increased precipitation and that the theory was at best "problematical." But he argued that trees did help to control the environment: "The principal effect of tree planting on the climate of western Kansas will be to check the winds and lessen evaporation in the immediate vicinity of the plantation." Additionally, the Forest Service enthusiastically maintained that the Kansas National Forest would "ameliorate the dryness of the atmosphere" so that the agricultural land to the east would receive a greater amount of precipitation.[50]

In April 1906, planting began for the Kansas National Forest, with more than 81,000 deciduous trees, such as Osage orange, Russian mulberry, and hackberry, as well as conifers, such as yellow pine and red cedar shipped from the Nebraska National Forest. A year later, prairie fire destroyed almost all of the seedlings. Even so, in early April 1908, the Forest Service extended this reserve to 302,387 acres and officially named it the Kansas National Forest; only about 1,000 acres had been replanted.[51]

Although the U.S. Department of Agriculture claimed that the expansion of the Kansas National Forest resulted from the desires of local residents, who favored reserving the entire sand hills region for forestry, in reality the Forest Service confronted the same opposition that it had encountered in Nebraska. Residents complained that the reserve removed good agricultural land from homesteading, ruined the tax base, and drained money from the area that ranchers paid for grazing permits. The federal government essentially ended these complaints by opening ten thousand acres to homesteading under the provisions of the Forest Homestead Act of 1906 and, in 1908, by returning 10 percent and later 25 percent of the revenues from the national forests to the state treasuries to support road construction and education in the affected counties.[52]

In spring 1908, with public support and agency confidence that a national forest could be created in western Kansas, the Forest Service sent a "permanent" staff to establish an office in Garden City and a nursery capable of producing 300,000 seedlings annually. The foresters planted 128,000 trees, primarily yellow and jack pine, in April and hoped for the best. It was not forthcoming. A year later, despite irrigation, only an estimated 32 percent of the honey locust and 27 percent of the yellow pine seedlings had survived, because of scorching summer temperatures and nearly constant hot winds. In 1910, Representative William A. Reeder of Kansas, however, reported that farmers in western Kansas had stopped irrigating "because our cultivation and tree planting have produced such an atmospheric condition that the rains came frequently." Reeder and others still firmly believed that tree planting could change the environment of the Great Plains.[53]

Despite this heavy loss, the Forest Service remained optimistic. Foresters planted approximately 125,000 trees annually for the next three years, emphasizing deciduous trees (such as honey and black locust, Osage orange, and cottonwood) transplanted from the Garden City nursery, because the Bessey nursery specialized in coniferous species. When drought destroyed the deciduous trees in 1911, the Forest Service decided to emphasize evergreens. In 1913, after introducing new nursery and planting techniques, the Kansas foresters optimistically contended that "only exceptional and unusually damaging conditions can bring failure." Nature rather than the Forest Service, however, prevailed, destroying the trees with continued drought. On October 14, 1915, a decade after Theodore Roosevelt had created the Garden City Forest Reserve, President Woodrow Wilson issued an executive order abolishing the Kansas National Forest. These forestry experiments proved, although few paid much attention, that the people of the Great Plains had to adapt to the environment: they could not make it adapt to them. The concept that nature in the Great Plains could be controlled had been demolished by the environment itself.[54]

In mid-January 1900, the local newspaper in Hays, Kansas, reported that residents would be able to enjoy telephone service within six months. At that time, only two free phones served the community: one at the local flour mill for alerting about fires and the other in the room of the city council. A year later, more than one hundred residents in Amarillo, Texas, had phone service, and, in 1911, the local phone company counted fifteen hundred subscribers, with lines reaching Canyon, Hereford, and Tulia, Texas. While modern technology and communications began to affect life in the Great Plains, some traditional activities remained, such as cutting ice on local streams, lakes, and ponds for storage and use in "ice boxes" during the remainder of the year, particularly in summer. Residents across the Great Plains welcomed progress and opportunity while taking comfort in the familiar. Social life often revolved around church and school activities, but the turnover rate for school attendance proved high, particularly during the summer months. Often, one-room country schools had too little room to accommodate all the children scattered across a range of ages and grade levels. Isolation and low salaries encouraged teachers to leave. During the 1915–16 school year, teachers in South Dakota and Nebraska earned salaries that averaged less than $440 annually. In 1912, only 8 of 148 schools in North Dakota had electric lights, and only 120 provided communal drinking cups at the well for students. In 1918, 91 percent of the schools in South Dakota still had outdoor toilets.[55]

Despite these limitations, the land drew many, even while the newly developing oil fields attracted those who cared little for farming. Between 1900 and 1904, Kansas gained national prominence in oil production by increasing pumping rates from 75,000 barrels from 103 wells to 4 million barrels from 3,300 wells. Drillers focused on southeastern Kansas, and Neodesha became *the* oil town, with Standard Oil operating the state's only refinery. Residents spoke of "oil and gas fever" and the money it would bring. Despite dry holes, wildcatters believed that the next well might bring their fortune. Chanute, Independence, and Garnett also became oil towns, with workers and oil service companies driving the boom-time economy. By 1909, every town in the southeastern oil counties had at least one refinery. Some Kansans wanted a state-owned refinery operated by convict labor to counter the exploitative practices of Standard Oil. The state legislature argued that municipalities already operated electric, gas, and water plants, and many Kansans saw nothing wrong with this form of socialism, but the state supreme court declared the act unconstitutional as a violation of the Fourteenth Amendment.[56]

By June 1916, pumps were drawing oil from 250 wells near El Dorado and Augusta. The El Dorado field had 600 wells by the end of the year and another 1,000 drilled in 1917. The oil fields lured thousands of people and created a boom-time economy. One observer noted that "the speculator can look for miles at an endless field of derricks set out in rows with all the regularity of a new apple orchard." These wells produced 9 million barrels in 1916, constituting 3 percent of the total national production of crude oil. In 1917, production reached 36 million barrels (11 percent of national production), then 45 million barrels (13 percent of the oil pumped in the nation) a year later. Optimists thought that Kansas might soon become known as the oil state.[57]

In 1902, oilmen began exploring the Texas Panhandle. Soon they discovered an oil and gas field 120 miles long and 20 miles wide that included seven panhandle counties, primarily north of the Canadian River. Known as the Panhandle Oil and Gas Field, it would become one of the most productive fields in the United States. By 1905, oilmen such as Harry F. Sinclair had located good drilling locations in Indian Territory and soon pumped 1,000 barrels per day from the best wells. In 1914, 900 wells pumped oil from the Cushing field in Oklahoma, and drilling continued at a frantic pace as oilmen worked to take what they could get before encroachment by others and the depletion of the field. Ten refineries converted the crude to useable oil and gasoline. These fields supported an economic boom and jobs for wildcatters, drillers, and roughnecks while fueling a host of refineries for most of the twentieth century. The oil business, however, did not attract manufacturers to the Great Plains. The petroleum and gas markets lay elsewhere, where a greater population and consumer demand prevailed. But oil patch payrolls stimulated construction for housing and increased tax revenues that helped improve schools and roads.[58]

During the first two decades of the twentieth century, the population increased by at least a quarter of a million in each Great Plains state except for Wyoming, whose population rose from 92,531 to 194,402. Oklahoma had the largest gain, increasing from a population of 790,391 in 1900 to 2,028,283 in 1920 and in the process qualifying the territory for statehood in 1907. Statehood for New Mexico followed in 1912. By 1920, Oklahoma City and Tulsa had become busy, fast-paced oil towns. Other cities with populations of more than 10,000 also grew rapidly. In 1900, San Antonio had a population of only 69,422. Twenty years later, it totaled 202,096, while Wichita increased from 24,671 to 72,217 people. Dallas and Fort Worth reached the 100,000 mark in 1910. Omaha expanded from a population of 140,590 to 266,074 during that period. Denverites considered their city the equal of any on the East Coast. Omaha became a major railroad city for both the Union Pacific and the Chicago and Great Western Railway, and strikebreaking became a way of life as workers and management battled for advantage in the transportation and meatpacking industries. The cities of the plains gave the region considerable economic and social diversity with a host of ethnic groups and growing industries.[59]

The largest cities on the rim of the Great Plains such as Cheyenne, Billings, and Denver in the northern and western part of the region and Omaha, Kansas City, and Fort Worth to the east and south served as entrepôts, or "gateway" cities, that serviced the interior. If a railroad bypassed a town or failed to build a branch line to it, this "inland" town was likely to fall into a slow economic decline. Railroads brought lumber, agricultural machinery, and household supplies and linked people and towns to the world beyond, simultaneously making life less isolated. In the eastern Great Plains, town dwellers enjoyed running water, sewer services, and paved roads that often made them feel superior to those whose lives in the western plains seemed at best dismal.

Despite urban growth, most of the plains towns had populations of only a few thousand. The towns built along railroads had a distinct T-shape, with the main street running perpendicular to the tracks. Grain elevators occupied land on the outside of the tracks. In the northern Great Plains, the harsh environment and the grain and milling industry in Minneapolis–St. Paul played major roles in curbing the development of urban centers. The major agricultural companies made the decision to keep their headquarters in the Twin Cities. Wheat would flow out, but urbanites would not flood in to build agricultural marketing and processing cities. To the south, railroads led to Omaha and Kansas City, where businesses served the central Great Plains from afar with no need to establish operations in the interior towns. Denver dominated the western plains, and its business leaders did not encourage town development that would offer competition along the Front Range. Summer temperatures of more than 100 degrees and winter temperatures of 40 degrees below zero discouraged companies from relocating to the plains. Business people and entrepreneurs often chose to live elsewhere.[60]

In the Dakotas, a half million new settlers arrived between 1900 and 1915; approximately one-quarter million were foreign born. In the northern Great Plains, farms, towns, and grain elevators began to dot the land. In the West River Country, these towns (like others built before them) depended on the railroads, which gave them life — or at least a fighting chance for survival — and, more important, kept the promise of the Great Plains alive despite a harsh reality. By World War I, more than 100,000 of these Dakota settlers were foreign born and more than half (approximately 54 percent) were male. Overall, the population of the Dakotas increased 61 percent during the first decade but slowed to 11 percent growth between 1910 and 1920.

Wyoming offered its open plains as a nirvana for farmers (provided they irrigated the land) and a haven for the tubercular. Settlers flocked into eastern Colorado and New Mexico, where land speculators offered an "ideal" world. Railroad construction and easy Texas land laws aided the expansion of cattle ranching and cotton farming from San Saba to Lubbock and wheat and cattle raising north to Amarillo. Trainloads of prospectors, speculators, and investors all eager to buy land spread into West Texas.

Across the western plains from Bismarck to Odessa, small towns, county seats, and capital cities provided goods, services, and government that drew people and kept them there. Men, women, and children scattered across the enormity of the land. By 1920, though, many homesteaders had given up. Beaten by drought, bitter winters, and crop failure and with a desperation born of poverty, inexperience, and dashed hopes, they moved on.[61]

Those who stayed primarily supported the Democratic and Republican parties based on heritage and issues. In 1900, for example, the Republican Party carried five of the eight Great Plains states (Oklahoma and New Mexico remained territories until 1907 and 1912, respectively), while Colorado, Montana, and Texas supported William Jennings Bryan. During the next presidential election, only Texas supported Democratic candidate Alton Parker. In 1908, the Democratic Party carried Colorado, Oklahoma, Nebraska, and Texas for Bryan, while voters in the other states cast their support for William H. Taft. In 1912, the Democratic Party carried Woodrow Wilson for the presidency in every Great Plains state except South Dakota, which favored Theodore Roosevelt, the Progressive Party candidate. In 1916, South Dakota supported Republican Charles Evans Hughs, but the other Great Plains states cast at least plurality tallies for Wilson.[62]

Often, presidential elections indicated greater interparty divisions than overwhelming preferences for either the Democratic or Republican parties, although gubernatorial races usually, but not always, followed the presidential results. In 1912, for example, Woodrow Wilson carried Kansas with only 39 percent of the popular vote, while William Howard Taft and Theodore Roosevelt polled 53 percent of the vote between them. Four years later, Wilson received 50 percent of the vote—the only time during the Progressive Era that the Democrats polled a majority. The Republican Party still dominated the state elections because voters favored its positions, particularly antiwar pronouncements regarding Germany and Mexico. In 1916, most Great Plains voters considered Wilson less likely than Charles Evans Hughes to engage in war, because of the president's reform record with Congress.[63]

Between 1900 and the end of World War I, hope, greed, and a will to conquer the land and the environment brought men and women to confront a capricious region that demanded adaptation. Often they expected and asked more than the land could give, and they tried to control the environment to meet their needs. But the environment proved impossible to control, although they did not accept that reality. The environment of the Great Plains would repeatedly teach this hard lesson throughout the twentieth century. While they learned it, Great Plains men and women built an economy, primarily agricultural, and pursued a host of social, political, and economic reforms that would seem radical to those who crafted a far more conservative region later in the twentieth century. At the same time, their belief that the Great Plains offered the promise of a better life was fraught with tension, violence, and shame, none more so than regarding matters of race and ethnicity.

CHAPTER TWO

The Ethnic and Racial Divide

The promise of a better life lured men and women to the Great Plains during the early twentieth century and reaffirmed faith in the future for those who already lived in the region. Settlers came for a variety of reasons. The Mexicans who began migrating to the Great Plains after 1910 were not interested in homesteading. Although many had agricultural backgrounds, they sought wage work. The Great Plains offered the opportunity to make money and improve their standard of living. By 1910, approximately 293,000 Hispanics lived in Texas and 166,000 in New Mexico. At the same time, several thousand Mexican immigrants made Trinidad and Pueblo, Colorado, Oklahoma, and South Texas home; they worked on the railroads and labored in the cotton fields and coal mines. Soon they could be found working in the sugar beet fields in Colorado and western Kansas. With their native homeland relatively close, their rate of assimilation and acculturation proved slower than that experienced by the Germans and Norwegians in the northern Great Plains. Most were young, with a median age of twenty compared to the U.S. population of twenty-six; if married, they produced more children than did nearby Anglos. Anglo Texans considered Mexicanos (Mexican Americans and Mexicans) as nonwhite and worried about the effects of this immigration on white civilization in the southern plains.

In 1900, Hispanics, that is, people of Iberian Spanish descent, primarily lived in New Mexico, with clusters in Colorado and the panhandles of Oklahoma and Texas. They resented being called Mexicans. Often they held positions of power in local governments and operated businesses, but as more Mexicans entered the southern Great Plains, these Hispanics suffered increasing discrimination by Anglos. In 1924, one Hispanic man in Walsenburg, Colorado, complained, "The Americans think we are no good; they class us with this trash that comes over from Mexico; we are greasers and nothing more. We have suffered much from these Mexicans, for the Americans lump us all together because we speak Spanish."

Mexicans immigrated to the Great Plains in rapidly increasing numbers after 1900, particularly following the Mexican revolution in 1910. Many Mexicans fled social upheaval and economic collapse. With Asian immigrants targeted by the Chinese Exclusion Act of 1882 and the Japanese with the "Gentleman's Agreement" of 1907, followed by the immigration acts of 1917, 1921, and 1924 (the latter two of which also curtailed southern and eastern European immigration), railroad, mining, and agricultural employers beckoned Mexicans. Movement across the border into the southern plains was easy and unrestricted by the American border guards. By 1929, the Mexican population in Kansas had come to trail only the Germans as an ethnic group with sufficient numbers to create permanent communities (called barrios) within larger towns, such as Topeka, Wichita, Emporia, and Garden City. They found employment with the railroads, in the salt and coal mines, and in the oil fields. Mexican children endured segregated and inferior schools, and the assumption by whites that they were suitable only for menial labor slowed their economic improvement. The stock market crash in 1929 further added to the grimness of their lives. In 1930, Mexicans were the largest immigrant group in Colorado. Until 1930, most native-born Mexican Americans and Mexican immigrants called Texas home.[1]

In the southern plains of Texas, farmers depended on Mexicano labor because few whites pursued the backbreaking work and low wages in the cotton and onion fields. One farmer observed, "A lot of white men would come down from the north and set onions, but they can't do it at Mexican prices, and we can't afford to pay more at the present prices of onions." Cotton farmers often preferred Mexicanos to "poor white trash," because they worked for lower wages than whites, and they were docile and did not demand good treatment. One Nueces County cotton farmer spoke for many across the southern plains when he said, "You can't beat them as labor. I prefer the Mexican labor to the other classes of labor. It is more humble and you get more for your money. The Mexicans have a sense of duty and loyalty, and the qualities that go to make a good servant." What the Mexicanos earned, they spent for necessities and a few pleasures. One South Texas merchant who liked their business said, "I don't want the damn Sicilians coming in." Racism and discrimination permeated Anglo and Mexicano relations in the southern plains during the early twentieth century in a world where white farmers, merchants, and Mexicano workers needed each other.[2]

As Mexicanos moved into the cotton and vegetable fields in the southern plains, white resentment increased because landowners began replacing their tenant farmers with Mexicano field-workers. Similar resentments emerged in the oil fields and among construction workers, when Mexicano workers took jobs at lower wages than white workers, who often lost their jobs. As race relations became worse, one commercial farmer addressed the matter of education by saying, "Educating the Mexicans is educating them away from the job, away from the dirt. He learns English and wants to be a boss. He doesn't want to grub." A white sharecropper put it differently, asking, "Why don't we let the Mexicans come to a white school? Because a damned greaser is not fit to sit [by the] side of a white girl." In Colorado, one superintendent of schools expressed the conviction of most Anglo residents when he said that "the respectable people of Weld County do not want their children to sit alongside of dirty, filthy, diseased, infested Mexicans." A Dimmit County, Texas, education official deciphered the essential truth from such racial remarks, saying, "The lower down the white man is the more he will object to the Mexicans. The higher class American knows that going to the same school doesn't imply equality."[3]

Between 1900 and 1930, then, where Mexicanos lived and worked, Anglos dominated the economy and permitted them access only to the lowest-level service and general-labor occupations, essentially labor niches at the bottom of the social scale. Yet wages that whites considered low seemed high to Mexicanos compared to their earning opportunities in Mexico. The coal-mining towns of Trinidad and Starkville in southern Colorado also drew Hispanics from New Mexico, and wives and daughters found work as cooks and domestic servants. By 1910, Hispanics and Mexicanos were working the sugar beet fields along the Arkansas and South Platte rivers in Colorado. During the mid-1920s, the Great Western Sugar Company in the Bitterroot Valley near Billings, Montana, also targeted Mexicanos, as did Wyoming beet farmers and processors near Lovell and Torrington, where approximately 7,200 workers of Mexican descent made their home in 1930. Racial discrimination in Wyoming was as bad as that experienced in the southern plains. Worland mandated a "Mexican" school, and at the Catholic Church in Lovell, Mexicanos were relegated to the back pews. Still, these workers preferred laboring in the beet fields because, unlike railroad or mine labor, beet work was family work. Wives and children could labor in the fields hoeing, planting, topping, and harvesting and thereby keep the family together. Migratory during the summer, the Mexicanos often wintered in Denver, waiting for the next sugar beet crop and the railroad work seasons.[4]

Sugar beet work and living conditions proved considerably more difficult in the central and northern plains than the labor recruiters promised, although many farmers had little better housing and sanitation themselves. Most Colorado growers, however, believed that conditions for their Hispanic and Mexicano workers were better than these workers experienced in their home communities in New Mexico or Mexico. One observer spoke for many when he said that "the peon has always lived like a pig and he will continue to do so." Eighteen-hour days during harvest time and poor living conditions wearied these working men, women, and children. Workers of Mexican descent in the central Great Plains remained economically vulnerable and socially marginal. While they were clearly lower class, their treatment moved them dangerously close to caste status. Such discrimination against them would not end soon.[5]

These Mexicanos made limited ventures into the economic world of the Great Plains, and they remained protective of their culture by withdrawing into their own often newly created communities when seasonal work ended. Anglos preferred this relationship because it confirmed the Anglos' belief in the dead-end status of the Mexicanos and helped keep them out of sight and out of mind. This settlement pattern established new regional Mexicano communities that began to spread northward. Whites might consider all Hispanics and Mexicanos alike because they spoke Spanish, but the American-born Mexican Americans and other Hispanics tried to separate themselves from the new Mexican arrivals for matters of social status. Integration into the older Mexicano and Hispanic communities by the newcomers proved difficult if not impossible.[6]

The demand of the railroads for workers, combined with rising wages for Anglo workers, who also increasingly rejected menial labor, made Mexicano workers attractive. The Santa Fe, Rock Island, Frisco, and Katy railroads carried these immigrants north from El Paso and Laredo, nearly 16,500 in an eight-month period between 1907 and 1908 alone. They were cheap, unskilled, and hardworking. In 1928, the Santa Fe alone employed some 14,300 Mexicano workers, and railroad labor seemed to be their employment of choice. Mexicanos who took railroad employment seldom advanced beyond low-level positions. Employers contended that lack of skill and fluency in English relegated them to lower-paying positions, but prejudice in the racially conscious society of the Great Plains was the real

Mexican and Mexican American workers began moving into the central Great
Plains during the early twentieth century for employment opportunities with the
railroads. In 1913, this Mexican section crew worked for the Atchison, Topeka
and Santa Fe Railway near Pauline, Kansas.

reason for keeping Mexicanos in subservient, menial jobs. Kansas City
served as the major distribution center for Mexicano workers, and with
a 300 percent attrition rate annually, the flow of migrants from El Paso
became continuous, and their dispersion systematic into the Great Plains,
no matter whether they were wanted.[7]

In contrast to European immigrants, who sought land, established
farms, formed ethnic communities, and became permanent residents and
citizens, Mexicano immigrants seldom became landowners. Railroad and
agricultural employment required mobility, even transience, and their
work remained seasonal. When the harvests ended and the cold and snow
prevented railroad maintenance, many returned to Mexico or South Texas
and waited for spring. Most of these Mexicano workers were single or married men traveling alone. In time, they brought their families north with
the intent to stay when the railroads began seeking a reliable and permanent workforce. Between 1900 and 1930, the Mexicano population in the
northern and central Great Plains increased from approximately 182 to
8,452. Yet these numbers are no doubt low because the census for the years

of 1910, 1920, and 1930 were taken during the late winter and early spring, when many Mexicans remained south of the Rio Grande.[8]

By 1910, Mexicanos were primarily living in towns that bordered the major railroads and in the cotton-farming area of southwestern Oklahoma and South Texas. In Kansas, they also worked for the meat packers in Kansas City, Wichita, and Topeka. The salt mines of central Kansas and the sugar beet fields in western Kansas also drew Mexican families. By 1920 Mexicanos were also seeking employment in Omaha's meatpacking plants and in the sugar beet fields in the North Platte River valley, while others had migrated to the Belle Fourche area of western South Dakota, the Red River valley of North Dakota, and Wyoming for agricultural, particularly sugar beet, work. By the 1920s, the terms *beet workers* and *Mexicans* had become nearly synonymous. Late in the decade, Mexican field hands constituted as much as 90 percent of the workforce in the sugar beet fields. Companies such as the Great Western believed that they could not survive without Mexicano and Hispanic workers, and they actively recruited them from offices in San Antonio, Fort Worth, and El Paso.[9]

Across the Great Plains, Mexicanos endured racial prejudice, discrimination, and violence. Many, if not most, whites considered them inherently criminal with a natural propensity for stoop labor and felt that they would intermix with whites if given the opportunity. The invasion of Mexico by U.S. Marines in 1914, followed by Pancho Villa's raid into New Mexico, and another American invasion under the leadership of General John Pershing in 1916 only encouraged and perpetuated racial prejudice against people of Mexican descent. Transgressions of the law or social norms also brought the risk of lynching and mob violence in the name of justice.[10]

Because of the Anglo power structure, political organization for protection and support proved difficult even in the cities that had large concentrations of Mexicanos. Even the Catholic Church proved ambivalent in helping the Spanish-surnamed population. Although the church supported schools and helped perpetuate Hispanic culture, it too discriminated against its Mexicano followers. During the 1920s, for example, the diocese in Dallas, with 46,000 white Catholics, received almost as much financial assistance from the Catholic Extension Society as did Corpus Christi, which had a church membership eight times as large, most of those believers Mexicanos. The Catholic Church also permitted segregation within the church and often looked the other way (in part, to avoid antagonizing farmers and businesses that employed the Mexicanos) when Mexicanos suffered discrimination at the hands of the Anglo population.[11]

Homesteading also remained an irresistible lure for many immigrant groups. Jewish homesteaders, for example, came in families and groups, particularly to the northern Great Plains, to escape lives of oppression and want in Europe. Russian Jews especially sought the economic freedom that landownership promised. It became an anchor, a foundation of stability, something that gave them a sense of refuge and security in an empty and sometimes forbidding land. Between 1900 and 1908, the Jewish Agriculturalists' Aid Society of America (JAAS) provided assistance for the settlement of 144 families in twenty-six townships in North Dakota. Most of these homesteaders settled along the Missouri River in the north-central portion of the state because the eastern area had been claimed by farmers prior to the turn of the twentieth century.

The JAAS attempted to ensure success by placing Jewish farm families in communities and by assisting other family members who arrived several years later. Mutual social and cultural support, especially regarding religious practices, proved essential for the survival of these rural settlements. The Homestead Act, however, created dispersed settlements rather than permitted the re-creation of the Jewish village, or *shtetl*. Dispersed homesteads, limited train transportation, and poor roads often posed insurmountable stress for the maintenance of cultural continuities. In the absence of synagogues, rabbis, kosher butchers, and schools, Jewish women took responsibility for maintaining cultural traditions. Jewish immigrant women whose lives had been circumscribed by the village market and home also found themselves working in the fields as a matter of necessity. Moreover, the financial limitations that hindered all homesteaders were particularly severe for those from Eastern Europe, who had little money for the purchase of horses, plows, grain drills, binders, harnesses, wagons, and household necessities. The JAAS estimated that homesteaders needed $600 in cash to begin farming; other agencies estimated as high as $1,500, that is, triple the average annual income of an industrial worker in the United States during the early twentieth century. Although Jewish immigration societies often loaned money to help their farmers get settled, by 1910 the Jewish homesteading experience had peaked in North Dakota at 250 farms and 1,200 men, women, and children.

The environment and cultural odds proved overwhelming for most Jewish homesteaders. Many of these men and women who endured and "proved up" chose to sell their land when they acquired the deed. They used the capital to move to nearby towns along the Northern Pacific Railway. There they regained their sense of community and established businesses, such as bakeries, general merchandise stores, and harness shops, and more-traditional divisions of labor once again prevailed between men and women. The decline of Jewish homesteaders preceding World War I indicated that their contribution to the history of the Great Plains would be in the towns and cities of the region and not as farmers. Although the Homestead Act had lured them to the Great Plains, other occupations and lifestyles that were more traditional kept them there. They reaped the promise of the land indirectly or circuitously. For Jewish homesteaders, "proving up" meant moving on rather than remaining on the land.[12]

In 1907, Wichita had a large Jewish population, many of whom had recently emigrated from Eastern Europe. In contrast to the established Jewish community in Wichita, they were poor, devout, and without a command of English. They did not have blood or marriage or place-of-origin ties with the German Jews who immigrated during the late nineteenth century. They differed in dress, manners, and mannerisms from the educated, acculturated, and assimilated German Jews who had preceded them, and they introduced a strong sense of *Yiddishkeit*, that is, Jewish culture, to Wichita. These new Jewish immigrants primarily were young, single men and without a means of support. The established Jewish community, however, gave them strong social and religious support and found them jobs and a place to live. If the men were married, their wives worked alongside them in their businesses. The Eastern European immigrant Jews embraced education, which they recognized as the road to Americanization, and eventually moved into the business and professional classes. The established Jewish community provided an economic, cultural, and religious support network. Despite the tendency of the immigrants to be Orthodox rather than Reformed, the established residents welcomed them as relatives rather than strangers, and they received little resentment from the Jewish community or systematic discrimination from the non-Jewish residents. Although the National Origins Act of 1924 essentially ended further immigration by European Jews, the oil and natural gas boom in south-central Kansas brought Jewish migrants from other towns, and Jewish neighborhoods soon developed in nearby El Dorado and Hutchinson. The business success of the first and second generations of German Jews enabled social acceptance and permitted them to hold political offices in Wichita, which facilitated the acceptance of the Eastern European Jews during the early twentieth century.[13]

The Great Plains also continued to lure other immigrant groups. On the western edge of the region, Albuquerque became a promising destination for foreign-born Italians as family and friends who had previously settled in the city urged them to come via a host of letters, which contributed to the phenomenon of chain migration. Italian Americans also found Albuquerque a destination of choice, in part for the healthful climate in a tuberculosis-ridden age and in part as a promising city for economic gain, that is, a higher standard of living. They did not, however, seek an agricultural life, although most Italian immigrants had been farmers. Most of these immigrants chose white-collar employment in restaurants, saloons, and stores of various types, in contrast to the blue-collar, unskilled jobs that many Italian immigrants held in eastern cities. In 1907, the Consolidated Liquor Company, owned by Oreste Bachechi and Girolam Giome, for example, conducted a thriving business selling Kentucky whiskies and imported Italian olive oil. Others worked in the repair shops of the Santa Fe railroad. In Albuquerque, Italian immigrant women often labored as domestics and operated boardinghouses and grocery stores. Most of these Italian immigrants avoided the ethnic prejudices and discrimination of eastern cities, because they were accepted as part of the white working class (as distinguished from Mexicans and Asians). Moreover, they arrived about the same time as and in comparable numbers to immigrants of northern European ancestry, and their shared settlement experiences fostered bonding rather than division.[14]

Other immigrants, although not necessarily foreign born, also confronted discrimination, particularly in the oil and gas boomtowns of the central and southern Great Plains. In 1904, for example, the Kansas Natural Gas Company hired several hundred Italian, Austrian, and Greek workers to lay a pipeline from its wells in Montgomery County to consumers in Kansas City. When residents, businessmen, and town leaders in Coffeeville and Independence learned that they would not be able to control local distribution of the natural gas, they used violence to frighten away many of the workers. In mid-December, these "anti-pipers" hooded themselves and rode into the immigrant camp, threatened the workers with guns, and blew up a portion of the pipeline with dynamite. Many of the workers left the next day, the victims of local hostility against the Kansas Natural Gas Company. These immigrant workers experienced other forms of harassment, even bigotry. In Garnett, for example, the newspaper editor reported that "Dagos of all kinds and sizes" were "jabbering" on the streets. Residents did not consider the Italians "desirable citizens" and were glad to see them leave. Kansans treated these immigrants as outsiders and a threat to the improvement of wages and benefits. Harassment became part of their daily lives as it did in the coal-mining areas. In April 1905, a reporter for the *Kansas City Times* wrote, "There are more than 500 Greeks and Italians laying the pipeline in Allen County. . . . The men work about six feet apart in trenching . . . [and are] bossed by Irish foremen. . . . There are interpreters too . . . because the men do not speak enough English even to order a meal."[15]

Italian immigrants also experienced discrimination in the coal-mining area of southeastern Oklahoma. There, native-born whites resented their ethnicity and Catholicism; often called them "niggers," "dagos," and "wops"; and believed that they more than likely were bomb-making socialists. These Italians kept to themselves and made little effort to learn English or assimilate. This was particularly true of the southern Italians, who, if Sicilian, had a reputation for fighting among themselves. Only the Catholic Church offered a sense of security and solidarity.[16]

In October 1915, when the Wichita Natural Gas Company made a major oil strike in the El Dorado vicinity, workers flooded into the small towns looking for work. Many of the men were immigrants. With housing at a premium, locals gouged them for rents, which were often 300 percent higher than before the strike. In Butler County, however, a contemporary observed that "the population of Oil Hill is 100 percent American. Every employee is white, and 'none speak a foreign language and all are native-born Americans!'" Greek and Jewish immigrants did soon establish businesses in El Dorado. When World War I began, Kansans considered these immigrant workers spies and saboteurs. These "foreigners" sought social protection by establishing an American identity through education, by learning English, and by adopting new cultural traditions. In so doing, they began to lose their ethnic ties.[17]

During the early twentieth century, the ethnic and cultural distinctions so prominent during the late nineteenth century had blurred north of Indian Territory. The central and northern Great Plains had become an amalgam of peoples from the Old Northwest, New England, and the Mid-Atlantic states. Below the Red River of the South, migration patterns from the Upper and Deep South and corresponding cultural traits held true. In the central and northern Great Plains, immigrant Norwegians and ethnic Germans from Russia dominated the cultural distinctiveness of the settlers, with the Norwegians predominating in North Dakota and large pockets of German Russians scattered from North Dakota to Texas, where they had sought large blocks of cheap land to ensure community support. These ethnic clusters maintained cultural identity through marriage within their group.[18]

Ethnic identity among the German Russians and Norwegians remained well into the twentieth century, although the Norwegians acculturated and assimilated more readily, because they adopted the English language relatively quickly. The German Russians from the Black Sea area settled in the northern plains of the Dakotas and Canada, while the Volga Germans migrated to the central Great Plains of Kansas and Nebraska. They tended to remain aloof, preferring to retain their language and cultural cohesion. Pejoratively called "Rooshuns" by Anglo neighbors and looked down upon by the Reichsdeutsche, or Germans from Europe, they gave their loyalty to the land, church, and family while avoiding English, politics, and cities. They perpetuated their culture in a nearly closed society. The Black Sea and Volga German Russians were skillful farmers but kept to themselves and usually practiced Catholicism, while many of the Reichsdeutsche were Lutherans. They gained a reputation for resisting acculturation and assimilation. Locals considered them "hard-headed and stubborn." Above all else, they cared about the land—owning it, farming it, and living on it.[19]

In 1920, nearly 70,000 first- and second-generation Catholic German Russians from the Volga region lived in the central and southern Great Plains. Protestant Volga Germans had established the community of Dreispitz in Oklahoma and a colony in West Texas's Lipscomb County. In Kansas, they settled Protestant and Catholic communities, the latter primarily in Ellis County. Others settled in Laurel, Montana, and near Lingle, Wyoming. In Colorado, the Volga Germans preferred the rich farmland in the Arkansas and South Platte River valleys. In these and other immigrant communities, the church provided stability and cultural continuity as well as spiritual comfort. Immigrant families remained patriarchal and productive units in which women and girls followed gendered roles. By the 1920s, however, immigrant cultural ties to the past had steeply declined as they adopted English, attended public schools, and integrated into mainstream daily life. Only the church remained as a functioning cultural link to the past.[20]

The ethnic composition of the Great Plains during the early twentieth century also can be seen in relation to employment in the meatpacking industry. In Omaha and Kansas City, ethnicity characterized the workforce, while homogeneity marked the evolution of labor in small meatpacking towns such as Wichita, where the industry primarily attracted rural whites and only a few immigrants, African Americans, and Mexicans. In other packing towns such as Topeka, African Americans moved into the labor force after being drawn to the region as strikebreakers for other industries. Race relations between white, nonwhite, and immigrant workers often proved tense, particularly during times of union organizational activities.

Prior to World War I, large numbers of native whites held the majority of meatpacking jobs in Kansas City and Omaha. In 1911, Eastern Europeans constituted only 15 percent of that workforce in Kansas City and 29 percent in Omaha. American-born workers of German and Irish heritage dominated the American Federation of Labor's Amalgamated Meat Cutter and Butcher Workmen, constituting 41 percent of Kansas City's and 33 percent of Omaha's membership by 1914. During the 1920s, the meatpacking industry in Kansas City and Omaha increasingly employed African Americans and Mexican Americans. Eastern Europeans, who were at least second generation, constituted the largest group of packinghouse workers, with Czechs and Poles the most prominent in Omaha and Croatians in Kansas City, where Poles, Slovenes, Russians, Greeks, and Lithuanians also worked. By 1930, Mexican Americans had declined to 6 percent of the packinghouse workers in Kansas City and slightly less in Omaha. Mexican American and immigrant meatpacking workers lived in neighborhoods close to the stockyards, such as Little Bohemia and Little Poland in Omaha. Racial and ethnic divisions, such as the Anti-Greek Riot of 1909 in South Omaha (which resulted from festering grievances against Greek strikebreakers five years earlier), occasionally caused violence. Meat packers primarily hired African Americans as strikebreakers in Omaha and Kansas City. Throughout the early twentieth century, then, ethnic tensions born of economic competition and racism prevailed.[21]

At the turn of the twentieth century, the African American population in the Great Plains remained small, but it soon increased in several states because of the pull of wartime opportunities and the continued push of racial discrimination and violence in the South. At the time of statehood in 1907, blacks in Oklahoma constituted approximately 10 percent of the population but accounted for one-third of the lynching victims. Between 1907 and 1915, fifteen blacks were lynched in the state, with another thirteen illegally executed during the next fifteen years. Charges of rape and murder incited white vigilante action, but other social fears contributed to this violence. As the black population increased, African Americans became more visible and thereby more vulnerable to discrimination. They also increasingly competed for jobs and land, and many whites resented the economic rivalry and appearance of a subservient people rising above their station in life. Most whites who lived below a line that transected the state through Oklahoma City generally had migrated from the Democratic South, while Republican midwesterners primarily settled northern Oklahoma, but their racial views differed little. In Oklahoma, whites lynched blacks when they deemed that such violence was necessary to deter crime or to exact vengeance.[22]

At the same time, black towns provided a measure of safety and employment. In 1910, 37 percent of the black women in Oklahoma held jobs. In black towns, such as Boley and Langston, they held clerical positions. They also worked in the fields alongside their husbands and children. Local schools and churches provided a sense of progress and place. The best upward mobility for blacks meant enrolling in Langston University to become a teacher. Black ministers and women teachers usually served as community leaders. For the most part, however, urban and rural African Americans experienced poverty and discrimination. The Oklahoma legislature enacted Jim Crow laws, provided inferior education, prohibited miscegenation, and used the Grandfather Clause to deny blacks the right to vote. Social and economic change would not come for another half century. In the meantime, the coming of the Great Depression in 1929 marked the end for many black towns because the cotton and wheat crops suffered from drought and government acreage allocations that hurt small-scale farmers. Many African Americans left their farms, and the black towns collapsed.[23]

Although the African American population did not substantially increase until World War II when black workers and families began moving into the cities with war industries, the larger cities had an African American presence during the early twentieth century. In 1910, Denver had a black population of 5,400, which increased by 1929 to 7,000 (approximately 2 percent of the city's population); the men worked as railroad porters and janitors while the women held jobs in domestic service and as cooks and laundresses. Despite abuse from the police and discrimination in employment and other aspects of daily life, African Americans considered Denver a receptive city. The schools were not segregated, they were not relegated to the backs of streetcars or separate railroad cars, and blacks were not denied the right to vote by poll taxes, literacy tests, and property ownership. In 1921, the National Association for the Advancement of Colored People considered Denver a "utopia" for African Americans despite the strong presence of the Ku Klux Klan. African Americans confronted far more discrimination in the rim cities to the east, such as Omaha, where by 1920 the black population had increased to 5 percent of the city's residents. Racial discrimination in employment and housing developed to the point of segregation, all of which contributed to the race riot in 1919.[24]

In Nebraska, most blacks had migrated from the South, where 77 percent (in 1910) of the African American population of Omaha had been born, with nearly 23 percent claiming a Deep South origin. They had fled the pervasive racial violence in the region and sought jobs with the Union Pacific Railroad and the Cudahy, Armour, and Swift meatpacking plants in Omaha. Soon, however, they complained about segregation and job discrimination. Although only 13,000 blacks in a population of approximately 1.3 million lived in Nebraska, and while Omaha had an African American population of about 10,315 out of 191,000 in 1919, whites increasingly feared the rapidly growing black community. Many African Americans also had recently moved to Omaha fleeing race riots in Chicago and East St. Louis. Others came as strikebreakers for Omaha's meatpacking industry. White hostility, prejudice, and labor unrest increased from these social and economic threats based on racial hatred. Realtors used covenants, known as red lining, to restrict their living areas while employers relegated them to the lowest-paying jobs, and police harassment became customary.[25]

Racial tension in Omaha erupted in late September 1919, when a mob entered the jail in the Douglas County Court House and seized a black man accused of raping a white woman. Before the rioting ended, the mob had burned a portion of the building, nearly lynched the mayor, prevented firemen from putting out the flames of the burning courthouse, and attacked policemen. When calm returned, the victim burned on a pyre of lumber, two rioters lay dead, and nearly three dozen nursed injuries. The city administration lost the next election, more policemen were hired, and the city bosses tightened political control. Race relations did not change. The new city government sought amicable race relations, which meant no racial confrontation, nothing more.[26]

No racial violence elsewhere exceeded that in Tulsa during 1921, where vigilante justice prevailed. According to one editor, "In Oklahoma among thousands of people it is not considered a crime for a mob to kill a negro." Whites did not fear legal retribution, and the newspaperman thought vigilante action would not end soon. "If the past is to be made a criterion for the future," he wrote, "it is perfectly safe at any time and at any place for any considerable number of men to gather, take a prisoner from the hands of an officer and inflict the penalty of death." Race relations in Tulsa proved this rule. In this rapidly growing oil boom city, whites called the black part of town "Little Africa." They considered no race relations as good race relations. Racism, discrimination, and segregation had prevailed since territorial days, and white Oklahomans considered this social trilogy the natural order of society.

As a result, when an alleged attack of a white woman by a black man occurred, rumor spread quickly and incited a hatred that demanded vengeance in the name of justice, and a mob seized the alleged perpetrator from jail and hanged him. Then the mob systematically looted and burned the African American neighborhood and prevented firefighters from giving assistance. Blacks fought back in the streets. The violence escalated beyond the ability of the police to control it, and a full-scale race riot quickly developed. With the local police unable to prevent or end the rioting, the governor summoned the National Guard. The commanding general, Charles E. Barrett, recalled that when he arrived in Tulsa at the height of the rioting on June 1, "Twenty-five thousand whites, armed to the teeth, were ranging the city in utter and ruthless defiance of every concept of law and righteousness. Motor cars, bristling with guns swept through [the] city, their occupants firing at will." Operating on the governor's declaration of martial law, the guardsmen confiscated weapons and arrested looters.

By the time civil order had been restored on June 3, more than a thousand people had been treated for injuries and at least twenty-six blacks and ten whites had been killed. Fire had destroyed a more than thirty-block area, with 1,115 homes burned and another 314 looted but not torched. With thousands of Tulsa's African Americans homeless, city authorities opened the convention hall and McNulty Park for detention or refugee locations before moving some four thousand people to the fairgrounds, where city and county officials provided food and shelter. The detention center became virtually an incarceration camp, with blacks permitted to leave only for work. Police officers arrested African Americans on the streets if they did not wear green tags that listed their name, employer, and place of work. Many blacks fled the city never to return.

The white community blamed the black community for the riot, but the reasons are complex, and the violent confrontation between blacks and whites did not begin with the lynching, which was only a symptom of a racist society founded on regional cultural tradition, disparity of wealth and education, discrimination, exploitation, disrespect for the law and its officers, a tolerance (even an expectation) of violence in personal and community affairs, and irresponsible leadership. These features of a racist society were not unique to Oklahoma but existed between blacks and whites from Texas northward, particularly where cities brought both groups together in numbers large enough to provoke confrontations.[27]

As late as 1930, mob violence against blacks accused of assaulting white women ended with lynching. The southern tradition of using vigilante justice to maintain white supremacy in a culture where the public considered the lynching of blacks for punishment or vengeance as justifiable remained firmly embedded in a cadre of people who often had time on their hands and hatred of blacks on their minds. Law enforcement officers often proved unwilling or unable to prevent this violence and occasionally acquiesced. The culture of racial prejudice would not end soon in the Great Plains.[28]

Racial prejudice also contributed to the reorganization of the Ku Klux Klan (KKK), which made a brief, intimidating mark on the social and political affairs of the Great Plains. In 1915, William J. Simmons, an Alabama Methodist minister, resurrected the Ku Klux Klan at the same time that D. W. Griffith produced the silent film *The Birth of a Nation*, which portrayed blacks as ignorant degenerates. The new Klan embraced white racism, championed "100 percent Americanism," and identified Catholics, Jews, Asians, immigrants, and African Americans, among others, as detriments to the social and moral order. It also championed reform, by which Klansmen meant preserving and restoring the status quo, that is, white supremacy, Protestant fundamentalism, capitalism, and the separation of church and state as well as marital fidelity, premarital chastity, and respect for parental authority.[29]

The Klan gained strength and influence for its brief life in Texas following its emergence in Houston during 1920. Centered in Dallas, the Invisible Empire drew 75,000 robed Klansmen at a state fair. In 1922, Klansman Earl B. Mayfield won a seat in the U.S. Senate, and the KKK elected the lower house of the state legislature, gained a host of state and local offices, and elected the entire ticket in Dallas County. The Klan's previous reputation for night riding and violence gave extralegal support for its rather amorphous political and social agenda of supporting morality and opposing ethnic groups as well as Catholics and Jews. Kidnappings, whippings, and brandings, particularly of African Americans, became commonplace in the Texas plains. With police and city officials often members, the KKK operated with impunity during the early 1920s. In 1922, the KKK in Dallas flogged sixty-eight people in a special Klan flogging meadow along the Trinity River. Protestant ministers ranked among the best-known Klan leaders in Texas and Oklahoma. In Dallas, many businessmen and city leaders (including the police commissioner and police chief) considered it just another fraternal organization.[30]

Texans soon revolted against the Klan violence. The mayor of Dallas ordered the local Klan to disband, judges began sending Klansmen to jail. Chambers of commerce, American Legion posts, and the Texas Bar Association as well as the Masonic Lodge and the Daughters of the American Revolution denounced the Klan. In an attempt to change its public image, the Klan began emphasizing political action rather than tar-and-flogging parties, particularly in Dallas. In 1924, it became the major issue in the election, and Miriam "Ma" Ferguson and Dan Moody gained the governorship and attorney general's office, respectively, with anti-Klan campaigns. Soon thereafter, Texas became a staunchly anti-Klan state, but not before it had gained considerable support in the plains cities of Dallas, Fort Worth, and San Antonio.

After the 1924 election, the Democratic administration purged Klansmen from state government, and the legislature passed a law prohibiting parading in masks. In 1926, the Texas Klan faced bankruptcy and a rapidly declining membership. Sensible Texans saw it as a racist, divisive organization that brought embarrassment to the state and dissention to communities. It also prevented the Democratic machine from focusing on political issues that did not emphasize flagrant discrimination imposed by violence. The Klan lasted less than six years as a major quasi-political, extralegal, and moral force, and while most Texans probably agreed with the Klan's views on racial, religious, and moral affairs, the whippings and killings had been too much, and they were glad to see it go.[31]

By 1918, the Ku Klux Klan also had organized in Oklahoma, but it did not become an organization of consequence until 1921, when membership reached about 70,000. By 1923, an estimated 103,000 Oklahomans had joined the Klan. Oklahoma probably had a greater Klan membership than any other Great Plains state, and the state organization found a favorable atmosphere for recruitment following Tulsa's race riot in September 1921. Positioning itself as a law-and-order organization that took responsibility for aiding local law enforcement officers, the Klan's membership included the vice president of the University of Oklahoma, who served as the Grand Dragon. In 1922, the Catholic and farm vote gave Democrat Jack Walton the governorship, but Klan violence, with hundreds of floggings intended to ensure social reform, soon became a political issue. Most Klan victims were not African Americans, Catholics, or foreigners, but native-born, white Protestants, women, and teenagers as well as men. Whipping squads kidnapped and flogged anyone whom the Klan considered a moral transgressor in need of punishment to encourage good behavior. One Oklahoman spoke for many when he said, "I joined the Klan because it was doing the things that needed to be done. . . . It was cleaning up. . . . It was the only crowd that was doing anything decent." Klan violence in Oklahoma may have exceeded any other Great Plains state, with more than 2,500 cases reported in 1922 alone, along with nine deaths attributed to it. In the Sooner State, the Klan emphasized ending bootlegging, followed by promiscuity and criminal activity. Police officers did nothing to discourage Klan violence, and juries failed to convict. The Klan made a particularly violent mark in Tulsa, Okmulgee, and Enid, where the mayor said, "Our watchword is 'Keep your mouth shut tight and keep out of the hands of the Klansman.'" In August 1923, Governor Walton proclaimed martial law in

Tulsa and later across the state, suspended habeas corpus, and used the National Guard to enforce the law in the city, where a military court began taking evidence and sentencing floggers to jail.[32]

Oklahomans rejected Governor Walton's response to the Klan as much as many rejected the Klan itself. With newspaper headlines reading "neither Klan nor King," the state legislature impeached Walton for suspending habeas corpus, for improper use of the National Guard, and for malfeasance relating to election and governing issues, as well as incompetence. By 1923, however, Klansmen no longer needed to resort to violence to gain their objectives, because the order had a large membership that wielded considerable influence in municipal, county, and state government as well as law enforcement agencies, and it used its power for social ostracism and economic boycott with skill and efficiency. When the Klan-dominated legislature passed an unmasking act in December, the KKK welcomed the legislation because it would help ensure peaceful demonstrations that otherwise might turn violent if members could maintain anonymity behind their masks. The KKK, then, would be a law-and-order organization by ensuring proper behavior while members practiced it themselves.[33]

Yet at the height of its power and influence, the Oklahoma Klan fell into dissention, dividing over the support of legislative candidates and Martin Trapp, the new governor. Klan solidarity cracked, and its political opponents took advantage of the order's increasingly apparent disintegration. Critics called the Klansmen "bed sheet sheriffs" who exhibited "pillow case manhood," while dispensing "cow pasture justice." By the election of 1926, Klan membership had declined to less than twenty thousand, and internal conflict divided the organization. The Democratic State Central Committee reported Klan activity only in ten of the state's seventy-seven counties. The Protestants had begun to reassert their self-professed responsibility for mortality, voiced from the pulpit rather than enforced at the whipping post. They might divide bitterly over the Catholic Alfred E. Smith on the national presidential Democratic ticket and carry the state for Republican Herbert Hoover, but they would do so without violence delivered in the dark of night.[34]

In 1922, the Ku Klux Klan arrived in Kansas heady with its success in Oklahoma and at a time when labor trouble gripped the coal mines in the southeast and the railroads across the state. With the railroads hiring African American strikebreakers and a new state industrial courts system that clearly favored business, the Klan, working out of an office in Kansas City, Missouri, found a fertile ground for recruitment. The railroad towns of Arkansas City, Coffeyville, and Pittsburg proved ready for the organizational work of the Invisible Empire. With the Klan advocating open Bibles in school classrooms, support for Jim Crow laws, abolition of secret societies of African Americans, investigation of the Knights of Columbus, ballot control to prevent the election of Catholics, Jews, and the foreign-born to public office, boycotts of immigrant businesses, and denial of employment to blacks, among other goals, the Klan had a full agenda for social, political, and economic reform.[35]

Governor Henry Allen, however, moved quickly against the Klan. Using the state attorney general's office, he contended that the organization was a Georgia corporation that operated illegally without a charter in Kansas and with no purpose other than to cause civil disorder and religious and racial animosity "for the purpose of intimidation and threats against persons who did not conform to [its] plans, doctrines, theories, or practices." The State of Kansas would use the law and judiciary to ensure social control. The Klan, in turn, contended that it was a fraternal and charitable organization and did not need a state charter.

The law-and-order message of the Klan brought police officers into the organization, and many Kansans liked the Klan's message. Soon it began claiming success for electing political candidates for public offices. Although Klan membership alone probably did not win elections for candidates, it helped them identify with causes that won votes. The Klan endorsed candidates and expected members to vote for them. In 1924, its peak year in the state, most communities had a Klavern, or local chapter, and the state had about 100,000 members. With 25 percent of the population being African American, Jewish, or Catholic, the public soon recognized Klan activities as considerably less than benevolent. Klan members criticized racially integrated school activities, stopped cars on highways and searched for liquor, and invaded homes in Emporia to prevent card playing on Sundays. Klan members also whipped and beat individuals for a host of moral transgressions, and they considered themselves to be their brother's keeper.

Not all Kansans agreed with the Klan or cowered in its presence. Governor Allen, for example, called the Klan the "greatest curse that comes to a civilized people," while William Allen White, the nationally respected editor of the *Emporia Gazette*, referred to Klansmen as "moral idiots" and the Klan as an "organization of cowards." When Ben Paulen, a Klan sympathizer, if not member, received the Republican nomination for governor, White ran as an Independent, not expecting to win but intent on revealing Klan influence in the Republican Party. On the campaign trail, White reiterated this theme: "The gang rule first came into the Republican Party last May when a flock of dragons, kleages, Cyclopes, and fussy furies came to Wichita from Oklahoma and held a meeting with some Kansas terrors and whambedoddles." White could sting with his voice as well as his pen.

Although Paulen won the election, White claimed a moral victory because he had "spit in the face of the Klan" and brought considerable public awareness about KKK activities to Kansans. In January 1925, the state supreme court ruled that the Klan needed a charter to conduct business in the state, thereby ousting it from Kansas on a legal technicality. The Klan ignored the decision and (with the state's Grand Dragon urging members to "stand firm" and "fight to the last breath and the last drop of blood") attempted to gain exemption through the legislative process, which caused a contentious debate before the bill met defeat by a close vote. The Klan then turned to the federal courts but could not gain the right to operate without a charter.

Unable to maintain a legal identity, the Klan could only influence public behavior through intimidation and violence, but the people that it tried to intimidate were not without legal protection, as had been the case with African Americans in the South during the late nineteenth century. In Kansas, blacks, Jews, and Catholics stood their ground. By the mid-1920s, most Kansans had come to consider the Klan nothing more than an organization that lived on bigotry and violence, and they shunned it publicly and fought it through the legal process. At the same time, Kansas Klansmen, like their Oklahoma counterparts, fell into internal bickering over the organization's finances, and members who had joined to support law and order drifted away after learning about floggings, mutilations, and murders. They had their own view of a peaceful, moral society, and they would not support atrocities by those who advocated violence to achieve it. By 1927, the KKK no longer had a voice or power in Kansas.[36]

In 1921, the Klan also organized in Omaha with outside recruiters who professed that a basic principle of the Klan was "adherence to law and order." One Klansman speaking for the organization contended, "We are an organization of Americans. We are non-everything that is un-American . . . We are a secret organization of Protestant, white, gentile Americans, ready to uphold the constitution." Within the year, twenty-four local Klans had been organized in Nebraska, and reports claimed that 800 people were joining the KKK per week.

In mid-1922, Omaha's black newspaper, the *Monitor*, estimated Klan membership at 1,100, but the next year, Klan headquarters in Atlanta reported the membership statewide at 45,000. The Klan had the greatest strength in Omaha, Fremont, Lincoln, York, Grand Island, Hastings,

North Platte, and Scottsbluff, locations of recognized urban status (at least in the Great Plains), rather than rural communities. By 1924, Klan parades and cross burnings had become common. A year later, approximately 1,500 Klansmen paraded in Lincoln during the state convention, while an estimated 25,000 curious observers attended a Klan-sponsored picnic. Patriotic speeches and cross burnings accompanied KKK activities, which gave the organization a semblance of legitimacy as well as ominous power or, as one organizer put it, conveyed "a dignified, dependable agency for the achievement of civic righteousness." In 1925, an estimated 2,000 members of the Women of the Klan, an auxiliary, met in Lincoln, where they, too, paraded and listened to speeches and discussed Christianity, Prohibition, strikes, and white supremacy. Boys and girls could join the junior Klan. The Women of the Klan were active in Lincoln, York, Norfolk, Fremont, and Weeping Water, while the organization proved most attractive in Lincoln, with an estimated 5,000 members.

In Nebraska, people joined the Klan for many reasons: some were motivated by fraternalism, others by excitement, and still others by opposition to the teaching of evolution or to the Catholic Church. If anything, the Klan was a heterogeneous organization composed of all classes, income groups, and political parties. Klansmen and women particularly argued that Catholics gave their allegiance to the Pope, not the Constitution, and that the Vatican would end the separation of church and state and destroy religious freedom; additionally, the Klan charged that Jews could never be assimilated into American, that is, Protestant, life. By 1926, these beliefs had created growing opposition to the Klan as men and women of reason attacked the organization in the press and from the pulpits as an un-American, undemocratic, and un-Christian organization, seeing Klan attacks on Catholics, Jews, and African Americans as blatant prejudice, racism, and bigotry.

Most Nebraskans and residents of the Great Plains would have held the same prejudices against blacks, Jews, Catholics, and immigrants had the Klan not existed, because they worried, even feared, for the preservation of their social and economic welfare. They favored the status quo in an age of great change, and the Klan offered the willing and susceptible Nebraskans the security of a white, native-born, Protestant society. The race riots in Omaha and Tulsa and similar confrontations elsewhere in the region clearly indicated that the Great Plains had a race problem; the Klan seemed to be an organization that could help maintain law and order and keep the undesirable and the unwanted in their place. Moreover, the Klan sought the support of farmers by advocating a grain-export corporation, federal aid to cooperatives, government purchase of surplus wheat, fixed prices for farm commodities, better credit, and the development of the St. Lawrence Seaway to improve trade and with it farm income. The Klan also opposed the Industrial Workers of the World (IWW), whom Nebraska farmers often feared at harvest time for fomenting strikes and damaging property to gain higher wages. The Klan considered the IWW a revolutionary organization, while the KKK promised to ensure Americanism.

From the early 1920s until the end of the decade, Nebraska newspaper editors either attacked or ignored the Klan; none supported it. The chancellor of the University of Nebraska promised the expulsion of any student who joined the organization. Public officials also spoke against the Klan as an organization that promoted mob rule and violence. In Omaha, the mayor prohibited public meetings of the Klan. By 1926, the KKK had peaked in the Cornhusker state. Without clear evidence that it influenced politics and policy, it remained a social organization with only bluster and no power. Nebraskans knew that change came through the political process, and they increasingly ignored the Klan and considered it a rough, fringe organization that caused more dissention than harmony and social order.[37]

In contrast to the limited influence gained by the Klan in the other Great Plains states, the Klan enjoyed exceptional success in Colorado. Arriving in 1920, it lodged in the cities on the western fringe of the Great Plains. Denver served as the Klan center; one in seven people in that city gave allegiance to the Invisible Empire. Avoiding its mistake in Kansas, the Klan filed for incorporation in Colorado, stating that its intent was to "unite white male Gentile native-born citizens of the United States into a fraternal militant society" to support and maintain the principles of "true Americanism." Two years later, it became a major force in Denver politics. In 1923, the Klan elected the mayor, who then used his power to appoint Klansmen to city offices, including the police, legal offices, and courts. Denverites liked the Klan's demands for law and order, particularly in the Jewish, Mexican American, African American, Italian, Polish, German Russian, and Austrian communities. With few Jews and fewer African Americans in the state, Catholics suffered the brunt of Klan animosity, reinforced in November with a twenty-three-foot-high burning cross on the steps of the capitol. Businessmen apparently joined to prevent the Klan from boycotting their stores, while politicians saw the advantage of block votes. In 1924, the Klan controlled the Republican Party, captured state and municipal offices, controlled the lower house of the legislature, and elected two Klansmen to the U.S. Senate. Klansman Clarence Morley won

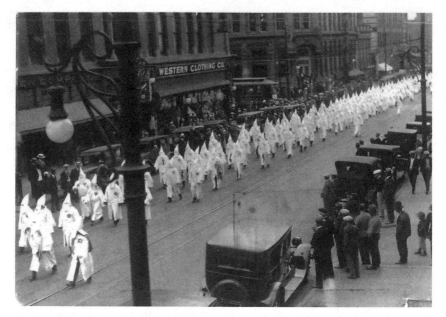

The Ku Klux Klan became popular during the early 1920s, particularly in Colorado. On May 31, 1926, these Klansmen paraded down Larimer Street in Denver on their way to a state convention.

the governorship, and the Klan-infested Republican Party carried Colorado for Coolidge, bolstered by the economic comfort of a good sugar beet crop. With more than sixty thousand Klansmen robed in Colorado, they wielded considerable political power.[38]

During the 1924 campaign, Klansmen broke up opposition meetings and denied free speech to opponents. At a citizens' meeting in the Denver City Auditorium, Klan men and women hooted down District Attorney Philip Van Clise when he attempted to speak before the Invisible Government League. One observer reported the behavior of Klan women, saying that "they paid ten dollars to hate somebody, and they were determined to get their money's worth." Insurgent Republicans and Democrats elected to the state senate, however, blocked all significant Klan-sponsored bills. Moreover, by 1925, internal fighting had seriously weakened the Klan's ability to act, and the regular Republicans saw an opportunity to purge the Klansmen. By nominating anti-Klan slates to oppose Klan tickets in the primary election, along with an anti-Klan voter backlash, a host of non-Klan Republicans gained a number of offices. By 1928, neither the Democrats nor Republicans needed to pander to the KKK, and the organization essentially ceased to exist, but not before Colorado had earned a reputation for supporting the KKK that was superseded only by Indiana, Georgia, and Alabama.[39]

Where the Klan organized in South Dakota, anti-Catholicism became its attractive and unifying platform. In 1921, the KKK went to Sioux Falls, South Dakota, to help confront the Catholic menace in the northern Great Plains. By 1925, the Klan had established a presence in every major town in South Dakota. The Klan found willing members, and cross burnings, tarring and featherings, and mass rallies and parades became common, particularly in the West River mining towns such as Rapid City. By 1928, however, few South Dakotans still cared about the Klan. The Nonpartisan League no longer proved a threat and therefore no longer a Klan issue. Even the election of 1928 could not energize the Klan in the two Dakotas. South Dakotans considered it an irrelevant, hateful organization, and by the mid-1930s it had disappeared from the state.[40]

The Klan enjoyed more success in Grand Forks, North Dakota, where its members came from the business community and considered the schools vulnerable to Catholic teachings. The Catholic threat to the social order proved nonexistent where Protestant, particularly Lutheran, congregations dominated the town's religious order. Yet these middle- and upper-class Protestants gave the North Dakota Klan political power. In 1926, the Klan gained control of the school board, which mandated Bible reading in the classrooms, as well as of the city commission and police court. Quickly, the city commissioners fired some city employees, thereby foiling a perceived Catholic threat to gain control of the town. Thereafter, the Klan ceased as an organization of political consequence once the imagined danger to the social order had passed. The people of Wyoming and Montana also showed little interest in the Klan, and New Mexico (as a Catholic, Hispanic state, with a Jewish governor) gave it little support.[41]

Thousands of middle-class citizens in the Great Plains, then, had joined the KKK because they believed that a host of economic, social, and cultural changes as well as dangers from Communists and other political radicals required a militarist organization to help ensure law and order and enforce the practice of moral principles based on Protestantism. Soon, however, they discovered that the KKK (with its secret membership rolls, masked members, and penchant for violence) attracted a host of grudge holders and fanatics. The extralegal activities of the KKK soon became unacceptable to many plains men and women, and in the late 1920s they gave little thought to the KKK. While members of the order increasingly fought among themselves over finances, positions, and power, they could not counter the growing public apathy that gave new meaning to the term "Invisible Empire."[42]

At the turn of the twentieth century, education remained the principal means by which the federal government intended to assimilate and acculturate the Indians of the Great Plains. Government-sponsored reservation day and boarding schools along with off-reservation residency schools would enable Indian children to learn white social and economic practices and reject their cultural legacy. In time, a new culture would become their own. On the Kiowa-Comanche-Apache Reservation in Oklahoma, one government official considered the effect of the reservation boarding school like the "constant dripping of water [that] wears away the headstone": little by little, the reservation schools would wear away Indian culture in the Great Plains. In time, Indian children would become Americanized (that is, white) except for skin color and would serve as models for the complete transformation of their people. They would learn Christianity, farming, and homemaking as well as the concept of private property. Most Indian children would attend reservation day and boarding schools, but off-reservation schools, such as Chilocco (which primarily served the Ponca and Pawnee reservations in Oklahoma) and the Haskell Institute in Kansas (which drew a variety of children from the plains tribes) gained reputations for providing better education for Indian children than most schools across the plains.[43]

Assimilation and acculturation through education, however, cost money, and neither the federal government nor interested religious denominations committed the necessary resources. As a result, by the early twentieth century, the Bureau of Indian Affairs (BIA) essentially had given up its plans to use education to transform the Indian people. During the Progressive Era, Indian schools became mere way stations while students matured, learned English, and trained for manual labor within a white society that would not accept them as equals. Teachers often proved incompetent and maintained order with cruel punishments. Turnover (of both teachers and students) plagued the Indian schools. At the Rainy Mountain school on the Kiowa-Comanche-Apache Reservation in Oklahoma, teachers averaged only six months on the job. School administrators, cooks, farmers, and laborers also came and went with considerable frequency, largely because of low pay and the isolation of the schools. The dedicated employees who persevered on energy and devotion meant the difference between a miserable and a caring environment for the children. Private and denominational schools suffered similar problems. Inadequacies in the areas of sanitation, clean drinking water, and medical care as well as in classrooms, dormitories, and food and clothing, along with outdated instructional materials, hindered learning. The BIA measured education success by the number of children taught and the perceived effect of destroying Indian culture.[44]

In 1907, Indian Commissioner Francis Leupp favored placing Indian children in public schools to save money. During the Progressive Era, BIA officials also lowered educational expectations for the Indians. At the reservation schools, Indian children had essentially two tasks — learn English and a trade (usually outmoded, such as blacksmithing and tinsmithing, as well as the more practical vocational practices of carpentry and farming and, by the 1930s, automobile mechanics). For the girls, education meant learning housekeeping in the white tradition and various domestic arts such as sewing and cooking, with their training geared for employment as domestic servants. At Chilocco, for example, the girls learned to make dresses, curtains, and rugs in the sewing rooms and conducted drudge work in the laundry and kitchen.[45]

In 1919, the BIA planned to terminate twenty-five reservation boarding schools in Oklahoma alone to reduce costs; this would force Indian children to attend public schools despite the wishes of their parents. White school officials often complained that their schools suffered from overcrowding and too few teachers and that Indian children were not ready for their classrooms and could not keep up with the work. In addition, white parents and children did not want to associate with Indians. Kiowa children often discovered that white teachers in the public schools would not permit them to enter the classrooms. One school superintendent reported that "with few exceptions the Indian children who attended the Hobart schools are unwelcome and repulsive to whites."[46]

In the end, the Indian schools did not destroy tribal cultures but instead taught Indian children to negotiate their lives in both the white and native worlds. During the Progressive Era, BIA educational policy turned from its original intent to destroy Indian culture to preparing Indian children for lives on the fringe of white America. Although unwanted by white society, the Indians would be useful servants looking in. As a result, Indians would remain marginalized by policies based on racism, segregation, and isolation.[47]

While failing to destroy Native American culture, the off-reservation boarding schools with multitribal students created a "pan-Indian" identity that resulted from the intermixture of students from many tribes. At these schools, the federal government did not make allowances for tribal cultural differences: Indian children were merely Indians. As a result, Indian children became less Kiowa, Cheyenne, and Sioux and more "Indian." At the same time, the boarding schools also had the dual effect of strengthening tribal loyalty as students from the same tribe, confronting great stress, bonded for mutual support in groups based on shared language and culture. In addition, the Great Plains reservation boarding schools became institutions of last resort to provide care for children of financially destitute parents when BIA assistance to those living on the reservations became insufficient. Basic learning occurred, of course, despite militaristic regimentation that stifled independent inquiry and creativity. In 1919, the superintendent reported good discipline during the year: "I doubt if there is an educational institution anywhere that is freer from vice, evil habits and general misconduct than is the Chilocco school." Little wonder, then, that those Indian children sometimes fled for home.[48]

Despite the mental and physical cruelty inflicted on Indian children at the boarding schools, certain beneficial and unintended consequences of this forced educational system developed that aided and strengthened the tribal groups on many reservations. In Indian Territory, where the BIA established boarding schools on the reservations, the children were not separated from their families by great distances. Parents and family members could visit their children relatively easily, and the students often returned home on weekends. At the boarding schools, Indian children could associate with each other, despite the controlled environment. Close proximity and contact with family and friends during a time when the BIA worked to allot land and end the reservation system enabled these Indian children to maintain tribal identity.[49]

The boarding schools also became a symbol of government responsibility to the Indians. The tribes, having sold their lands, considered their treaty rights sacrosanct. Educational benefits or promises, then, became not only practical but also inalienable rights. In time, many Indians worried that the BIA would close the schools. This fear was not unfounded, not only because critics began to question the cost of Indian education (particularly at the off-reservation boarding schools) but also because of a growing social thought that held that inherited racial characteristics could not be changed by the environment. Other critics argued that these schools encouraged dependency, because students received the benefits of civilization, such as hot water, electricity, and steam heat, without working for these conveniences. Even so, the boarding schools remained as the last federal hope to do what war, destruction of the bison, disease, starvation, allotment, and missionaries had failed to do, that is, destroy the Indian way of life in the Great Plains. By the end of the 1920s, only the schools still offered any hope of achieving that goal.[50]

Indian children and parents also used reservation day schools to reinforce cultural traditions. Between 1900 and the waning of assimilationist educational policy during the 1920s, approximately 15 to 20 percent of Indian children attended a reservation day school annually. Reservation day schools could teach more students for less cost than off-reservation or reservation boarding schools. Moreover, the lessons taught at the day schools could be shared with parents at night, thereby achieving assimilation policy on a wide scale. The young and the old would learn as a result of the reservation day schools. At these schools, such as at Pine Ridge in South Dakota, the teachers were not omnipotent. They lived among the Indians and relied on the tribe for daily assistance, friendship, and security. Moreover, reservation day schools prevented separation of students and parents and created a more comfortable, less threatening, learning environment. When the students returned home at night, they reimmersed into Oglala culture. Given this situation, cultural makeovers in the day schools proved impossible. With home close by, Oglala children also felt considerably more freedom to challenge their teachers or to refuse to speak English, in contrast to those children who lived under more authority at the off-reservation or reservation boarding schools. Day schools, then, gave Indian children the tools, particularly English, that were necessary to negotiate the white world, but the schools also unintentionally helped maintain Indian culture. Indeed, the day schools primarily served individual bands for which kinship bound the community together. Consequently, the day schools strengthened bonds of kinship and community by educating the children, who essentially and intentionally were segregated and reliant upon themselves but were not separated from their communities. Moreover, the day schools provided meals, clothing, and care, and the teachers often served as advisors and social workers for their communities, thereby strengthening them.[51]

During the first three decades of the twentieth century, federal officials and friends of the Indians also believed that an agricultural way of life would help the Great Plains tribes become economically independent and assimilated into American, that is, white society. Yet federal support always proved insufficient to meet policy goals. Unless the Indians received adequate equipment, livestock, and seed as well as credit and training, the goal of making Indians into white farmers had no chance of success. Moreover, the harsh environment often ruined government plans to make Indians into small-scale farmers in the white tradition. As a result, reservation Indians continued to rely on the federal government to meet nearly all of their food needs.[52]

Increasingly, the Indians leased their allotted and heirship (that is, inherited) lands to whites, who pressured the federal government to declare more Indians competent to receive title to their allotments, which meant that those lands could be sold to whites. In May 1906, the Burke Act enabled the secretary of the interior to declare an allottee competent to manage his or her own affairs prior to the termination of the twenty-five-year trust period. This act authorized the secretary of the interior to grant a patent in fee simple (in other words, a title) to an allotment. Francis Ellington Leupp, the commissioner of Indian affairs at the time, believed that the Burke Act would help solve the "Indian problem," because Indians who held title to their land would no longer have claims upon the federal government for support. In 1914, the BIA began organizing commissions to survey reservations and determine which Indians were competent to receive title to their allotments. The commissioners often issued patents to incompetent Indians or to those who did not want title because they would be obligated to pay property taxes. Once issued, these land titles could not be refused. Friends of the Indians, however, believed that Indian lands of "great value" would soon be sold to whites. They were correct. Soon the reservations were checkerboarded by white landholdings. Moreover, without access to irrigation, much of the tribal and allotted land in the Great Plains could not support self-sufficient farming. Leasing to cattle ranchers, however, provided a dependable, though limited, income for Indian landowners, and many allottees preferred earning some money to none at all. Until the end of the administration of Herbert Hoover, most policy makers and those who influenced Indian affairs remained convinced that an agricultural way of life for all Great Plains Indians would ensure assimilation and end their dependency on the federal government.[53]

At the same time, intertribal divisions began to emerge. Among the Blackfeet, for example, full- and mixed-bloods began dividing over the best land-use practices for the tribe. The full-bloods favored further development of agriculture, while the rapidly growing population of mixed-bloods advocated development of the tribe's oil reserves, livestock operations, and engagement in other business practices. The mixed-bloods or assimilated Blackfeet favored dissolution of the reservation, while the full-bloods sought to keep the tribal estate intact. By 1914, with the number of full- and mixed-bloods nearly equal, the political stakes for power and influence within the tribe had become increasingly divisive.

Although the Blackfeet Reservation had been allotted by 1920, considerable debate existed about the tribe's use of the remaining tribal land. With the collapse of the livestock industry and wheat prices during the early

1920s, the Blackfeet Tribal Business Council sought the development of reservation oil reserves in hope of generating income similar to the oil-producing nations in Oklahoma, particularly the Osage, which in one day in 1916 earned $2.3 million in oil royalties from the lease of tribal lands. The Bureau of Indian Affairs, however, had little interest in developing the oil reserves on Indian lands in Montana. By the late 1920s, the lack of government support for the development of the natural resources on the Blackfeet Reservation had led full- and mixed-bloods to believe that the tribe would have to solve its own economic problems. But precisely who composed the tribe — only full-bloods, or mixed-bloods too? And could their cultural differences be bridged to enable combined action to address their political and economic problems? Other Great Plains tribes would face the same dilemmas, particularly after the federal government gave them the opportunity to take increasing control of their own affairs.[54]

In contrast, among the Osages to the South, each tribal member (including mixed-bloods) was entitled to an equal share of all mineral income. As oil royalties grew with the expansion of drilling and production after 1900, money flowed into Osage bank accounts. In 1920, oil and gas royalties reached $8,090 per person, which meant that a family of five had an income of $40,450 and, in 1925, $65,000. Yet, in the late 1920s, most Great Plains Indians earned less than $200 annually. Individual wildcatters and oil companies inundated the Osages and brought social disruption including trespass, theft, and murder to their lives and families, which gave new meaning to the term "Roaring Twenties." While some Great Plains tribes approached starvation and abject poverty and want, the Osages lived lavish lifestyles, enjoying automobiles, expensive houses, and fine china and silverware. The Osages had oil money, and they spent it embracing the cultural materialism of white society, but at a cost to Osage family cohesion and kinship relationships. The oil industry, then, brought wealth and confrontation to the Osages in the southern Great Plains. During the 1920s, one government agent reported, "If their oil should fail the Osage people would be in a hard predicament more so than any other Indian Tribe because they have lived expensively and have become accustomed to it." His words proved prophetic.[55]

Changes in Indian culture can also be seen in relation to the BIA's prohibition of native dancing (meant to change Indian traditions) while tribal members discovered ways to maintain their values related to religion or spiritualism. Among the Great Plains tribes, particularly the Lakotas, Cheyennes, Kiowas, Blackfeet, and Arapahos, the annual Sun Dance affirmed their place in the world, and the ceremony strengthened intratribal relationships and fulfilled tribal obligations to the Creator. Consequently, the Sun Dance served as an essential religious, social, and political event for the well-being of the tribes. The Sun Dance involved fasting, dancing, and lessons regarding the ritual. Among the Cheyennes, Lakotas, Blackfeet, and Arapahos, however, it also involved self-sacrifice in the form of bodily mutilation by piercing the breasts or back with skewers attached to rawhide strings attached to a pole. The dancers attempted to pull the skewers through their flesh, thereby making a sacred sacrifice of flesh to the Creator. Those who undertook the Sun Dance brought great prestige to themselves, and the scars that they bore for the rest of their life testified to their loyalty to and consideration for the tribe.

The BIA considered the Sun Dance militaristic and banned it as early as 1883, but the Great Plains tribes kept the ceremony alive. In 1907, after Cheyenne leaders at the Tongue River Reservation in Montana argued that they had the constitutional right to practice their religion, BIA officials recanted and lifted the ban. Shrewdly, the Cheyennes scheduled the Sun Dance on the Fourth of July and eliminated the aspect of self-sacrifice. Whites considered it an exciting example of native culture and tribal identity, but the BIA reinstituted the ban in 1911. The Cheyennes, however, continued the Sun Dance, stressing its social value before whites but emphasizing its religious significance when they danced out of sight and mind of reservation officials.[56]

During the early twentieth century, the Great Plains tribes also resurrected other dances that the BIA had banned because officials believed that dancing, singing, and drumming hindered assimilation. By scheduling these activities on major holidays, however, the tribes seemingly emphasized the educational and entertainment value of the performances for whites while also ensuring their cultural, social, and religious heritage and maintaining individual, clan, and community identities. The Lakotas convinced BIA officials that only the old people (that is, "lost causes"), not the young people, wanted to dance. By 1922, however, the superintendent at the Standing Rock Agency could report that "nearly every male adult of the reservation" participated in tribal dances. Commissioner of Indian Affairs Charles H. Burke admitted that the federal government could not prevent the Indians from dancing on their own allotments, or property. Moreover, Congress passed the General Citizenship Act of 1924, which gave the Indians the legal right to oppose BIA prohibitions on dancing, singing, and drumming. By the 1930s, the Great Plains tribes had become masters at using dancing as a social and political mechanism of cultural resistance under the guise of education and patriotic fidelity to whites and the federal government.[57]

In the 1920s, BIA officials also came under increasing criticism from friends of the Indians. As a result, in 1926, Secretary of the Interior Herbert Work asked the Institute for Government Research (present-day Brookings Institution) to conduct a comprehensive study of the social and economic conditions on the reservations and provide recommendations for changes in federal policy. Two years later, the institution issued the Meriam Report, which found that the reservations were plagued by inferior education and housing, chronic poverty, poor sanitation, disease, and malnutrition, which limited the average life expectancy to forty-four years, during which time they lived "below any reasonable standard of health and decency." The report attacked the efforts of the BIA to destroy Indian culture and force assimilation and acculturation, along with the boarding schools and allotment policies. As the nation approached economic collapse, the Great Plains Indians, who had been enduring poverty and want since having been driven onto the reservations in the late nineteenth century, neared cultural disintegration. Few realized, from their homes in the Great Plains, that federal policy would soon change, bringing new hopes and new problems.[58]

In the meantime, most Great Plains residents considered African Americans, Mexican Americans, and poor working-class whites as undesirables and unwanted in their communities. The cities and towns attracted the unskilled (of color, of suspicious ethnicity, and whites alike), while the farms and oil fields drew those with grievances who sought retaliation against those who paid them little and worked them hard. As a result, poverty, violence, and desperation often prevailed among these groups, much to the concern of the middle- and upper-class whites. Segregation and discrimination against nonwhites, which included Catholics and Jews, commonly occurred across the region in response to these concerns. The sharp dichotomy between hope and despair, law and justice, and peace and violence gave a hard-edged reality to life in the Great Plains, where expanding agriculture, manufacturing, and transportation as well as growing cities and towns made the region economically prosperous, socially diverse, and politically volatile.[59]

CHAPTER THREE

The Age of Uncertainty

Fear stalked many Germans in the Great Plains during World War I. Most Great Plains residents (like most other Americans) identified with Anglo-Saxon Protestantism, and Anglo-Americans were the largest ethnic group in the nation. At the same time, most German Catholics, Lutherans, and Mennonites who lived in the Great Plains considered themselves Americans. Although they enjoyed their German cultural heritage, such as church, language, and social life, they had no loyalty to the German imperial government. The Anglo population, however, took pride in its dominant language, political institutions, religion, and democratic practices. These plains men and women considered Germany to be militaristic and autocratic and, by extension, suspected that anyone of German descent would be supportive of the German government. Some people of German heritage, by accepting Germany's explanation about the causes of the war or by showing too much sympathy for Germany, did not help to dispel this suspicion. In Kansas, for example, one farmer of German descent flew the German flag over his house and received the critical judgment of the residents in the surrounding area. In the Nebraska Synod, many German Lutherans denounced Great Britain while defending American neutrality, particularly in relation to an arms embargo. Many German Catholics also expressed strong pro-German sentiments and exhibited a defensive attitude about their cultural heritage. All efforts to defend Germany's political and military goals, however, brought increasing hostility from other residents and groups in the Great Plains.[1]

Overall, German Americans by birth or descent responded to World

War I with little uniformity. Some flaunted German heritage, while others emphasized their Americanism and respect for the law. Government officials and superpatriots, however, increasingly demanded expressions of loyalty. By 1917, German-language newspapers and education made this group suspect, even guilty, of insufficient support for the war effort. In Kansas, the *Topeka Capital* demanded the silencing of every German-language newspaper in the state, because the editors allegedly hoped that Germany would win the war and, therefore, were disloyal. Similarly, by the autumn of 1917, the majority of Great Plains residents hated Germans and any symbols of German culture, and they proceeded to eliminate all vestiges of German identity. City officials changed the names of streets, schools, and parks, even the names of towns. Germantown, Nebraska, became Garland; Berlin changed to Otoe; and Potsdam was rechristened Potts. In May 1918, the editor of the *Yankton Press and Dakotan*, however, questioned calling sauerkraut "liberty cabbage," asking, "Aren't we overdoing our anti-Germanism when we jump on this helpless vegetable?" Undeterred by such reasoning, the German State Bank became the Avon State Bank. In Sioux Falls, officials changed the name of Germania Hall, the site of three state constitutional conventions, to Columbia Hall.[2]

In Nebraska, the Germans constituted the largest group by immigration and descent, which made them conspicuous as an enemy within. Approximately 40,000 of the state's 1.2 million people had been born in Germany. In thirty-four counties, from 10 percent to 25 percent of the population were born in foreign countries, particularly Germany, Austria, and Hungary. Approximately 60 percent of these foreign born were naturalized citizens. Given these numbers, the danger from German subversives became apparent to most Nebraskans. Indeed, with forty German-language newspapers in Nebraska alone and with Lutheran ministers conducting church services in German, teachers in the parochial schools using that language extensively, and approximately 6 percent of the population in the Cornhusker state unable to speak English, the danger to the public seemed obvious.[3]

On April 18, 1917, the legislature created the Nebraska State Council of Defense to encourage agricultural production, provide aid to the Red Cross, and support Liberty Loan drives as well as provide work for the Home Guard. Like other state councils of defense, the Nebraska body possessed broad and unusual powers, such as the right to subpoena witnesses, punish for contempt, and compel the presentation of evidence. With these powers, the council became the most active and dangerous organization in the Great Plains in the violation of civil liberties. In July, the council announced that many German residents and "conspicuous leaders" of the

Lutheran church had committed dangerous acts, ranging from "utterances of a treasonable character to direct acts and words of disloyalty." The council accused Nebraska's Germans of opposing the sale of war bonds and the work of the Red Cross. Moreover, the council charged that the Lutheran church had no organized war relief activities, that many of its leaders exhibited "dangerous tendencies," and that church officials favored the German cause. The publisher of the *Lincoln Star* warned that the Lutheran church served as an outlet for German propaganda. When Lutheran representatives met with the council of defense, they reiterated that church doctrine prevented the clergy from advocating the purchase of Liberty Bonds and participating in Red Cross and food- and fuel-conservation programs because to "preach up" such activities would violate their commitment to the separation of church and state as well as individual conscience. The council disagreed with those excuses and prohibited the use of German in schools, churches, public meetings, and over the phone and demanded the removal of German-language books from the state traveling library. It also encouraged school boards to inspect textbooks for pro-German sympathies and enforced the state Sedition Law that required teachers to promise not to use a foreign language in the classroom. This same restraint applied to ministers.[4]

Disloyalty, if not clear cases of treason, seemed to abound among the German population in Nebraska, and the council of defense urged law enforcement officials to station guards at public meetings, inspect packages for bombs, and arrest suspicious people. The council also encouraged county councils to guard water supplies, food storehouses, and other critical sites and buildings, and it ordered the confiscation of all guns and ammunition from Germans who were not citizens when they registered as enemy aliens, as required by federal law in late 1918. Because Nebraska's Germans voted overwhelmingly for candidates who pledged to protect their civil liberties, the Republican governor and legislature repealed the open primary and reinstated the nominating convention for the selection of state party candidates, thereby removing German influence from the selection process.[5]

In Denver, on the western edge of the Great Plains, Mayor Robert Speer placed armed guards at the pumping plants of the Denver Union Water Company while Governor Julius Gunter ordered the National Guard to patrol the reservoir and prevent German sabotage at the Colorado Power Company. Lutheran schools in Colorado and the Denver high schools also stopped teaching German. In Weld County, a rumor spread that Mexican agents planned to enlist migrant workers to join any German attack on the

United States. Residents responded to such rumors by forcing the deputy county clerk to resign, upon learning that he had been born in Germany. The city and county clerks in Denver suffered the same fate. Residents of German heritage also received blame for cattle rustling and the opposition of some Indian tribes to the military draft. In December 1917, a mob in Hugo forced a naturalized citizen from Austria to kiss the U.S. flag or be hanged. Only incarceration in the local jail saved him from a beating or death at the hands of local residents, who considered their actions a "demonstration of patriotism."[6]

In Colorado, harassment, intimidation, and invasion of privacy became common for German Americans. In 1917, the Colorado 100 Percent American Club formed women's branches. Members had the responsibility to locate pro-German women and give their names to federal officials. They canvassed neighborhoods and asked women to sign a pledge that they would observe one meatless and one wheatless meal each week. Another group asked women to sign a pledge promising to aid the federal government if their service proved necessary. Those who refused were reported to club officers. Several statewide women's organizations worked with the Women's Committee of the state council of defense to lead a campaign for food conservation and the prevention of waste as well as to encourage the planting of "war gardens," working in hospitals, and selling Liberty Bonds. But they also prided themselves on their efforts to discover subversives. One Nebraska group, the Women's Benefit Association of the Maccabees, reported, "Secret service work has been done in unearthing German plots and reporting same to government." Nor was private property safe. In Sterling, a German American junk dealer had his business raided by local patriots to determine whether he harbored stolen property. Most Great Plains residents demanded loyalty, and they were not beyond violating the law and Constitution to ensure it, particularly regarding people of German descent.[7]

The South Dakota Council of Defense, supported by the legislature, ordered an end to all German-language instruction from the elementary to the college level. Many communities also organized groups of vigilantes to guard against disloyalty and sedition. In Sioux Falls, the Patriotic Legion of Loyalty Society claimed 1,500 members who pledged to support the government and put down disloyalty. Five of South Dakota's six German-language newspapers ended publication. In early 1918, the American Defense Society operated in the Black Hills and urged South Dakotans to "telegraph, write, or bring us reports of German activities in the district." Law enforcement authorities arrested some Germans for criticizing the war effort in a manner considered seditious. In Dell Rapids, residents forced residents of German heritage to salute and kiss the U.S. flag. South Dakotans also dispensed horse whippings, tar and feathering, and other violence against those German Americans whom they judged unpatriotic. In June 1918, the Sanborn County Council of Defense distributed posters that read "Cut out the Kaiser's tongue — Anything civilized can be said in the American Language — If you don't know it, learn it or move out." In South Dakota the most extreme reactions against residents of German heritage occurred in areas where few Germans lived, and the violation of civil liberties and constitutional rights continued as long as the war lasted. When the war ended, however, the anti-German sentiment, if not hysteria and paranoia, quickly faded away.[8]

Across the Great Plains, German teachers often lost their jobs if they could not be assigned other duties or refused to sign loyalty oaths. German Catholic and Protestant schools came under harsh public attack. The *New York Sun* reported that Nebraska teachers "whip children who speak English in German schools," which some believed proved the need to "put a stop to Kaiserism in the schools." In Nebraska, the state legislature prohibited anyone from discouraging enlistment in the armed forces, and the state joined Montana to prohibit anyone from advocating strikes or lockouts in war industries. Kansans, Nebraskans, and South Dakotans also amended their state constitutions to abolish the voting rights of unnaturalized aliens. In 1918, hatred against residents of German descent became worse. Congress responded by using Montana law as an example to prohibit any infringement of the sale of war bonds; utterances or writings that indicated contempt for the federal government, the Constitution, or the U.S. flag or uniforms; actions that hindered the production of war materiel; or any work or deed that aided a nation at war with the United States. Those found guilty of such infringements were subject to a $10,000 fine and twenty years in prison.[9]

In Nebraska and Texas, Lutheran ministers suffered mental intimidation and physical attacks, and an arsonist destroyed the Lutheran parochial school in Herington, Kansas. Officials often could not prevent terrorism from vigilante mobs acting under the guise of patriotism. Many Germans avoided intimidation and violence by supporting the war effort, joining patriotic organizations, or keeping a low profile as well as changing their names. Yet intimidation seemed to abound. In Nebraska, the council accused several professors at the University of Nebraska of insufficient support for the American war effort. Ultimately the educators appeared before a court, where they were charged with harboring unpatriotic sentiments, but the case collapsed when the chairman of the board of regents denied that any faculty were unpatriotic. On July 4, 1918, officials in Shawnee, Oklahoma, organized a book burning for German texts. In Montana, the state council of defense also prohibited the use of German in the pulpits and in private and parochial schools and ordered the removal of all German-language books from school and public libraries. In Butte, bullies forced some residents of German descent to kiss the U.S. flag, and Montana's governor announced, "There shall be no temporizing with treason in Montana." Despite these irrational and vicious attacks, when the war ended, German Russian ethnicity remained intact. German no longer served as the language of instruction in the schools, but Volga German and Black Sea German communities remained. Their homogeneity of settlement and tightly knit communities had isolated them from outside political oppression. The war ended and life went on.[10]

In 1920, Democratic presidential candidate Joseph Cox received less than 20 percent of the German vote in North and South Dakota, far less than his 34 percent vote nationwide. In heavily German-settled Stark County, North Dakota, the Democratic vote dropped from 39 percent in 1916 to 23 percent in 1920. In Ellis County, Kansas, where the Democratic Party prevailed among the voters of Volga German descent, Cox received only 27 percent of the vote compared to Wilson's 65 percent in 1916. German voters essentially wanted less government intrusion in their lives, and the Democratic Party had a poor record in that regard during the war years. As the German population aged and died, however, and with their children American born, they ceased to be perceived as a problem in the Great Plains states by the onset of the Great Depression. The betrayal of their constitutional rights because of ethnicity and in the name of patriotism and democracy, however, remained an indelible stain on the region's history.[11]

The Mennonites experienced the greatest distrust and resentment among the German sectarians. Most of the Mennonites had descended from people who came directly from Europe. These German speaking Mennonites kept to themselves and maintained their pacifist culture, including nonconformity and nonresistance, and they gained control of the local schools. In 1914, when World War I began, the Mennonites in Kansas sympathized with Germany based on culture and language, but their support was not unanimous. In 1916, during the presidential election, Mennonites (who usually voted Republican) supported Charles Evan Hughes, who received 59 percent of the vote from fourteen townships with a high Mennonite population. Woodrow Wilson garnered 34 percent of the vote, a decline of 6 percent from the presidential election of 1912, primarily because the Mennonites believed that he would lead the nation to war, and they remained staunch conscientious objectors.

In 1917, when Congress passed the Conscription Act, Mennonite leaders informed government officials that they would not accept military service. Secretary of War Newton D. Baker, however, assured them that once drafted no Mennonites would be required to accept work that violated their conscience. Upon arrival at the military camps, however, Mennonite conscripts learned that the army intended to force them into military service, although in noncombatant roles. These young men had expected to be assigned to work outside the military to fulfill their service obligations while reconciling their noncombatant status. Mennonite leaders particularly worked to get their young men furloughed for farm labor or other civilian occupations.

Upon arrival at a military base, such as Fort Riley, near Junction City, Kansas, the Mennonite conscripts soon found themselves pressured to accept military service based on biblical teachings and patriotism. Those who balked received assignments hauling garbage. The Mennonites who refused this detail, which they considered military service, experienced beatings and deprivation of food. Overall, the Kansas Mennonites endured this abuse; only 23 of 323 draftees accepted army service and rejected their status as conscientious objectors. The army imprisoned the Mennonites that it considered insincere in their resistance to military service, although most of the conscientious objectors received furloughs for farmwork beyond the Great Plains.

The Mennonites believed that they could demonstrate their patriotism by efficiently and productively cultivating the soil. Some sects contributed to the Red Cross, Young Men's Christian Association, and Salvation Army, because they considered such support to be in harmony with their religious principles, in contrast to the purchase of war bonds. Pressure by the federal government and non-Mennonite neighbors, however, compelled most Kansas Mennonites to purchase a few Liberty Bonds, but they donated those bonds to the Red Cross, rationalizing that the purchase of Liberty Bonds was a form of taxation that their creed permitted paying.[12]

When some Mennonites refused to purchase war bonds, they suffered being tarred and feathered and their bodies, homes, businesses, and churches splashed with yellow paint. The mobs that levied retribution reportedly were composed of successful, respected, and orderly citizens, some of whom the Mennonite victims had considered friends but who became vigilantes to force support of the war effort. One Mennonite farmer near

McPherson, Kansas, who had already been tarred and feathered, reported that the vigilantes returned and "called me out and threatened to pound me to pieces, using the most abusive and ungodly language." In Nebraska, Mennonite women proved particularly obstinate by refusing to sign food-conservation cards because the wording offended their religious principles. Finally, the council changed the text to make it sufficiently innocuous so that they could sign the pledge in good conscience, thereby ending the council's embarrassment from bringing so many Mennonite women before it for reprimands and fines. In Oklahoma, Mennonites and other German Americans endured similar violence.[13]

Not all Great Plains residents, however, persecuted the Mennonites. In Whitewater, Kansas, the business community disavowed the violence used against them in an attempt to avoid the boycott of their businesses by local Mennonites. In Burrton, a yellow-paint-splattered and beaten Mennonite was saved from hanging when the head of the town's Anti–Horse Thief Association drew a revolver and kept the mob at bay until the defiant farmer could be placed in jail for his own protection. One observer likened him to Christ, saying, "They'd slug him on one side of the face and he'd turn his cheek on the other." When the court acquitted him of espionage, bitter feelings between the patriots and the pacifists lingered, with tension and distrust between Mennonites and non-Mennonites still observable during the late twentieth century, particularly in Burrton.[14]

By spring 1918, local law enforcement authorities had restored order in Kansas, and the chairman of the McPherson Red Cross rejected donations "secured by night riders." For many non-Mennonites, however, justice and revenge were distinctions without a difference. In May, the editor of the *Marquette Tribune* believed that anyone who failed to support the war should be "reported to the proper officers, taken to detention camps, their property confiscated, and then at the end of the war they and their families be banished forever from living under the flag they have denounced in war time." Although Kansas governor Arthur Capper never attacked the Mennonites for disloyalty, he urged them to purchase war bonds to avoid problems. In general, many Kansans believed that people of German heritage, particularly Mennonites, supported "Kaiserism." Ironically, had the federal government taxed the Mennonites, even to support the war, they would have paid the taxes, because the Bible permitted them to do so. By making the purchase of war bonds voluntary, the government gave them an option that challenged their patriotism and pacifism. These Mennonites responded by essentially withdrawing from politics; even their newspapers avoided political commentary.[15]

The Hutterites in South Dakota attempted to avoid problems by volunteering to contribute money to charities provided the funds were used for relief rather than to buy war bonds. Although they contributed $30,000, the Yankton County Liberty Loan Committee demanded more support, then raided the colony and stole two hundred cattle and one thousand sheep, which the members sold at auction for about 40 percent of their value. The committee used the $16,000 from the auction to purchase war bonds for the Hutterites. Most South Dakotans believed that the Hutterites got what they deserved and recommended the "Yankton way," that is, intimidation and violence, to other communities where Mennonites refused to purchase liberty bonds, reasoning that if they did not like such treatment, they could leave South Dakota. Twelve of the state's seventeen Hutterite communities felt so threatened that they took that advice and moved to Canada.[16]

In retrospect, the religious pacifist Germans who maintained their own schools and organizations to foster group solidarity resisted giving up their language or letting their churches and organizations serve secular purposes. Although they did not threaten American society, they suffered more intimidation and violence than did the "club" Germans, that is, those who maintained cultural attachments only for social, recreational, or loose identity purposes. In the Great Plains, the most persecuted Germans were peaceful Mennonites and Hutterites. They were rural, separatist, and pacifist as well as apolitical and often traced their heritage to Russia rather than Germany. They were the Germans who were most ridiculed, harassed, beaten, painted, tarred, and robbed in the name of patriotism.[17]

Labor strikes over wage increases and union recognition and the continuing ramifications of the Russian Revolution occupied considerable public attention after the Treaty of Versailles ended World War I. Bombings by anarchists and Socialists at home and abroad created public apprehension that Bolsheviks and other radicals, such as the Wobblies, would attempt a revolution. In 1919, a full-fledged Red Scare swept across the newspaper pages, if not the nation, and Attorney General A. Mitchell Palmer saw the opportunity to enhance his political ambitions while fighting Bolshevism. On November 7, the second anniversary of the Russian Revolution, Palmer authorized Justice Department agents to raid offices of radical organizations in twelve cities, where they seized files and made arrests and began deporting alleged radicals. A Palmer raid occurred in Denver, but it netted only eight suspected radicals. In January 1920, he also closed every known office of the Communist Party. These Palmer raids were short-lived, as complaints mounted against his agents and the Department of Justice for violating civil liberties and circumventing legal procedures. That summer, his warnings about a Bolshevik revolution in the United States brought scorn and apathy.[18]

Overall, the Red Scare alarmed few people in the Great Plains, but the Wobblies remained a concern because people believed that they would burn wheat fields, destroy farm machinery, and unionize workers in the oil patches and mining areas. Plains men and women essentially considered Wobblies more dangerous radicals than Bolsheviks and treated them with considerable cruelty and violence in Kansas, Oklahoma, and Montana. In spring 1918, the *Daily Oklahoman* labeled radicals and antiwar advocates "defectives," while the *Tulsa World* demanded the deportation of foreigners who had criticized the government.[19]

State legislative response to perceived Bolshevik radicalism proved more dangerous than Palmer raids in the Great Plains. By 1920, Colorado had enacted a rigid sedition law, which made speaking or printing abusive language against public officials or the government illegal. Red flags or banners had become the symbol of revolution, and many states enacted Red flag legislation. In Oklahoma, the Red flag law prohibited the display of banners "indicating disloyalty or a belief in anarchy or other political doctrines." Punishment involved a small fine or brief jail sentence. By mid-1920, most plains men and women, like others across the nation, had come to realize that no danger of a Bolshevik revolution existed in the United States. Whether any Great Plains resident had ever seen a Bolshevik in the region was arguable, but plains men and women could be remarkably intolerant in a utilitarian way, and Socialists, Nonpartisan Leaguers, and Wobblies, in the absence of Bolsheviks, would do. By autumn 1920 most people were treating the Red Scare as a hoax. The public was tired of wartime fears and tension, they were ready for peace, and radicalism in the form of the Socialists and Wobblies had essentially been stymied. Palmer, however, would not be the last to spread fear of communism in the Great Plains.[20]

In the Great Plains, farmers primarily depended on wheat for their livelihood. Yet by specializing in single-crop agriculture, they placed themselves at the mercy of the railroads that transported their grain and the elevators that bought and stored it. They also appeared as supplicants before bankers, who provided credit for the purchase of seed and equipment and living expenses to tide them over until the harvest brought income into the farm home. By 1915, however, this dependency (along with high interest rates and shipping charges) had convinced most North Dakotans, more than

70 percent of whom were farmers, that government needed to protect their interests through greater regulation of corporate America.

Populists and Socialists had argued for federal ownership of the railroads; the Progressives had advocated stricter regulation of the railroads and banks; and North Dakota farmers had formed cooperatives to promote improved marketing and gain purchasing power through strength in numbers. One manifestation of this shift toward regulation and cooperative action can be seen in the American Society of Equity, which gained considerable support in the northern plains after 1909 by advocating a cooperative farmer-owned terminal grain elevator in Minneapolis–St. Paul or Duluth-Superior. Only by operating their own grain elevator, Equity members believed, would they be able to end the pricing and grading inequities of the privately owned "line" elevators located along the railroads. Despite the importance of the cooperative movement, which had come to extend across North Dakota by World War I, farmers recognized that economic unity alone would not improve their conditions. Only political solidarity and government ownership of certain businesses that had a public trust would solve their problems. In January 1914, the North Dakota Socialist Party advocated the creation of state-owned terminal grain elevators, mills, and processing facilities. By midsummer, Arthur C. Townley, a Socialist state organizer, was beginning to aggressively campaign to recruit farmers into the party. Later that year, however, Socialist Party loyalists tried to end his recruiting campaign because they did not believe that property-owning farmers could become good socialists. Townley contended that a farmers' organization could achieve the regulatory and ownership goals sought by the region's major farm organizations, particularly a terminal elevator, banks, mills, and cold storage plants. In February 1915, when the North Dakota legislature defeated a bill for a terminal elevator, Townley and others began organizing a Nonpartisan League (NPL).[21]

Townley understood that North Dakota farmers wanted fair treatment when they sold their commodities, and they listened when he explained the goals of the Nonpartisan League: state ownership of terminal grain elevators, flour mills, packinghouses, and cold-storage plants; state inspection of grain; exemption of farm improvements from taxation; state hail insurance; and rural credit banks operated at cost. Farmers welcomed this Populist creed and paid their $6.00 membership fee. In little more than a year, some forty thousand farmers had joined the League.[22]

The League pursued its agenda by nominating supportive candidates in the primary elections of the Republican and Democratic parties when party candidates proved unacceptable to the League. Alternatively, it ran

Arthur C. Townley provided the leadership for the organization of the Nonpartisan League, which became a strong political force in North Dakota. The moderate socialist programs of the Nonpartisan League appealed to farmers who believed that the railroads, grain elevator companies, and credit institutions cheated them. Here, Townley is speaking to a large crowd at Crosby, North Dakota, circa 1920s.

independent candidates on the ballot. The NPL, then, had to convince enough Progressives as well as party regulars to vote for NPL candidates, thereby winning a majority vote with a minority of NPL voters. By using the party primaries for its own purposes, the NPL controlled North Dakota politics for five years, elected officials in other states on a piecemeal basis, and demonstrated the political power of an organized minority.[23]

In 1916, the North Dakota Nonpartisan League presented a slate of candidates for election through the direct primary, including William Langer for attorney general and Lynn J. Frazier for governor. All candidates except one had been Republicans, and most won election in November. In 1917, when Governor Frazier opened the legislative session, with the NPL holding a majority in the state House of Representatives, he called for the enactment of the Nonpartisan League platform. The legislature responded by providing a state grain grading system, a bank deposit guarantee law, a nine-hour workday for women, woman suffrage, reduced tax rates on farm machinery and improvements, and the prohibition of rate discrimination by railroads regarding long and short hauls, among other reforms.[24]

Amidst this heady success, the NPL planned even greater achievements, but the beginning of a world war created problems from which it never recovered. Townley opposed American entry into the war and demanded the nationalization of basic industries. The Republican Party charged the NPL with disloyalty, and business leaders organized the Independent Voters Association (IVA) to challenge the patriotism and loyalty of Townley and Leaguers. Even so, the NPL carried the election in 1918 and used the legislative session the next year to establish the Bank of North Dakota to provide low-interest rural credit and to finance state industries, such as the mill and elevator; to exempt farm improvements from taxation; to authorize a department to inspect weights and measures; and to establish an industrial commission to manage and operate all state-owned industries. In 1920, however, IVA attacks, an agricultural depression, and waning interest in the NPL caused its political crusade to spiral downward. A recall election in 1921 removed Governor Frazier, Attorney General William Lemke, and Commissioner of Agriculture John N. Hagan from office.[25]

Although the NPL offered the most radical solutions to the "farm problem," in reality it provided mild socialist solutions for persistent economic problems. The NPL gained many supporters, particularly among the Norwegians in the northern part of North Dakota, even though only farmers could become members. Many farmers had lost faith in the Republican Party, and they believed that the election of nonpartisan candidates who supported NPL goals would end political favoritism for big business. Although the NPL no longer remained a political force in North Dakota after it collapsed in 1922, the physical symbols of its achievements are still manifest in the state bank, mill, and elevator; its legacy also includes the use of the direct primary to make the major political parties, particularly the Republican Party, responsive to the will of the majority, the farm men and women of North Dakota.

In June 1917, the NPL also recruited in Nebraska with a North Dakota agenda, but the Farmers Union (FU) considered it an "apolitical movement brought from the outside by persons unfamiliar with Nebraska conditions." The FU urged farmers to reject the League, because it would diminish their political voice by diluting it in multiple organizations. The state council of defense established to promote loyalty during the war questioned the patriotism of League members as well as their friendly overture to farmers of German descent. This opposition prevented the NPL from moving beyond the stage of rudimentary organization in Nebraska. Indeed, the state council of defense made the NPL its "special whipping boy" and denied it meeting places for organizational activities in the counties. The council also proclaimed that no "self-respecting farmer, no patriotic American could belong to the Nonpartisan League" and charged it with "doing the

Kaiser's work." Governor Keith Neville refused to restrain local authorities who disrupted or prohibited League activities. In the summer of 1918, the state legislature struck the NPL with an amorphous Sedition Bill, which, when approved, enabled construing almost any League activity as illegal. Democrats further weakened the NPL by charging that Republicans had been primarily responsible for its founding in North Dakota.[26]

The NPL achieved even less success in the other Great Plains states. In July 1917, the League moved to Kansas, established its headquarters in Topeka, and sought "justice for all and special privileges to none," which essentially meant achievement of the North Dakota agenda. In March 1918, League activists provoked violence at Great Bend when approximately two hundred members of nearby American Legion posts tarred two NPL speakers. One victim reported, "We were taken to a lonely place. Two men were stationed to each of our arms, holding them up while we were fearfully beaten by others." Most Kansas newspapers condemned the violence as an infringement of free speech but opposed the NPL as a radical organization that sought class warfare, particularly during the "Red Scare" that swept the nation after World War I. Most Kansans believed that if Leaguers were beaten, they merited such treatment, which indicates a remarkable shift to the political right from the Populist years. With the agricultural depression beginning in 1921 — and bracing against charges that the NPL was socialist, radical, and disloyal — most farmers remained affiliated with the Republican or Democratic Party. In the end, the NPL remained an organization in the spring wheat country where farmers felt aggrieved by their treatment by the grain dealers in the Twin Cities. Yet the violence among Kansas farmers over agricultural economic issues indicated a conservative and dark side of the body politic.[27]

The NPL had similar difficulties organizing in South Dakota, where farmers felt less aggrieved by the economic system than did their neighbors to the north. One observer noted, "The Nonpartisan crowd is coming down from the North like a swarm of grasshoppers." The Leaguers met the considerable political abilities of Peter Norbeck (soon to be elected governor) and the progressive Republicans, who did not intend to concede their power. Norbeck quickly sought low-interest state loans for farmers on real estate to put money in their pockets, state hail insurance for crops, the acquisition of water and power sites, and state-operated terminal grain elevators — essentially the NPL program. The state legislature approved a rural credit act and a workman's compensation law and began studying the feasibility of Norbeck's other recommendations. Norbeck and the Progressive Republicans also supported state-owned enterprises by constitutional amendment and attacked the League as an organization of radical socialists who were disloyal for opposing the war. Norbeck told voters that South Dakota had a more progressive legislature than North Dakota and that they did not need NPL "agitators" to deal with social and economic issues. Essentially, South Dakota, under Norbeck's leadership, supported the NPL program and outmaneuvered the League.[28]

In Oklahoma, Townley and NPL leaders believed that the strong presence of the Socialist Party, particularly among wheat farmers, would provide a firm base for recruitment. Essentially, the NPL attempted to impose North Dakota's solutions to the farm problem upon the Sooner State. By May 1919, approximately three thousand Oklahoma farmers had joined the NPL, but they hailed from wheat country, not the cotton area. NPL secrecy brought considerable public disapproval as it worked to gain control of the Democratic Party in Oklahoma. By the 1918 election, the Socialist Party had faded, and the Republican and Democratic parties vociferously attacked the NPL. Farm organizations and many state newspapers opposed the NPL and its political activities, the former because of competitive jealousy and the latter because the League seemingly advocated class legislation, that is, laws that benefited only farmers. Additionally, most Oklahoma farmers preferred to remain in their own party. Amid these problems, the NPL self-destructed by not supporting the war effort, particularly after Townley's indictment in February 1918 for obstructing the draft and opposing enlistments in the military.

By Election Day in November 1918, most Oklahomans had come to consider the NPL a disloyal socialist organization of German sympathizers. The NPL generated no interest in the primary election and essentially disappeared. In general, Oklahoma farmers still enjoyed prosperity generated by high wartime prices, with wheat bringing more than two dollars per bushel and cotton more than thirty cents per pound. In Oklahoma, the NPL had little to protest. When the Farmer-Labor Reconstruction League organized in September 1921, the few remaining NPL diehards gravitated to the organization, and the NPL never reemerged in Oklahoma. Moreover, cotton farmers never supported the NPL, in part because cotton gins had been public utilities since 1915 and railroad rates for wheat shipped to gulf ports proved less expensive than for North Dakota farmers, who transported their grain to St. Paul. In the end, the Oklahoma farmers saw little merit in the NPL and rejected it. Agrarian radicalism in the Great Plains seemed to be on the wane.[29]

During the 1920s, the federal government, though urged by farmers to intervene in the marketplace, would not formulate an agricultural policy to raise prices and set a course for recovery. Both Congress and the executive branch preferred that farmers resolve their own economic problems, largely through the creation of cooperative associations designed to market agricultural commodities more effectively. Between 1929 and 1931, however, the government spent nearly $400,000 through the Federal Farm Board, which loaned money to agricultural marketing cooperatives to help these organizations purchase farm surpluses and keep them off the market. Nevertheless, farm surpluses overwhelmed the cooperatives, and agricultural prices continued to slide.

Great Plains farmers had used high wartime prices to purchase more land and equipment, often on credit at high interest rates. As agricultural prices continued to rise into the summer of 1920, these farmers believed that their prosperity would long endure. In Nebraska, wheat rose to $2.07 per bushel, and to $2.71 per bushel in the Texas Panhandle. Corn brought $1.45 per bushel, and cattle $11.50 per hundredweight. Hay prices increased to $16.90 per ton. By 1920, however, European agriculture had begun to recover from wartime conditions; demand for American farm commodities fell and with it agricultural prices. Wheat brought $2.40 per bushel in Montana, then fell to $1.25 per bushel in October 1920. Between 1919 and 1925, approximately 11,000 farms (or 20 percent of the state's total) were vacated, some 20,000 mortgages were foreclosed on, and one of every two farmers lost their land. Montana had the highest bankruptcy rate in the nation. Sixty thousand people left the state during the decade. In 1921, farmers had only two-thirds of the purchasing power that they had enjoyed prior to the war. They had become victims of an agricultural depression that would last through the 1930s. In 1922, wheat brought only $.92 and corn $.62 per bushel and cattle $6.50 and hogs $8.10 per hundredweight. At the same time, the Federal Reserve Board contracted credit. In Nebraska, the value of crops dropped 39 percent, from $507.4 million to $198.3 million before rebounding to $238.8 million a year later. The agricultural index for prices received in Nebraska averaged 213 in 1918 and 115 in 1922 for all commodities (1909–14 = 100). State banks, the assets of which primarily involved real estate and crop mortgages, found payments difficult to collect, and bank failures became increasingly common. More than half the banks in Nebraska closed their doors between 1920 and 1932. In Montana, 214 banks (more than half of the state's total) failed between 1920 and 1926. In North Dakota, 573 banks failed between 1920 and 1933, largely because of the faltering agricultural economy. In South Dakota, 71 percent of the state banks failed between 1920 and 1934. Depositors across the region lost millions of dollars. Credit disappeared, and real estate values collapsed, often dropping to less than half of their highest value during the decade.[30]

One North Dakotan described these desperate years: "Wheat was the sole source and meaning of our lives. . . . We were never its masters, but too frequently its victims. . . . It was rarely long outside a conversation." Drought and low prices kept wheat and economic survival on most farmers' minds. As agricultural prices fell, farm costs and everyday living expenses increased, and purchasing power plummeted. In 1929, the per capita income in North Dakota was $375 compared to $703 nationally. Many plains men and women began to live on savings as the economic crisis worsened. In 1932, wheat brought $.25 and corn $.10 per bushel and cotton less than $.05 per pound. Hog prices plunged from $11.35 per hundredweight in 1931 to $3.00 per hundredweight a year later. These were the lowest prices since the 1890s. Between 1929 and 1933, agricultural prices dropped 63 percent and farmers had only 58 percent of the purchasing power that they had enjoyed from 1909 through 1914. One South Dakota farm wife reported, "My husband had to buy a pair of shoes. To pay the price ($4) we brought to town twenty pounds of butter and twelve dozen eggs. That just paid for the shoes." On December 28, 1932, William DeLoach, a farmer near Lubbock, Texas, wrote in his diary, "If I could sell 'any thing for any thing' it would not be so hard, but will do the best I can."[31]

Confronted with problems such as these, many midwestern farmers became convinced that they needed to take "direct action." The most radical members of the Farmers Union advocated a government policy that would guarantee cost-of-production prices plus a small profit for farmers. The Hoover administration, however, refused to permit the federal government to artificially raise prices by purchasing crop surpluses. Faced with government inaction, many midwestern farmers prepared to man barricades to win by force what their desperate appeals had failed to achieve.

Milo Reno led the extremists of the Farmers Union in advocating cost-of-production legislation and the use of economic coercion to achieve it. By February 1932, growing demand had developed within the FU for a farm holiday—a time during which farmers would neither buy nor sell. This withholding action, Reno believed, quickly would close food processing plants and empty grocery store shelves. The inevitable result would be federal intervention guaranteeing farmers the cost of production prices plus a profit of about 5 percent. Once that happened, farmers would return to their fields.

On May 3, 1932, Reno (a veteran of the Populist revolt during the 1890s) persuaded some two thousand farmers to gather on the state fairgrounds in Des Moines, Iowa, to organize a Farmers' Holiday Association (FHA). Delegates from Nebraska and Oklahoma attended the gathering, and state organizations soon formed in North and South Dakota. The delegates, inspired by Reno's fiery oratory and his evangelical fervor, chose him as president of the association and vowed to strike on July 4. Naively, Reno called for the strike to last either thirty days or until government intervention guaranteed the cost of production, that is, about $.92 per bushel for corn and $11.25 per hundredweight for hogs. The FHA also advocated an inflationary monetary policy and demanded enactment of the Frazier-Lemke Bill, pending before Congress, which would provide refinancing of farm mortgages by the federal government.

These were bold demands, but to many farmers the economic crisis warranted drastic action. John A. Simpson, president of the Farmers Union and an FHA supporter, believed that unless Herbert Hoover was defeated for the presidency in November 1932, and unless a new president provided farmers with economic relief, he would be "the last president of the United States"; a revolution would sweep across the land and a dictator would gain the support of the people. FHA members agreed. These were revolutionary times, and the existence of the republic was at stake. Although Reno, Simpson, and FHA members overstated the danger, their miscalculations are clear only from hindsight. Many at the time believed that the specter of revolution loomed beyond the farmers' gates.

In Nebraska, the Farmers' Holiday Association was organized on August 18, 1932, primarily by the corn and hog farmers in the northeastern counties. It had little appeal among wheat farmers. The corn and hog farmers had enjoyed price stability and prosperity since World War I, and the collapse of prices and loss of income were unprecedented. Insurgent farmers who demanded higher agricultural prices responded by halting an interstate freight train and uncoupling its cars. On the outskirts of Omaha, farmers fought with deputies throughout the nights of August 30 and 31 and September 1, while supporters blockaded the Omaha market from the Iowa side of the Missouri River. In October, a small group of Madison County men, known as the "red army" (because they supposedly were under the control of the Communist Party), strengthened the opposition to farm foreclosures by beginning "Sears-Roebuck" and "penny auction" sales. These sales occurred when a farmer could not pay a debt that had been secured by personal or farm property. Sears-Roebuck sales were used not to satisfy real estate debts or mortgages but to discharge debt on personal property. The first such sale in Nebraska occurred at the farm of a widow confronted with a debt foreclosure. When the auction began, the farmers in attendance bid $.05 for every item offered for sale. The sale produced a paltry $5.35, and the bank representative wisely judged from the angry mood of the crowd that the sum should be accepted for full settlement of the debt. At one "Sears and Roebuck" sale on a farm near Milbank, South Dakota, the auctioneer netted only $6.30.[32]

Similarly, farm auctions held to meet mortgage debts through foreclosure sales were known as "penny auctions." Usually the bidders present at the penny auctions were the friends and neighbors of the farmer who faced the loss of his home and land. Generally, everyone understood the simple procedure. Frequently, friends made arrangements with the auctioneer for him to accept only one bid, and when someone bid a nickel for a tractor, the gavel came down. In Steel County, North Dakota, the executive board of the Farmers' Holiday Association visited a local banker who intended to foreclose on a woman whose husband had recently committed suicide; the chairman told him, "If you foreclose on that woman, we'll hang you." Quickly the penny auctions became the most visible activity of the Farmers' Holiday Association, and they involved more farmers than any other aspect of the association's protest activity. Like the farm strike, the penny auctions were the spontaneous reaction of a small group of farmers to events that seemed beyond their control.[33]

In some cases, the antiforeclosure activities of the Farmers' Holiday movement fostered violence. Deficiency judgments stimulated many confrontations. Although deficiency judgments could be levied if a foreclosure sale did not return the amount of indebtedness or at least a significant portion of it, the farmers present at the penny auctions frequently bullied creditors to accept as full payment whatever was bid. In Nebraska, the state legislature put a ceiling on deficiency judgments, while Governor Langer of North Dakota proclaimed a moratorium on farm foreclosures and ordered the National Guard to prevent foreclosure sales. These measures enacted while the FHA actively interfered with the foreclosure process gave farmers the appearance of possessing far greater power than they had in reality, and a growing public perception arose that they were abusing their power.

The Farmers' Holiday Association, lacking leadership, organized in roughly the eastern third of South Dakota but had little appeal in the conservative and sparsely populated West River Country. South Dakota governor Warren Green hosted a conference for regional governors and farm leaders on September 9, 1932, in Sioux City for the purpose of developing an "orderly, practical, legal, and nonviolent program for raising

The collapse of the agricultural economy during the late 1920s and early 1930s gave rise to the Farmers' Holiday Association. The association often aided economically distressed farmers whose personal property and land was subject to foreclosure, by bidding only a few cents on items of personal property and a few dollars on land while demanding that creditors accept the returns in full payment of the mortgage. This photograph shows a crowd of Farmers' Holiday sympathizers at an auction in Nebraska.

farm prices." When the conference assembled, the only other governor to attend was George Shafer of North Dakota (though representatives from Oklahoma, Nebraska, and Wyoming observed). The delegates did not address the concerns or demands of the FHA and only recommended improved tariff protection for farm products, expansion of the money supply, reorganization of the agricultural credit system, and voluntary restraint by creditors. In response, the FHA decided to strike on September 21 but not picket. The withholding action would apply only to livestock and grain, but it would be expanded to include eggs, butter, and cream if prices did not increase within thirty days. Although some grain sales declined in Rapid City and Huron and hog sales fell in Sioux Falls, agricultural marketing soon returned to normal because farmers needed income. In the November presidential election, Franklin Delano Roosevelt carried South Dakota with 64 percent of the vote; voters also elected Democrat Tom Berry as governor, and the Democratic Party captured both houses of the state legislature. Farmers looked to the incoming Roosevelt administration for economic relief.[34]

The Farmers' Holiday Association organized in North Dakota on August 7, 1932, after considerable discussion through the summer when farmers sought a dollar per bushel for their wheat and advocated using "direct action," "armed resistance," and "night ride[s]" to achieve it. North Dakota farmers also believed that a farm strike would "bring industry to its knees before the farmer whose supplications have gone unheeded for years." When the North Dakota farm strike began in thirty-six counties (where the FHA claimed a total of fifty thousand members) in September, no pickets blocked the roads or markets, in a disciplined response to its leadership in the state. Farmers continued to market grain and cattle in Minot, which soon led to full-scale picketing in northwestern North Dakota, where strikers turned back trucks of grain and cattle from reaching market. Public support soon waned because local businesses opposed the strike, and the public ridiculed picketers as being communists. When a mid-October snowstorm struck, enthusiasm for picketing flagged and the strike collapsed. The farm strike, however, strengthened the ties between the Farmers' Holiday Association, the Farmers Union, and the Nonpartisan League, the collective goals of which drove North Dakota politics in the future.[35]

In the meantime, the FHA worked with bankers to help resolve delinquent loan issues that involved scaled-down repayment plans that met the needs of both farmers and lenders. Indeed, the most important long-term achievement of the Farmers' Holiday Association was not the withholding action or the penny auction but the creation of "councils of defense" or "committees of action" on a county-by-county basis. These organizations brought creditors and debtors together to work out refinancing and payment of delinquent debts. Despite this success, the FHA quickly lost its credibility because of the violence that often occurred whenever it picketed during a withholding action. Overall, however, FHA members in South Dakota showed restraint in demonstrations for change in the agricultural economy. Residents of the towns and cities supported FHA goals, and politicians spoke in its favor. Moderation, not radicalism, characterized their participation in the Farm Holiday Movement in the Great Plains, even though a picketer shot and killed a farmer near Jefferson when he tried to run the road blockage with a truckload of milk.[36]

Great Plains farmers believed that they deserved assistance. Emil Loriks, leader of the Farmers' Holiday Association in South Dakota, expressed that sentiment best when he said, "We have the right to ask the government for aid and assistance in times of great emergencies," and he held, "It is the duty of government to come to our aid." Great Plains farmers wanted federal aid that would enable them to maintain their profitability, independence, and freedom to make their own operating decisions, particularly in time of economic crisis. Soon a new approach to the farm problem would dissipate much of the feeling of anger and desperation in the countryside, at least for a time.[37]

Despite the farm depression of the 1920s, agricultural expansion in the southern Great Plains continued at a rapid pace, particularly in the region that would soon become known as the Dust Bowl. The increases in acres planted and harvested meant that less grass remained to protect the soil from the nearly constant winds, and few farmers applied the best soil conservation techniques. In 1914, the European war caused wheat prices to soar from $.91 to $2.06 per bushel by 1917, and wheat prices remained above $2.00 per bushel until 1920. When the United States entered the war in 1917, southern plains farmers responded to the "Wheat will win the war!" campaign by planting more acres. Precipitation remained sufficient to allow, even encourage, that expansion. After the war, farmers planted more wheat, and grazing land appraised at $10 per acre increased 100 percent in value when planted. The earnings of a good crop year might equal the income earned from a decade of cattle raising. When wartime agricultural prices collapsed nationwide in the early 1920s, plains farmers broke more sod and planted more wheat to offset the economic loss. New technology and depressed farm prices stimulated southern Great Plains farmers to break 32 million acres of sod between 1909 and 1929 for new cropland, and wheat acreage expanded 200 percent between 1925 and 1931; in some counties, this expansion ranged from 400 to 1,000 percent.

By the early 1930s, most of the good farmland had been planted in the southern Great Plains. In southwestern Kansas, more than 50 percent of the range had been plowed for cropland, and in Baca County, Colorado, about 60 percent of the sod had been broken for wheat. More cropland meant less protective grass cover to hold the soil against the nearly constant winds. Continued plowing by farmers in the Great Plains pulverized the soil, and in little more than five years after the native sod had been broken, it was in an excellent condition for blowing. Moreover, after a farmer plowed under his grassland, the productivity of the soil steadily decreased because of continual loss of organic matter, and that decrease made the soil more susceptible to wind erosion because it could not absorb as much moisture and support the growth of vegetation that would hold the soil against the wind.

Rapid agricultural expansion also occurred in the northern Great Plains, and drought struck the area in 1917 and lasted into the early 1920s. Crops failed and grasshoppers consumed much of the grain that survived. As postwar agricultural prices collapsed, many communities confronted a severe economic recession, which Great Plains residents hoped would not become an economic depression. Others guardedly hoped for the best. The expansion of the wheat lands in the Great Plains, however, went un-noticed. Had a similar amount of forest been cut down, the threat to soil erosion would have been obvious. In the southern plains, though, once the grass had been plowed under, the land still looked much the same, as giant wheat fields trailed off to the distant horizon. In the spring and autumn, the land was green with wheat. Only later, when a severe drought parched the region, was the damage noticed. By the early 1930s, dust storms had become warning signs of a pending environmental disaster for the Great Plains.[38]

Although the agricultural economy became increasingly weak, not all residents of the Great Plains feared the future. In 1920, the Gulf Oil Company made a strike in the Texas Panhandle. Other discoveries followed, including the Permian Basin field in 1923. Odessa, Midland, and Fort Stockton became oil towns, and drillers pursued black gold into eastern New Mexico. In 1926, the Panhandle Oil and Gas Field produced 25 million barrels, compared to only 1 million barrels a year earlier. In March, new discoveries caused an oil and natural gas boom and created the city of Borger nearly overnight. Where there had been only three hundred registered voters before the boom, some thirty thousand people quickly descended on Hutchinson County to find work and make their fortunes.[39]

Early in 1926, Oklahoma businessmen Asa P. Borger and John R. Miller purchased 240 acres for twelve thousand dollars from a rancher, marked off town lots, and at the end of the first day of sales on March 8, counted more than sixty thousand dollars. At first, people called the town "Little Oklahoma," and more than one thousand people often arrived per day—roughnecks, merchants, and barbers as well as prostitutes and gamblers. All sought easy money; most found failure. Gas fumes irritated eyes, noses, and lungs, while raw sewage collected in cesspools where residents dumped their garbage. Stench, flies, and mosquitoes soon became commonplace. Water sold for $1.50 per barrel. Tents, sheet-metal buildings, and clapboard siding gave structure to a grim-looking town. City officials did not have the power to tax to support schools. Red Burton, a Texas Ranger, called Borger "The most perfect picture I ever saw of my dream of hell." By 1927, however, city commissioners had provided health, zoning, and safety ordinances, although the residents still did not enjoy running water or a sewage system. The Santa Fe railroad had linked Borger to the panhandle and the world beyond, a newspaper was published daily, and a chamber of commerce held regular meetings. The federal government also promised a post office, but the police protected bootleggers, prostitutes, and gamblers for a price. More than two thousand prostitutes paid a weekly "misdemeanor fine" to save time with arrests and prosecution. Typhoid fever made matters worse. The Texas Rangers could not control crime or adequately protect the citizenry. In February 1929, they left Borger, blaming its problems on the fact that so few Texans lived there. Governor Dan Moody proclaimed martial law and sent troops from the National Guard and a new contingent of Texas Rangers to occupy the city and county. The local editor worried about Borger's image, particularly after *Time* magazine described it as "a slovenly clutter sprawling over the prairie." By 1930, however, the drillers had departed, and Borger no longer essentially served as a place of recreation when the oil-field workers had free time. Others left when quick fortunes eluded them, and the National Guard and Texas Rangers brought a semblance of law and order to the town. By the end of the year, two-thirds of the population had gone. Those who remained thought the town had a bright future.[40]

In December 1926, some forty thousand people likewise lived in the tent city of Panhandle, Texas, and relied on oil companies such as Gulf, Texaco, Conoco, and Phillips 66 either directly or indirectly for their living. Many farmers and ranchers drew a second income from oil and gas leases, money that would soon prove essential during the dust-laden, depression years of the 1930s. Oil companies also drilled a thousand wells per year in Kansas during the 1920s, and production reached 40 million barrels annually. More cars and trucks plied the roads, and demand forced the price of gasoline to sixteen cents per gallon in 1923. The Hugoton natural gas field in southwestern Kansas fed pipelines that stretched to consumers in Detroit and Chicago. In the northern Great Plains, the discovery of the Kevin-Sunburst field near Shelby, Montana, also proved significant.[41]

The oil boom of the 1920s created winners and losers. Land near Ranger, Texas, which farmers had bought for twenty-five cents per acre before the oil strike in 1917, was leased to oil companies for several thousand dollars per acre annually. Banks and businesses expanded, lured by the earnings of oil-field workers. In Tulsa, 800 oil companies and 140,000 people gave the city claim to the title "oil capital of the world" in 1930. The oil fields drew people like a magnet. Families that arrived overnight placed their children in schools without notice, taxed city services, and often departed as quickly as they came when the oil boom ended. Until then, the oil-field towns accommodated tough, hard men and women who hoped they had found the opportunity for a better life. One observer reflected that "they was good people, and the worst—all together."[42]

In the oil towns of the Permian Basin, Midland had the most Mexican Americans (totaling 14 percent of the population in 1930), but because of discrimination, they rarely held drilling or production jobs. Native-born white workers, usually Texans, prevailed. Few Indians worked in the oil fields. Most oil-field workers were young and unmarried. Women soon followed their husbands either alone or with families in tow. Most working women held jobs as waitresses, teachers, clerical employees, and sales clerks. These jobs paid higher wages than could be earned in the non-oil towns. Many women saw an opportunity to improve their lives, and they took it. Oil money and boomtowns created jobs for women, especially for blacks and Mexican Americans in domestic service. One woman remembered, "If you wanted a job you could get it." Still, most women in the oil-field towns did not work outside the home.[43]

Although blacks and Mexican Americans were relegated to traditional menial labor, the oil boom still created new jobs for laundresses, cooks, domestic servants, and general laborers. In this segregated society, the oil boom expanded even limited employment opportunities for minorities, but these low-status jobs required hard work and long hours for low pay. African Americans also migrated to the Permian Basin during the 1920s, drawn by the expansion of cotton farming. Anglos, Mexican Americans, and African Americans often held more than one job, and while earnings improved lives, the long hours and hard work had personal and social costs. Oil boom opportunities were unequal and discriminatory, but they were welcomed, even needed, opportunities that many plains men and women sought and took.[44]

Improved roads, though not necessarily paved, expanded across the plains, and automobiles and telephone lines helped to improve communication, particularly in rural areas. Increasingly, automobiles enabled residents to bypass local, small-town businesses for county seats and regional trade centers, thereby contributing to economic and population decline in lower-population areas. Flying services began linking the larger towns with the world beyond the Great Plains. In the late 1920s, the Amarillo Airport linked West Texas with Denver and Dallas, while Omaha, Lincoln, and Cheyenne also benefited from air mail and passenger service. In September 1929, the *McCook Daily Gazette* reached subscribers only hours after it came off the press when contract pilots dumped bundles of newspapers from the air to waiting carriers in thirty-three towns in southwestern Nebraska and northwestern Kansas; the first arrival of the newspaper in this way eclipsed the news of the day.[45]

The Great Plains also had become less isolated but not less intolerant as its urban and rural population grew during the 1920s. Many western plains counties from North Dakota to Texas gained population. In South Dakota, the population of the West River counties increased by 20 percent to 112 percent. Mining helped boost this population growth in the Black Hills counties. Agricultural service and regional shopping centers, such as Lubbock, boomed. Increasingly, county seats became retail centers. In 1920, Lubbock and the neighboring South Plains (a thirty-thousand-square-mile area of West Texas and eastern New Mexico) had a population of 4,051 and 64,974 respectively. A decade later, Lubbock's population had increased 406 percent to 20,520, while the population of the South Plains jumped to 173,699, largely because of agricultural and oil-field expansion, retail shopping, and educational and cultural opportunities. From Bismarck on the northern plains through Wichita and Oklahoma City in the southern plains and to Denver and Albuquerque on the region's western rim, cities rather than agriculture were responsible for the major population growth. In contrast, North Dakota and Montana began experiencing a persistent out-migration. North Dakota would not exceed its 680,845 population of 1930 during the remainder of the twentieth century. After the 1930 census, it lost a third of its representation in the U.S. House of Representatives, and its delegates were reduced to two, elected at large. Thereafter, only Colorado, New Mexico, Texas, Wyoming, and Montana continued to gain population until the late twentieth century, while the other states would require decades to surpass the peak year of 1930.[46]

By the early 1920s, most plains men and women had lost faith in government ownership of industries and state regulations, and the Progressive movement began to wane. Feuding over state fiscal problems enabled conservative Republicans to regain political influence. In 1924, progressivism was dead in South Dakota, and Republican infighting led to the election of Democrat William J. Bulow to the governorship in 1926. South Dakotans then gave overwhelming support to presidential candidate Herbert Hoover two years later. Yet during the 1920s, conservatives were often comparatively liberal, particularly in North Dakota. Plains men and women generally supported federal aid for agriculture in the form of the Federal Intermediate Credit Bank, the McNary-Haugen Bill, and the Federal Farm Board. Many North Dakota Republicans opposed Calvin Coolidge for the presidency in 1924, preferring Progressive Party candidate

Robert M. La Follette. Coolidge carried the state only with the support of the conservative Democrats. In 1928, Hoover won North Dakota with the urban vote. Internal, state-related issues divided and united Republicans and Democrats on the state level, with the Republican Party secure north of Oklahoma.[47]

In Montana, from 1925 until 1931, conservatives prevailed in the Republican-controlled state legislature, but the state had a conservative Democratic governor who won election on a platform promising economy and efficiency in government through retrenchment and good business practices. Montana also sent liberal Progressive Democratic senators Thomas J. Walsh (1913–33) and Burton K. Wheeler (1923–47) to Congress, where they soon gained a reputation for attacking Republican malfeasance in office at the presidential level. Many politicians in the Great Plains states balanced conservatism and liberalism with compromises dependent on the issues and personal gain, not party ideology.[48]

Politically, then, between World War I and the Great Depression, Great Plains residents, with few exceptions, sought to solve their economic problems on the national level primarily by supporting the Republican Party and its presidential candidates. Texas supported Democrat James Cox in 1920 and, along with Oklahoma, John W. Davis in 1924. The region supported Republican Herbert Hoover in 1928 and Democrat Franklin Delano Roosevelt in 1932. State politics often depended on factional strife and personalities rather than issues. Perhaps more important than national party support, however, was the general agreement by the men and women of the Great Plains during the first three decades of the twentieth century that the purpose of government was to aid the general welfare. When the stock market crashed in October 1929, however, grim days lay ahead for the people of the Great Plains. During the decade of trials that followed, they would recast their vision about the proper role of government in their lives. The Great Depression and the New Deal years of the Franklin Delano Roosevelt administration would provide the foundation for a new way in which the men and women of the Great Plains viewed the purpose of and their relationship to the federal government.[49]

CHAPTER FOUR

The Anxious Years

Drought, wind, and a lack of soil-holding vegetation brought dust storms to the southern Great Plains during the spring of 1932. These storms primarily swept over sandy lands where drought had caused wheat, corn, and cotton crop failures and where livestock raisers had overgrazed their cattle on the grasslands. Much of the native sod had been plowed during the 1920s, much of it was submarginal land, that is, land that given the current price of wheat did not merit planting. Yet farmers in this region and across the Great Plains tried to make up for lower prices and decreased income by planting more wheat to regain lost income with a greater volume of production. Precipitation also remained above normal during the 1920s, and farmers plowed the grassland with a rapacious speed, knowing that large wheat crops would return more income than raising cattle would. Tractors and sod-slicing and pulverizing one-way disc plows tore open the land, more than 5.2 million acres between 1925 and the first dust storms of the early 1930s. Farmers and agricultural economists measured the wheat harvests in the millions of bushels. With rainfall adequate and the price of wheat tolerable at about one dollar per bushel, most men and women of the southern plains thought that life could be worse. One agricultural extension agent in southwestern Kansas called the twenties "a period of plenty." Little did they know that near-desert conditions would soon descend upon the region. From 1931 through 1936, the region averaged less than twelve inches of precipitation. Dust storms soon became common from spring to autumn, until near-normal precipitation returned during the late 1930s and early 1940s.[1]

Although dust storms became more common during the spring of 1933,

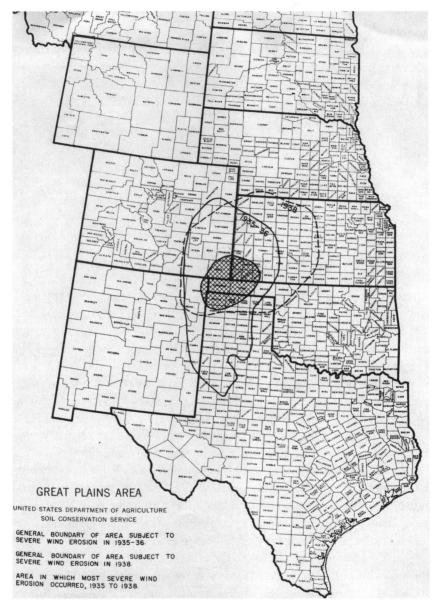

GREAT PLAINS AREA

UNITED STATES DEPARTMENT OF AGRICULTURE
SOIL CONSERVATION SERVICE

GENERAL BOUNDARY OF AREA SUBJECT TO
SEVERE WIND EROSION IN 1935-36.

GENERAL BOUNDARY OF AREA SUBJECT TO
SEVERE WIND EROSION IN 1938.

AREA IN WHICH MOST SEVERE WIND
EROSION OCCURRED, 1935 TO 1938.

During the 1930s, the southern Great Plains suffered serious prolonged drought and dust storms that gave the region the sobriquet of the "Dust Bowl." This map shows the area of the most severe wind erosion.

residents of the Great Plains were not particularly alarmed, because blowing dust occurred periodically in the region. They worried more about crop failures and low agricultural prices than soil erosion until November 1933, when a dust storm swept beyond the Great Plains and deposited soil as far east as Lake Superior. By spring 1934, the entire nation had become increasingly alarmed about the growing menace of blowing dust. An April storm blew out of the southern plains and reduced visibility to less than one mile in Baton Rouge, Louisiana, and in May the wind removed an estimated 300 million tons of topsoil from the Great Plains and sifted it over the eastern half of the nation, including Washington, D.C., New York (where the press called it "Kansas dirt"), and ships five hundred miles out to sea.[2]

Dust storms of considerable severity continued to blow from 1934 through 1938. In the southern Great Plains, residents covered windows with a translucent glasslike cloth, sealed windows with tape, wedged rags beneath doorjambs, and covered furniture with sheets, but the dust sifted into homes through keyholes and cracks and made housekeeping nearly impossible. Many people hung wet sheets in front of living room and bedroom windows in attempts to filter the dust-laden air. Plates, cups, and glasses remained overturned on the table until the meal could be served directly from the stove and the pans quickly re-covered to keep out as much dust as possible. Surgeons and dentists fought the problems of sterilization. Railroad engineers sometimes failed to see the stations and had to back up their trains. Occasionally, dust drifted over the railroad tracks and train crews had to scoop the rail clean so the train wheels could maintain enough friction to move forward, as well as to prevent derailment.[3]

Electric lights dimmed to a faint glow along streets, and drivers turned on their lights during midday dust storms. The wind-driven dust scoured the paint from automobile bodies and pitted windshields. Poor visibility caused motoring to become particularly hazardous during a dust storm. Static electricity also accompanied the storms and caused automobile ignition systems to fail. Many cars stalled along the roadside until the storms passed. In addition, the dust storms caused respiratory problems, the most serious cases of which doctors called "dust pneumonia." The Red Cross tried to prevent breathing problems during dust storms by distributing masks not unlike those used by the army to combat poison gas during World War I.[4]

During the spring of 1935, "black blizzards" swept across the southern plains. In March, a woman in Garden City, Kansas, reported, "All we could do was just sit in our dusty chairs and gaze at each other through the fog that filled the room and watch the fog settle slowly and silent, covering everything." Following the storm, she reflected, "Our faces were as dirty as if we had rolled in the dirt; our hair was gray and stiff and we ground dirt between our teeth." Dust storms had become so common that residents began accepting them as a basic aspect of daily life — even going to bed in dust-laden air only to shake off the covers in the morning. In Hays, Kansas, hospital nurses placed wet cloths over the faces of their patients. In Dallas, many people covered their mouths and noses with cloth masks to help filter the dusty air.[5]

The frequency and severity of the dust storms during the 1930s became major news items, and journalists from various newspapers and magazines traveled to the southern plains to describe the region. After one of the most severe black blizzards that ever struck the plains (which residents remembered as the "Black Sunday" of April 14, 1935), Robert E. Geiger, an Associated Press reporter, released a series of articles, the first from Guymon, Oklahoma, for the *Washington (D.C.) Evening Star.* In his story, Geiger inadvertently but appropriately used the term *dust bowl.* Geiger ignored the term in his next two articles, and in his last story from the area, he referred to the region as a "dust belt." The public and the Soil Conservation Service, however, adopted the term *Dust Bowl* almost immediately and used it when referring to the windblown, drought-stricken southern Great Plains.

Although wheat prices declined because of overproduction and although drought and dust storms ruined crops and caused additional economic hardship, farmers did not exit en masse from the Dust Bowl. Steinbeck was wrong; the Okies and others like them were products not of the Dust Bowl but of the cotton region east of the most drought-stricken areas. Certainly, *The Grapes of Wrath* is an important social commentary on the plight of the dispossessed in California during the Great Depression. Many families like the Joads fled the Dust Bowl over Route 66, but most did not leave. Most California migrants were products of the drought across the entire Great Plains and Midwest, not just from the Dust Bowl.

This is not to say that many Okies did not enter California during the drought years. Of the 43,180 migrants in need of employment who entered the state between June 16 and December 15, 1935, more than 7,000 (16.5 percent) came from Oklahoma. This number doubled the migrant total from the second-ranking state — Texas. More Oklahoma migrants followed. From July 1935 through June 1939, 22.7 percent of the emigrants in need of manual employment in California migrated from the Sooner State, but most of these Okies came from the cotton region, where the economy had totally collapsed. While most wheat farmers owned their own land, more than 60 percent of the Oklahoma cotton farmers were tenants and sharecroppers. Because of low prices and decreasing harvests, many landowners in the cotton-producing region preferred to release their tenants, reduce

In the southern plains during the 1930s, dust storms often reduced visibility to zero. The dust drifted across fields, sifted into houses, and caused respiratory illnesses. The worst dust storms, such as this one that swept across southwestern Kansas, were known as "black blizzards." Notice the lack of soil-holding vegetation, which resulted from prolonged drought.

production, and purchase tractors. As a result, thousands of tenants and migratory farmworkers were forced onto the highways in search of employment elsewhere. Displaced cotton tenants and field-workers, then (not the Dust Bowl wheat farmers), were the migrants we think of as Okies; only 2–3 percent of the 500,000 Oklahomans who migrated during the 1930s actually came from the Dust Bowl.[6]

During this parched, windblown decade of hard times, nearly 190,000 people left South Dakota, and the federal government spent $400 million to help the others stay. South Dakota lost a greater proportion of its population than any other state in the nation with 7.2 percent, followed by North Dakota, Kansas, and Oklahoma. By 1940, 14 percent, or 22,000 people, had left the West River Country during the 1930s. In North Dakota, the population declined 121,000 through out-migration during the decade, with approximately 86,700 departing between 1935 and 1940. Forty-three of fifty-three counties lost residents, and the farm population declined by 17 percent, although the urban population increased by 17 percent. The Texas Panhandle lost approximately 20,000 people. From 1935 to 1940, a sixteen-county area of southwestern Kansas lost an average of 30.5 percent of its farmers, while the rural nonfarm population declined by 7.4 percent and the town population by 8.6 percent. Overall, 212,503 people migrated from Kansas between 1935 and 1940, but 162,437 people moved from farms to a nearby town or an adjacent county. Although the major cities gained modestly in population, overall out-migration along with drought and dust characterized the plains during the 1930s.[7]

Although many people left the Great Plains during the 1930s, not all migrants fled the dust storms. Most people stayed because they had no place to go, were unwilling to try life somewhere else, or preferred to remain where family and friends gave them a sense of security in hard times or where they were comparatively better off economically. Others stayed because they believed that life would eventually improve, optimistically hinging their fate on three little words: "If it rains." The people who experienced the dust storms would never forget them. Alfred M. Landon, Kansas governor and Republican presidential nominee in 1936, reflected, "They changed thousands of lives permanently." The Dust Bowl years became an indelible mark on the minds of residents.[8]

Drought, dust storms, and grasshoppers also plagued the northern Great Plains. A farm woman from Lyman County, South Dakota, remembered 1931 as "the first grasshopper year, the beginning of bare earth farming." On her farm, "the earth was alive with them . . . even the leaves of the trees were stripped. . . . There were so many piled dead in our potato patch that they stank." In November 1933, the Greater North Dakota Association held a regional conference to discuss the measures to eliminate this crop-destroying menace. Ultimately, the delegates secured federal funding for a poison control program. Three years later, North Dakota also created the State Grasshopper Control Committee and provided state funds for poison control methods.

In the northern plains, as in the southern plains, agricultural prices fell and remained low during the early 1930s. In Meade County, South Dakota, a farm woman remembered selling cream for $.10 a pound and eggs for $.10 per dozen, down from $.38 and $.24, respectively, only a few years before. In Pennington County, wheat brought $.16 per bushel, down from $1.26 per bushel in 1926. Farmers burned corn in their stoves because it was cheaper fuel than coal or wood. Economic and environmental calamity seemed to prevail. For South Dakotans in the West River Country, the 1930s brought a brutal struggle for survival and a decade of lowered expectations. Great Plains residents reverted to the pioneer regional tradition of making do or doing without.[9]

As unskilled workers began losing their jobs and as credit contracted, city, county, and state governments and local charitable organizations and relief agencies could not meet the needs of the destitute. Tax revenues declined or went unpaid. Governments and schools slashed budgets and, like businesses, fired employees. Increasingly, the financially solvent public considered those in need of public assistance to be morally inferior. They expected those who suffered hard times to find work, while the business community provided minimal public relief. Yet Great Plains residents also felt uneasy about government relief programs that brought federal regulations, even though local committees often had the responsibility of enlisting public support and administering the relief programs. Workers essentially remained dependent on their employers and hoped for the best.[10]

Where race colored relief, as in San Antonio, Mexican Americans and African Americans suffered more than whites as they sought jobs and economic assistance to help weather hard times. Both groups experienced discrimination based not only on race but also on gender. Latino women primarily found limited employment in manufacturing or businesses, the latter of which serviced their ethnic community. Black women predominated in domestic employment, which whites considered their station in life. Gender and ethnicity segregated the workforce and relegated Mexican American and African American women to low-paid jobs. Overall, one local newspaper called San Antonio a "pesthole of low paid labor." Because San Antonio and Bexar County did not provide public relief, Mexican American and African American women and men ultimately depended on federal programs to help support their families.[11]

Indeed, substantive public assistance for the region did not come until the federal government under the Roosevelt administration began a host of programs administered through a variety of agencies to restore the economy in a multiplicity of ways. Created in 1935, the Works Progress Administration (WPA) provided work relief projects such as improving roads, laying sewers, and painting public buildings, while women received employment in WPA sewing rooms making clothing for the needy, at canning projects, and in nursery schools, all of which provided essential wages that kept families and communities viable until better times and jobs returned. The WPA became the most popular agency to provide work relief for unskilled and semiskilled workers, often on small-scale make-work projects.

WPA workers built swimming pools and helped construct the post office and federal building in Amarillo. In South Dakota, the agency provided $35 million to hire workers for the construction of 131 buildings and the refurbishing of 250 more. In North Dakota, the WPA built more than 20,000 miles of streets, 721 bridges, 503 buildings, and 680 outdoor recreation areas, among other projects, as well as a baseball stadium for the Fargo Public School District. At one time, more than 53,000 North Dakotans

During the New Deal years of the 1930s, many federal assistance programs attempted to provide income and employment for men and women to stimulate the economy until better economic times returned. The Federal Emergency Relief Administration, Works Progress Administration, and Public Works Administration funded various projects that benefited local communities. On July 20, 1935, this public works project funded by the Federal Emergency Relief Administration involved paving a street with bricks in Omaha, Nebraska.

earned $40 per month while working on WPA projects, and they used that income for groceries, fuel, and the basic necessities of life. In Ellis, Kansas, the WPA built a limestone wall around the cemetery. Near Amarillo, the Civil Works Administration paved an 18-mile section of Route 66, the last unpaved portion of the highway between Amarillo and Chicago. Across the Great Plains, the Civilian Conservation Corps (CCC) hired young men to plant trees, built shelters in city parks, and assisted the Soil Conservation Service and local farmers. Overall these temporary work relief projects made lasting improvements for towns, cities, and the countryside.[12]

In March 1934, more than 37 percent of North Dakota's population received some form of government relief. In December, South Dakota had 39 percent of its people on relief (a higher percentage than any other state), and more than 50 percent of its farm families depended on some form of public assistance. Between 1932 and 1937, the worst years for drought and dust, the per capita income of North Dakota was 47 percent of the national average. Most families had only $145 in disposable income for

Many cities and towns used federal emergency relief funding to establish sewing centers for women, who received a wage for making clothing, rugs, and quilts that would be sold at low cost or provided to those in need. This sewing center in Fairbury, Nebraska, advertised its dresses as "fashionable" with no duplicates.

the year. By 1940, one-third of South Dakota farmers had lost their land to foreclosure, and tenancy reached nearly 50 percent. In North Dakota, one member of a county welfare board who "detested Roosevelt" admitted that "the people of Cass County . . . were glad there was money coming in that they didn't have to provide." Another North Dakotan reflected that "federal money was like rain in a drought," because it benefited local governments and citizens alike. State and county officials might complain about federal regulations that came with government programs, but their opposition was not enough to reject New Deal funding, which increased purchasing power and strengthened the local economy. Increasingly, state and local governments looked to the federal government for relief. By the end of the decade, they, like the farmers, had begun to consider government assistance a matter of entitlement rather than as temporary financial and economic programs, and local and state officials did not hesitate to ask the federal government for more money.[13]

Many people across the Great Plains, however, refrained from participating in federal relief projects because of shame and embarrassment that they could not provide for themselves or their families. One North Dakotan reflected, "It was a disgrace to go on relief, it really was." He spoke for many in saying, "People were ashamed of themselves if they went on relief. It was a sin if you had to accept welfare. People were very, very proud." One Kansas family with eleven children and a single mother no doubt benefited from federal relief of some form, and while the children held jobs, no one later talked about the Great Depression other than to say that times were hard and that many suppers consisted of bread and gravy. Otherwise, they professed a lack of memory or only, "We got by." One North Dakotan probably spoke for many across the Great Plains in saying, "Most people who needed help were too proud to ask."[14]

At the same time, problems remained. The $40 monthly wage set by the WPA for common labor in 1935 hardly met the needs of a family, and other public or charitable assistance became necessary. Although the government agencies, with a few exceptions, gave priority to the employment of heads of families to help as many people as possible, the WPA technically could not provide work relief for farmers because agency officials did not consider them unemployed. Farmers also objected to work relief projects, arguing that such government employment deprived them of labor, particularly at harvest time, all the while accepting federal dollars in other forms of government programs and assistance. One North Dakotan put it succinctly in saying that the government "bid against farmers" for labor. Although public relief and agricultural assistance projects and programs were never efficient, they effectively provided the people of the Great Plains with hundreds of thousands of dollars. Simply put, the federal government saved many plains men, women, and children from destitution.[15]

Although the Public Works Administration supported unions and the National Recovery Administration guaranteed workers the right to organize and bargain collectively, organized labor often confronted a hostile public across the Great Plains, particularly where small-scale family businesses and retail and service occupations predominated. Even so, workers seeking higher wages and better working conditions increasingly joined unions in Great Plains cities during the 1930s. In 1937, Fargo painters, bakers, and barbers as well as truck drivers struck for higher wages and shorter working hours. Some strikes proved long and violent. Many union members did not have experience or a tradition of membership, and their support and enthusiasm often waned. With few large-scale industries or employers across the region, many plains men and women preferred steady employment and a regular paycheck to no job at all or the risks of unionization. Certainly they feared the loss of their job because of strikes. Great Plains men and women generally preferred the right to work or an open shop at worst, rather than closed-shop employment. African Americans and Mexi-

Not all farmers and ranchers suffered from the economic effects of the Dust Bowl and Great Depression. In the southern Great Plains, oil production contributed substantial income to landowners who leased their land to oil companies and drew royalties from the pumped crude. In 1937, the Mansion Extension Area to the Oklahoma City Oil Field boomed.

can Americans seldom even had that choice. These workers often became the first fired or had their wages substantially reduced when the national economic collapse reached the Great Plains.[16]

Only the federal government could provide the resources, expertise, and organization to bring some semblance of economic and social relief to the drought-stricken, windblown, economically wavering Great Plains. The most significant agricultural aid came in May 1933 with the Agricultural Adjustment Act (AAA), which created the Agricultural Adjustment Administration. The federal government intended to use the AAA to pay farmers to reduce crop production, thereby eventually eliminating surplus agricultural commodities and raising farm prices, particularly for wheat, cotton, corn, and hogs in the Great Plains states.[17]

Nearly all Great Plains farmers participated in the AAA program. Indeed, they could not afford to do otherwise. Although they preferred to plant as much wheat as possible and hope for rain, they had little choice but to accept AAA checks: they needed the money. The only significant opposition to the New Deal program came from the large grain dealers, commission men, and food processors (who were taxed to pay for the first AAA program), rather than from the farmers. As a result, AAA payments became the major form of income for many farmers between 1933 and 1937. In 1936, one South Dakotan observed, "The AAA saved the west river country."[18]

The AAA became one of the most significant and popular agencies for Great Plains farmers. Most important, the AAA marked the beginning of the federal government's active role in regulating the agricultural economy. Certainly, the AAA laid the foundation for an agricultural policy that affected nearly every farmer until the late twentieth century. Whether they approved of such government intervention in agriculture, they became dependent on AAA-inspired policy that built on its income generation, allotment, and marketing methods for the remainder of the century.

Most Great Plains farmers used their AAA payments to meet essential needs and pay bills, bank loans, and taxes as well as purchase daily household and farm necessities such as food, clothing, and seed, as well as equipment, thereby improving their credit. Women played a major role in determining the expenditures of these checks, which farm families considered a windfall. On January 6, 1936, however, the U.S. Supreme Court held the Agricultural Adjustment Act unconstitutional because the tax on food processors used to fund the program was not a real tax but rather an agricultural production control system that was voluntary in name only.

Despite the Supreme Court's ruling, the Roosevelt administration was unwilling to allow the AAA to expire because many Great Plains farmers had become dependent on allotment checks for daily living and farm operating expenses, and because the presidential election would be held that November. Consequently, the administration moved quickly to have Congress pass new legislation, known as the Soil Conservation and Domestic Allotment Act, and the president signed the bill into law on February 29, 1936. AAA payments were then based on the agreement of farmers to plant soil-conserving crops for production control rather than for acreage reduction, although the end result was the same.[19]

Great Plains farmers also participated in the Emergency Livestock Purchase Program of the Drought Relief Service. In this program, the federal government purchased cattle to provide income for livestock producers who could not feed their starving cattle and to provide work relief at local slaughterhouses and canning plants that would then provide beef for needy people. In 1934, South Dakota stockmen sold more than 900,000 cattle, most of which were processed at local slaughterhouses in Aberdeen, Huron, Mandan, Mitchell, and Rapid City for relief assistance and distribution by the Federal Surplus Commodities Corporation. The federal government required participating farmers to limit production, and despite the reputation of cattle producers for having fierce independence and hostility toward any government regulation, they (like others) took the money because they needed it.[20]

The Soil Conservation Service also provided farmers with funds to apply emergency wind-erosion mitigation techniques, such as contour listing, strip cropping, and terracing to hold the soil against the wind and keep any moisture from running off and further eroding the land. The Farm Credit Administration helped farmers refinance their mortgages with long-term, low-interest loans, while the Bankhead-Jones Farm Tenant Act of 1937 provided low-interest loans to tenants who wanted to buy land. Farmers also received financial aid from the Resettlement Administration, which Franklin Delano Roosevelt created in April 1935 to help ease the problem of rural poverty. Only those farmers who had exhausted all other forms of credit could apply for aid from the Resettlement Administration in the form of "rehabilitative" loans. These loans allowed farmers to purchase necessities — food, clothing, feed, seed, and fertilizer — for the purpose of making the farm operator self-sufficient once the drought ended. Before making a loan, the administration designed a farm management program that budgeted the farmers' expenses so that the operator could know how much to spend and still meet other loan and mortgage obligations. Resettlement Administration loans made in the southern Great Plains averaged $700 per farm family. These loans substantially helped farmers cope with dust, drought, and depression and by so doing enabled them to maintain their operations until the rains and good times returned. The Farm Security Administration (FSA) that replaced the Resettlement Administration in 1937 also made loans to farmers who could not obtain credit from other sources. The FSA granted loans to farmers whose operations promised to be self-sustaining, provided they had adequate access to equipment, seed, and livestock. The FSA loans were also designed to enable farmers to shift emphasis from cash grain farming to mixed farming with greater emphasis on raising livestock.[21]

Even so, life was difficult at best for Great Plains farmers. Government aid alone could not return the region to prosperity; only rain could do that. Yet during the 1930s, the federal government took responsibility for agricultural programming that ranged from price supports to acreage reduction to conservation to fiscal policy. The federal government became an agricultural organizer, lender, and regulator. It did not coerce participants, but few farmers could refuse the federal programs and opportunities. Certainly, this government support aid gave farmers buying and refinancing power that they would not have had otherwise. No farmer got rich from governmental aid, but without it the Great Plains agricultural community would have suffered far more even than it did.[22]

It did not take long to reaffirm the idea that trees were important to environmental control on the Great Plains. By the summer of 1932, drought together with the plowing up of the southern Great Plains created the most severe wind-erosion problem in the history of the region. As dust storms swept across the plains, darkening the skies, destroying crops, and drifting soil like snow, plains residents and federal officials alike began thinking about controlling the environment once again. Only with environmental control, they believed, could humans live in harmony with nature in the Great Plains.

In March 1933, the Forest Service began new efforts to control the Great Plains environment after President Franklin Delano Roosevelt asked the agency to investigate whether a major tree-planting program could substantially reduce wind erosion in the region. Roosevelt and others contended that the early attempts at forestry in the plains provided encouragement and offered a partial solution to the wind-erosion problem. The president believed that tree planting would ameliorate drought conditions by slowing the force of the wind and would ease economic hardship by saving cropland from ruin by drifting soil. At the same time, the forestation of a major portion of the Great Plains would require a considerable workforce, and the federal government could use it as a work relief project as well as a conservation program. While the drought and dust storms dramatized the wind-erosion problem on the Great Plains, a large-scale forestry project also would dramatize the human and institutional response to environmental conditions out of control.[23]

Working at record speed, the Forest Service concluded its preliminary investigation and sent its report to the president on August 15, 1933. In that document, Robert Y. Stuart, chief forester, argued that a monumental forestry program for the Great Plains was not only feasible but also warranted. In contrast to Roosevelt's suggestion that a one-hundred-mile-wide forest be planted from the Canadian border to Texas, the Forest Service advocated planting a Shelterbelt Zone. The shelterbelts, planted by local labor, would be spaced one mile apart across a hundred-mile section of the Great Plains. These shelterbelts would run north–south to check the "prevailing dry winds," protect fields and livestock, reduce evaporation, hold snow, reduce wind erosion, and eliminate dust storms. For many foresters, a tree-planting program for the Great Plains offered the solution to periodic wind erosion caused by drought and cultivation and would provide some control over the environment.[24]

But not everyone agreed. Some foresters argued that the plan was not only too grandiose but also environmentally impossible. Grass, not trees, grew naturally on the Great Plains, and drought would doom any major forestry program to failure. The result would be a great embarrassment to the Forest Service. One forester wrote, "We might cover the High Plains with trees, and we might carpet the state of Maine with buffalo grass, but if we are sensible we shall try to do neither." Other critics considered the project an oversimplified conservation plan, and they contended that no matter what measures government agents and farmers used to keep the soil from blowing, only rain would end wind erosion and blowing dust in the Great Plains. Still others believed that the project would be too expensive and that it would benefit individuals rather than the general public.[25]

Foresters at the Lake States Experiment Station in St. Paul, Minnesota, where the feasibility study had been conducted, however, cogently championed the project. They contended that large-scale tree planting in the Great Plains was not just a "make-work" project. Rather, a forestry program would ameliorate the local effects of an unfavorable climate. While forestry would not change the climate of the Great Plains, it could help control the environment by reducing wind erosion. Forestry thus was not simply possible but necessary, and Raphael Zon, the Lake States Station director, believed that "it is absurd for anyone to say that man cannot accomplish this on a considerable scale." These foresters agreed that "[i]f merely the surface velocity of the wind over a wide territory can be broken and decreased in the slightest degree, soil will be held in place, the moisture of soil will be conserved, havens of shelter will be created for man, beast and bird, and much future suffering and property loss will be averted. Meanwhile, a harassed people will be given new courage and a pittance on which to subsist, without recourse to charity and loss of self-respect."[26]

Before the project could begin, however, the Forest Service revised the plan and announced on May 28, 1934, that the project should extend, one hundred miles wide, from Canada to Texas but would be neither a solid block of trees nor a systematic string of shelterbelts spaced one mile apart running north–south. Rather, the shelterbelts would be planted on an east–west line at the center of each section of land. The western boundary would follow the eighteen-inch line of precipitation and extend from Bismarck, North Dakota, to Amarillo, Texas. The Forest Service also projected a budget of $60 million to plant 700 million trees across six states in ten years; nearly half of that budget would cover the cost of land purchases from farmers.[27]

Based on the advice of the Forest Service, Roosevelt established the Shelterbelt Project by executive order on July 11, 1934. F. A. Silcox, chief of the Forest Service, proclaimed, "This will be the largest project ever undertaken in the country to modify climate and agricultural conditions in an area that is now consistently harassed by winds and drought." Shelterbelts would slow the winds that dried the soil and crops and modify temperature extremes in the same way that green fields cooled the air. Raphael Zon at the Great Lakes Experiment Station, however, emphasized that the Shelterbelt Project was "only part of a broader plan of water conservation and erosion control for the entire Great Plains region." Shelterbelts alone could not eliminate the black blizzards; the dust storms could be stopped only by a comprehensive soil conservation program that included withdrawal of cropland, reseeding grass, controlled grazing, terracing, strip cropping, and agricultural diversification as well as shelterbelts.[28]

Although many Great Plains farmers did not think that shelterbelts would end the dust storms, most regional newspaper editors favored the project, because trees had proven merits and the project offered the opportunity to experiment with a work relief program on a major scale across the region. The *Amarillo Globe* noted that if the Great Plains environment could not be controlled, the region would become another semiarid wasteland like China. Still, opponents remained numerous and vocal. One opponent argued that "only God can make a tree . . . [and] . . . if He had wanted a forest on the wind-scoured prairies of Nebraska and Kansas, He would have put it there . . . and that for FDR to rush in where the Almighty had feared to tread was not only silly, but possibly blasphemous!" In contrast, embarrassingly supportive statements came from officials such as C. A. Russell, secretary of agriculture for South Dakota, who wrote that "the greatest good derived from [the] proposed shelter belt would be [the] tendency to increase rainfall." Similarly, F. C. Conn, state forester in North Dakota, believed that the Shelterbelt Project would favorably affect the climate beyond the Great Plains. As a result, the Forest Service began making a concerted effort to distance itself from any ideas that the Shelterbelt Project would change the climate and that it was just another "rain-making" scheme. Instead, the agency worked hard to emphasize the concept of environmental control because trees, properly planted according to a precise plan, would "ameliorate the effects of weather on a large scale"—but not change it.[29]

In August 1934, amid both criticism and optimism, the Forest Service established field headquarters for the Shelterbelt Project at Lincoln, Nebraska, with state offices in Jamestown, North Dakota; Brookings, South Dakota; Lincoln, Nebraska; Manhattan, Kansas; Oklahoma City, Oklahoma; and Wichita Falls, Texas. Two months later, the U.S. Department of Agriculture announced that preliminary work had begun to determine

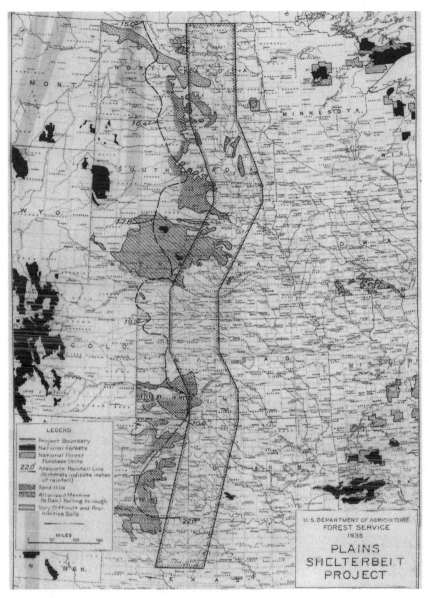

The U.S. Forest Service attempted to halt wind erosion and dust storms in the Great Plains by planting a one-hundred-mile-wide zone of trees from North Dakota into the Texas Panhandle. In this area, the Forest Service worked with farmers to plant rows of trees called shelterbelts to help slow the wind and protect croplands. The Prairie States Forest Project (or Shelterbelt Project) proved controversial, but some of these shelterbelts remain as historical footprints to a time of major state planning in agriculture.

suitable sites in terms of soil conditions and terrain as well as species for one thousand miles of shelterbelts. The Forest Service intended this work to establish the scientific base for the project. Yet despite this work and the Forest Service's tree-planting experience on the Great Plains, the agency did not know how to go about establishing forestry on such a grand scale. The foresters knew that if they planted the trees too far to the west, the seedlings would die, but if they planted them too far to the east, the trees would not be necessary. Moreover, the Forest Service contended that all farmers in the zone had to participate in the project to ensure success.[30]

Survey work performed in the autumn of 1934 caused the Forest Service to revise its shelterbelt plan. This time the agency advocated a 100-mile-wide belt that would stretch 1,150 miles from the Canadian border through the eastern third of the Dakotas, east-central Nebraska, west-central Kansas, western Oklahoma, and into northern Texas. The western boundary would skirt the ninety-ninth meridian from Devil's Lake, North Dakota, to Abilene, Texas, an area that averaged sixteen inches of precipitation in the north to twenty-two inches in the south and that totaled 114,700 square miles. Shelterbelts would not be planted in continuous strips spaced a mile apart. Rather, the Forest Service had determined that only 56 percent of the projected area proved suitable for trees. If the shelterbelts were planted on the appropriate soils and in the best locations, they would help control wind erosion on nearby fields. Raphael Zon also contended that "highly stabilized control of the land dedicated to the shelterbelts is essential." Moreover, the project might require fifty years before the public recognized any benefit. Consequently, long-term federal control of the land was essential.[31]

In 1937, the Forest Service made simple cooperative agreements with landowners who furnished their property and fencing materials in return for the planting of a shelterbelt, the erection of fences, and rodent control provided by the agency's WPA workers. By doing so, farmers bore about half of the project costs. Comptroller J. R. McCarl, however, refused to release funds for the program because money provided by the Emergency Appropriation Act of June 18, 1934, could be spent only for emergency work relief. McCarl interpreted the law to mean that those funds could not be spent to purchase land, trees, or supplies. Although Roosevelt succeeded in getting the release of $1 million to begin the project, the Works Progress Administration began financing it in 1936. Because the WPA required that 90 percent of its funding had to be spent in work relief, however, the Forest Service necessarily gave up any hope of purchasing land for the shelterbelts from the farmers.[32]

Moreover, the Forest Service received criticism not only from those who considered the program nothing more than financial irresponsibility but also from the nursery owners on the Great Plains. The Forest Service knew from its experiences in planting the Nebraska and Kansas national forests that only trees raised in local beds or seeds gathered in the vicinity would survive. Because they could not purchase seedlings or collect seeds from outside the area with much chance for success, the Forest Service planned to purchase seedlings from nurseries in the Shelterbelt Zone until it could establish its own nurseries. The Forest Service, however, ran into trouble almost immediately. Although several nurseries sold some planting stock to the agency, nursery owners refused to participate after 1935 because the federal government could not incur obligations beyond the fiscal year. With trees taking several years to sprout and reach sufficient size for transplant, the nursery operators hesitated to incur expenses that they were not guaranteed to recover through government contracts. As a result, the Forest Service leased private nurseries to raise transplant stock. Employees also dug up wild cottonwood trees along creek bottoms, and the experiment station at Woodward, Oklahoma, became a leader in seed collection. By 1936, the federal government had established twenty nurseries on the Great Plains that saved an estimated $15 million over the life of the project, but nursery owners did not like the situation.[33]

The Forest Service also struggled in the field. When workers planted the first shelterbelt near Mangum, Oklahoma, on March 19, 1935, few farmers on the Great Plains were convinced that the project had merits. Many believed that drought, poor soils, and unsuitable topography would quickly destroy the trees. In the southern Great Plains, farmers gave little support to the project; only twenty-five miles of shelterbelts were planted in Kansas, while the foresters planted a scant fourteen miles in Oklahoma and merely two miles in Texas during the first year.[34]

Despite a slow start, Forest Service agents, known as "land examiners," continued to hold local meetings to enlist support from community leaders and organizations and provide newspapers and radio stations with news releases. In Kansas, the Forest Service had considerable success working with county farm bureaus, local Granges, and Farmers Union organizations. This public relations work, together with visual evidence that the shelterbelts reduced wind velocity and soil erosion, gained support of the project from other landowners, who then agreed to participate in the program.[35]

In Kansas, Charles A. Scott, state project director, reiterated in no uncertain terms, "The shelterbelts will not change the general climate of the entire region." But the shelterbelts would, in his judgment, "modify temperature, humidity, and wind velocity on portions of the adjoining farms." Shelterbelts would not prevent drought but would lessen its effects. Moreover, shelterbelts would not increase the total amount of rainfall, but they would help conserve the moisture. Simply put, the shelterbelts would help control the environment. Scott also deviated from the announced purpose for the shelterbelt program — to help prevent wind erosion. Although he believed that the shelterbelts would check wind erosion and protect croplands, he envisioned the project in social as well as environmental terms. He wrote, "We are doing it to improve living conditions; to improve farm conditions in the western half of the state. We want to make conditions livable. We want to develop a rural sociability, a rural happiness, a rural contentment which we think such plantings will bring about." Scott contended that the shelterbelts would "raise the living conditions in the plains region for thousands of people to a higher level of permanence and stability." The project would also encourage farmers to plant more trees. Less idealistically, Scott also noted that another important benefit of the project would be the "cash wages" that the federal government would pay farmers for preparing their land for planting, fencing, and cultivating the shelterbelts — a "benefit" that could not be underestimated by "anyone familiar with the Middle West in its present condition."[36]

By the autumn of 1937, the Forest Service had also moved to eliminate the perception that it arbitrarily told landowners where the shelterbelts had to be planted. In Kansas, for example, project officials worked with the county agents to appoint township tree committees. These committees had the responsibility to develop plans that would benefit the local community as well as the farmer. Township tree committees developed and mapped ideal shelterbelt locations and encouraged landowners to participate in the project.[37]

Despite problems, then, the project continued. In late March 1935, Forest Service employees planted shelterbelts at the rate of 2 miles per day in Collingsworth County, Texas, with 60 miles projected and with shelterbelts also planned for Wheeler and Childress counties. In Oklahoma, the Forest Service targeted sixteen counties for 10 miles of shelterbelts. North Dakota had 35 and South Dakota 28 miles of shelterbelts. By the end of 1935, 129 miles of shelterbelts had been planted on 263 Great Plains farms. In the Dust Bowl states, the survival rate of the planted seedlings averaged as high as 70 percent. In 1936, the Forest Service estimated that nearly 1,278 miles of shelterbelts had been planted on 876 farms. The Forest Service estimated the survival rate for the 1936 plantings at 90 percent by the autumn despite continued drought. This success encouraged the Forest Service to report that the Shelterbelt Project "constitutes complete refutation of the theory that trees will not grow on the Plains." By that time, some of the shelterbelts planted in 1935 allegedly had made a "marked influence" on nearby cropland, making production possible where it had been hazardous or impossible before the shelterbelts had been established; this served as a solid indication for some of the "entire feasibility" of the project. It was a modest but important beginning.[38]

Because many landowners soon became convinced that shelterbelts could help protect their fields from wind erosion and because farmers outside the Shelterbelt Zone pressured their congressmen to include them in the program, on May 18, 1937, Congress passed the Norris-Doxey Cooperative Farm Forestry Act, which widened the Shelterbelt Zone to two hundred miles. Essentially, this legislation authorized the Forest Service to plant shelterbelts to help control the environment between the 96th and 101st meridians. Essentially, however, this act gave the Prairie States Forestry Project, as it became known, "functional authorization" but no funding. As a result, the WPA continued to finance the Shelterbelt Project.[39]

Because of the project's expansion and increased precipitation, the Forest Service planted 4,266 miles of shelterbelts during 1938, the peak year for the project. With the survival rate of the trees reaching 80 percent in some of the most drought-stricken and wind-eroded sections of the Great Plains, the foresters believed that the agency had begun to gain control of the environment, and farmers began to request increased plantings. The success of the Forest Service in reducing wind erosion, however, did not translate into financial support from Congress. The life of the Prairie States Forestry Project continued to rely on the Works Progress Administration for funding, and with the return of normal precipitation and government concerns about renewed war in Europe, the project received increasingly less attention. When the United States entered the war, work relief projects were no longer needed, and on July 1, 1942, Secretary of Agriculture Claude R. Wickard officially transferred the project to the Soil Conservation Service (SCS). By that time, 30,233 shelterbelts containing 220 million trees stretched for 18,600 miles on the Great Plains.[40]

The SCS, however, considered tree planting to be part of its other conservation work, rather than a major independent activity. SCS officials also preferred to plant smaller windbreaks to protect farmsteads and livestock rather than the larger shelterbelts primarily designed to protect croplands, and the agency preferred that the newly organizing soil conservation districts provide the initiative for tree planting. Unfortunately for the Prairie States Forestry Project, these districts had been organized across only about 25 percent of the Shelterbelt Zone. As a result of budget reductions due to military needs during World War II and the transfer of the project to the SCS, the Prairie States Forestry Project could not survive. Only 1,750 miles of shelterbelts were planted in 1942, and 65 miles the next year, and the project thereafter ceased to exist.[41]

At the same time that the Forest Service worked to plant shelterbelts to help control the environment, much of the Great Plains lay beyond any precipitation line that promised even marginal success for large-scale tree planting. In 1933, many New Dealers believed that the time had come for the federal government to purchase submarginal, wind-eroded lands in the Great Plains to institute a massive conservation program and gain at least some control over the environment. The purchase of submarginal lands also would enable federal social scientists to consolidate farms to ensure that the farmers who remained would have enough acres to earn an adequate living, although these scientists could not precisely say what that meant. Those farmers who sold their lands could be moved to federal resettlement projects elsewhere, or they could take their money and do as they pleased.

The federal government began the submarginal land-purchase program in the autumn of 1934 under the land policy section of the AAA. Federal land purchases for the retirement of cropland were made in southern Otero County, Colorado; Harding County, New Mexico; and Morton County, Kansas. In Otero and Harding counties, a high percentage of the land remained in native grass, and the government leased it back to cattle raisers under a controlled grazing program to ensure wise range management, enable expansion of operations, and encourage the shift from cash crops to livestock. In southwestern Kansas, where the sandhills of Morton County had been badly abused, grazing lands and croplands alike were subject to severe wind erosion; public support for a government land-purchase and conservation program grew primarily because the lands under consideration for purchase produced little wheat and few cattle, and land prices had plunged. Many farmers preferred to sell their land to the federal government because it had become basically worthless in terms of productivity. Kansas senator Arthur Capper supported the federal land-purchase program and hinted of the possible need to expand it when, in July 1936, he said, "It may be that thousands . . . of acres should be purchased by the federal government and returned as public grazing lands, utilized at times for growing crops to meet some emergency that requires abnormal grain production for a year or so."

Although the submarginal land-purchase program, known as the land utilization project, began slowly in July 1937, land acquisitions quickened after the passage of the Bankhead-Jones Farm Tenant Act. Title III of that legislation authorized the secretary of agriculture to purchase submarginal lands not suited for agriculture in the Great Plains. The purchases would be selective. Only those lands beyond the control of private owners would be acquired, and county planning committees would determine the areas where the federal government could make land purchases. All federal land acquisitions would coordinate with other agricultural conservation programs designed to help restore the area.

No one knew how much land might be taken eventually, but it could not be taken against the owner's will. After identifying the "problem" areas where wind erosion had severely damaged the land, government officials surveyed the area to determine which lands should be restored to grass under government control and which lands should remain in private ownership. If a farmer wished to sell, the government sent appraisers, and both parties tried to arrive at a fair price based on soil conditions and improvements. The farmer retained the mineral rights, and the government paid all back taxes. Upon purchase of the land, government officials began reseeding plowed fields and wind-blown pastures and using strip cropping, terracing, and various tillage techniques to slow the wind and hold the soil on croplands.

As a large land-purchase program began, some Great Plains farmers became fearful that the government intended to move them from the land purchase areas at all costs, but federal officials only wanted "wild land," that is, severely wind-eroded land not under lease or cultivation. The croplands purchased by the government would be retired to grass and eventually used for "controlled grazing," wildlife refuges, and public recreation areas. Although that task would require years of work, and although some Great Plains residents thought the outcome was "dubious," most agreed that the objective was commendable.

The soil conservation work planned for the land utilization projects should not be confused with the work of the Soil Conservation Service to help farmers end wind erosion on their croplands and gain some control of the environment. Although federal officials proclaimed that the land utilization projects would return windblown croplands to soil-holding grasslands, most of the submarginal lands purchased remained in grass. The Little Missouri Land Utilization Project in the Badlands of western North Dakota provides an example. In this region, drought was a perennial threat, and landowners primarily grazed cattle rather than plowing the land for wheat. In contrast to what occurred in the southern Great Plains, few dust storms plagued the region because lower temperatures and evaporation rates along with soil-holding spring snow cover helped keep the prevailing winds from creating dust storms.

The land utilization administrators were determined to use agricultural science and best practices in range management to restore or, rather, improve those grasslands and ensure systematic and controlled grazing practices. In 1936, with little cropland in the Little Missouri Land Utilization Project, the federal government purchased more than 268,500 acres of grazing land (approximately 93 percent of the project area). To the south on the Mills Project in New Mexico, the federal government purchased approximately 73,000 acres, of which only 26 percent was in cropland. Despite the efforts of the Soil Conservation Service to reseed the land utilization project grass-lands, however, drought, insufficient funding, and inadequate knowledge prevented federal officials from achieving much environmental control.

Despite limited success in reseeding the grasslands, federal officials used the land utilization projects to ensure sustainable grazing practices by reg-ulating the number of cattle on those lands through grazing associations organized by local ranchers who, to gain access to the project grasslands, had to follow federally mandated grazing practices. The Soil Conservation Service had more certainty than success in helping farmers prevent soil erosion on cultivated lands in the southern Great Plains, for enhancing grass cover on the rangelands of the land utilization projects did not solve the problem. Wind erosion, of course, damaged the grasslands, but the soil-erosion problem was the worst (and most treatable) on croplands where the planting of soil-holding vegetation, such as wheat or grass, and tillage techniques slowed the wind and held even scant precipitation in the soil. In the end, the dust storms would continue until the drought ended. Soil conservation techniques, including the reseeding of the grasslands on the land utilization projects, helped, but nature, not man, primarily created and ended the Dust Bowl.

Insufficient funding always hindered the land utilization project's land-purchase and conservation program. By 1939, however, the submarginal land-purchase program had fallen into disrepute because the government reportedly was buying good lands, which forced tenants into town and onto relief rolls. Local governments also feared additional losses to the tax base, and others resented the government destroying improvements that were often worth more than the land when it purchased farms. The real reason for dissatisfaction with the government's land-purchase program, however, was the return of near-normal precipitation for crop raising in most areas during the late 1930s. In January 1939, Morton County, Kansas, had the best wheat prospects of any county in the state. The war in Europe also forced Congress to curtail many programs in favor of boosting defense. As a result of these influences, the federal government terminated the submarginal land utilization program in February 1940. By that time, nearly 1 million acres of submarginal land had been purchased since 1935, at an average price of $3.56 per acre. Although 250,000 acres were still subject to wind erosion, 350,000 acres had been restored to grassland, which the government leased to cattlemen.

Certainly the land utilization projects in the Great Plains were not capable of solving all agricultural, economic, and social problems, but as part of a broad soil conservation program designed to gain control of the environment, the federal government's land utilization program played a major role in helping reduce wind erosion across the region. The Soil Conservation Service, which became responsible for the land utilization projects in 1938, administered them until November 2, 1953, when Secretary of Agriculture Ezra Taft Benson transferred the projects to the Forest Service. And on June 20, 1960, the U.S. Department of Agriculture created national grasslands from the land utilization projects in every Great Plains state. The national grasslands, like the shelterbelts, remain a visible historical footprint of an unprecedented experiment in state planning and land reclamation to control the environment of the Great Plains.[42]

On April 21, 1933, John Collier became commissioner of Indian affairs, and his appointment placed the bureau on a new course. Collier had been an activist for Indians during the 1920s, and as the director of the American Indian Defense Association he served as the most persistent and visible critic of the Bureau of Indian Affairs (BIA). After the election of Franklin Delano Roosevelt to the presidency in 1932, he became the leading candidate for the office of commissioner of Indian affairs. When Collier accepted the position, he and many Indians and reformers believed the time had arrived for an "Indian New Deal."[43]

Under Collier's leadership, the BIA had the opportunity to steer Indian policy on a revolutionary course that would change Indian-white relations for all time. Collier had a far different view of the Indian world and its place within white society than did other friends of the Indians. He believed that all efforts to acculturate and assimilate the Indians had failed. Instead, federal policy had destroyed the inherent strengths of tribal life. Henceforth the Indians would retain their cultural uniqueness; no longer would they be forced to acculturate and assimilate into white society. Cultural pluralism would solve the Indian problem. Tribal communalism rather than private individualism, Collier contended, would create viable social alternatives to life based on the cultural traditions of white society. To achieve that goal, Collier proclaimed that the federal government would help the

Indians become self-supporting and politically independent within their own ethnocentric world. Collier championed the preservation of Indian civilization by the creation of a "Red Atlantis." Only by doing so, he argued, could the Indians live self-sufficiently and with dignity. As commissioner of Indian affairs, Collier believed that agriculture remained a cornerstone of his program to ensure Indian economic survival. He planned to guarantee the land base for future generations, preserve the soil, and extend federal aid for many programs, thereby creating a sound economic base that would make self-sufficiency possible within the tribal community. To achieve these goals, Collier first sought the creation of the Indian Conservation Corps not only to provide needed work relief by creating thousands of federally supported jobs but also to help prevent soil erosion and restore reservation lands to full agricultural productivity. President Roosevelt supported Collier's plan, and the new agency began work in July 1933. Officially known as the Indian Emergency Conservation Work, it became known unofficially as the Civilian Conservation Corps–Indian Division, or CCCID. On the premise that reservation problems differed from those found elsewhere, the BIA, rather than the Civilian Conservation Corps, maintained control of this agency. Moreover, the work of the CCCID was directed not toward improving the public domain (as was that of its parent organization) but toward conserving and restoring reservation lands and training the Indians to use their lands wisely.[44]

In the Great Plains, most of the work for the CCCID was scheduled for reservations in Oklahoma, South Dakota, and Montana where "relative need" and "relative poverty" determined the expenditure of funds. Collier believed that the erosion problem was "acute" on the reservation grazing lands in these states, and he called upon the Indians to diversify their crops and to institute better range-management practices. Indians employed by the CCCID built stock watering ponds and terraces that checked runoff and prevented gullying; poisoned rodents, such as prairie dogs, gophers, and ground squirrels; and drilled wells for irrigation. They also seeded crested wheatgrass on wind-eroded lands to promote natural reseeding, and they built fences to permit the rotation of rangelands for livestock grazing.[45]

Among the Sioux, committees selected by the tribal council chose men over eighteen years of age for enrollment in the CCCID, where they received $30 per month, or $1.50 per day for twenty days of work per month. Indians who brought their own horses to the job received an additional $1 to $2 per day. At Pine Ridge, Rosebud, Standing Rock, Cheyenne River, and Lower Brulé reservations, the CCCID emphasized soil and water conservation projects. East of the Missouri River where drought posed a lesser problem than in the West River Country, CCCID men on the Crow Creek, Yankton, and Sisseton Sioux reservations constructed roads, strung telephone lines, and built fences as well as prepared communal gardens and developed irrigation systems. Overall, the CCCID employed 8,405 Indians over nine years and spent more than $4.5 million on the Rosebud, Standing Rock, and Pine Ridge reservations. In 1940, 97 percent of the population at Standing Rock depended on the CCCID for approximately half of their federal relief income. The CCCID also provided some training for off-reservation employment. For a comparatively brief period, the CCCID served as the most important relief agency for many Great Plains tribes, in part because it prevented starvation.[46]

World War II ended even the feeblest commitment of the federal government to improving the economic, social, and political problems of the reservation Indians. On July 2, 1942, Congress terminated the CCCID. During its nine years of existence, it contributed vital economic relief for families and training programs for individuals. Yet in the latter case, the CCCID contributed to off-reservation migration, as Indian men trained for semiskilled and skilled jobs and moved to urban areas for employment or joined the military. Overall, the conservation work of the CCCID on the reservations significantly improved tribal lands, but the agency did not exist long enough to achieve substantial change.[17]

While the BIA became increasingly involved with soil conservation, Collier also made it responsible for the administration of a new land policy. He believed that the allotment policy of the previous administrations had destroyed the well-being of the Indians. Allotment, together with heirship and leasing policies, continually eroded the Indian land base, and he intended to reverse that policy. On August 12, 1933, Collier ordered his superintendents to halt the sale of all Indian lands held in trust or otherwise restricted by the federal government. This decree covered both allotted and inherited or heirship lands, and it prohibited reservation superintendents from issuing fee patents (titles) and certificates of competency and from approving requests for the removal of the restrictions that prevented the sale of Indian lands except in cases of severe individual distress or emergency.[48]

Collier's order merely served as a stopgap procedure designed to halt the sale of Indian lands. The Indian lands that remained, Collier believed, had to be brought under a new system of Indian ownership to ensure productive use by the Indians, not whites, and to be "permanently safeguarded against voluntary or forced alienation." To achieve that goal, the Indians needed to make "deep adjustments" supported by legislation. He also argued that the lands that the Indians had lost because of allotment policy had to be "recaptured" to enable them to live full and productive lives as subsistence farmers. Henceforth, all Indian lands not under individual control would be subjected to communal use. Tribal rather than individual development of these lands, he believed, would guarantee the preservation of their landed estate. Indeed, a reversal of BIA land policy was essential if the Indians were to avoid generations of, if not permanent, poverty. No allotments, for example, had been made at the Sisseton Agency in South Dakota since 1892; Fred A. Parker, agency superintendant, reported that all land subject to allotment had been allocated and that within a generation all reservation land would be in heirship status and controlled by whites, and the Sisseton would be relegated to "wanderers over the face of the earth" with no future but to "perish miserably in dire poverty."[49]

Because allotment policy had turned the Indians into "paupers" instead of making them responsible, self-sufficient farmers and because many whites still supported past policies, Collier believed that legislation would be necessary to guarantee protection for his land-policy decree. By February 1934, Collier had developed an extensive plan, which included most of the recommendations of the Meriam Report, to redirect the course of American Indian policy. Submitted to Congress in mid-February, it became known as the Wheeler-Howard Bill. It called for governmental organization on the tribal level, improved education, the establishment of an Indian court, and the abolishment of the allotment system, thereby ending the BIA's "great experiment in social engineering," as well as the restoration of surplus lands to tribes and the acquisition of new lands with a $2 million annual fund. It also authorized the secretary of the interior to transfer privately held Indian lands to the tribe if he deemed such action necessary for the consolidation of Indian lands. Moreover, the bill enabled the tribes to assume control of restricted lands upon the death of the owner, rather than having the land divided among the heirs. The heirs, however, would maintain a proportional interest in tribal lands. In addition, the bill authorized the secretary to sell current heirship lands to the tribe, and it provided for an Indian agricultural and industrial credit fund. Collier believed that the Wheeler-Howard Bill would ultimately enable the Indians to control their own affairs, prevent future allotments, and consolidate and expand Indian lands.[50]

In sharp contrast to the past, Collier's new Indian policy sought communal, rather than individual, ownership of property. While many Indians supported the Wheeler-Howard Bill, however, others feared that the government would force them to return their allotments and their heirship rights to the tribe. Some, particularly those who ultimately were the most acculturated and assimilated (such as the Indians in Oklahoma, who were not included in the bill), objected to Collier's plan to renew tribal sovereignty, because this policy might mean a deprivation of their rights to own property. Many Sioux also feared the loss of their treaty rights. Friends of the Indians, such as the American Indian Rights Association, also objected to the Wheeler-Howard Bill, because it would segregate Indians (rather than integrate them into the white community) by stressing tribal self-development and self-government. The reservation missionaries also contended that the Wheeler-Howard Bill would undo a century of work because the tribes could revert to paganism, that is, the worship of non-Christian gods or spirits.[51]

To win congressional approval for his program, Collier sought compromise. Even so, opposition within the Indian community, as well as in Congress, remained strong. Before the bill became law on June 18, 1934, the Wheeler-Howard Act, also known as the Indian Reorganization Act (IRA), had been redrafted in the House and heavily amended in the Senate. The revised bill, in part, extended the trust period indefinitely for Indian lands, authorized the return of unallotted and surplus lands to tribal ownership, made possible the voluntary return of allotments to tribal control, and provided for the addition of lands to the reservations with an annual fund of $2 million, but it did not ban inheritances of land. It also authorized a $10 million revolving credit fund for economic development. In addition, the IRA authorized the tribes to organize their own government and adopt a constitution and bylaws. The tribes could then employ legal counsel, receive a charter of incorporation, and mortgage their own property.[52]

After Congress approved the IRA, Collier solicited support from the various tribes by hosting a series of tribal congresses where the Indians would vote whether to accept or reject it. Collier hoped that an educational campaign would convince the Indians that the acceptance of the IRA would mean self-governance, protection of their property, and cultural and economic independence, whereas rejection would mean a continuation of the old problems of allotment, heirship, inadequate credit, economic destitution, and BIA domination. Congress excluded the Oklahoma Indians from the provisions of the act. Senator Elmer Thomas and Representative W. W. Hastings, a Cherokee, had opposed Collier for commissioner of Indian affairs and also opposed the IRA. At the congresses held in Oklahoma, the tribes did not want to return to tribal landownership and segregation on reservations, and they considered reservations to be communistic or socialistic. This position excluded them from federal loans, extension of the trust period, and the right to incorporate for business purposes. Senator Thomas said, "The Oklahoma Indians having made progress beyond the reservation plan, it was thought best not to encourage a return to reservation life."

In Oklahoma, the Kiowas opposed the IRA while the Comanches, Pawnees, Kaws, Otoes, Tonkawas, and Ottawas feared the loss of their allotments, especially those containing lead and zinc mines. The Five Civilized Tribes also rejected the IRA for the same reasons. In 1935, however, Congress, led by Senator Thomas and Representative Will Rogers, essentially applied the IRA to Oklahoma Indians of one-half blood or more. Their property would remain in trust status, while Indians of less than one-half blood would have any government restrictions on their land removed. The Oklahoma Indians could voluntarily organize tribal governments and incorporate and receive federal funds for advancing credit. This legislation also promised health care and educational facilities. Known as the Oklahoma Indian Welfare Act, this legislation passed Congress on June 26, 1936; however, the Osages remained excluded.[53]

The Sioux at Crow Creek, Yankton, Sisseton, and Standing Rock reservations also rejected the IRA, primarily because political factions emerged and voted against acceptance. Some Sioux believed that the new tribal governments would threaten older power groups, such as tribal claims committees, which sought restitution for past grievances, including the Wounded Knee massacre in 1890 and the violation of treaty rights. Moreover, the IRA did not grant complete tribal sovereignty, because the commissioner retained authority to review and approve various tribal ordinances. The Sioux who opposed the IRA believed that it would continue wardship status. Overall, the Sioux full-bloods rejected this legislation because it would return their restricted allotted lands to tribal ownership, while the mixed-bloods usually had sold their allotments. The Sioux at Cheyenne River argued that the days of communal ownership had passed, while the full-bloods at Standing Rock said that they were "getting accustomed to the allotment system." The Assiniboines and Atsinas at the Fort Belknap Agency in Montana favored the establishment of a community government but opposed the return of allotted lands to the reservations without compensation.[54]

Many Great Plains Indians believed that tribal governments would favor the mixed-bloods. Among the Blackfeet, the mixed-bloods outnumbered the full-bloods by a ratio of four to one. After the tribe approved the IRA, the mixed-bloods elected most members of the tribal business council that was chartered under the provisions of the law, and they served on the boards that distributed livestock and federal funds for various programs and tribal revenues. The full-bloods divided and did not vote in a block, and the chiefs and elders who had previously spoken with authority lost power and influence. Tribal unity disintegrated, much to the chagrin of the "real Indians," who constituted the "real tribe." Moreover, the full-bloods believed that they were the "rightful owners" of Blackfeet oil royalties, while the tribal government (controlled by mixed-bloods) spent those funds for other collective purposes. The BIA considered the full-bloods a "rebellious minority" and urged them to work out their problems with the newly created tribal government.[55]

The IRA was the most significant legislation passed by Congress on behalf of the Indians during the twentieth century. Fundamentally, Congress intended the IRA to return government and decision making to the tribes, which would become formal institutions for the management of all tribal economic, political, and social affairs and ensure the recognition and validity of tribal cultures in a white world. The new tribal constitutions, however, imposed Anglo political organization and structures, including tribal councils and the election of officers, on the tribes. Moreover, the problems of the past could not be remedied quickly. By 1935, however, Collier believed that the Sioux at the Cheyenne River Reservation had gained "fundamental political and economic education through the process of working out their constitutions." Even so, the process of political organization moved slowly. Years would be required to change the tribal governance process and create a sense of self-determination. Significantly, the IRA ended land allotment, returned surplus lands to the reservations, and provided money for the purchase of lands to help block in reservations that had many scattered white holdings. In the Great Plains, the restoration of surplus lands primarily benefited the Kiowa, Comanche, and Apache Reservation in Oklahoma, the Pine Ridge Reservation in South Dakota, and the Standing Rock Reservation in North and South Dakota.[56]

Ultimately, missionaries, reformers, and bureaucrats as well as insufficient funding and World War II prevented the IRA from significantly benefiting the Indians in the Great Plains. Moreover, Congress refused to authorize the compulsory return of allotment and heirship lands to communal, tribal control in the confines of the reservations. Collier's most severe critics charged that the IRA supported segregation and isolation instead of acculturation and assimilation and that it imposed communism and a dictatorial reign of Indians on other Indians. In expecting to impose a tribal government and a tribal economy, Collier failed to take into account the importance of Indian bands and villages in the Great Plains. In the end, however, the Indian New Deal ended the allotment process and enabled substantial soil conservation work on the reservations. The elected tribal councils also eliminated autocratic rule by agency superintendents, and although the IRA did not achieve most of its provisions, it confirmed the Indian right of self-government.[57]

Still, the federal government had failed to stimulate economic improvement on the reservations. The BIA could not overcome the problems caused by drought and depression. The relief projects of the Civil Works Administration, Public Works Administration, and Works Progress Administration helped, but in 1939, with a per capita income of $150.50 on the Rosebud Reservation, with the average family income at only $458 in 1940, and with 95 percent of the Sioux still receiving some form of relief by 1942, economic improvement seemed far beyond the ability of BIA officials. Even off-reservation and military employment during World War II would not cause substantive improvement in the reservation economies of the Great Plains. As a result, significant tribal economic initiatives would await the last half of the twentieth century, but poverty served as the common denominator for the majority of the Indians of the Great Plains, while the tribes wrestled with the conflicting desires of sovereignty and the protective security of the federal government.[58]

On the eve of World War II, then, the Indians of the Great Plains (especially those on the reservations) remained rural, isolated, and poverty stricken, and the reservations ensured their segregation from white society. The tribes, however, were linked by the common bondage of federal policy that facilitated intertribal communication about similar problems and interests that laid the foundation for post–World War II ethnic resurgence and political activism. At the same time, many members of Congress and employees in the executive branch believed that the time had come for full assimilation of the Indians into white society. To achieve their goal, they spoke about the necessity to terminate all Indian relationships with the federal government. The future loomed ominously for the Indians in the Great Plains.[59]

Despite grumbling and resentment, Great Plains residents essentially welcomed the New Deal and its agents, politically as well as economically. The Great Plains states supported Roosevelt in the presidential election of 1932, when the New Deal was merely a promise. They supported him again in 1936, by which time the New Deal had become a reality through government jobs, loans, and price supports, among other assistance. During the 1940 presidential election, however, Kansas, Nebraska, and North and South Dakota returned to the Republican camp, which indicated that voters there felt sufficiently economically secure so that they could have both government-issued checks (derived from a Democratic administration) and a Republican political ideology. Moreover, despite complaints about the New Dealers devising a host of alphabet agencies, which often duplicated or worked at cross-purposes with each other—such as the AAA and RA (later the FSA)—as practical people, the men and women of the Great Plains appreciated the experimentation of the Roosevelt administration. Something (indeed, much) needed to be done, and the New Dealers sought the art of the possible in planning by accepting and rejecting ideas until they found something that worked, at least enough to improve the lives of plains men and women. For the people of the Great Plains, given the hard times of drought, dust, and depression, change offered the promise of progress and the improvement of their daily lives.[60]

The 1930s, the decade of the Great Depression, drought, and dust storms, culminated with fundamental changes to the economic system, social structures, and cultural values. The New Deal agencies and programs of the federal government gave plains men and women a choice between their customary independence and local control and that government economic aid that came with regulations and obligations. They chose government aid to remain on their land, stay in business, and endure until better times returned. Having made the choice to cast their fate with the federal government for economic survival, they could not go back to the independence and self-reliance of the past. The 1930s, and specifically the New Deal, became watershed years. Life in the Great Plains would never again be the same, whether residents liked that situation or not.

Even so, the people of the Great Plains suffered severe hardship during the 1930s. In November 1933, South Dakota journalist Lorena Hickok wrote to Harry Hopkins, President Roosevelt's confidant and New Deal programs administrator, saying, "This is the Siberia of the United States. A more hopeless place I never saw." North Dakota she believed was "drying up and becoming a desert." From Wyoming, she reported, "I saw a range that looked as though it had been gone over with a safety razor and stacks of Russian thistle put up for winter feed." Yet in Kansas she reported that the people did not want "rehabilitation"; they wanted rain. Although this attitude indicated hope, she saw "[m]iles and miles of burnt brown pastures."[61]

In the end, Great Plains residents welcomed federal assistance but not "help." In this context, the cultural differences between them and the eastern and Washington, D.C., bureaucrats who came to remake the land often caused both groups to see the economy of the region differently. The government's social and agricultural scientists dealt with ideas and optimistically believed that they could change the Great Plains for the better. The men and women of the plains considered pragmatism and decentralization of government to be the keys to success, and they often looked at federal officials, agencies, and programs with skeptical eyes. While federal agencies often improved their lives, Great Plains men and women retained their guarded distrust of government officials who were outsiders and who they believed did not understand their land, communities, and culture but had the power to impose programs that would change their lives. They particularly stiffened when ideas and progress seemed defined and directed by Roosevelt and his "Brain Trust." For the men and women of the Great Plains, the problem with the New Dealers was that they were not sufficiently practical. In April 1933, one Dakotan remarked, "The world is leaning too heavily on college professors. They are well meaning and have excellent book education but they draw overly much on the field of theory. They are removed from the practical aspects of life." Another North Dakotan, less diplomatic, described them as "white-collared, supercilious nincompoops."[62]

In retrospect, no greater calamity has struck the Great Plains than the triple plagues of drought, dust, and depression during the 1930s. Many people left the region, but most remained, whether by misfortune or choice. Yet a traditional and often unjustified spirit of optimism remained. During the depth of the Great Depression, one farmer wrote, "Western South Dakota is still a poor man's country, the land of promise to him who has the pioneering spirit." Another held a slightly different perspective, saying, "we have taken so many lickings that another defeat or failure means little to us." By the end of the 1930s, most Great Plains men and women had proved that they were "stickers." They were a "next year" people even though the future looked no better than the past. While they struggled with and against the federal government, which sought to gain technical control of the environment and to impose a new social and economic order on the plains, many took a hopeful wait-and-see approach to life. In Wheeler County, Texas, a panhandle woman wrote, "Oh, God, again to feel wet wind."[63]

The world of Great Plains men and women, then, became fundamentally altered during the 1930s. By the time the rains returned and World War II primed the economy, not a man, woman, or child remained untouched by the intervention of the federal government into the region. Never again would they be as independent and self-sufficient as before the years of the Great Depression and New Deal. In the end, the federal government changed everything except the isolation of the region and the environment. But now the Great Plains bore the brand of the federal government.[64]

CHAPTER FIVE

The Age of Certainty

The people of the Great Plains expressed an overwhelming sentiment for isolationism, including the variations of noninterventionism and neutrality, during the 1930s. Like most Americans who felt betrayed by the European powers at the Versailles Peace Conference in 1919, many also agreed with Senator Gerald P. Nye of North Dakota that the United States had been led to war in 1917 by the bankers, financiers, and munitions manufacturers solely for economic gain at the expense of thousands of American lives. Nye called the Great War "incorporated murder," and many men and women in the Great Plains agreed.[1]

In 1938, when Germany annexed Austria and seized the Sudetenland of Czechoslovakia, Great Plains residents expressed sympathy for the oppressed Europeans but nothing more. They generally supported the Neutrality Act of 1936, which prohibited loans and credits to warring nations, except for ordinary commercial business. In 1937, however, Congress amended the Neutrality Act, in part to authorize the president to list certain goods that could be traded to belligerents on a cash-and-carry basis. The Neutrality Act of 1937 was hardly impartial, because it favored Great Britain, which had a large navy capable of protecting its merchant ships transporting goods from American ports. Even so, the people of the Great Plains hoped the act would keep the nation out of war.[2]

In general, Great Plains leaders and their constituents voiced isolationist sentiments. Senator Lynn J. Frazier from North Dakota, like many other men and women of the Great Plains, believed that only trouble could come from entangling alliances, collective security agreements, and international organizations, such as the League of Nations. Frazier also contended that military appropriations and preparedness could only lead to an international arms race that made war inevitable. Senator Arthur Capper of Kansas advocated his own brand of isolationism, but in contrast to Nye and Frazier, he considered himself an internationalist who opposed war. Capper supported trade agreements with Latin America but not Europe and Asia. His isolationism sprang from George Washington's admonition to avoid entangling alliances and Thomas Jefferson's embargo prior to the War of 1812. He opposed strengthening the army and navy because, in his judgment, a military buildup would lead to war. Capper argued that the United States needed the army and navy only for the defense of American shores. He did not believe that a new European war would endanger American security, as long as the nation remained truly neutral. Many Great Plains people agreed.[3]

As Europe sped toward war, many representatives and senators from the Great Plains states adamantly favored isolationism and, after the German invasion of Poland in September 1939, noninterventionism and neutrality. Few gave much attention to Japanese expansion and militarism. Instead, their congressional representatives constantly made the case that isolationism, however defined, meant staying out of European wars. A foreign policy based on isolationism, noninterventionism, or neutrality would protect the nation.

In mid-October 1939, only weeks after Germany invaded Poland, Senators Edward Burke of Nebraska, William J. Bulow of South Dakota, and Burton K. Wheeler of Montana addressed the danger of repealing the arms embargo of the Neutrality Act and entering a new European war. In that discussion, Senator Wheeler made the riveting remark that the American people "do not want to see the bodies of their boys hung on the Siegfried Line." Once again, the people of the Great Plains agreed. At that time, Senator Frazier also opposed repealing the arms embargo of the Neutrality Act. He believed that such an action would enable the munitions manufacturers to commit the United States to war, just as they had in 1917.[4]

After the fall of France in June 1940 and Germany's invasion of the Soviet Union, the people of the Great Plains saw a greater danger of American entry into the war than ever before, and they used their congressional delegations to support neutrality, even isolationism, if such action would keep the peace. In November, the Wichita Council of Churches urged Senator Capper to support their desire for the federal government to prohibit the sale of scrap iron, aviation fuel, and other war materiel to any nation that might go to war with the United States. Significantly, the council considered Japan a danger to the security of the United States.[5]

In early 1941, Congress debated the merits of the president's proposed Lend-Lease Bill, which gave the president the authority to provide military aid to any country with payment in some form after hostilities ended. Many Great Plains men and women considered the Lend-Lease Bill no less than another ruse by the Roosevelt administration to commit the nation to war on behalf of Great Britain. Representative Harry B. Coffee of Nebraska opposed the Lend-Lease Bill because it would give the president unprecedented power to commit the nation to war, and Representative Clifford Hope of Kansas believed that the bill would enable the president to become a dictator. Senators Lynn S. Frazier and Gerald Nye of North Dakota also strongly opposed the Lend-Lease Bill. In May 1941, Senator Nye attacked President Roosevelt's foreign policy and told his radio listeners, "If we get into this war it will not be because the President tried to keep us out."[6]

In the late summer of 1941, many Great Plains residents feared that President Roosevelt would commit the nation to war more than they feared Germany. Japan still did not seem a major threat to them. The December 7, 1941, attack by the Japanese on Pearl Harbor and the declaration of war on the United States by Germany and Italy four days later, however, destroyed all sentiments of isolationism, noninterventionism, and neutrality. The nation had been attacked. The people of the Great Plains had wanted peace, almost at any price; they now wanted revenge.

Although most Great Plains residents would have preferred to avoid becoming involved in the new European war, nearly everyone saw the economic advantages that could be gained as the federal government increased spending to aid the national defense. In May 1940, President Roosevelt had asked Congress for $1 billion for the addition of fifty thousand planes to the national arsenal, and by mid-1941, Congress had appropriated $60 billion for national defense. Soon the term *defense industries* became part of everyday reference to the economy, and Great Plains chambers of commerce and congressional delegations worked hard to gain their share of any federal war-related appropriations. Military installations meant jobs and large payrolls during the construction and operation of the bases. Local chambers of commerce, congressmen, and governors, among others, saw the coming war as a great economic opportunity, and they aggressively lobbied the War Department for the establishment of military bases, airfields, and hospitals for their neighborhoods and states. Although city officials preferred air bases, their communities were delighted to receive any military training facility. Soldiers and sailors had money to spend, and fortunate local electricians, plumbers, and secretaries often gained employment at the military installations. Bank deposits mushroomed. These economic opportunities born of war helped end the economic hardships of the Great Depression.[7]

Once the nation officially entered the war, military needs expanded rapidly, and towns that had been bypassed with defense contracts received new opportunities to participate in the wartime economy. Soon, Nebraska received federal war industry contracts to build planes, make small arms, and load ammunition. Business leaders and city officials welcomed an announcement by Senator George W. Norris that the federal government planned to build a munitions plant between Grand Island, Hastings, and Kearney. With construction costs estimated as high as $28 million and payrolls of $100,000 per day, seven days a week, the wartime boost to an economy still weak from the problems of the Great Depression promised to put hard times behind. Between January 1940 and August 1, 1944, at least 118 new war industries, employing 102,000 workers, began production in Kansas. These workers averaged wages of $109 per month in 1940 and $225 per month in 1944. Contemporary observers considered Wichita one of the "hottest" defense boom cities in the nation. Defense industries in Oklahoma City and Dallas–Fort Worth also grew rapidly.[8]

As federal funds reached employees in the Great Plains via defense industry contracts, women entered the workforce on a scale larger than ever before. Nationwide, between 1940 and 1945, the number of women in the workforce expanded by more than 50 percent, from 11.9 million to 18.6 million (37 percent of all working women). About 75 percent of these newly employed women were married, and nearly 50 percent of all women took employment at some time during the war. High pay, patriotism, and increased status lured them to the defense industries. At the Cornhusker Ordnance Plant in Grand Island, Nebraska, women worked at every job (including pouring liquid TNT into bomb casings), except the most physically demanding positions. Overall, these women knew that they filled traditionally male jobs and that they would lose their positions when the war ended and men returned from the military. Even so, World War II gave many Great Plains women their first job outside the home. Most liked the freedom, independence, and money.[9]

Women of the Great Plains, however, did not immediately enter the wartime workforce. When the war began, employers believed that the male labor supply would remain adequate, and they doubted the physical and

World War II brought prosperity and an end to the Great Depression in the towns that received defense-industry contracts. The aircraft industry in Wichita, Tulsa, and Dallas–Fort Worth expanded and drew employees, often women, from the small towns and countryside. Although the central and southern Great Plains profited from the war, the northern Great Plains, which had fewer people and resources and comparatively greater isolation, did not enjoy the economic benefits of the war. Notice the women workers on this bomber assembly line in Wichita, Kansas.

mechanical ability of women to handle many defense industry jobs. By late 1941, however, the labor situation had changed dramatically, and employers welcomed women workers. At first, they were mostly young, unmarried, and unskilled, although the records do not precisely indicate their number other than to suggest that thousands of women in the region held wartime jobs. As the war progressed, nationwide, women workers tended to be married (with husbands in the military) and older (with approximately half of this workforce over thirty-five years of age by the end of the war).[10]

These women anticipated that the United States would become involved in the war, and they began preparing for it by enrolling in training programs that would qualify them for war industry jobs. In 1941, some Oklahoma City women enrolled in the Oklahoma Aircraft School, where they learned the craft of riveting. The National Defense Training School in Wichita began accepting women, who, upon completion of their training, took jobs at the Cessna aircraft plant, where they made wooden ribs for planes. Women who took short vocational courses through various training programs, such as the National Youth Administration, received job offers for quick employment upon completion of their training. By mid-January 1942, women had taken many specialized positions in the Great Plains aircraft plants, where they worked "men's jobs" and received "men's pay," that is, $.60 an hour at entry. At Fort Crook, near Omaha, women trained as mechanics and earned $4 per day as civilian employees at army ordnance depots and shops where they repaired cars and trucks.[11]

As the war progressed, more women were needed to replace men in almost every occupation. They drove taxicabs, worked in banks and department stores, and pumped gas at service stations. Many of these jobs had been solely the domain of men before the war. In time, male employees apparently accepted female workers as equals, with a prevailing paternalism or sexism characteristic of that period. Women, however, did not always work in large-scale defense industries. A host of subcontractors employed women to help fill orders for the larger plants. Even if a company did not have a war industry–related subcontract, the lack of male employees because of military service opened new employment doors for women. As women left the small towns and farms for defense industry jobs in the cities, such as Omaha, secretarial schools could not meet the demand because so many women left private employment for newly created civil service positions related to the war effort. The women who enrolled at the secretarial schools tended to be older housewives who chose to return to paid employment. Hotels began employing women in their business offices and at reservations and customer services desks. Waitresses soon enjoyed receiving generous tips from soldiers and sailors from nearby military bases.[12]

Defense industry jobs also lured women schoolteachers who preferred high-paying jobs over the low income of teachers. As a result, many rural schools closed or consolidated because school administrators did not have enough teachers to meet classroom needs. In Nebraska, school superintendents and school boards often blamed the federal government for enticing teachers from their classrooms for war industry jobs. When teachers broke contracts, sometimes during the school year, resentment occurred. In Norfolk and other Nebraska towns, school boards asked the state legislature to revoke the license of any teacher who broke a contract for another job. In 1942, the Nebraska State Department of Public Instruction attempted to solve the problem by compiling a master list of inactive teachers and offering recertification if they would take a summer refresher course in their field. By the autumn of 1943, approximately 1,500 rural schools had closed in Nebraska because of the teacher shortage, which plagued all of the Great Plains states during the war.[13]

For many women, employment proved not only an opportunity to earn a high income but also a chance to participate in the war. By July 1943, women constituted 30 percent of the fifty-four-thousand-person workforce in sixty-four of Nebraska's largest essential industries, with the exception of railroad and construction (although a few women also worked in those sectors). At the Glenn L. Martin Company, women constituted more than 40 percent of the bomber plant's employees, which made the company Nebraska's largest employer of women. Still, 83 percent of the women who were hired held positions with the lowest classification: as drill operators, bench electricians, and maintenance staff as well as clerks, cafeteria workers, and general helpers. They averaged wages of $96 to $172 monthly, but they had a higher turnover rate than men, perhaps because of family responsibilities.

Although the federal government glamorized the movement of housewives to the defense industries and transformed them into the symbolic Rosie the Riveter and Wendy the Welder, most working women in the Great Plains and across the nation did not labor in defense industries. Although many women worked because they were patriotic and wanted to contribute to the war effort, they also worked because wartime jobs paid high wages that enabled them to improve their standard of living. Some women worked because they lost income when their husbands left for military service. Many women wanted to keep their jobs when the war ended. In 1944, the Wichita Chamber of Commerce conducted a survey that indicated that 26 percent wanted to continue their wartime employment. Another poll indicated that approximately seven out of ten women in Omaha wanted to keep their jobs after the war.[14]

Wartime working women enjoyed the extra income if they were married and also gained a new independence that came from financial security. Still, most women, including those living in the Great Plains, remained housewives. Many middle-class women rejected blue-collar jobs and preferred to stay home, where they believed they could best aid the war effort by nurturing the family. The war also segregated women in certain jobs, such as secretaries, store clerks, and bank tellers, but most middle-class women could not afford to quit these jobs or accept termination at the end of the war. Blue-collar women workers who wanted and needed to keep their high-paying jobs often lost their employment and income when peace arrived.[15]

World War II, then, provided new employment opportunities for women, but many jobs disappeared when the defense industries closed as the war ended. Women lost high-paying jobs that had given them independence, and many had no alternative but to return to domestic life and labor.

Overall, however, World War II enabled the permanent addition of women to the labor force on an unprecedented scale in government as well as civilian jobs. The war gave Great Plains women new employment opportunities, but when the war ended, the status of women workers was not improved much over that of the prewar years. They remained a cheap labor force that could be easily exploited regarding pay, hiring, and promotion. When peace came, many women remained employed but at lesser jobs. Even so, Great Plains women who worked outside the home during World War II were subtly and sometimes profoundly changed. Thereafter they had different expectations about work, independence, and self-worth that would be lasting. Because of racism, however, black women often became employees of last resort. Few war industries across the Great Plains employed African American women and men. For the most part, black women worked as janitors in the defense industries.[16]

As the war progressed, volunteerism became a community activity. Communities particularly became active in the collection of scrap metal to aid the war effort. Soon after the war began, the Office of Production Management urged the collection of scrap metal for the "victory program." Quickly, Great Plains communities organized scrap metal drives and collected rubber and paper, and local newspapers frequently published photographs of donors and volunteer collectors before various scrap piles. Although scrap drives began before Pearl Harbor, they became a major wartime activity. Junk dealers collected, sorted, and shipped metal scrap to smelters where they received the payment of the highest prevailing price. Sales to smelters also were made under the auspices of the city or town that sponsored the collection drive, with the earnings restricted to use for civilian defense. In Nebraska, Joe W. Seacrest, state salvage chairman, considered the collection of metal scrap a patriotic responsibility, calling the salvage of scrap metal the "job of every man, woman, and child." He urged teachers to organize their students to help collect it. Soon, scrap drives became venues for competition between schools, classes, service clubs, towns, counties, and states. Boy Scout troops, citizens' groups, and local defense committees also conducted rubber and scrap drives as a public service activity. Collection drives for wastepaper, tin cans, and cooking fats also occurred across the plains in conjunction with metal scrap and rubber drives; women often organized these patriotic activities.[17]

Oil companies often sponsored the scrap rubber drives and provided storage and transport of old tires to government reclamation or processing plants. The oil companies covered the transportation and collection costs. The federal government authorized automobile service station operators to pay $.01 per pound for the salvaged rubber, then sell it to the government for $2 per ton or $.0125 per pound with the profit donated to the United Service Organizations (USO), army and navy relief funds, and the Red Cross. Salvage committees made the donation of scrap metal and rubber a "patriotic duty."[18]

The supply of gasoline also dwindled during the war for drivers on the Great Plains. On December 1, 1942, the Petroleum Administration for War imposed a nationwide gasoline rationing policy. Most drivers could only receive four gallons per week; the amount was reduced to two gallons in March 1944. Everyday drivers received coupon books labeled "A," while individuals who drove more than sixty miles per week to war industry jobs received "B" coupons. Professionals who held essential jobs, such as doctors, received "C" coupons. County rationing officers distributed the coupon books upon driver registration.

Originally the intent for gasoline rationing had been to preserve rubber tires. The federal government hoped that the rationing of gasoline and tires would limit drivers to five thousand miles annually. In order for drivers to purchase a new tire, they had to have their old tires inspected. If a new tire or retread was warranted, the driver received a certificate for presentation to the local rationing board. If the board approved, the driver could purchase a tire. Rationing also would help ensure that East Coast drivers would receive ample and fair supplies of gasoline refined in the Great Plains. The shortage of gasoline also resulted from the increased needs of the military, particularly for aviation fuel. As refiners worked to meet their supply contracts for the military, civilian gasoline supplies diminished. Most Great Plains drivers, however, considered the federal government's gasoline rationing program unfair because of the large oil fields and many refineries in the region. Drivers complained about gasoline and tire rationing throughout the war but had little choice but to accept it.[19]

Food also became an important part of the federal government's wartime rationing policy. The Office of Price Administration (OPA) developed a food rationing program designed to limit consumption yet give everyone some choice and control over food purchases. The OPA distributed coupons or stamps through local rationing boards. Consumers presented these coupons at grocery stores, and the coupons allowed them to purchase a certain amount of a specific food during a particular time period. Sugar and beef became two major foods subject to wartime rationing. Although Great Plains farmers produced an abundance of sugar beets, much of it went from the processing plants to the munitions industry, where it was converted into alcohol for making smokeless powder. Soon sugar supplies for consumers dwindled. Sugar bowls disappeared from restaurants. As a result, sugar rationing for consumers began on May 5, 1942. Across the Great Plains, schools served as registration sites for sugar stamps. These stamps permitted consumers to purchase about a half pound of sugar per family member per week, or about half of the prewar level of consumption. Ration stamps proved annoying, but Great Plains consumers took most food rationing in stride.

Meat rationing, particularly for beef, also caused considerable complaining and violation of OPA rationing policy. In 1942, government officials urged the public to limit their maximum consumption to 2.5 pounds per week, or 130 pounds per year, to ensure that military men and women received 1 pound of meat per day. Soon the military took about 30 percent of the beef supply from the meat packers across the Great Plains. Consumers complained about beef shortages, and cattle producers argued that they had more cattle to sell. The meat packers also charged that they could not make a profit by supplying the civilian market, because the Office of Price Administration fixed prices too low for retail meat. Soon a black market for beef developed because consumers bought meat from non–federally inspected packers who operated beyond the regulatory control of the federal government. The meat shortage, particularly for beef, remained for months after the war ended. In the meantime, some meat packers urged consumers to eat horse meat, which they believed could be made readily available. Great Plains consumers rejected that idea as an unacceptable solution to their desire for more meat, particularly beef.[20]

The booming wartime economy, however, brought problems as well as profits. Although the great inflow of workers to build military bases, for example, brought economic benefits to local communities, the arrival of several thousand workers and, later, military men and women caused many problems. Housing became difficult for workers and their families to locate, rents escalated, and price gouging became common. Expanded water, sewer, and street systems became necessary but costly. While the housing construction boom gave a host of workers employment, contractors often struggled to get needed materials, particularly lumber, and they usually rushed their jobs, particularly if they fell behind schedule because of shortages of material. Housing built for the federal government often proved shoddy. In Salina, Kansas, housing promoted as temporary soon became permanent and lowered the property values of nearby private homes. Social problems also emerged on a greater scale than had been previously experienced. Military men and women often drank too much in the nearby cities, and prostitution became a problem. Young men and women took a live-for-the-moment approach to life, which often caused difficulties for local authorities and embarrassment for nearby residents.[21]

In Bellevue, Nebraska, a town of 1,184, residents did not have paved streets, streetlights and street signs, or sanitary or storm sewers. On December 6, 1940, when residents learned that a bomber assembly plant would be located at nearby Fort Crook, everyone knew the proposed workforce of 27,000 people would transform the community. Omaha officials a dozen miles away had worked hard to secure the plant, and President Roosevelt wanted the plains states to receive defense contracts to dampen complaints that the federal government had ignored them during World War I. Omaha seemed a likely source for labor and housing. Quickly, however, property values increased in Bellevue. City house lots that brought $15 prior to the arrival of the Glenn Martin bomber plant sold for as much as $825 in 1941. Bellevue officials attempted to implement a zoning plan to avoid "discord and confusion." In February 1941, the town hired an engineer and attorney to assess community needs and draft codes and ordinances. Bellevue officials particularly worried about controlling the number of trailer homes of workers because they would decrease property values and give the community a transient appearance. By April, Bellevue officials had zoned the town for future growth, separated the trailer camps from the better homes, and established building codes that met Federal Housing Authority requirements for loans. Bellevue also secured assistance from the Works Progress Administration to improve the sewer and streets as well as from the Public Works Administration for an improved water system, a health center, and a new elementary and an expanded high school. When the bomber plant began operations in January 1942, the town boomed with new residents and money, although housing and road problems remained.

The war then increased urbanization in the Great Plains, particularly where war industries flourished. In Kansas, approximately 40 percent of the population lived in urban areas when the war began, but this increased to 52 percent by the war's end. In 1941, miles of new homes lined Wichita's new streets. Contractors were building thirty-five houses each week by mid-May. With an average of twelve men working on the construction of each house, the building tradesmen reportedly were "reaping a golden harvest." Grocery stores and gas stations opened for business to service the new workers, and automobile traffic became a major problem for city officials.[22]

During the war, the conservation of resources (whether tires, gasoline, vegetables, or other items of daily living) and the philosophy of getting along or doing without became daily guiding principles. State and federal governments and their respective agencies consistently reminded the public of those maxims. Most Great Plains residents exercised self-discipline as consumers, but they built pent-up demands for goods and services that they intended to satisfy when the war ended. To discourage hoarding, which no one precisely defined but which involved exceeding community standards of one's fair share, the federal government urged families to keep no more than a four-day food supply. The editor of the *Great Falls Tribune* in Montana responded to this recommendation by saying, "We don't want hoarding, but Washington should not talk scary stuff to the housewife." In Omaha late in the war, to prevent hoarding, retailers agreed to require the exchange of an empty pack of cigarettes before a full pack would be sold. Merchants hoped for the best, and some cynics predicted that the regulation would only keep teenagers, who were prohibited by law, from acquiring cigarettes. During the war, neighbors reported neighbors whom they suspected of hoarding by sending anonymous letters and phone calls to the district Office of Price Administration. Plains residents were willing to do their share, but they did not want to sacrifice when others violated the rules. The matter of comparative sacrifice determined their patriotic judgments, whether in relation to government policy or in comparison with the activities of their neighbors. In the small towns across the Great Plains, neighbors really were their "brother's keeper," although such observations intruded on privacy and freedom of action.[23]

During the war, most of the workers for the defense industries came from the farms and small towns in the Great Plains. In many areas, the population loss occurred quickly, with California an ever-popular destination for men and women seeking high-paying, steady jobs. The war also increased urbanization in the region, particularly in the aircraft manufacturing towns of Wichita, Oklahoma City, and Dallas. Still, when the war ended, the major federal contracts and funds remained in the Far West, not the Great Plains. In the Great Plains, farming and agricultural services industries continued as the mainstay of the economy. Defense industry contracts largely disappeared, and residents often confronted loss of income while they adjusted to a peacetime economy. Essentially, the Great Plains was an agricultural region when the war began; it remained so when peace returned. The war could not change the dictates of geography.[24]

When the war ended, many defense plants began canceling contracts and closed. Men and women soon returned from the military and sought their previous jobs. Employees of various war-related state and federal agencies lost their jobs. City and town planners struggled to provide housing and city services as the men and women from the armed services returned home from the military. Many businessmen, businesswomen, and farmers feared a postwar economic recession. Gasoline rationing abruptly ended, but worn tires kept many drivers off the roads. Food rationing also soon ended. Bank deposits and agricultural production had expanded during the war, and Great Plains residents had considerable disposable income to spend on a host of goods that they had been unable to purchase during the war because of rationing or unavailability. Everyone hoped the good times would continue with the peace. Only time would tell.

Often isolationist when the war began in 1939, the people of the Great Plains became staunch supporters of the war after the Japanese attack on Pearl Harbor. They embraced the wartime economy and welcomed high-paying jobs. They dealt with social and economic change that proved disruptive to their lives, but few wanted to return to the economic conditions of the 1930s no matter whether they lived in the cities or on the farms. For most Great Plains residents, World War II became an indelible, transforming moment. It would be their central reference point for the remainder of their lives and a defining social, cultural, and economic moment in the history of the Great Plains. After the war, life in the region would never be the same as it had been prior to the German invasion of Poland and the Japanese attack on Pearl Harbor.

Mexican Americans who lived in the Great Plains continued to experience discrimination and segregation during World War II, but the conflict provided employment opportunities that enabled many men and women to leave agricultural work, domestic service, and other unskilled, low-paid jobs. Even so, in Texas, Mexican Americans in particular experienced racial discrimination and harsh treatment because of racism. In San Antonio, the schools remained segregated, and business often refused service. Across the region, but particularly in the southern Great Plains, where the Mexican American population was the largest, discrimination prevailed in real estate transactions, employment opportunities, and police protection. Selective Service boards in Texas also threatened to draft all Mexican American workers who refused to pick cotton for $1 per day, a wage that kept them in dismal poverty. Mexican Americans often fled racial discrimination in the southern Great Plains by seeking better-paying agricultural work in the sugar beet fields of the northern plains. Yet even there they could not escape discrimination, although farmers welcomed them for their labor. In the northern plains, Mexican Americans often experienced segregation in or exclusion from restaurants, movie theaters, barbershops, and other businesses and public places.

In Albuquerque, located on the western edge of the Great Plains, wholesale and retail businesses, followed by state and federal governments, provided the most employment for Hispanics. In 1940, the greater metropolitan area had a population of 69,391, of which about half were Hispanics. During World War II, Hispanic men and women gained employment in comparatively high-paying jobs at nearby military facilities, although many positions remained semiskilled and clerical.

Through the 1940s and into the 1960s, Mexican Americans lived in poverty and experienced segregation and hostility across the Great Plains. Most Great Plains residents did not consider them whites, but instead viewed them as racially and culturally inferior. For the foreseeable future, Mexican American workers would only qualify for unskilled, low-wage jobs. Mexican Americans who had moved to the cities during and after the war did improve their economic fortunes, which helped them develop an increasing socially conscious voice. They, along with the returning Mexican American veterans who demanded the comparative equality that they had enjoyed in the military, increasingly used that voice to advocate for their civil rights. Nearly a half century would pass, however, before this racial prejudice against Mexican Americans began to disappear.[25]

The situation was not much better for African Americans. Preceding World War II, the Urban League had functioned as a social, economic, and educational service organization dedicated to providing opportunities for the African American community. During the war, however, the national Urban League began addressing civil rights issues. In Lincoln and Omaha, Nebraska, for example, the Urban League followed that lead and began pursuing the national goals for equality in education, housing, and employment. This departure from its former emphasis on promoting the activities of black churches, social events, and public forums caused many African Americans to leave their local organizations because they disagreed with the changing mission of the Urban League. Greater employment opportunities and a larger African American population in Omaha, however, enabled the Urban League to emphasize a civil rights agenda during the war. In those years, the Omaha Urban League (OUL) worked closely with the National Association for the Advancement of Colored People (NAACP) to resolve complaints by African Americans about their treatment at theaters, restaurants, and other businesses, and the OUL advocated improved housing conditions. By the end of the war, the OUL had made the transition from a local recreational and service agency to an increasingly powerful organization that fought discrimination and segregation against African Americans. The OUL no longer served as an administrator of social services. By 1945, largely because of job opportunities at nearby defense plants, it had become a mediator in the search for social justice, and it sought the success of African Americans in everyday social and economic life. By so doing, the OUL became an advocate for civil rights. Yet decades of struggle for equal opportunities remained for the African American communities in cities such as Omaha, Wichita, and Dallas, and redlining clearly marked the white and black parts of Great Plains cities and towns where the presence of a large African American population seemed to warrant it. Even so, the social voice of the African American community grew louder after the Great Depression and World War II.[26]

In general, Great Plains men and women accepted racism against African Americans, Latinos, and Indians, and they accepted Jim Crow laws. Racism against blacks was more prevalent in the central and southern plains, where the African American population was the largest; Kansas provides an example. There, racial exclusion gave form and function to the color line that wound through towns and cities and marked where African Americans were not welcome. In Kansas and across the Great Plains, civil rights and segregation were "compatible concepts," and at least in Kansas, limited or partial segregation prevailed. In the Sunflower State, schools in first-class cities with populations greater than fifteen thousand segregated schoolchildren, although smaller second-class communities also often followed that practice. A racial hierarchy existed in the state but not the all-encompassing separation or segregation of the South. With comparatively few African Americans in Kansas and the southern Great Plains, their demand for equality as guaranteed by the Fourteenth Amendment was not readily apparent or threatening to most whites.

During the late 1940s and 1950s, however, African Americans began challenging the color line. In Wichita and Lawrence, Kansas, and Oklahoma City, for example, they organized sit-in demonstrations, picketing, and other forms of nonviolent, direct action to gain integration of local lunch counters, theaters, and swimming pools. During the late 1950s, the sit-ins in Wichita and Oklahoma City began a form of protest that spread into the South during the 1960s and, most important, responded to similar conditions of racial exclusion.[27]

Although some groups had opposed segregation in Wichita during the 1950s, the city remained segregated except at the cafeterias at Wichita University and the YMCA. During the summer of 1958, some young African Americans planned to conduct a sit-in at the Dockman's Drug Store lunch counter in downtown Wichita. On July 19, the sit-in began — without NAACP support, because the national office did not yet approve such tactics. Some whites intimidated the demonstrators and generally held the opinion that blacks could not be served, arguing that "that's the way things are in Wichita." On August 11, the owner recanted and told his employees, "Serve them. I'm losing too much money." This order desegregated all nine Dockman's drugstores in Wichita, followed by all Rexall Drug stores in Kansas. In 1959, students at Southwestern College in Winfield also staged a successful sit-in at a local barbershop that observed a "whites only" policy. These and other civil rights activities spread to other towns across the state that had an African American population large enough to merit action with a justifiable expectation for success.

Despite the success of the lunch counter sit-ins, residential segregation prevailed. In 1962, the Wichita-Sedgwick County Metropolitan Planning Commission reported, "Wichita is one of the most tightly segregated cities in the nation in terms of residence," with the city more than 95 percent segregated. Civil rights demonstrators also continued to picket downtown stores, such as Woolworths, carrying signs that read "Don't Buy Where You Can't Work" and "Don't Put Your $ in Cash Registers That Your Hands Can't Ring." This organized persistence, plus a 1961 state law banning employment discrimination and support from the NAACP, achieved modest success. In 1963, the state legislature also prohibited discrimination in public accommodations and restaurants, but little change occurred in Wichita and other cities when blacks sought to buy a home. Not until 1970 did the state legislature pass a fair housing law that prohibited discrimination in the sale and rental of property and in the terms of mortgages. The Civil Rights Act of 1964 and the Voting Rights Act of 1965 also increased access to the courts for African Americans who suffered discrimination. Segregation in the Wichita schools remained unresolved, however, through the early 1970s, and repression and limited accommodation continued to epitomize race relations in Wichita.[28]

In August 1958, segregation in Oklahoma likewise suffered a blow when the Youth Council of the NAACP, inspired by the Wichita sit-ins, organized a lunch counter sit-in. During the sit-in, the council negotiated with the owners while urging blacks to deny business to the stores with segregated lunch counters. The boycott proved effective; one businessman reflected, "It had a depressing effect on business." Even so, Oklahoma City's restaurants would not be totally integrated until the Civil Rights Act of 1964 compelled owners to serve African Americans.

The first sit-in demonstrations of the civil rights movement occurred in Wichita and Oklahoma City. On August 26, 1958, African Americans occupied the lunch counter at a Katz Drug Store in Oklahoma City. This peaceful sit-in demonstration eventually gained them the right to be served.

In retrospect, the Oklahoma City sit-ins did not generate violent reactions from whites comparable to similar situations in the South. In Oklahoma City, the NAACP used elementary school children to occupy the lunch counters, and whites felt less threatened and generally unwilling to risk public censure and criminal charges for threatening and assaulting children. Moreover, when whites threatened adult African Americans, they responded nonviolently rather than aggressively. The police also exercised restraint, protected the protesters, and generally kept white hecklers at a distance. A sympathetic Governor James Howard Edmondson and the city council also helped control a potentially volatile racial situation. In addition, business owners quickly learned that the black community had economic power that hurt sales during the lunch counter sit-ins at the department stores, and they soon accepted the equality of all customers having money to spend. Moreover, no segregation laws prohibited integrated lunch counters. Oklahomans practiced this segregation and racial exclusion based on custom, not law. By the time of the Civil Rights Act of 1964, racial segregation had largely disappeared in Oklahoma. It had succumbed to nonviolent activities that dramatized the shameful, embarrassing Jim Crow practices in the Sooner State, and a generally reasonable white public saw no reason to perpetuate segregation when no law mandated such separation.[29]

Desegregation in education proved more difficult to achieve. Many white men and women of the Great Plains believed that Kenneth MacFarland, superintendent of schools in Topeka, Kansas, spoke for them when in the early 1950s he stated that Topeka was "not ready for integration." Whites generally ignored segregation and believed it to be beneficial to African Americans. Yet to abide segregation by custom, even inadvertently, meant acquiescence, even support, as well as legal sanctioning in the elementary schools. When Kansas became part of the NAACP-filed Brown case (Brown v. Board of Education) to desegregate the schools, most Kansans were bewildered. They lived in a state founded on blood and iron for the abolition of slavery, and they were surprised that their romanticized notion of Kansas as a land of the free was, in fact, not true, because skin color limited freedom for many who lived there. Many Kansans believed that segregation concerned the South, not a preeminent free state, despite state law that permitted segregation in some schools. Yet many Kansans and Great Plains residents could easily accept the denial of service to African Americans and Mexican Americans, based on custom rather than law, that required them to order food only for carryout or to sit in "Peanut Heaven" (that is, the seats reserved in balconies for blacks in theaters) or for them to obey signs that read "Colored Entrance" or to play on segregated sports teams.

In December 1953, the superintendent of the Augusta Public Schools wrote a letter to Governor Edward Arn about the pending *Brown* case, saying, "I am surprised and I must say chagrined to learn that Kansas now classifies itself as one of the White Supremacy states as indicated by the case now before the United States Supreme Court." For him, the history of "bleeding Kansas" had been "thrilling and glorious," but it was so no longer. "I wonder," he wrote, "how we suddenly find ourselves represented before the Supreme Court opposed to those human rights for which our early settlers bled."[30]

In large part due to embarrassment, the Topeka School Board had voted in September 1953 to end segregation in the schools before the Supreme Court ruled on May 17, 1954, that segregation was unconstitutional. Even though the State of Kansas defended segregation before the Supreme Court, it did not advocate segregation for educational purposes; rather, it argued the constitutional right of the state to regulate education. Even after the Supreme Court handed down its decree, most Kansans did not believe that segregation existed in the state. Topeka and other Kansas towns that practiced segregation, however, began to implement desegregation plans; this goal was not achieved until 1999, and even then de facto or privatized segregation remained because parents could send their children to neighborhood schools located in traditionally white or black neighborhoods. Put differently, the Supreme Court agreed that parents could not be compelled to send their children to segregated or integrated schools. They had the free choice to associate with whomever they pleased regarding education and, thereby, perpetuated an invisible segregation that Kansans considered not only acceptable but also right.[31]

Certainly, Kansas and other Great Plains states to the north did not have the history of racial violence that was characteristic of the South, nor did it experience mass demonstrations to end segregation, because the black population was relatively small and blacks often, but not always, lacked the economic power to force social change through economic protests or sit-ins. Moreover, many black teachers in Topeka did not support the NAACP and its challenge of segregation in the *Brown* case; they believed that they would lose their jobs if the Supreme Court ordered the school district to integrate, because white parents would not want them teaching their children. They were correct.[32]

Discrimination in Oklahoma also lingered where the separation of races occurred by custom and law. In the 1950s, the city government in Tulsa passed laws prohibiting whites and African Americans from living in the same block and provided school boundaries that ensured segregation. In Oklahoma City, housing policies kept the schools segregated until a 1965 court order forced the school administration to develop a plan for integration. Even so, the white schools did not quickly integrate black teachers. In 1959, only ten black teachers taught in integrated schools; 350 had lost their jobs since the *Brown* decision, and the state legislature permitted white students to relocate to a school of their choice. Oklahoma public schools, then, remained predominantly black or white as a result of this skillful circumvention of the *Brown* decision.[33]

In Oklahoma, with its Southern tradition built on nineteenth-century immigration patterns and racial prejudices more typical of the Deep South, segregation also prevailed in higher education. When a graduate from Langston University, the state's all-black school, applied for admission to the School of Law at the University of Oklahoma, however, the state's racial boundaries received a major challenge. Upon the denial of admission, the student filed suit arguing that a separate but equal law school did not exist in Oklahoma as required by the 1896 U.S. Supreme Court case of *Plessey v. Ferguson*. The student's attorneys, including Thurgood Marshall (destined for the Supreme Court), argued that Oklahoma prevented her from receiving equal protection under the law as guaranteed by the Fourteenth Amendment because the state denied her an education equal to that received by white students. On January 12, 1948, the Supreme Court agreed, holding that she was "entitled to secure a legal education afforded by a state institution." Confronted with a dictate to either admit her to the School of Law at the University of Oklahoma or establish an equal law school for African Americans, the state responded by providing legal training at Langston University because the Supreme Court did not strike down Oklahoma statues that permitted segregation.

Many Oklahomans approved the admission of blacks to the law school at the University of Oklahoma, although this approval did not necessarily extend to equal rights in all aspects of life. One editorial writer contended, "We've always been convinced that because Negroes are American citizens they are entitled to equal rights. However, in Oklahoma and other states it has been the practice to extend equal rights through separate school facilities." For him and many other Oklahomans, the Supreme Court's decision was "not in keeping with the way Oklahomans, all races considering, have been living." A survey of students at the University of Oklahoma indicated that only 43.6 percent favored the admission of blacks to graduate school, although 50 percent favored separate but equal educational facilities at the undergraduate and graduate levels. Eighty-two percent of the law students favored admission, while 70 percent of the business students disapproved. Most Oklahomans, however, believed that segregation in all educational institutions was not only just but also necessary.[34]

In 1948, the University of Oklahoma agreed to follow a district court order to admit a black man to the College of Education. The court had ruled that Oklahoma's segregation statutes were unconstitutional and unenforceable. The University of Oklahoma, however, required him to sit at a separate table in the library and cafeteria as well as apart from white students in the classroom. Many Oklahomans considered this compromise acceptable, if it did not lead to mixed marriages. When the U.S. Supreme Court held (in the case of *McLaurin v. Oklahoma State Regents* [1950]) that the student must receive equal treatment in order to "learn his profession," however, the university had no choice but to accept the admission of black students to the state's graduate schools on an equal basis with whites. Chief Justice Frederick Moore Vinson held that "state-imposed restrictions which produce such inequities cannot exist." This ruling along with the *Brown* case still did not convince the state board of regents to abolish segregation in Oklahoma's institutions of higher education until 1955. In June, the *Daily Oklahoma* observed, "Segregation in our Oklahoma institutions of higher learning was abolished years ago by a supreme court decision. That decision was preceded and accompanied by certain dire predictions of trouble. But none of those predictions were fulfilled," The reporter observed, "Negroes entered the state university, but the heavens did not fall. . . . Interested parties quietly adjusted themselves to the new conditions, without disturbance — not even a minor one." At the same time, however, the majority of white students at Oklahoma A and M did not want to live with or socially interact with African American students outside the classroom, although veterans had a more favorable opinion of desegregation in Stillwater. A pattern of nonacceptance prevailed, but it was not of the "Deep South variety." Overall, Oklahomans accepted court-ordered desegregation in education, but they thought it would have come anyway, gradually, based on "time and patience." Other racial barriers would slowly fall.[35]

Racial prejudice in Oklahoma, however, festered into the 1960s. Churches remained separate, and swimming pools and restaurants were off-limits for blacks. Rural towns, such as Lindsay and Marlow, posted signs at the city limits well into the 1970s warning blacks to leave town by sundown. Ironically, desegregation eventually contributed to the demise of many African American towns in Oklahoma. Black schools often closed because they were inferior to white schools where African American students were permitted to attend. The black population moved closer to the white schools in the larger towns, and African American businesses failed from the loss of customers in rural communities, because blacks received services at white-owned businesses and restaurants. Thus, Jim Crow and the black towns died together, the exception being the African American Baptist, Methodist, and Holiness (Church of God) churches, which remained lasting social and support centers for black communities in Oklahoma. Revivals of black towns came only in the twenty-first century.[36]

Other racial problems developed that indicated support for segregation and integration. In 1960, for example, the Lawrence League for the Practice of Democracy (LLPD), an organization committed to racial equality and social justice, pressured the city of Lawrence, Kansas, to integrate a swimming pool that restricted admission to whites. When city officials refused, students from the University of Kansas began picketing the facility in July. This picketing began a decade of increasingly confrontational social polarization between liberals and conservatives and between those who favored racial equality and those who were racists. This confrontation clearly showed that many Great Plains residents defined freedom and equality in different ways, and they disagreed about the role of the state in guaranteeing each as well as the manner in which new racial boundaries were created and old boundaries maintained.

Many Lawrence residents, like other white men and women across the Great Plains, supported the principle of equality, but they often placed individual freedom above the regulatory constrictions of civil rights whether exercised in custom or in law. Rather than argue against integration based on white supremacy and African American inferiority, they championed individual freedom as a natural right that the state could not infringe. Indeed, in the latter view, the state had the obligation to protect and defend individual freedom and property rights rather than the collective rights of minorities. This was a seemingly rational, dispassionate defense of segregation on a plane highly elevated from the violent confrontation between rabble whites and African Americans in the South. By so contending, the Lawrence segregationists and others like them across the Great Plains challenged a liberal and activist state.

Although most of Lawrence had been integrated between the late 1940s and 1960 because of the efforts of the NAACP, Congress of Racial Equality (CORE), and LLPD, as well as leadership from the University of Kansas, the movement for full integration no longer existed in 1960. Many businesses excluded blacks at the owner's discretion based on the principle that they had the right and freedom to deny service to anyone. In March

1960, however, the lunch counter sit-ins in Wichita, Oklahoma City, and Greensboro, North Carolina, inspired the Lawrence League for the Practice of Democracy to target a privately owned and segregated swimming pool, called the Jayhawk Plunge, which the owner advertised as "socially selective and friendly," with admission available to anyone who correctly completed a form that asked for the name, address, age, and race of the person wanting to purchase a ticket to swim. The owner claimed the right to use her property as she saw fit. In 1959, she had declared her business a "private club," under the regulations of the Kansas Criminal Code, which in 1949 permitted private clubs to discriminate based on race (in contrast to new legislation that prohibited discrimination in any place of public entertainment based on race, color, religion, or national origin if the business had been licensed by the city). She considered her swimming pool to be not a "place of entertainment or amusement" but a private club that the law exempted. When the LLPD asked her to integrate the pool, she refused, fearing "racial troubles" and a loss of income, because white parents would not let their children swim with black children.

When some members of the LLPD began picketing the pool in July 1960, the owner asked, "What happened to the personal rights of private industry to operate at a profit?" She also believed that "outsiders" from the university were causing all the trouble. Other residents agreed. Before the city could devise a new ordinance that mandated integration of a privately owned pool that was licensed to operate by the city, and amidst harassment and threats against her, the owner closed the pool, citing financial losses because white parents had been frightened into not sending their children to swim. One supporter of the owner argued that private property rights had been attacked, which resulted in closing a business and costing people their jobs. Until this incident, he and others had seen no racial problem in Lawrence, and he contended, "This community has advanced far since the days when Negroes were hanged from the Kansas river bridge." Clearly, the citizens of Lawrence privileged private property rights above equal opportunity or equality while defending their own freedom against the liberal state and special interests. By so doing, they gave a "moral" voice to segregation in Lawrence. These segregationists believed that they were decent, honest, hardworking people who did not have a race problem.

This belief did not end soon. In December 1965, Justin Hill, president of the Lawrence Paper Company, contended that African Americans were "demanding housing in suburbs developed by whites, jobs in companies developed by whites, the right to eat in restaurants and go to stores owned and developed by whites." He believed that "the coloreds should earn the right to these things." Those residents of Lawrence and across the Great Plains who believed that property rights superseded individual rights and that the state was morally and legally bound to protect private property could not be swayed. For the moment, the interpretation of the Constitution by the segregationists and their commitment to mainstream conservatism prevailed, thereby maintaining traditional racial boundaries while challenging a growing postwar liberalism that advocated an interventionist, activist state. Many, if not most, Great Plains residents held those conservative beliefs. For the most part, grassroots liberalism met its match. Only federal law would compel these conservatives to change their business practices — if not their beliefs. Lawrence would not have a public, integrated swimming pool until 1969, with the years in between characterized by growing racial animosity, violence, and death.[37]

Across the Great Plains, racism died slowly, if at all.

Many problems remained for the Great Plains Indians at the end of World War II. On the reservations, they needed more land and agricultural training through demonstration and extension work, as well as credit for the purchase of equipment, seed, and livestock. Indian farmers often were unable to continue their agricultural operations on the meager level of the past. Heirship lands so divided the reservation that finding enough acreage to support cattle ranching became nearly impossible. As a result, the agency superintendents leased much of the reservation land, sometimes without the heirs knowing about it or receiving their portion of the rental fees, because they could not be identified or located. In the absence of heirs or with the inability of the heirs to agree to lease their lands, white stock raisers grazed cattle on Indian lands without making payments. With problems such as these, the Indian stock raisers did not have the incentive to improve their agricultural operations. In addition, inadequate welfare services, low income, and hunger sometimes prompted the Indian cattle growers to butcher breeding cattle for food, thereby further limiting their ability to increase the size and profitability of their herds.

Between 1950 and 1960, whites leased two-thirds (or 600,000 acres) of South Dakota's Rosebud Reservation. Reductions in BIA funding forced Rosebud ranchers to seek needed credit from private sources, but lack of collateral and the inability to establish credit ratings, combined with discrimination, prevented them from receiving adequate funding. Lacking the necessary capital to buy cattle, many Sioux cattle growers sold their land to the tribe, which, in turn, leased it to non-Indian ranchers. Even if the Sioux had utilized all of their trust lands for grazing purposes, cattle ranching would have supported only one-third of the reservation's population. In many respects, then, an inadequate land base became a more serious problem than the lack of adequate credit, both of which Indian cattle raisers needed to make existing operations more productive. The Sioux at the Pine Ridge Reservation experienced similar problems; in 1956, only 21.4 percent of the Oglala considered themselves farmers. In general, whites leased most of the productive reservation lands in North and South Dakota by 1960.

To the west, whites also leased approximately 80 percent of the Crow Reservation in Montana. During the 1950s, Crow farmers had too few cattle and too little machinery to maintain viable agricultural operations. The most successful cattle raisers shared or rented lands with family members or partners, although not all of the land might be contiguous. At least seven tribal grazing associations used Indian lands and raised "good quality" Hereford cattle. The Crows sold most of their livestock in Billings, but they also made shipments to Omaha, Nebraska, and Sheridan, Wyoming. In the early 1950s, cattle provided 81 percent of the cash income for these Indian ranchers. To the South, in Oklahoma, not more than a dozen Kiowas, Comanches, Apaches, and Wichitas remained full-time farmers in 1950. They, like many small-scale white farmers, simply could not compete in the postwar world, where the extensive use of land and capital often meant the difference between success and failure. By the end of the decade, white farmers had gained leasing rights to most of the Quapaw, Cherokee, Chickasaw, Choctaw, Creek, Cheyenne, and Arapaho lands.[38]

Given these and other problems, some government officials and alleged friends of the Indians renewed their call for the termination of all government responsibility for the reservation tribes. In January 1945, John Collier's pressured resignation (followed by the end of the war in August) brought an end to self-determination and cultural preservation and restoration as the foundation of Indian policy. Quickly, the assimilationists in the executive branch and Congress reinstituted the policy of the past, which sought the inclusion and acculturation of the Indians into white society, thereby to achieve the other goal of terminating federal responsibility for Indian affairs. Termination meant repealing laws that treated Indians differently from other citizens, cancelling services that the BIA provided the tribes, and ending federal supervision of, guardianship of, and responsibility for the tribes.[39]

Termination also reflected a belief by some government officials that the Indian New Deal had failed to solve the problems created by the Dawes Act of 1887. Although the Dawes Act authorized the president to allot 160 acres of reservation land to each head of an Indian household, it did not provide the technological and financial support, training, and sufficient land base to ensure successful agriculture. Therefore, a new direction and a new solution were needed to solve the problems of Indian poverty and dependence on the federal government for subsistence, education, health care, and other basic needs. Supporters of termination believed that it would liberate the Indians from the bonds of reservation life by forcing them to rely upon themselves rather than depend on the federal government for their livelihood. Termination also would save taxpayers money or at least divert it for other purposes. Many whites who supported termination believed that state governments could handle the services that the BIA provided and that the Indians could protect their interests under state and federal law. Supporters of termination also correctly argued that some Indians favored the termination of federal trusteeship.[40]

In 1949, the movement for termination gained support when the Commission on the Organization of the Executive Branch of the Government, commonly known as the Hoover Commission, reported that "assimilation must be the dominant goal of public policy." The commission contended that the basis for Indian cultures no longer existed. Few Indians remained, and assimilation could not be prevented. The Indians needed integration into white society as taxpaying citizens. Commissioners of Indian Affairs John R. Nichols and Dillon S. Myer (the latter of whom assumed office on May 5, 1950) supported assimilation, and termination became the basis of Indian policy during the eight-year presidential administration of Dwight D. Eisenhower.[41]

On August 1, 1953, Congress, with strong leadership from the Wyoming, Montana, Nebraska, and South Dakota delegations, unanimously passed House Concurrent Resolution 108 (introduced by Wyoming congressman William Henry Harrison), which declared that "it is the policy of Congress, as rapidly as possible, to make the Indians within the territorial limits of the United States subject to the same laws and entitled to the same privileges and responsibilities as are applicable to other citizens of the United States, to end their status as wards of the United States and to grant them all the rights and prerogatives pertaining to American citizenship." Simply put, the trust status of the tribes would be terminated. In the Great Plains, the government singled out the Potawatomis in Kansas and Nebraska for the earliest possible termination. During the next five years, the Peorias, Ottawas, and Wyandots in Oklahoma would lose their trust status, and in 1962, the Poncas in Nebraska also lost that protection.[42]

Upon termination the Northern Poncas lost their federal recognition as

Indians and their right to participate in the programs and services guaranteed by their trust status. The BIA sold their land and divided the income along with the remaining trust funds for a per capita payout of $450. Dispossessed of their land and cultural and tribal identity, the Poncas suffered almost immediately from a serious decline in their economy and health care and welfare benefits. In 1989, the Northern Poncas had an unemployment rate of 57 percent, and 31 percent of their people fell below the poverty line. They also reported that 40 percent had not been able to seek health care during the previous year, because of the lack of financial resources and health insurance.[43]

Faced with these problems, in 1987 the Northern Poncas sought congressional restoration of their tribal identity based on their deteriorating economic and health conditions. Congress recognized their plight and agreed to reinstate them as a tribe provided that they would not seek a residential reservation. Congress then approved tribal restoration on October 31, 1990. This legislation permitted the Northern Poncas to purchase 1,500 acres that the federal government would hold in trust, but that land could be used only for federally sponsored housing programs and would not entitle the Poncas to any jurisdictional authority that was characteristic of other reservations. Moreover, the federal government would not provide funds for the land purchase. Most important, the Northern Poncas became eligible for federal health, education, and economic programs through the BIA. Even so, the tribal board of directors had difficulty compiling a tribal roll, drafting a constitution, and providing the organization for the delivery of BIA services. When the twentieth century ended, the Northern Poncas still labored to reestablish their trust benefits.[44]

The drive for termination, however, slowed in 1956, when the Democratic Party increased its congressional membership, thereby changing the committee structure. Indian and white opponents of termination, including Senators James E. Murray and Mike Mansfield of Montana and Senator Joseph C. O'Mahoney of Wyoming, also became more critical of a program that ensured destitution and poverty rather than freedom and liberation for tribal members. State and local government officials feared that federal budget reductions and the great financial need of the Indians would create insurmountable problems that they would inherit. The tribes also dreaded the continued loss of their land base, sovereignty, and disregard of their opinions about policy. They argued that the Bureau of Indian Affairs should provide massive economic aid for the reservations — because the states did not have the financial or organizational resources to meet their economic, social, and political needs — rather than sever all relationships with the tribes. In short, the BIA needed to expand its involvement with the Indians, rather than abdicate its responsibility. On January 7, 1957, Senator Murray contended that the BIA should "assist American Indian communities to reach the level of well-being enjoyed by other communities in the United States," but "without exacting termination of Federal protection of Indian property or any other Indian rights as its price."[45]

In response to these critics, Congress and the Department of the Interior backed away from the termination policy. By the autumn of 1958, the Eisenhower administration had deemphasized termination as much as possible. Fred A. Seaton, secretary of the interior, declared that termination was merely an objective, not an immediate goal, and that no tribe should have its relationship with the federal government ended unless the tribe supported termination and had developed a program to ensure its success. For Seaton, forced termination was nothing less than a "criminal" action. With this change of attitude within the government, termination ended by the early 1960s, but the term remained a volatile, emotionally charged word that Indians used to criticize or oppose unwanted proposals from and actions by the federal government. Thereafter, the Kennedy and successive administrations emphasized a policy that enabled self-determination without the severance of all tribal ties to the federal government.[46]

The policy of termination, however, had a positive effect because it encouraged greater Indian advocacy for self-determination within the federal system. Moreover, as many Indians left the reservations for urban employment, they expanded their contacts with other Indians from different tribes and, to an extent, created a pan-Indian bond. During the 1950s, multicultural Indian powwows were held in the plains. These powwows enabled the Indians to celebrate past traditions while building new ones. These cultural revitalizations worked contrary to the efforts of assimilationists, who sought termination and the destruction of Indian cultures.[47]

In 1964, the newly established Office of Economic Opportunity (OEO) created new antipoverty programs that provided important assistance and permitted local decision making. While providing increased access to federal support, OEO programs also weakened the control of the BIA because other agencies gained responsibilities for dealing with the reservation Indians. A year later, the Economic Development Administration sponsored the building of industrial parks on the Crow and Pine Ridge reservations. By the late 1960s, unemployment had dropped from 88 percent to 35 percent on the Rosebud Reservation, primarily because of government-sponsored projects. Increasingly, Indian managers took control of these new businesses. In 1972, William Houpee, tribal chairman at Fort Peck, boasted, "We are developing a number of budding executives." The failure rate of these new businesses, however, remained high because of a host of factors, such as mismanagement by Indians and whites, inadequate capitalization, and Indian cultural resistance, as well as changing political divisions within the tribes.[48]

During the late 1960s, federal attempts to encourage Indian self-determination through economic development brought immediate skepticism and often suspicion and rejection by the Great Plains Indians, who saw those efforts as renewed plans for termination. They had good reason for their concerns because Congress still considered House Concurrent Resolution 108 as official Indian policy. In April 1969, Commissioner of Indian Affairs Robert L. Bennett foresaw continued debilitating problems that divided the Indians on the reservations and BIA officials and Congress. He could only say, "Most of the problems are of longstanding duration with little prospect of immediate solution." Still, in September 1968, the tribes welcomed Richard Nixon's campaign pledge that "termination of tribal recognition will not be a policy objective and in no case will it be imposed without Indian consent. . . . The right of self-determination of the Indian people will be respected and their participation in planning their own destiny will be actively encouraged." Upon election, Vice President Spiro Agnew affirmed this policy. "The Administration *opposes* termination. This administration *favors* the continuation of the trust relationship and the protection of Indian lands and resources." Federal Indian policy became based on the premise that the Indians could become independent yet maintain their tribal communities and federal support. Even so, grievances, voiced through growing Indian activism, festered on the reservations. By the end of the 1960s, Red Power had become a loosely organized political movement, and the 1970s became a decade of protest and violence.[49]

In the 1940 presidential election, the northern and central Great Plains states held firmly Republican, except North Dakota, Montana, and Wyoming. Franklin Delano Roosevelt garnered strong Democratic support in the southern Great Plains. The return of normal precipitation, higher agricultural prices stimulated by the new European war, and successful New Deal programs had stabilized the economy, although the many government agencies had not solved the myriad of economic and social problems created by the Great Depression. Even so, many Great Plains residents felt sufficiently optimistic to return to the Republican Party. The strong Democratic vote in the southern Great Plains continued to reflect not only support for Roosevelt's New Deal programs but also migration patterns from the South that helped spread attachments to the Democratic Party into the southern Great Plains. In 1944, Roosevelt and the Democratic Party again prevailed in all the Great Plains states except Kansas, South Dakota, and Wyoming, where anti–fourth term sentiment probably contributed to his loss. Truman's support for agriculture was not enough for him to carry Kansas, Nebraska, and North and South Dakota in the closely contested presidential election of 1948 against Republican Thomas E. Dewey. Dwight D. Eisenhower, elected as a Republican, strongly carried every Great Plains state in 1952, but his support from traditional Democratic states such as Oklahoma, Texas, and New Mexico reflected his popularity as a revered wartime military leader; this support held four years later.

The 1960 presidential election became divisive for many Great Plains voters because the issue of religion tainted the campaign with the Democratic nomination of Catholic John F. Kennedy. Although Kennedy carried Texas and New Mexico, the widespread and powerful Baptist church voiced considerable opposition in the Lone Star State. In Texas, the *Baptist Standard* acknowledged John F. Kennedy as being "a clean young man with intelligence, ability, and competence," but it urged Baptists to reject him on election day unless Kennedy renounced allegiance "to the foreign religio-political state at the Vatican" and declared "freedom from the domination of the clergy by American Catholic citizens," a sentiment combining the traditional question of Catholic loyalty as well as Baptist belief in the priesthood of all believers. Baptists opposed Kennedy not because he was merely a Catholic but because he was a member of an institution that was both a church and a state.

Other Great Plains residents who were not Baptists held a similar view that if Kennedy became president he would take orders from the Pope. In May 1960, a public opinion poll showed that 76 percent of Texans knew that Kennedy was a Catholic and 60 percent considered him a political liability for the Democratic Party. As late as mid-September, a poll commissioned by the Kennedy-Johnson campaign indicated that 58 percent of all Texans polled favored the Republican candidate, Richard Nixon. When the votes were tallied, Kennedy carried Texas and New Mexico by only 2 percent and .8 percent margins, respectively. The efforts of the Texas *Baptist Standard* to determine the outcome of the presidential election portended a growing body of religious conservatism in American politics.[50]

In many respects, this political development can be seen in the southern Great Plains, particularly in the Texas Panhandle, where conservatives pursued their own brand of politics that gave solid allegiance to the Republican Party. With zealous beliefs in the necessity for limited government and unrestrained capitalism to ensure individual freedom and prosperity, both pursued with the righteousness of Protestant values, Republicans used politics and government for the good of themselves and their communities. They considered an activist federal government along with its social programming for the betterment of the commonweal not only interventionist but also a danger to individual freedoms. By 1970, these self-proclaimed "cowboy conservatives" had created a local Republican Party based on grassroots organization and ideological rigor. A decade later, their political assumptions and goals provided the core values of the national Republican Party. They opposed communism, deficit spending, and strong centralized government but supported the protection of American interests abroad on the national level. Locally, however, they championed morality, hard work, and Protestantism as well as whiteness. In 1970, 82 percent of Panhandle Texans considered themselves conservative. Their politics looked to the past and essentially became exclusionary.

At the same time, however, the demography of the Texas Panhandle began to change. The Latino population increased rapidly. In 1980, whites constituted 90 percent of Amarillo's population, but a decade later this had fallen to only 80 percent. In 1990, whites constituted merely 68 percent of Lubbock's population. Latino and African American voters had different individual and community needs. In 1968, conservative Democrats and many other residents of the Texas Panhandle believed that the national Democratic Party was taking the wrong side of the civil rights movement. Panhandle conservatives believed that both Alabama's Governor George Wallace and Republican presidential candidate Richard Nixon spoke for them on racial and social issues. During the 1970s, the politics of race came to the southern Great Plains. School bussing, affirmative action, and immigration restrictions as well as the redrawing of local precincts, among other locally sensitive issues, became major political issues because the racial population had changed sufficiently to require that government meet different public needs. As the population of the southern Great Plains became more Latino, Catholic, and working class, the politics of the region teetered on the edge of great change.[51]

On the state level, politics often diverged from national issues and was circumscribed by geography, that is, state boundaries within which unique political issues often developed. In Kansas, landowners, the public, and the state contested the right to use underground water. In 1945, the legislature passed the Kansas Water Act, which declared all water within the state to be public property subject to regulation by the state. This legislation privileged domestic and municipal use, to the consternation of farmers and industrialists, among others. The right to divert water depended on the date of priority for appropriation of the water when the supply proved insufficient to satisfy all water rights dependent on it. Groundwater (rather than just surface water) thus became part of the public domain; it also became a commodity for the economic development of Kansas. Farmers who invested heavily in irrigation equipment during the 1960s and 1970s, however, contested all efforts to limit their pumping. In 1991, one farmer spoke for many in saying, "We all went into that investment knowing that the water wasn't going to last forever, maybe 30 years. We didn't go into it with ideas that we would face artificial constraints."

Urbanites, however, wanted the regulation of water usage. Wichita's population continued to increase after World War II, and the city increasingly relied on groundwater to meet public needs. Wichita pumps decreased the water supply for nearby farmers, who demanded protection by the legislature from urbanites attempting to "steal" their water. Animosity between both groups lingered for the remainder of the twentieth century. Environmentalists also demanded clean water and its conservation to prevent "shameless water gluttons" from wasting it on their lawns. By 1990, Kansas had come to rely on eleven state agencies to oversee ninety water-management programs. When disagreements occurred, opponents fought in court over their differences, and the large-scale water users continued to effectively influence the legislature, which essentially meant the provision of water law. Considerable political fighting continued between agricultural and urban interests, the latter of whom after 1950 constituted the majority of the population and, after reapportionment of the state legislature during the mid-1960s, formed the largest political interest group in the state. When the twentieth century ended, Kansans clearly understood the axiom of the West that "Whiskey is for drinking and water is for fighting over."[52]

In contrast, in 1947, Nebraska politics became entangled in "right-to-work" issues, antistrike legislation, and the right to sue unions, all emanating from Omaha. The labor movement sought to repeal what workers considered oppressive legislation, but without success. At the same time, union membership increased; in 1969, state employees in Nebraska gained the ability to engage in collective bargaining (in contrast to North and South Dakota, where this right remained limited or did not exist and other issues drew voter attention). In North Dakota, for example, following World War II, politics was transformed from the pursuit of agrarian radicalism, such as Governor William Langer's declaration of a moratorium on farm foreclosures in 1933, and political defensiveness to perceived second-class status in the family of states, that is, as an outsider in the national mainstream of political events. Geographically isolated with an extractive, colonial economy, North Dakota relied on outsiders for capital, markets, and political largesse, that is, benefits dispensed by the federal government. Instead of lashing out defensively against North Dakota's enemies, both real and imagined, a new breed of politician emerged after the war who understood the benefits of federal programs, which meant funding for projects in the state that North Dakotans would otherwise do without. North Dakotans would seek military bases that provided civilian jobs and military pay, spent locally, as well as a host of agricultural programs that brought federal funding into the state, and they used politics to achieve those goals as never before.[53]

At the same time, progressives became increasingly comfortable ideologically in the Democratic Party, and a two-party system emerged during the late 1950s, with the Democrats becoming fiscally moderate or conservative and mildly progressive on social issues — in a word, centrists. Yet while the Democratic Party dominated the governorship and congressional delegations in North Dakota, voters had supported the Republican Party in every presidential election since 1964, partly because of support from conservative Democrats who rejected national party positions on ethnic groups and labor unions, among other issues, and their preference for the positions of the national Republican Party. Moreover, conservatism to North Dakotans meant conserving federal programs and funding for the state. Put differently, after the New Deal the federal government had something to give and North Dakota no longer opposed taking it, all the while keeping a watchful eye for outsiders, usually easterners, who might take advantage of them. Moreover, they kept a tight rein on their elected officials by using the initiative and referendum as a natural right.[54]

Oklahoma also emerged as a two-party state following World War II, with the Republican Party created, in part, on the popularity of Dwight D. Eisenhower and the Catholicism of John F. Kennedy, as well as dissatisfaction with Lyndon Johnson and the Vietnam War. The ideological attractiveness of the national Republican Party on domestic social and economic issues also contributed to party development in the state. By 1962, the Republican Party had shed its legacy of the Great Depression; Henry Bellman became the first Republican governor of Oklahoma. Soon, Republican Oklahomans gained congressional seats. Oklahoma politicians then began focusing on securing federal support rather than personal fighting and obstruction of the governor's initiatives. At the same time, Oklahoma re-

mained a Democratic state except when voting for Republican presidents
and senators, and Republicans contributed little to policy making on the
state level. The residents of the Old Indian Territory, roughly those living in the eastern half of the state, where political culture linked them to
the Old South and the Democratic Party, dominated Oklahoma's politics
while the western half, or the Old Oklahoma Territory, reflected northern
Republican settlement and political culture.[55]

In contrast, the Republican Party with few exceptions dominated politics
in South Dakota because party members were not doctrinaire capitalists.
They supported socialism in the form of state ownership of game lodges
and resorts and state subsidization of the Burlington Railroad, and municipalities owned and operated power plants, airports, telephone systems, and
liquor stores. Fiscal conservatives supported low taxes and a reliance on
the federal government to fund services from highway construction and
maintenance to aid for senior citizens, dependent children, agricultural
programs, military installations, and Indian reservations. Overall, South
Dakota politics centered on issues involving road construction, education,
and social services.[56]

Indian cultural groups in South and North Dakota became Democratic bastions in conservative Republican states. Yet, while generally supporting Republican presidential candidates, the voters of both states have
sent liberal Democrats to Congress to gain federal programs for farmers.
Otherwise, North and South Dakota have remained among the most conservative states regarding domestic issues and international relations. In
North Dakota, voters of Norwegian heritage remained primarily isolationist, conservative, and Republican, while the eastern, urban areas of North
and South Dakota were comparatively more liberal on political issues than
were voters in rural areas.[57]

In Wyoming, the Republican Party dominated politics after World War II
while sharing similar conservative views with the Democratic Party. State
politics often centered on economic development and, increasingly as the
twentieth century neared its end, environmental regulations of mineral
companies. Although Wyoming politicians focused on agricultural issues
and the mineral industries while standing up to the federal government, at
the end of the twentieth century the state remained isolated and economically dependent on the federal government. Economic and environmental
issues, then, dominated politics, but Wyoming's political voice and power
remained essentially nonexistent on the national level.[58]

Similarly, in the big, largely empty state of Montana, the Anaconda
Copper Mining Company (AMC), the Montana Cattlemen's Association,

and the Montana Farm Bureau, along with the Great Northern, Northern Pacific, and Milwaukee railroads, and a few other companies, dominated the state's politics. By the early 1970s, however, Montanans were increasingly voting to punish industry and business for past exploitation through the tax code while resisting efforts to provide a state sales tax. Although the AMC was terminated in 1977, in part because of the nationalization of its deposits in Chile, Montanans still resented its exploitative corporate power of the past, and they used politics to foil any indications of its reemergence. In the 1980s, industrial and agricultural economic challenges encouraged out-migration, which resulted in the loss of two congressional seats. With the miners and small-scale farmers gone, Progressives migrated intellectually to the Democratic Party in the urban areas of western Montana, where their political concerns involved labor and environmental issues, while the Republican Party represented the farm, ranch, and country club conservatives. When the twentieth century ended, the political voice of Montana's plains residents remained weak, if not nonexistent.[59]

In the mid-twentieth century, the political voice of the Great Plains was neither the movement culture of the late nineteenth century nor politics in service of the commonweal but instead reflected small-scale interest group politics, the politics of personal gain for individuals and their groups rather than for the benefit of society.

In retrospect, the immediate postwar years involved readjustment to a peacetime economy. By the late 1940s, food rationing and wartime earnings had come to mean disposable income that men and women could spend on automobiles, housing, clothes, and farm equipment, among other needed and desired consumer goods. Federal funds once again became available to support various projects, such as soil conservation and rural electrification. In 1950, 69 percent of South Dakota's farms had electricity, up from 18 percent three years earlier because of the expanded work of the Rural Electrification Administration. In addition to enjoying electric lights, rural families bought electric hot water heaters, washing machines, and equipment for the barn.

While plains men and women adjusted to peacetime, they also confronted national issues that involved the perceived threat of communism. As Eastern Europe and parts of Asia came under communist control, plains men and women followed the newscasts about the impending threat to the West. They supported the Marshall Plan to help Europe recover from the war and combat the communist threat to Western democracies. In South Dakota, Congressman Karl E. Mundt became the leading "cold warrior" in the region. Mundt used his positions on the House Un-American Activities and Foreign Affairs committees and on the Senate Foreign Relations Committee to warn the public about the threat of communism.

In March 1947, Congressman Mundt, ever vigilant against "godless communism," urged the public to investigate library and school materials to determine whether children were "being victimized by communist propaganda." In 1949, with Mao Tse-tung capturing Beijing and the Soviet Union testing an atomic bomb, followed by the conviction of Julius and Ethel Rosenberg for spying, the communist threat seemed a clear and present danger. In 1950, Mundt blamed the Roosevelt administration for this state of affairs and charged that since the election of Franklin Roosevelt to the presidency in 1932 the country had been "run by New Dealers, Fair Dealers, Misdealers and Hiss dealers, who have shuttled back and forth between freedom and Red Fascism like a pendulum on a cuckoo clock." Small wonder, then, that Mundt supported Senator Joseph McCarthy's (D, Wisc.) efforts to identify suspected communists in government and industry.[60]

Mundt represented the extreme conservative fringe of plains residents, who believed that communism had targeted the United States for extinction. Their fears and Mundt's work in Congress led to the Internal Security Act of 1950, also known as the McCarran Act (but which easily could be called the Mundt Law). It required the registration of communists, tightened existing espionage and sabotage laws, and provided for the detention and deportation of subversives. The states also quickly passed loyalty oaths for public servants to combat the communist threat. Plains men and women believed that through loyalty oaths, citizens should prove their fitness to hold positions in state and federal government and public and higher education.[61]

Not all plains men and women believed that protecting the United States from subversion was more important than the Bill of Rights. But until Senator McCarthy received censure in the U.S. Senate, plains men and women struggled to accept witch hunts for communists, both real and imagined, which seemed to violate the Constitution. Most plains residents could not have identified a communist if they tried, and in December 1950, the Federal Bureau of Investigation could locate only thirty-six communists in South Dakota. Although plains men and women signed the required loyalty oaths for employment, they were offended that the federal and state governments questioned their patriotism. Ultimately, they signed the documents as nothing more than a bureaucratic necessity to acquire and keep a job, and they soon forgot about it. Within a few years, plains men and women recognized Red Scare politicians such as Mundt and McCarthy as obnoxious fearmongers, and they soon gave their attention to other concerns.[62]

Although plains men and women generally supported the Korean conflict at first, they increasingly objected to the war. The old isolationist sentiments increasingly reemerged. Communities near military installations and cities with defense contracts, however, profited, in the same way that they had gained from the economic boost of World War II. In 1951, the federal government reactivated the old army airfield at Amarillo. This multipurpose facility, renamed the Amarillo Air Force Base, trained jet-engine mechanics, guided-missile technicians, and pilots and supported units of the Strategic Air Command. In 1965, the air base contributed a $2.5 million monthly payroll to the region's economy. The military also reopened the Pantax Army Ordnance Depot. Other Great Plains cities also profited from the cold war. From 1948 to 1992, the Strategic Air Command headquartered at Offut Air Force Base near Omaha. In 1950, it supported 20,000 servicemen and servicewomen and their dependents; this increased to 26,000 during the Vietnam era. Offut brought millions of dollars into eastern Nebraska. In the northern Great Plains, Air Force bases at Minot and Grand Forks, North Dakota, and Ellsworth near Rapid City, South Dakota, also provided new employment and payrolls.[63]

As cold war fears once again brought the military to the Great Plains, the Dakotas and Montana became sites for atomic and nuclear intercontinental ballistic missiles. These missiles targeted Moscow and other Soviet industrial and military locations. By the time of the Cuban missile crisis in October 1962, South Dakota alone had 150 Minuteman missiles hidden in underground silos. During the 1960s, North and South Dakota contained approximately 20 percent of the nation's intercontinental missile launching sites. North Dakotans joked that if the state became independent, it would become the world's third largest nuclear power. These military complexes brought millions of dollars into the local economy for construction workers and military personnel. Plains men and women generally did not object to the location of missile silos near their homes, because they were patriotic and worried about the communist threat to Western democracies. Ironically, these missiles located on the isolated, windswept plains placed residents in the bull's-eye of Soviet missiles, should first or retaliatory strikes occur due to a miscalculation in cold war politics. The quiet emptiness of the region deceived the eye.[64]

In 1980, the cold war world of civilian Department of Defense work provided employment for 20,000 workers in San Antonio and another 15,000 in Oklahoma City alone. In 1983, during the Ronald Reagan presidency, Dallas and San Antonio received more than $2 billion in defense spending, more than residents' taxes allocated for defense. Albuquerque and Denver, especially their universities, also received considerable research and development funding for military projects. Military contracts usually required a well-educated and highly skilled workforce. During the 1970s, Kansas and Colorado ranked among the leading states for high-tech, military-dependent jobs. Dallas and Lubbock benefited from the location of Texas Instruments, which also provided high-tech employment that helped boost population growth. Retiring military personnel increasingly called Colorado, New Mexico, and Texas home (especially Denver, Albuquerque, and San Antonio) because of access to social clubs, medical facilities, and, in the southern plains, relatively warm winter weather. These cities grew in size but also in age as the proportion of residents aged sixty-five or older increased.[65]

Plains men and women responded to the cold war, in part, by voting for conservative Republican candidates in the central and northern plains and conservative Democrats in the south. The scant political influence of the plains states on the national level came from leaders such as Republican Karl Mundt and Democrat George McGovern of South Dakota, Republican William Langer of North Dakota, and Democrat Robert Kerr of Oklahoma. On the state level, parties remained relatively weak and focused on fiscal conservatism and maintenance of the status quo. On the national level, congressional delegations strongly supported federal farm programs, including conservation. They favored low taxes but high federal returns to state coffers, and they aggressively pursued federal funding, particularly for agriculture as an entitlement. Many states received more federal dollars for programs than they paid in taxes. During the mid-1970s, South Dakota received about three dollars of federal funding for every tax dollar. In the late 1980s, South Dakota ranked second in the nation, behind Alaska, receiving approximately two dollars for every tax dollar paid.[66]

Great Plains farmers supported the federal government's efforts to solve the problem of overproduction and low prices with the Agriculture Act of 1956, which authorized the Soil Bank Program. This program enabled the federal government to pay farmers for removing land from short-term production of basic crops, such as wheat, as well as long-term withdrawals of land for a Conservation Reserve Program. Great Plains farmers participated in the Soil Bank Program to gain needed cash, but they generally removed their least productive lands from cultivation and increased their crop production with the use of more fertilizer on the acreage planted.

While farmers supported the Soil Bank Program, local merchants opposed it, arguing that farmers earned less from federal program payments for idling farmland than they received from crops. As a result, farm families spent less money in town. In 1959, Congress abandoned the program due to expense and complaints, but in the meantime, the Soil Bank Program further indicated that Great Plains residents would willingly accept federal dollars while professing the need for low taxes, fiscal conservatism, and limited government.[67]

After World War II, migration from the countryside increased because of a flagging farm economy. Farms consolidated and increased in size. By 1960, only 30 percent of South Dakotans were still living in the country-side. Cheyenne and Casper, Wyoming, Billings, Montana, and Dodge City, Kansas, among other towns, gained population during the 1950s and 1960s as people left the farms and small towns for job opportunities in the larger towns and cities, particularly where defense-related industries offered employment. The oil-field towns of Abilene, Midland, and Odessa, Texas, also drew new residents and became regional financial and retail centers. The strip-mining coal towns in western North Dakota, Wyoming, and Montana, controlled by distant corporations, gave hope in a barren and torn landscape. Social services, law enforcement, and education could not keep pace; the term *Gillette syndrome* was coined to describe the so-cial disarray and degradation spawned by rapid population growth in that Wyoming coal-mining town. As smaller towns and rural areas declined in population, schools consolidated and churches closed.[68]

Between 1940 and 1970, every Great Plains state exhibited a modest increase in population, except North Dakota, where the population declined from 641,935 to 617,761 (a loss of 24,174 people). North Dakota would not exceed its 1940 population until 1980, before declining once again. The metropolitan area of San Antonio increased from a population of 338,176 in 1940 to 864,014 in 1970. Lubbock grew from 100,085 to 201,550. During the same period, Oklahoma City increased from 244,159 to 640,889, while Wichita expanded from 143,311 to 389,352. Similarly, Omaha grew from 325,153 to 540,142 in population. After 1940, Albuquerque and Dallas–Fort Worth made the transition from small city to metropolis. During the 1940s, the population of metropolitan Albuquerque increased by 110 percent, the highest growth rate of all American boom cities. Lubbock followed close behind, with 95 percent growth. Although the rural areas of the Great Plains lost population, the cities grew because of internal migration and the arrival of newcomers drawn by economic opportunities or corporate assignment. The county seats increasingly became island communities and major retail trade centers amidst a sea of land. Between Albuquerque, New Mexico, and Amarillo and Lubbock, Texas, the plains remained comparatively empty, but only North and South Dakota and Montana remained predominately rural.[69]

Growth, however, did not necessarily mean progress or improvement. The political power structure in Denver resisted commercial real estate development despite its potential to further expand the economy: the past was good enough. Cheyenne, Wyoming, pursued the same status quo approach to the future. In 1949, one observer noted that "the men who run Cheyenne incline to the thinking that their town is large enough. . . . The real leaders, those who dominate the city's economic life . . . do not want competition, and are constantly on the alert to block newcomers who might someday pose a threat to their vested position." Regional tourism and the Cheyenne Frontier Days celebration met their needs for economic development. Voters in Omaha, Dallas, and Fort Worth saw little or no need for federal dollars to help their economies.

Some city leaders, such as those in Dallas, took a more forward-looking approach to economic development, largely in fear of a postwar recession. City planning became a hallmark for careful annexation and economic development in the form of new businesses, jobs, housing, and transportation as well as infrastructure improvements such as roads and sewage facilities. Reform-minded governments in Albuquerque and San Antonio also sought to reorder the power structure with council-manager forms of government, seeking efficiency and nonpartisanship, but the cities also continued to ignore the social and economic needs of blacks and Hispanics. Oklahoma City boomed on the postwar oil capitalism of Kerr-McGee, Oklahoma Gas and Electric, and the First National Bank. In the mid-1950s, Denver aspired to recognition as a "continental city," leaving Kansas City and Dallas behind in both influence and recognition. In 1955, leaders in Denver and Tulsa formed business coalitions to support city improvements. Great Plains cities that aspired to sustained prosperity and growth wanted skid row and other poor sections of their cities demolished and the poor moved out. One North Dakotan succinctly described the problem by noting that Fargo's North Pacific Avenue was "the central thoroughfare of the dingy feel-good roll of Indian bars, Western-wear stores, pawn shops, and Christian Revival Missions that Fargo was trying to eradicate." The same could be said for Larimer Street in Denver. In preparing for the HemisFair in 1968, San Antonio evicted 1,600 residents and built a theater, arena, and exhibition building and leased the remaining acreage from its 149-acre purchase. With H-bomb boosterism, San Antonio announced that it was a major modern city with hemispheric importance.[70]

Until the 1960s, most Great Plains towns had too few African American children to merit the cost of segregated education, but they could afford discrimination, even exclusionary policies, in housing, restaurants, and hotels as well as other public facilities, because private individuals, not the state, bore the cost of denying business to blacks and Mexican Americans. Although the *Brown* case legally ended segregation, racial prejudice in daily affairs prevailed, particularly among the Great Plains people who were politically conservative and poorly educated. As late as 1963, travelers could see signs outside various businesses in Oklahoma that read "No Beer Sold to Indians."[71]

For the remainder of the twentieth century, the economic, social, and political concerns of Great Plains residents involved agriculture, demographic change, and the depopulation of the countryside, familiar issues that brought new problems.

CHAPTER SIX

The Perils of Agriculture

In 1939 when World War II began in Europe, nearly all Great Plains farmers wanted to stay out of the conflict. They feared the loss of life, particularly of their sons, if the United States became involved. They also remembered the collapse of the agricultural economy after World War I. Still, many farm men and women considered the war an opportunity for the United States to sell surplus, price-depressing agricultural commodities to Great Britain and France. Wartime demands, they hoped, would increase farm prices and improve their income and the standard of living for farm families across the Great Plains. The editor of the *Nebraska Farmer* contended that a long war would bring prosperity to farmers because, to feed their people, the belligerent nations would turn to the United States for agricultural commodities that they could no longer produce.

Although agricultural prices for grain and livestock increased during the autumn of 1939, most farmers anxiously awaited major price increases for farm products. By early spring of 1940, however, the *Nebraska Farmer* reported that the war had not "lived up to the expectations of those who looked for a boom in exports of farm products." Britain and France continued to spend more for armaments than for American farm commodities. As a result, in late 1940, only government buying, commodity loans, and export subsidies kept agricultural prices from falling because of a loss of foreign markets, primarily due to German and British blockades.

By mid-1941, however, increased British demands for food as well as an expanding U.S. military had substantially increased agricultural prices. Farmers enjoyed 25 percent more purchasing power than during the previous year, and agricultural experts predicted another 25 percent increase the next year. In September 1941, Great Plains farmers became even more optimistic when Secretary of Agriculture Claude R. Wickard called for "the largest production in the history of American agriculture to meet the expanding food needs of this country and nations resisting the Axis." Farm income thus outpaced expenses, at least for the moment.

As the nation drifted toward war, Great Plains farmers worried about government price fixing for agricultural commodities, if the United States became involved in the conflict. On the eve of Pearl Harbor, Congress bowed to farm-state pressure and approved liberal maximum prices for farm commodities while promising farmers that agricultural prices would not be targeted for control if war came and consumer prices escalated. Nearly everyone understood that agricultural production would have to increase to feed an expanding military. Soon people began speaking of "Food for Defense," and federal and state officials met with farmers to encourage them to increase production by specific amounts.

Agricultural Adjustment Administration officials, who represented the federal government, visited farms and asked farmers how much they could increase the production of various commodities. Across the Great Plains, wheat and cotton production still seemed more than sufficient to meet the nation's needs for bread and fiber. Most observers believed that the European war might end soon, and farmers did not want to produce too much and suffer price-depressing surpluses and an economic depression like the one that had followed World War I. The Japanese attack on Pearl Harbor on December 7, 1941, however, ended the reluctance of most Great Plains farmers to increase production. Quickly, the army became the major buyer of flour from wheat and of beef produced in the Great Plains. Farm commodity prices skyrocketed by 42 percent, while farm costs increased only 16 percent from the previous year.

Great Plains farmers met the challenge of the U.S. Department of Agriculture and other government agencies to increase production by seeding more acres, raising more livestock, and working longer days. They also took pride in their achievements and couched their work in patriotic terms as their contribution to the war effort. In July 1942, the *Nebraska Farmer* touted the increased productivity of farmers in the Cornhusker State: "On every Nebraska farm there is a dramatic story of sacrifices, hard work and long hours, often made by women and children who took the place of sons and brothers in the military." One Oklahoma editor contended, "The war has made the farmer almost the most important person in the county, and farming has become as essential a war-time business as the manufacturer of planes, tanks, guns and ammunition." By early 1942, Great Plains farmers had become aware that the war would dramatically increase their income. In South Dakota, farmers and livestock raisers anticipated wartime profits because approximately 75 percent of the state's farm income came from sales to allied forces and civilians through the Lend-Lease program.

Yet as agricultural income increased, Great Plains farmers recognized a looming agricultural labor shortage as their sons and hired hands joined the military while the federal government expected them to increase production. In the spring of 1942, the U.S. Employment Service could not find enough workers for farm labor. Government officials recommended the employment of nonfarm women and men and boys and girls and also urged businesses to close during peak agricultural seasons, such as harvest time, to enable employees to help local farmers. In Colorado, some people opposed the organization of schoolchildren for farm labor because it required too much regimentation. Many schools and civic organizations, however, provided volunteers to help farmers.

Great Plains farmers knew that agricultural machinery would help them solve the labor shortage, improve efficiency and production, and reduce labor costs. But they could not purchase much equipment during the war because defense industry needs for iron, steel, and rubber had priority over agricultural machinery manufacturers. A farm implement shortage developed quickly, particularly for tractors, combines, and corn pickers, and forced Great Plains farmers to share equipment when an implement broke or wore out. During the summer of 1942, H. O. Davis, rationing director for Kansas, told farmers, "This is more than a question of 'neighboring'; it is a question of patriotic service for the country." By autumn, E. K. Davis, president of the Kansas Farmers Union, also urged members to share labor and machinery.

In September 1942, Secretary of Agriculture Wickard issued a rationing order for all new farm machinery, effective in November. As a result, Great Plains farmers used their well-worn equipment during the war. Implement dealers often could not keep pace with the demands for repair work. Great Plains farmers could only make do with the implements that they had when the war began, while recognizing the potential problems ahead. Throughout the war, insufficient farm machinery and labor hindered the efforts of farmers to increase production. Most farmers, however, confronted their problem and profited from increased productivity and high wartime prices.

While farmers endured without sufficient farm implements, they also contended with a labor shortage throughout the war. In Colorado, Governor John C. Vivian appealed to Secretary of War Henry Stimson to release men in the military provided that they worked on farms. He believed that the induction of farm men into the military by the Selective Service contradicted government appeals for farmers to increase production. Governor Vivian argued that only farmers knew how to farm, not city men and women, who might be hired as agricultural workers.

During the war, the farm labor shortage became serious across the Great Plains. Farmers could not compete with defense industry wages, and the military took away many of their usual workers. The construction of military bases and employment at the bomber and ordnance plants, air bases, ammunition depots, and flying schools further drained the agricultural labor supply in the region because the construction and war industries paid considerably higher wages than did farming. In Kansas, farmers paid approximately $50 per month with room and board for year-round help and $3 per day for seasonal harvest hands. In autumn of 1942, however, they paid $5 per day for inexperienced workers and at that could not employ enough of them, in part because the aircraft industry in Wichita paid wages as high as $12 per day.

In 1943, the state extension services and the U.S. Department of Agriculture began a major campaign to encourage farmers to employ boys and girls and men and women from the towns and cities to help meet their labor needs. The Kansas Extension Service reported, "It may take two boys to make one man, or three businessmen to replace one skilled farmer but the help that is here must be utilized." The extension service also observed, "It will take patience on the part of the farmer to train skilled help. It will also require that sacrifice be made by town people unused to farm work under the summer sun. All of this is incidental to getting the job done." In April, the Kansas State Extension Service appealed to the patriotism of town and country people alike to help solve the farm labor shortage.

The agricultural labor shortage remained critical across the Great Plains during the war years. The Dallas Chamber of Commerce asked business leaders to release their employees for fieldwork, but few business owners or their employees volunteered to chop, that is, weed cotton fields with a hoe. Similarly, farm labor officials urged Cheyenne business owners and their employees to spend their summer vacations on a farm within a fifty-mile radius of the city. In Nebraska, one county agent reported that interest among school boys and girls for farmwork lagged, and a survey of high school students in Oklahoma City clearly indicated that most had no intention of working on farms for patriotic reasons, because they could earn $100 or more per month in various city jobs. Few farmers could pay such high wages. Near Dallas, cotton pickers earned at best $5 per day, and few workers took that employment.[1]

In June 1942, O. M. Olsen, commissioner of labor for Nebraska, surveyed the labor shortage in the sugar beet region of western Nebraska. He supported the recruitment of seven hundred Mexican farmworkers to help farmers block, that is, thin sugar beets. In Wyoming, volunteers also helped farmers thin beets to ensure a crop. Some farmers hoped that Japanese evacuees from the West Coast who were relocated to Heart Mountain, Wyoming, could help harvest sugar beets. Given the inability of many Great Plains farmers to meet their labor needs locally, they increasingly sought Mexican and Mexican American workers, particularly for work in the sugar beet fields for cultivating and harvesting as well as to chop and pick cotton in New Mexico and Texas. Many Great Plains farmers were encouraged when the federal government negotiated an agreement with Mexico to support the temporary migration of workers to aid farmers with certain needs who met specific wage, housing, and working regulations; this agreement became effective on August 4, 1942. Soon, farmers and agricultural officials referred to it as the Bracero Program, and it lasted until 1964.

Mexican workers, called braceros, proved good workers in the Great Plains sugar beet fields. Sugar beet growers and nearby refineries quickly stereotyped them as a people who would work long and hard for low wages and not complain, and many came from rural areas and understood farmwork. Few local or white migrant workers sought this back-aching work, which paid about $10 per day. During the remainder of the war, Great Plains farmers, particularly sugar beet growers, sought braceros that they contracted through the federal government.

Braceros also worked for Great Plains farmers in other capacities: they harvested potatoes, shocked corn, threshed grain, and stacked hay. Because of racist prejudices, farmers wanted the Mexicans to leave their farms and the area when the job ended, and braceros and Mexican American migrant workers from the southern Great Plains confronted segregation in businesses and public places across the region. Great Plains farmers who employed braceros, however, praised their work ethic and productivity. Even though they sometimes lacked skills for harvesting corn and wheat or using machinery, they learned quickly and worked hard. South Dakota farmers particularly welcomed braceros during the war years. In Nebraska, an extension agent praised the ability of the braceros to learn any farm job. The Fillmore County agent observed that they were accustomed to working with their hands, which gave them an advantage over "most unskilled workers." He also urged farmers to help ensure good working relations for them. Great Plains farmers, particularly sugar beet growers, needed Mexican nationals in their fields, and the labor of these immigrant workers proved essential. Between August 1943 and August 1945, approximately twenty thousand braceros worked in the Great Plains, where they served as an important labor force.[2]

These workers, however, could not provide all of the labor needed on Great Plains farms. Some agricultural officials in the USDA and state extension services believed that women in the cities and towns could help ease the farm labor shortage by joining the Women's Land Army (WLA). Great Plains farm men and women appreciated patriotism, but they questioned whether nonfarm women could perform physical agricultural work. Few town women volunteered for the WLA, which Congress authorized in April 1943. In the Great Plains, farmers traditionally had not hired women for seasonal or harvest work, and recruitment proved difficult. In Nebraska, the extension service reported that farmers willingly accepted their wives and daughters in the fields, but they were reluctant to hire nonfarm women. Moreover, few nonfarm women sought agricultural employment, because they were not interested in this work and did not consider it a contribution to the war effort. Moreover, it did not pay as much as defense industry jobs.

During the war, many women did work on Great Plains farms. Women detassled corn and pitched hay in South Dakota, shocked wheat in North Dakota, and harvested potatoes in Wyoming, where the number of women driving tractors became noticeable. In Nebraska, women likewise drove tractors to cultivate corn, and they harvested grain and picked corn. Most of these women, however, were family members, not nonfarm urban or town women. Most of these farm women drove trucks and tractors during the harvest, with hauling grain their most common job. Implement companies, state extension services, and agricultural employment committees often sponsored training courses for farm and nonfarm women to help them learn to operate agricultural implements, particularly tractors.

Few farm women wanted city women working in their homes, unless these women cleaned and cooked. Farm women did not want nonfarm women working in the fields. Moreover, farmers were skeptical about hiring females, particularly nonfarm women. They preferred to entrust their machinery to their wives and daughters or other farm women, who had some knowledge about the operation of various implements. Consequently, the women working on Great Plains farms were in the following order, with decreasing frequency: first, the farmer's wife; second, his live-at-home daughter; third, the daughter who had moved away but returned during the harvest; fourth, a relative; fifth, friends; and sixth or last, town women who wanted to work on a farm, if the family accepted them. In the Great Plains, then, women conducted a considerable amount of agricultural labor but not as part of the WLA. At best, farm men approved of nonfarm women helping their wives with domestic chores, and farm women treated them as "hired girls" who did not know very much. Farm women considered fieldwork their responsibility in time of need. In the end, farm women, not town recruits of the WLA, made the greatest contribution of women to agricultural work in the Great Plains during World War II.[3]

When the war began, farmers optimistically had hoped that the new conflict would benefit them, because increased federal demands for greater production meant more money. In 1940, farmers received an index price of 84 (1910–14 = 100) for wheat, 83 for cotton, and 108 for livestock, while their cost of living reached 121. At the end of the war, the index wheat price was at 172, cotton, 178, and livestock, 210, while the cost-of-living index reached 182. Put differently, the index price received on all farm products was 95 in 1939 and 204 in 1945. At the same time, farmers paid an index price for commodities, interest, taxes, and wages of 123 in 1939 and 192 in 1945. Net income on a typical Great Plains wheat farm in Kansas, Oklahoma, and Texas rose from $558 in 1939 to $6,700 in 1945, a 1,102 percent increase. In Oklahoma and Texas, cotton farmers earned an average of $997 for their crop in 1939 and $2,894 in 1945, a 190 percent increase. Overall, then, Great Plains farmers benefited from World War II. They paid debts and mortgages, bought land, and saved. They hoped that any postwar economic depression would pass quickly. The war years had ended the price-depressing surpluses and low farm income of the Great Depression. Great Plains farmers agreed that war paid. Even so, operating costs increased, and they struggled with a cost-price squeeze after the war that plagued them for the remainder of the twentieth century.[4]

Prior to World War II, plains farmers often had preferred to hire short-term labor to limit farm operating costs instead of making long-term financial commitments to purchase machinery. Better-paying jobs and working conditions in industry fostered by World War II, however, forced farmers to mechanize to ensure their ability to plant and harvest. Fixed operating costs in the form of payments for machinery necessitated the cultivation of more acres to increase income, which, in turn, meant plowing pasture and grasslands or expanding farm size. New chemical pesticides, fertilizers, and herbicides as well as improved livestock disease control and government programs helped reduce the risks of farming, if a farmer could afford the investment. Tax laws and government policies also benefited large-scale farmers rather than small-scale operators.[5]

By the early 1950s, drought had returned; it made farm life more difficult as the "powder dry" soil and strong winds once again brought dust storms to the Great Plains. Dust storms swept across the southern and central plains with a frequency and intensity that surpassed the drought years of the 1930s, although black blizzards were more rare. Drought damaged croplands across most of the southern and central Great Plains, and dust drifted, once again, across roads, covered fences, and ruined crops. One western Kansas farmer remarked, "We'd probably give the land back to the Indians . . . if we had any Indians." By the mid-1950s, wind erosion had become a serious problem. Bare, submarginal wheat lands that should have remained in grass blew with the nearly constant winds, and the drought and the wind-erosion area extended far beyond the boundary of the old Dust Bowl. Some farmers had been negligent over the past decade, and "suitcase" farmers (absentee farmers who had to travel long distances from home to work their fields) contributed to the problem because they were seldom available to apply the proper emergency conservation methods when their lands started blowing.

Near-normal precipitation did not return to the plains until the late 1950s. During the 1950s, however, Great Plains farmers quickly took advantage of government soil-erosion-mitigation programs that provided financial support for emergency tillage practices to help slow and hold the blowing soil. Still, drought and dust ruined pastures and feed crops and brought economic losses to livestock raisers. The Oklahoma Cattlemen's Association urged the federal government to buy 100 million pounds of beef at a minimum price of twelve dollars per hundredweight. The association also sought a renewal of the canning program initiated during the 1930s. Shading its real motives for beef price supports under the cloak of patriotism, the Oklahoma Cattlemen's Association recommended that government-canned beef be distributed through the Office of Civil Defense "to guard against food shortage in the case of national emergency or disaster due to atomic attack." Cattlemen in the drought area also sought long-term loans at low interest rates, low-cost feed (subsidized by the federal government if necessary), and emergency transportation rates on feed for "bona fide" farmers and stockmen, indicating that their dependence on the federal government remained firm.

These demands did not go unheard. In late July 1953, the Commodity Credit Corporation began selling corn, wheat, oats, and cottonseed at below-market prices to help livestock producers maintain their basic herds.

Additional aid also was forthcoming. As part of the new drought relief program, the federal government agreed to purchase 200 million pounds of beef for the American and Greek armies and for the school lunch program. The U.S. Department of Agriculture also began cooperating with the drought states by providing funds to help pay railroad charges for transporting hay into designated drought counties. In addition, the department gained the cooperation of several railroads to reduce the freight rate by 50 percent on incoming hay. The federal government also provided special feed and livestock loan programs to help meet their expenses until market prices returned a profit. Although the drought of the 1950s became more severe and widespread than during the 1930s, the wind-erosion problem never became as serious, and fewer farmers abandoned their land. Many had adopted proper soil conservation techniques, the federal government provided a multiplicity of programmatic aid, and high agricultural prices kept them from destitution.[6]

Moreover, the economic situation was vastly different during the 1950s. Great Plains farmers had enjoyed profitable harvests and had accumulated financial reserves by the time the drought and dust storms returned, and many had diversified by the mid-1950s with the help of irrigation and no longer faced financial disaster if a wheat crop failed. As a result, these farmers were able to stay on their land and practice the appropriate soil conservation techniques. By 1957, precipitation had returned to nearly normal, the drought had broken, and the dust storms had essentially ended.

To the north, Great Plains farmers still complained about discriminatory railroad rates. Often transportation rates made the wheat from the northern Great Plains less competitive with grain raised in areas closer to processing centers, and northern plains farmers usually received lower prices where freight rates were high. In contrast to the late nineteenth century, railroads had begun to charge proportionally more for a long haul than a short one. Short-haul rates were usually lower because the railroads had to compete with cheap truck transport of grain to market. Over longer distances, however, the costs leveled out, and the railroads could charge more for a long haul. Intrastate shipments also cost more because the Interstate Commerce Commission could not regulate those rates.

Although Great Plains farmers confronted unique environmental problems, they also faced other difficulties and trends. Land sales, for example, usually increased the size of farms and decreased the number of farms and the agricultural population. Health, age, and financial situations were the most compelling reasons for selling or buying land. Usually the buyers lived nearby and paid higher prices than those who lived far away and bought land merely for investment. The farmers who bought land to expand their operations usually intended to pay for it with the agricultural income. They did not purchase the land merely to rent it to someone else. Land prices were determined by a host of factors, such as the wheat allotment, the amount of acreage in cropland and pasture, the availability of irrigation, the number of buildings, road quality, and distance to town. In some areas such as western Kansas and eastern Colorado, absentee owners became common.[7]

Many farmers who could not afford to buy land rented it from local landlords. This trend continued, and as land prices escalated, tenancy also increased, but this condition no longer implied limited profitability or resources. By 1970, tenants were among the most prosperous farmers in the central Great Plains because they had not overextended their capital investments, and renting land proved more cost-effective than buying it. The full tenants, those operators who did not own land, tended to be young entry-level farmers, while most landlords were retired farmers. As farm size increased, Great Plains farmers relied less on hired labor and more on technology, particularly tractors and combines, the latter of which saved considerable labor costs for threshing and reduced the number of workers (which necessitated big meals prepared by the farmer's wife)[8]

During World War II, Great Plains farmers began employing "custom cutters," that is, people who owned combines and trucks and were hired to harvest small grain crops, particularly wheat, and haul it to an elevator or storage bin. With farm implements (such as combines) and labor in short supply during the war, enterprising combine owners began the wheat harvest in the southern plains of Texas and Oklahoma in May and followed the ripening wheat northward, often returning after cutting sunflowers in North Dakota in late autumn. In 1947, some 7,800 custom combines operated in Kansas, while 5,117 cut wheat in Nebraska. When custom cutters finished a job, they loaded their combines on a truck and hauled them down the highway to the next orally contracted job. Farmers liked this service because it enabled them to forgo the purchase of expensive machinery and the recruitment of costly labor. Custom cutters charged by the acre plus a hauling fee and an assessment for crops over a certain level of bushels per acre. By the early 1960s, many farmers had given up their combines in favor of custom cutters. They preferred to avoid the costs of buying and maintaining a combine while ensuring a timely harvest at an affordable price. During the 1960s, custom cutters also developed a distinctive way of life for both cutters and farmers in the Great Plains, where technology and crops linked people and created lasting friendships. As a result, a new social and economic culture in plains agriculture emerged that remained part of farm life in the region for the remainder of the twentieth century.[9]

The relatively level fields in the Great Plains enabled the adoption of large machinery. Although expensive, over time it saved labor costs if commodity prices, particularly wheat, remained profitable. Often, however, large capital investments for technology and relatively low wheat prices placed farmers in financial jeopardy. In 1946, South Dakota farmers needed 836 bushels of wheat to purchase a tractor. In 1960, falling prices and increasing costs meant that they needed 1,748 bushels to purchase a comparable implement (although they usually made these purchases on credit, which meant that interest rates increased the cost of acquiring a tractor even more). Similarly, 1,513 bushels of wheat were required to purchase a combine in 1946 but 3,829 bushels in 1960. For the remainder of the twentieth century, farmers battled the cost-price squeeze, and many necessarily left agriculture for better-paying jobs in the towns and cities.[10]

In the Dakotas, especially, farm size often became the "critical factor" that determined success or failure, and livestock production increased while grain production declined. Farm consolidation resulted from increased labor shortages due to the lure of higher-paying jobs with better working conditions in the towns and cities or beyond the region. Farmers adjusted by purchasing more tractors, which enabled them to plow, plant, and harvest more land to increase production and decrease unit costs. Essentially, they substituted capital for labor and increased the economy of scale. Large-scale farmers also profited most from government programs that paid them for reducing production and practicing certain conservation measures. They could take advantage of government policies, tax breaks, and credit sources that favored them disproportionally compared to small-scale farmers. In addition, the work of the agricultural experiment stations favored the large-scale, capital-intensive farmers who could afford labor-saving technologies such as fertilizers, herbicides, and pesticides that freed them, in part, from the vagaries of the weather. Government programs protected them from price fluctuations. Large-scale, capital-intensive agriculture encouraged one-crop specialization, but it increased the risk of farming in the Great Plains.[11]

Farm consolidation did not occur uniformly or with equal consequence across the Great Plains, although it marked the general trend. The availability of labor, mechanization, irrigation, fertilizer, and capital played different roles, and not all farmers had equal access to them. Moreover, the climate of the Great Plains fluctuated, often violently, and made farming, even under the best of circumstances, a matter of risk and hope. More than one Great Plains farmer ruined his health over the years by worrying about oncoming storms before the wheat crop had ripened or the custom cutters arrived.

In the forty years following 1935, the number of farms in Kansas, Nebraska, North and South Dakota, and Colorado declined from more than 600,000 to fewer than 300,000. Many farms that remained across the Great Plains did not generate sufficient income to provide an adequate standard of living. As a result, farm families moved away, and the number of farms decreased rapidly, with loss rates varying between 38 percent and 59 percent in the ten plains states. Great Plains farmers were then operating on the premise of "get bigger or get out." As a result, the average farm size in the Great Plains increased from 454 acres in 1930 to 1,138 acres in the early 1980s. The farm population also declined. In South Dakota, it fell from 254,000 in 1940 to 213,000 in the mid-1960s, when only 30 percent of its people lived on farms. At that time, about 14 percent of the state's young adults, many reared on farms, left the state. In 1970, the farm population constituted only 25 percent of the state's population, with approximately half of that total living in towns with more than 2,500 people. Between 1950 and 1960, 59 percent of the towns in South Dakota also lost population.[12]

Farm consolidations along with depopulation across the Great Plains caused major economic problems for small-town merchants and brought increasing fears that large-scale corporations would soon own much of the farmland, to the detriment of the small-scale family farm. In 1982, the Nebraska legislature responded by warning large-scale corporations to keep out of the Cornhusker State and by passing Initiative 300, which amended the state constitution to permit only family farms to incorporate, to protect family assets from total loss if bankruptcy occurred. By the mid-1990s, a dozen Kansas counties had prohibited corporate farming, and South Dakota had prevented National Farms from establishing a large-scale, corporate livestock operation in the state. Great Plains farmers feared the loss of their farms to giant, international corporations, such as Tenneco, DuPont, and Standard Oil.

During the late twentieth century, many Great Plains farmers and politicians did not trust the U.S. Department of Agriculture, which they believed had been staffed, in the words of South Dakota congressman Jim Abourezk, by "retreads from the Benson era or recent recruits from the corporate board room." South Dakota senator George McGovern believed that Secretary of Agriculture Earl Butz was "thoroughly committed to the gentlemen farmers in agribusiness, who couldn't tell a chicken coop from a chain store." Oklahoma senator Fred Harris joined the criticism: "The government has continually sided with the giant agribusinesses, turning its back on the little man." For them and many of their constituents, the giant nonfarm corporations seemed poised to take over the family farm. Moreover, with Nebraska alone losing more than 73,000 people during the 1960s, the danger seemed clear. One North Dakota farm couple, echoing the fears of Thomas Jefferson nearly two centuries earlier, argued that farmers who lived on the land were the foundation of morality and democratic government. They believed that the corporations were "driving contented folks off the land to the already congested, crime-laden city life." For them, this was "not the way the Good Lord intended it to be." In reality, little corporate farming existed other than family farms that incorporated for tax purposes and to gain protection from bankruptcy. Moreover, most farm consolidations occurred from farms being purchased by other farmers, not by large, multinational corporations. Even so, the fear of corporate takeover remained strong throughout the late twentieth century.[13]

Serious financial and economic problems continued to plague Great Plains farmers. During the mid-1980s, low commodity prices, high interest rates, and declining land values combined to force an unprecedented failure of farms and flight from the land. Many farmers had used the prosperity of the 1970s to purchase more land and equipment, often at high interest rates. When the agricultural economy collapsed in the 1980s, they could not meet their financial obligations. Often these farmers had irresolvable debt-to-assets ratios, and bankruptcies and foreclosures became common. With 23 percent and 39 percent of all farmers in Texas and North Dakota, respectively, for example, having debt-to-assets ratios exceeding 40 percent (a ratio that agricultural experts considered difficult to manage) and with 33 percent of all Texas farmers and 24 percent of all North Dakota farmers spending more than they earned, these highly capitalized, mostly young farmers who rented their land confronted failure. As a result, more farm men and women sought off-the-farm employment to make ends meet.[14]

The work of women remained vital to the success of any Great Plains farm. In the early 1980s, North Dakota farm women worked more than twenty hours per week on farm tasks alone, except during the winter. At the same time, they also worked an average of forty hours per week on household tasks year-round. Women farmers across the Great Plains experienced a similar workload, although women on livestock farms worked more hours on farm tasks than did women on non-livestock farms (with the latter spending more time on household chores). At the same time, because of farm needs, less than one-third of these women held off-farm jobs, and most agricultural women did not receive a farm wage. Yet they conducted more than half of the farm tasks and provided at least one-third of the required farm labor, while their husbands contributed only about 20 percent of the household labor.[15]

Even with these problems, the cooperative movement remained strong, particularly for grain and petroleum associations. These cooperatives were the most influential and successful where the Farmers Union was strongest, as in North Dakota. Supermarkets and discount stores in the major towns and cities, however, had essentially displaced merchandise and grocery cooperatives for farmers. Population decreases continued to hurt the tax base and the maintenance of schools, churches, community services, and local merchants. Only the county seats or small cities with at least ten thousand people were able to provide adequate services to the farm community. With a rule of thumb that the loss of every seven farm families meant the loss of one business, by the 1980s many main streets had become a "disaster" across the Great Plains. Fewer people meant increased individual costs for services such as road maintenance.[16]

By the last quarter of the twentieth century, rising land and machinery prices and off-the-farm employment had slowed farm consolidation for agricultural expansion. Great Plains farmers had become highly capitalized, mechanized, and increasingly specialized. For the most part, they had achieved their desired efficiencies and economies of scale. Thereafter, further consolidation and expansion enabled only relatively small-scale improvements and efficiencies. By 1980, nearly a half century of rapid technological change, farm consolidation, and the loss of agricultural and rural population had made the Great Plains emptier than it had been only a few years before.[17]

By the mid-1940s, environmental control had come to mean more than slowing the wind, controlling the movement of the soil, and providing irrigation to permit bountiful harvests in a dry land. It also mandated taming the rivers, particularly the Missouri, which occasionally raged out of its banks, took lives, and swept away homes, crops, livestock, and millions of tons of topsoil. Record-setting floods during the spring of 1943, which inundated 1.8 million acres of bottomland and caused more than $47.3 million in property damages, primarily in the city of Omaha, caused residents of the drainage basin to demand federal aid for flood control. In May 1943, Congress responded by ordering the U.S. Army Corps of Engineers to prepare a flood-control plan. Colonel Lewis A. Pick, head of the Missouri River Division of the U.S. Army Corps of Engineers in Omaha, directed the study team that quickly reported the need to build storage reservoirs for flood control and gain the additional benefits of hydroelectric power, irrigation, recreation, and improved navigation.

The people in the northern and southern Great Plains, however, had different ideas about the purposes of dam building on the Missouri River and its tributaries. Senator Gerald P. Nye of North Dakota clearly identified the problem: "In the south end of the valley you have one problem and in the north end we have another. Some want control of these waters, some want access to these waters." In Montana, North Dakota, South Dakota, and Wyoming, farmers, ranchers, businesspeople, and politicians wanted dams for irrigation and hydroelectric power. In the lower Missouri River basin states of Nebraska and Kansas, the public wanted dams that would prevent urban flooding, improve navigation for barges, and provide cheap electric power. The lower-basin residents, particularly, believed that dams for irrigation in the north would deprive them of sufficient water to improve the river's navigation channel, while residents in the northern basin feared that those to the south would take their water for navigation.[18]

To gain control of the Missouri and prevent flooding while improving navigation, the Pick Plan advocated building five multipurpose dams on the river and eighteen dams on its tributaries, as well as a host of levees along 1,500 miles of the river and smaller streams, including the Yellowstone and Big Horn rivers in Montana. This staircase of dams would control flooding and enable adequate water flow for navigation downstream from Sioux City, Iowa. The corps confidently believed that technology and engineering could control the Missouri River. The major dams would be Garrison in North Dakota and Oahe, Big Bend, Fort Randall, and Gavin's Point in South Dakota. These dams, however, would not provide much irrigation or hydroelectric power. When major flooding again occurred in 1944, causing an estimated $100 million in damages, the necessity for a major flood-control plan seemed obvious to many Great Plains residents.[19]

The people of Wyoming, Montana, South Dakota, and North Dakota, however, protested that such a plan would deprive them of water for irrigation and that it would only benefit the residents of the lower Missouri River valley; they gained the support of the Bureau of Reclamation, the federal government's primary water development agency, which had its own interests to protect, as the federal agency responsible for the development of irrigation. In May 1944, the bureau submitted its plan to control the Missouri River. This plan, prepared by William Glenn Sloan (assistant regional director of the bureau in Billings, Montana), called for the construction of dams and reservoirs on the tributaries of the upper Missouri River, primarily for irrigation and electric power. These projects also would provide employment for returning veterans and displaced war industry workers.[20]

The Sloan Plan advocated the construction of the Oahe, Big Bend, and Fort Randall dams. Oahe and Fort Randall would provide irrigation for North and South Dakota, while Big Bend would generate electricity. The Sloan Plan did not provide for the other dams of the Pick Plan, and it kept much of the water in the northern basin. Sloan called the bureau's plan for the Missouri River basin "a solution of postwar problems which is more concrete, definite and practical than any plan heretofore proposed." He believed that the bureau's plan would create 53,000 new farms by opening dry, unproductive lands to irrigation and would support the creation of 13,000 new businesses in the upper basin. The rural population would increase by an estimated 212,000 and the basinwide population by 636,000.[21]

Not all residents of the northern Great Plains welcomed the Pick or Sloan Plan; they preferred the creation of a Missouri Valley Authority (MVA) modeled after the Tennessee Valley Authority (which Congress had created in 1933). Many residents of North Dakota and Montana supported the idea because they believed it would increase their access to electric power, boost regional economic development, and provide opportunities for irrigated agriculture. They also believed that an MVA would prevent people in the central plains of Nebraska and Kansas from dominating the river with flood-control projects and demanding large river flows to guarantee navigation on the Missouri, all of which would drain water away from the northern plains. Democratic senator James Murray of Montana and North Dakota's congressional delegation, including Republican senator William Langer, led the fight for a Missouri Valley Authority. The plan for an MVA further divided northern and southern Great Plains residents over water control as well as whether the federal government could manage the Missouri River for the benefit of the public good or whether such power would lead to unwanted federal intrusion in state affairs. North Dakotans particularly believed that an MVA would provide low-cost electric power needed to lure industry into the region. Without it, economic development and expansion would not occur and the region's economy would remain agriculturally based, with the wealth of the northern plains extracted by others in a colonial economy. In 1944, when President Roosevelt proposed an MVA, one administration official believed that it would be "the greatest thing for the region since Lincoln signed the Homestead Act."[22]

A Missouri Valley Authority, however, threatened the Bureau of Reclamation and the U.S. Army Corps of Engineers, both of which would be excluded from control of the river by the new agency. As a result, the bureau and the corps agreed to cooperate and accepted all proposed flood-control dams, irrigation projects, and navigation plans that had previously divided them. The bureau and corps also agreed on "spheres of influence," with the corps taking responsibility for the construction of dams on the river and its major tributaries and the bureau assuming control of all projects on the smaller, upstream tributaries of the Missouri. Congress merged the two plans and combined the essential features of both proposals in a compromise known as the Pick-Sloan Plan in the Flood Control Act of 1944. This plan called for the construction of four major dams in South Dakota—Oahe, Big Bend, Fort Randall, and Gavin's Point—and Garrison in North Dakota. In addition, an enlarged reservoir behind the Fort Peck Dam, an existing main-stem dam in Montana, would increase the storage capacity on the Missouri River to 77 million acre-feet. In all, Congress approved the construction of 107 dams on the Missouri and its tributaries for the primary purposes of irrigation in the upper basin and flood control in the lower basin. Both agencies could use their dams to generate hydroelectric power. The Pick-Sloan Plan became officially known as the Missouri River Basin Development Program.[23]

The National Farmers Union, however, opposed the Pick-Sloan Plan, favoring the MVA and calling the compromise between the two agencies "a shameless, loveless, shotgun wedding," in part because Garrison Dam would flood fifty thousand acres of irrigable land in North Dakota. Montana's Senator Murray similarly believed the Pick-Sloan Plan nothing more than a marriage of convenience to kill the MVA and protect the interests of two powerful federal agencies. In 1945, Murray introduced an MVA bill that would make it the only agency designated to manage the Missouri River. The MVA would be responsible for flood control, irrigation, and navigation as well as "the prudent husbandry of soil, mineral, and forest resources." In addition, the MVA would have the power of eminent domain to secure the best dam sites for irrigation reservoirs. Murray particularly wanted the MVA "to encourage the widest possible use of available electric energy" and "to prevent the monopolization thereof by limited groups or localities." Murray and the North Dakota congressional delegation also intended the MVA to generate and distribute electric power "to states, counties, municipalities, corporations, partnerships, and individuals."

As late as 1950, North Dakota ranked last in the nation for farmers with electricity, which meant that many residents did not have telephones, indoor plumbing, hot water heaters, and electric stoves. The Rural Electrification Administration, created in 1935, had not yet been able to provide electric power to most residents of the northern plains, because few farmers had organized the required cooperatives to run power lines and construct generating plants or buy electricity from private companies. One North Dakota farmer wrote to Senator Langer in support of the MVA, saying that "every farmer is entitled to lights and power on his farm" to lighten chores with electric equipment, brighten the darkness, and improve the standard of living. Murray agreed that "the people of the Missouri Valley have come to realize that industrial development, with its rich and more diversified economy and higher standard of living is possible only to the extent that we increase our electric energy resources."

Although the states legally claimed and distributed water within their boundaries, residents of the northern plains believed that an MVA would protect their interests and prevent federal encroachment on state water rights instead of privileging downstream navigation below Sioux Falls, South Dakota, and Sioux City, Iowa. Northern plains farmers wanted navigation extended the entire length of the Missouri River to enable cheap access to markets for their wheat and to free them from dependence on the railroads. An MVA, they contended, would work for all residents of the plains. At the same time, other northern plains residents wanted the dam building to begin even though the reservoirs might soon become filled with silt or fail to contain enough water to permit irrigation of farmland, because the economy would be boosted by a host of construction jobs and services. Opponents of the MVA, such as members of the North Dakota Reclamation Association, however, feared creeping socialism. "When" (in the words of its president, Roy Young) "we give them the right to control the waters, the soil, the forests, and mineral deposits, we practically give them all we have for that takes in everything above and below the ground." Others considered MVA supporters "Moscow sympathizers."[24]

In the end, states rights advocates, the electric power companies, and railroads, as well as the Bureau of Reclamation and U.S. Army Corps of Engineers, defeated the MVA. They were joined by the North Dakota Stockman's Association, whose members believed that an MVA would terminate their water rights. By the mid-1950s, the REA had begun to provide electric power on an affordable and equitable basis to nearly everyone who wanted it across North Dakota, or else the private power companies provided it to protect their market area from REA encroachment. The generators of the Garrison Dam also sent electricity across the state. Because the greatest attraction of an MVA had been to provide electric power, such an agency was no longer needed.[25]

Still, problems remained. Along the upper Missouri River and its tributaries, residents wanted flood control and irrigation but not large-scale dams that would inundate valuable, productive farmland. In 1949, many northern basin residents became particularly unhappy when they learned that 151 reservoirs had been proposed that would cover 2.5 million acres and displace four farm families for each 1,000 acres taken. The loss to local economies and tax bases seemed catastrophic. Bureau officials, however, contended, "Some land and improvements in river bottoms will be flooded, but, with few exceptions, reservoirs will cover lands of little or no agricultural value." For the bureau, the loss of farmland would be "insignificant compared with the area to be benefited." Farm tenants were the ones who experienced the most hardship as a result of the Pick-Sloan Plan. In 1945, tenants constituted 65 percent of the Missouri Basin farm families. In North Dakota, dam building threatened to displace 40–78 percent and in South Dakota 45–94 percent of the tenants in the construction areas. In the lower basin, farmers tended to own the land acquired for dam and reservation sites and did not face the eviction problems that would be inflicted on tenant farmers to the north.[26]

Other negative consequences soon became apparent. The decision to acquire dam and reservoir sites on Indian lands arose from financial factors, not technical reasons to control the river. The government did not want to purchase expensive agricultural land or urban real estate, but the acquisition of tribal lands seemed cost-effective. Government officials considered Indian lands "underutilized," "low quality," and "useless," that is, cheap. Furthermore, the cost of moving a relatively few Indians from dam and reservoir sites was considerably less than costs that would be incurred from moving urban populations, buildings, and railroads, among other expenses.[27]

The Indians whose lands would be affected by the dams and reservoirs were not included in the planning stages, hearings, and public forums that led to the Pick-Sloan Plan. Although Indian lands and towns in the northern basin would be covered with impounded water, the planners did not change any dam sites to accommodate the Indians, and the corps often began building on Indian lands before acquiring the property. Indian lands made the Pick-Sloan Plan affordable, which helped ensure federal funding for the dams. The residents in the northern basin would have irrigation and electric power and the people in the southern basin would have flood control and improved navigation, while the Indians lost considerable reservation lands from the impoundment of water. Moreover, the communities of Lower Brulé, Cheyenne River, and Crow Creek in South Dakota and Cannonball in North Dakota, required relocation. The Indians lacked the political, financial, and legal power to prevent the loss of their lands to the Pick-Sloan dams. Whites who had these powers gained the benefits, particularly electric power in the northern basin. A weak Bureau of Indian Affairs could not protect the Indians from the powerful corps.[28]

Although the Pick-Sloan Plan became a monumental project to control nature on the Great Plains, it also damaged the environment in the process and caused great social disruption for the Native Americans living along the banks of the Missouri. There, the five main dams — Garrison in North Dakota and Oahe, Big Bend, Fort Randall, and Gavin's Point in South Dakota — covered more than 550 square miles of rich agricultural land that belonged to the Sioux reservations of Standing Rock, Cheyenne River, Yankton, Crow Creek, and Lower Brulé in South Dakota and the Fort Berthold reservation in North Dakota, which belonged to the Mandans, Arikaras, and Hidatsas. The smaller dams on the tributaries built by the Bureau of Reclamation affected other tribal groups in Montana, Wyoming, and North Dakota and deprived the Indians of valuable cropland and grazing lands as well as woodlands for fuel and lumber. The livestock raisers at the Standing Rock, Cheyenne River, and Lower Brulé reservations were particularly hard hit by the loss of grazing lands.[29]

In 1952, the social and environmental dislocation of the Indians in the project areas along the Missouri, however, was inconsequential to whites, who renewed their demands for greater flood control after the Missouri River again swept through towns in the upper and lower basin. Bismarck, Pierre, and other urban areas received major flood damage. Although no loss of life occurred, when the floodwater receded, officials estimated the damage at $179 million. Lingering opposition to the Pick-Sloan Plan went downstream with the debris. Few people questioned whether the Missouri could be controlled; they only asked whether the Corps of Engineers had done enough to restrain nature. The corps responded by contending that if its flood-control plan for the Missouri River basin had been completely authorized, it "would have controlled the floods." In Kansas, Senator Frank Carlson agreed, and he advocated greater efforts to control the floodwaters of the Missouri River basin, saying, "Let's get the job done, but fast." A year earlier, after the floodwater from Tuttle Creek receded in Manhattan, Kansas, the city manager had told a reporter, "We wouldn't have the heart to begin the tremendous job of rehabilitation without assurance these disasters will not recur." When the rivers of the Great Plains raged out of their banks, local residents, particularly those who lived in the cities and towns in the floodplain, demanded that government bring nature under control. Congress quickly provided additional funding for the construction of Gavin's Point and Oahe dams and for the completion of Fort Randall.[30]

In September 1966, with the completion of the last major project, the Big Bend Dam in South Dakota, flood control and navigation had measurably improved along the river, but the desire to control the environment by harnessing the Missouri River was not an unmitigated good. The dams altered the ecology in the project areas by destroying timber, wildlife habitat, and agricultural lands, while they disrupted the lives of more than ten thousand Native Americans. The projects, particularly plans for expanding irrigation into the James River valley from Oahe, created considerable opposition and animosity that remained divisive for the remainder of the century. Moreover, during the summer of 1993, the Missouri River proved, once again, how difficult, if not impossible, it is to control. By that time, many of the dams also had begun to fill with silt, irrigation remained impractical for many areas, and the ecology of the Missouri River had been irreparably altered.[31]

The Indian tribes along the Missouri River in the northern Great Plains also had not received an equal share of the benefits of the Pick-Sloan Plan for flood control, irrigation, or electricity. The Sioux on the Yankton, Lower Brulé, Crow Creek, Cheyenne River, Standing Rock, and Fort Berthold reservations in North and South Dakota lost approximately 353,313 acres to the Pick-Sloan Plan. At least 3,538 Indians suffered forced removal from these lands, while another 6,900 Sioux had their lives permanently disrupted. Tribal economies, cultures, and government services could not escape the changes that came with the Pick-Sloan dams and the impoundment of water in the reservoirs.[32]

The idea that the environment of the Great Plains could be controlled also meant using one element of nature (water) to counter another (drought). Following the Dust Bowl years of the 1930s, farmers in the southern and central Great Plains turned to irrigation from groundwater supplied by the seemingly limitless Ogallala Aquifer. Aided by improved technology in the form of powerful turbine pumps, moveable sprinklers, and cheap power from electricity and natural gas, farmers began relying on the Ogallala Aquifer to provide supplementary water when normal precipitation failed. As irrigation costs became cheaper, they increased their irrigation beyond supplementary practices to change cropping patterns in dramatic ways by raising corn, sugar beets, and alfalfa where those crops could not be grown without heavy applications of underground water. Livestock production also increased once feed crops could be guaranteed with irrigation.[33]

The drought of the 1930s convinced many farmers that irrigation would stabilize, if not increase, crop production because it would give them some control of the environment, particularly during dry years. In southwestern Kansas, farmers invested heavily in irrigation technology for crop insurance because the shallow distance to the water table of the Ogallala Aquifer made drilling and pumping costs manageable. In the mid-1930s, farmers with pumping plants produced a nearly normal harvest while dryland crops failed. Where irrigation stabilized agricultural production, certain crops increased in value. Irrigated potatoes in Scott County produced 400 to 500 bushels per acre. With corn selling at $1.00 per bushel, and with irrigated corn producing 90 bushels per acre, many farmers began intensive cultivation on irrigated tracts ranging from 40 to 160 acres. Near Garden City, hay climbed to $20 a ton, with great demand by livestock raisers in the drought-stricken regions of the state. In 1940, some farmers believed that irrigation meant the difference between crop failure and a profitable year. One farmer claimed that the $100 to $200 per acre incurred in irrigation expenses was more than offset by the rise in land values—the increase often jumping from a low of $30 per acre to $280 per acre. Irrigation became a stabilizing factor not only for the farm but also for the general economy in southwestern Kansas.

Irrigation with groundwater from the Ogallala Aquifer proved attractive because it was more reliable than irrigating from a stream, it was not subject to weather fluctuations, and it provided limitless water during drought. As a result, irrigation farmers believed that with irrigation they could become independent of the weather so that drought would no longer pose the hazard of the past—at least as long as pumping rates (that is, the drawdown) did not greatly exceed the annual recharge. Few farmers were concerned with the depletion of the groundwater supply.[34]

During the late 1930s, then, Great Plains farmers increasingly turned to irrigation to control the environment, because irrigation could ensure profitable harvests during drought years. In the parlance of the region, irrigation provided "rain when you want it." New irrigation systems became more convenient with improved pumps, (usually powered by electricity or natural gas), aluminum gated pipes, and a host of sprinkler systems, especially center-pivot sprinklers during the 1960s. Soon irrigation permitted cotton and corn to grow where only dryland crops, such as winter wheat, had grown before, thereby changing the agricultural landscape while creating a problem of water mining and the rapid depletion of the Ogallala Aquifer.[35]

The Ogallala Aquifer underlies approximately 174,000 square miles spread across eight Great Plains states. It primarily is composed of unconsolidated clay, silt, sand, and gravel that worked down from the Rocky

Mountains about ten million years ago. The Ogallala feeds the Platte, Republican, Niobrara, Smoky Hill, Arkansas, and Canadian rivers. In the late twentieth century, the Ogallala contained an estimated 3.25 billion acre-feet of water. (One acre-foot covers one acre of land with one level foot of water.) This is the amount of useable water that can be pumped from an estimated 21.8 billion acre-feet in the aquifer. About 65 percent of the Ogallala underlies Nebraska, while Texas has access to 12 percent, Kansas 10 percent, Colorado 4 percent, Oklahoma 3.5 percent, and New Mexico, South Dakota, and Wyoming less than 2 percent each of the Ogallala. Approximately 87 percent of the Ogallala, then, is concentrated in Nebraska, Kansas, and Texas. The saturated area from which water can be pumped for irrigation averages about 200 feet thick, but in some areas of Nebraska the saturated area is more than 1,000 feet thick. The Ogallala's recharge rate is minimal, ranging from six inches annually in the Nebraska Sand Hills to about a quarter of an inch in Kansas and Texas. Recharge is minimal because the water is restored to the aquifer from precipitation, seepage from streams, and inflow from surrounding areas. The recharge also is slowed by high summer temperatures, low humidity, and persistent winds, and it depends on vegetative cover, land slope, soil permeability, and season rainfall. Because irrigation is heaviest in the area that receives only sixteen to eighteen inches of precipitation annually, water mining became a serious problem.[36]

By the early 1950s, high agricultural prices resulting from government policy and the Korean War had enabled Great Plains farmers to pay off mortgages, buy more land, and purchase new and additional farm equipment. In the southern plains, particularly in West Texas and southwestern Kansas, farmers began large-scale investments in irrigation technology. During the 1950s, drought and dust storms further encouraged them to drill wells, level land, and dig irrigation ditches and furrows as well as to lay gated pipe and set sprinklers. They believed that irrigation would solve the problem of drought by tapping the underground water supply.

As government restrictions continued to limit the production of wheat and cotton, southern plains farmers raised more grain sorghum for livestock feed, often with the aid of irrigation, chemical fertilizers, and tractors and combines. Irrigation also increased land values, which gave farmers more collateral for bank loans to cover operating costs and the acquisition of more land until harvest time. Farmland valued at $30 per acre in 1935 brought $300 per acre or more in the early 1950s. In West Texas counties where farmers made substantial investments in irrigation, populations stabilized or increased, while dryland counties lost residents.

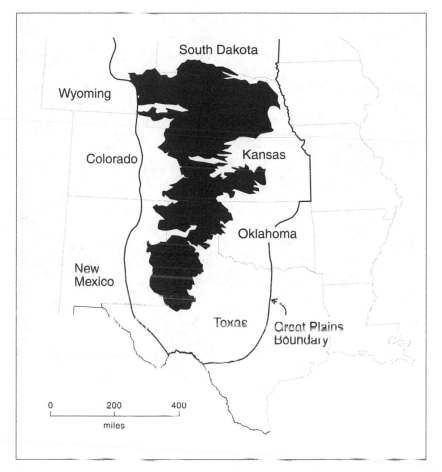

The Ogallala Aquifer lies beneath the central and southern Great Plains. It provides water for irrigation and industry, particularly cattle feeding and meatpacking, and it has changed the nature of agriculture in the region. Corn and alfalfa now grow where those crops could not be raised without irrigation. With the depletion of the Ogallala Aquifer, much of the region faced the return to dryland and less profitable agriculture.

Irrigation, or the lack of it, then, had economic and social consequences. By 1960, irrigated cotton, wheat, and grain sorghum had increased farm income to approximately $74 million in the plains area south of Lubbock, while the multiplier effect brought an estimated $68 million annually to businesses engaged in agricultural marketing and an additional $63 million to the farm-supply businesses, such as implement and fertilizer dealers. Businesses not directly associated with agriculture, such as automobile

Large sprinklers that pivot from a center well and powerful pump have changed the landscape of the Great Plains in the region of the Ogallala Aquifer. These distinctive circular fields can cover nearly a square mile, making the region the "land of the underground rain."

dealerships and appliance, clothing, and shoe stores, garnered another $125 million annually, for a total economic gain of about $330 million, all based on irrigation agriculture. During the 1950s, then, irrigation provided the foundation for economic and population growth in the southern Great Plains, where powerful pumps lifted the water from the Ogallala Aquifer. By the early 1960s, irrigation had given many farmers an important environmental control because it mitigated crop losses due to drought and ensured good harvests and a reliable income. For these farmers, "walking water" (that is, center-pivot sprinkler irrigation) made the southern Great Plains the "land of the underground rain."[37]

Irrigated crops of grain sorghum, corn, and alfalfa helped farmers raise more stock cattle and entrepreneurs establish commercial packing industries on the southern Great Plains. During the 1960s, large-scale feedlots began appearing in the irrigated area of the southern Great Plains, particularly in West Texas and Kansas. Cattle raisers who had previously sold their feeder cattle to feedlots in the Corn Belt found closer markets in the plains. Fattened cattle also drew meatpacking companies, which took advantage of the proximity of irrigated grain and forage crops and a system for fattening cattle. With corn-fed cattle nearby, the meat packers could reduce shipping expenses for fattened cattle. In 1965, approximately 436,000 cattle were "fed out" in West Texas feedlots. In 1970, 73 feedlots, ranging in capacity from 5,000 to 70,000 head, fed 2.8 million cattle for slaughter in the packinghouses at Amarillo, Lubbock, and Plainview, while other packers operated in Clovis and Roswell, New Mexico, Guymon, Oklahoma, and Garden City, Kansas.[38]

Irrigation (especially the rapid expansion of groundwater irrigation based on the Ogallala Aquifer) had important and unforeseen consequences for the Great Plains above the Ogallala. In the central and southern plains, as dryland wheat acreage changed to corn, the great harvests for livestock feed that lured the feedlot owners to the region also changed the region's demography. The combination of irrigated crop production, feedlots, and meatpacking drew relatively cheap unskilled labor, mostly Mexican Americans or Latinos. Soon, Latino communities developed in the towns and cities near the packinghouses. The Spanish language and the Catholic Church gave new cultural dynamics to these plains towns, as well as a potential political force that found the Democratic Party more attractive than the Republicanism of the plains. School districts confronted new challenges: not only more children but also students whose culture required adjustment of curriculums and teaching methods. Meatpacking towns faced shortages of adequate housing, and barrios created a poor side of the proverbial tracks. Skin color, accents, and skills as well as a host of economic, social, and political needs changed many towns in the central and southern plains. In addition, the expansion of irrigation from the Ogallala Aquifer created a booming agricultural supply and service industry. Hastings, Nebraska, became a major distribution center for irrigation equipment, and it soon became known as "The City of Liquid Gold."[39]

The drought of the 1950s and the rapid increase in irrigation across the Kansas plains from 1950 to 1970 caused farmers and scientists to reconsider the dangers of substantial groundwater depletion. Not only were farmers digging deeper wells, with average depths of more than 300 feet in some areas, but they were also pumping more water than ever before. In northwestern Kansas, farmers used 100 wells to pump 15,000 acre-feet in 1950; in 1973, they used 2,250 wells to pump 500,000 acre-feet annually. Consequently, the water table dropped significantly in some parts of that area, and several wells reached 800 feet by 1958. During the decade following 1966, the annual average decline in the water table in northwestern Kansas was one foot; in 1976, it dropped two feet. To the south, the drop for those same time periods was two feet and three feet, respectively.[40]

In 1980, 170,000 wells pumped 18 million acre-feet to irrigate 14 million acres, but the irrigated acreage had declined because of the falling water table and the increased cost of pumping water to the surface, particularly from energy costs. Some famers in West Texas returned their irrigated lands to dryland farming to reduce their costs. Nebraska and Kansas farmers, however, continued to expand their irrigated acreage. With only 15 percent of the water available for extraction or able to be extracted, the future of irrigation from the Ogallala became doubtful. Moreover, many farmers began removing their hedgerows and windbreaks to accommodate center-pivot sprinklers, which portended wind-erosion problems if their wells went dry.[41]

By attempting to control the environment of the central and southern Great Plains for new agricultural purposes, irrigation farmers took a calculated risk that the water would last forever. During the 1980s, the hydrological evidence proved that they had been mistaken. With more than 20 million acre-feet pumped annually from beneath 15 million acres of land, water levels dipped more than 100 feet in some areas of Kansas, Oklahoma, New Mexico, and Texas, with 50-foot declines common area-wide. With the recharge rate almost nonexistent, water mining became a serious problem. Control of the Great Plains environment with irrigation from the Ogallala Aquifer clearly had become a temporary rather than a permanent measure, and the eventual return of the newly irrigated lands to dryland agriculture became a "grim reality."[42]

By the late 1980s, the problem of groundwater conservation had become more complex, because the Environmental Protection Agency (EPA) considered agriculture a major cause of water pollution from chemicals. In 1987, the EPA reported to Congress that groundwater pollution by farmers who used heavy applications of chemical fertilizers, pesticides, and herbicides created "a problem which defies traditional regulatory solutions to resource protection."[43]

Although the customary conservation practices of terracing, strip cropping, and contour plowing remained viable through the late twentieth century, economic motives continued to shape the way plains residents used the environment. With most plowed soils tilled for between 75 and nearly

150 years in the Great Plains using "bare tillage" (known as "clean cultivation"), the common practice on most fields, organic matter and organic nitrogen concentrations had declined significantly, often 25–60 percent for soils cultivated for 30 years or more. Moreover, bare tillage practices promoted soil erosion. By 1960, however, after a decade of experimenting with the herbicide 2,4-D, researchers had begun developing crop production systems that enabled farmers to partially or completely eliminate the tillage of their fields. By 1980, some experts had begun to advise farmers on the Great Plains to practice "ecofarming," that is, adopt a crop rotation system that used herbicides and subsurface tillage to control the weeds and conserve subsoil moisture.[44]

At the same time, nonfarm residents on the Great Plains increasingly shaped their environmental concepts based on perceived needs that superseded economic concerns. They became concerned about the safety of drinking water and the preservation of wetlands and wildlife habitat. By the late twentieth century, environmental quality had become an important and highly visible public issue not only for urban areas but also for rural areas, and farmers in the Great Plains became more conscious of matters of environmental protection and preservation than ever before. And in 1986, the Nebraska legislature passed legislation that provided jail terms and fines for farmers who violated mandatory "best management practices" in special protection areas to safeguard drinking water for rural residents from pollution by agricultural chemicals. Given legislation such as this, many Great Plains farmers were surprised to learn that the public considered them partially responsible for environmental damage, and agricultural experts realized that they no longer controlled the environmental agenda (even though they did not know precisely who did marshal the environmental policy debates). Agricultural environmental policy, particularly for water quality, was no longer merely a farm problem or the provenance of farmers. Rather, it had become a national sociopolitical issue, reinforced by the rapid population growth along the Front Range of the Rocky Mountains. Ultimately, with voters controlling the environmental agenda, farmers (fewer in number than town and city dwellers) confronted policy issues over which they had no control. By the late 1980s, "voluntary" environmental protection practices for farmers had come to mean "optional," but optional really meant "or else," because if a sufficient voluntary adoption of appropriate farming practices did not occur, farmers confronted the real possibility of government regulations and mandates. As a result, during the late twentieth century, so far as the environment of the Great Plains was concerned, the public no longer considered agriculture "special" but rather thought it suspect at best, and the public often considered farmers to be the major environmental polluters in the countryside.[45]

Throughout the late twentieth century, the concept of environmental preservation continued to cause debate, because it mixed economics, science, politics, and philosophy and because it involved individual liberty and social responsibility and the idea that "nature has rights that humans should respect as part of an extended code of ethics." Some environmentalists even argued that "natural rights should extend to and encompass the rights of nature," in a recognition of the fact that, historically, residents of the region have exploited the land, often unmercifully. Moreover, in the late twentieth century, conservation and environmental concerns were not synonymous. Minimum tillage practices helped conserve soil moisture and prevent wind and water erosion, but this agricultural practice required heavy applications of herbicides that often polluted groundwater. When the century ended, policy makers had not yet determined how to mesh conservation practices with environmental protection.[46]

Despite potential problems, irrigation from the Ogallala Aquifer increased production of corn, cotton, wheat, and sorghum, expanded agribusiness, and improved the region's economy. Still, the problems of water mining remained at the end of the century, particularly for those farmers who considered irrigation from the Ogallala to be indispensible. By the late twentieth century, the ability of irrigation to sustain agricultural productivity through intensified farming practices also had come to depend on urban demands for water and the ability of farmers to adapt their use of water to availability as a result of increased urban demands. At the turn of the twenty-first century, the issues of water pollution, usage, and control portended economic and political difficulties that had social ramifications far beyond those confronted in the past.[47]

CHAPTER SEVEN

The Inevitability of Change

A persistent, unmistakable decline in the rural population occurred in the Great Plains following World War II. Between 1950 and 1990, 45 of 105 counties in Kansas lost population. During the 1970s, South Dakota's population decreased in 43 counties; a decade later, North Dakota's population dropped in 38 counties; Nebraska experienced a population loss in 50 counties; and 22 counties in Oklahoma also declined in population. The Texas Panhandle likewise lost population. Increased agricultural mechanization after the war meant that farmers needed fewer workers. As many farms consolidated, families moved away. The rural counties across the Great Plains had few attractions for retirees, and the senior population essentially aged in place as young people left for better opportunities outside the region. Only the growing Hispanic population proved the exception to the rule.

Chain migration to metropolitan areas, such as Lubbock, Abilene, and Amarillo, also contributed to the decline of rural towns and counties, which experienced business closures and school consolidations. Local identity, particularly based on the school, began to disappear. The rural counties tended to have populations that were not only older but also poorer, less educated, and with fewer gainfully employed; these counties suffered greater population loss than did nonmetropolitan counties. Employment usually involved low-paying, unskilled jobs related to agriculture. The more education the children received, the more likely they were to leave their rural counties for employment beyond the Great Plains. Yet their departure served as evidence of their parents' success in providing for their education. But then, this has been an age-old story since settlement, and it became a truism of the region that parents who educated their children would lose them.[1]

The long-term population decline in the Great Plains resulted from a host of economic push and pull factors that included the inability of the land to provide an adequate living for the people. The carrying capacity of the land no longer supported or sustained the population that lived there, and as a result, people departed. This trend was particularly obvious among the young, who sought better educations that would enable them to acquire higher-paying jobs than were available in the Great Plains. Although this generalization reflects broad historical patterns of demographic change and movement, exceptions keep it from becoming an absolute rule. Between 1980 and 1990, for example, a study area of 184 counties in the Ogallala region showed that the population increased in western Kansas, eastern New Mexico, and the Texas Panhandle where irrigation from the Ogallala Aquifer expanded.

During that period, the population above the aquifer in Texas increased 10.4 percent, followed by a 6.6 percent gain in New Mexico and a 5.7 percent gain in Kansas. In Nebraska, however, the Ogallala area lost 3.8 percent of its population; in Oklahoma, 1 percent; and in Colorado, 11.9 percent. The major areas of population growth included the Platte River valley in Nebraska, southwestern Kansas, and the northern and western counties of the Texas Panhandle. The greatest population losses occurred in the Sand Hills and south-central portion of Nebraska, northwestern Kansas, eastern Colorado, and the eastern counties of the Texas Panhandle. Town populations often increased where irrigated agriculture and dryland farming gave continuous support to service-related businesses, such as cotton gins, feedlots, and meatpacking plants as well as feed, seed, fertilizer, herbicide, and pesticide distributors, along with agricultural machinery dealers. Overall, across the six-state Ogallala region, the population increased by 4.1 percent. Nonfarm employment contributed more to population growth than did irrigation in the comparatively depleted area of the Ogallala in Texas, Oklahoma, and New Mexico.[2]

Indeed, irrigation was not the primary reason for population growth in many areas. In fact, it ranked second to the attractiveness of the largest city in a county. A study of ninety-one western Kansas towns between 1960 and 1990 indicated that only places with fewer than 500 residents lost population, while towns with more than 1,000 inhabitants tended to gain residents. During that time, Dodge City, Garden City, and Liberal, Kansas, had a population increase of nearly 58 percent. The regional stereotype of economic decline, social marginality, and political irrelevance did not apply to these towns. In many respects, these and other towns like them, but particularly towns with a population ranging from 500 to 1,000, were Ogallala oases. These oases of population growth occurred on seemingly "empty lands" where only a few farm families tended irrigated and dryland crops. But in these small towns, irrigation from the Ogallala encouraged and supported a host of agricultural services that increased their populations. Consequently, a portion of the declining population in the open areas really involved only the shift of people from the countryside to the towns and cities.[3]

Moreover, by 1980, the dire predictions that the Ogallala Aquifer would soon dry up had not proven true. Some experts estimated that only 5 percent of the aquifer's 3.25 billion acre-feet of water had been used. At the same time, little expansion of irrigated acreage had occurred since the late 1970s, because of falling crop prices and the cost of irrigation technology. Federal agricultural programs also paid farmers to remove land from production, and farmers used less water for their remaining crops or returned irrigated lands to dryland farming. As a result, the Ogallala oases remained. These agricultural service towns gave little indication that they would economically collapse. During the 1990s, irrigated acreage even increased in some areas, although farmers tended to use irrigation to supplement rainfall rather than replace it. As a result, water use often declined in some areas even though irrigated acreage increased, depending on the weather and because the newer irrigation systems applied the water more efficiently.[4]

In the northeastern plains of Montana, the Dakotas, and Wyoming, the population increased to approximately 600,000, an increase of 26 percent, between 1970 and 2000, although more than half of the sixty-four counties in this region lost population. In the plains, west of the hundredth meridian, the population increased 28 percent to approximately 2.57 million during the same period. Here too, the urban areas accounted for most of the population gain while the rural areas and small towns with fewer than 10,000 residents often suffered a population decline. Yet the population change often meant redistribution rather than decline because of the multiplier effects of the agricultural economy based on groundwater irrigation that provided new employment opportunities in the agricultural service towns and cities.[5]

The redistribution of population in the Great Plains based on access to the Ogallala Aquifer can be seen in another fashion. Irrigated acreage can produce more than dryland acreage can. This increase required greater applications of fertilizers, pesticides, and herbicides; more energy to power the pumps; additional machinery such as tractors, trucks, and combines; expanded maintenance and repair services; and more cotton gins, warehouses, and livestock. All of these translated into an increased demand for labor by the creation of a host of jobs related to and dependent on irrigated agriculture. From the center-pivot kingdom in Nebraska to the cotton fields in the southern plains, water meant agricultural abundance and sufficient profits to provide an acceptable standard of living for farm families as well as to support a host of businesses and residents in the towns. Observers, however, believed that a population increase outside of the major towns and cities was unlikely.[6]

Certainly the Great Plains remained a sparsely populated region. In a 184-county study area of the Ogallala Aquifer, 131 (71 percent) of those counties had a population density of fewer than ten people per square mile by the late twentieth century. Moreover, the population of that entire area totaled only 2.2 million, which was less than the population of metropolitan St. Louis. Even so, in 1980, 60 percent of those inhabitants lived in urban areas. Only 16.4 percent resided in a town with fewer than 2,500 people, and only 23.8 percent lived in the country. Moreover, while the Great Plains remained sparsely populated, the towns were relatively isolated. Few were located within 50 miles of an interstate highway. People often lived 150 miles or more from a metropolitan area, although telephones, televisions, and computers provided linkages to the world beyond and helped mitigate their isolation. Even so, physical isolation, empty space, and few people remained a reality.[7]

Since the 1950s, the residents of the Great Plains also have been older than the national average. In 1950, more than half of the counties had a higher percentage of the population aged sixty-five or older than did the nation as a whole. In 2000, 84 percent of the counties fell in that category. In nearly 90 percent of the counties, there were more residents sixty-five years of age or older than residents in their twenties, and in one-third of the counties, the number of residents aged sixty-five and older exceeded the number of people in their twenties and thirties combined. Whereas 5 percent of the population was over seventy-five years of age in 1970, twenty years later 6.4 percent of the people were in that age group. The median age also had increased from 32.9 years in 1990 to 35.2 years by 1998. Ninety-seven of the ninety-nine counties in the nation with the highest percentage of residents aged eighty-five years or older were located in the region. Nine of the twenty-five poorest counties in the nation also were located in the Great Plains.[8]

The rural population of the Great Plains peaked between 1930 and 1940. Thereafter, agricultural change that involved mechanization and farm consolidation began the rural population decline that continued for the remainder of the twentieth century. Although the Great Plains states span 20 percent of the territory of the lower forty-eight states, 61 percent of the towns with fewer than 2,500 people in the Dakotas, Kansas, and Nebraska lost population during the 1990s, while 71 percent of the towns smaller than 250 people also experienced population declines. As the young left, an aging population remained. Although the population density for the Great Plains always had been low, averaging 8 people per square mile in 1930, by 2000 it had declined to 5 people per square mile, and 20 percent of the rural counties had population densities of fewer than 2 people per square mile, while two-thirds of the counties had fewer than 8 people per square mile. In 1990, Kansas had more land with fewer than 6 people per square mile than a century earlier, and much of the region had the same empty appearance. Substantive variations in population did occur, however. Wallace County (in the western part of the state) had a population density of 2 people per square mile, but Johnson County (on the eastern border near Kansas City) had a population density of 900 people per square mile, and nearby Wyandot County was 99 percent urban. Overall, though, fewer than half of the counties in the Great Plains had an urban population, that is, towns with more than 2,500 people. By 2000, the rural people of the Great Plains had become fewer, older, and more isolated than at any time since the Great Depression.[9]

During the same time period, the total population of the Great Plains increased nearly 12 percent, from 10.12 million to 11.33 million between 1990 and 2000, but most of that increase occurred in the region's 40 metropolitan counties, while 56 percent (281 of the 477 counties in the study area examined by the USDA's Economic Research Service) lost population. As a result, tax bases declined, businesses closed for want of customers, and schools consolidated. Mechanization eliminated the need for many farmers and agricultural workers, and paved highways led to urban areas or at least county-seat towns where a Wal-Mart and other businesses drew customers. People moved away and schools, stores, and churches closed. Doctors departed and hospitals shut down or greatly reduced services. Casey's markets replaced the grocery store, cafe, and gas station. Ministers often became the equivalent of nineteenth-century circuit riders serving several congregations across many miles. Where many towns once bustled during the week, including shopping on Saturday nights, closed and abandoned stores lined main streets. Television and automobiles along with the declining economy gave people little reason to make their customary weekly Saturday shopping trip to town.[10]

Another study of 293 Great Plains nonmetropolitan counties from 1950 to 1990 revealed a substantial population loss (except during the 1970s). During those decades, the counties that consistently lost population primarily depended on agriculture for employment. Between 1960 and 1970, 2.8 million people left these counties. During the 1970s, about 4 million moved into the nonmetro counties, a population increase of 5.2 percent. The nonmetropolitan counties that gained population, however, already had large populations, higher median incomes, and diverse economies, and they bordered metropolitan counties; in many respects, these nonmetropolitan counties were bedroom communities. During the 1980s, outmigration again increased, and nonmetro birth rates declined. In some rural counties, the number of deaths exceeded the birth rate. Approximately 84 percent of the nonmetropolitan counties lost population in the 1980s. During that time, a net out-migration of 344,523 persons occurred, for an average loss of 1,170 per county, which was mitigated by a natural population increase of 226,430 births. In all, 96 percent of the counties had greater out-migration than in-migration during the decade. As a result, tax bases and services declined.[11]

The migrants from the rural counties often relocated to the metropolitan areas on the eastern and western fringes of the Great Plains. A study area of 358 nonmetropolitan counties from the Kansas-Oklahoma line to the Canadian border showed a population of 8 million in 1990, a 4 percent gain over the 1980 population. The metropolitan counties had a population of 4.7 million (an 11 percent increase), while the nonmetropolitan counties declined to a population of 3.3 million (a loss of 4.8 percent). During the 1980s, agricultural employment in the nonmetropolitan counties declined from 8.3 percent to 6.6 percent of all employment. At the same time, employment in mining (coal in eastern Wyoming, oil and gas in Kansas, and gold in South Dakota) declined 31.5 percent and construction jobs dropped 20.17 percent in the nonmetropolitan counties, partly because of a collapse of the energy boom and the farm crisis during the 1980s. Manufacturing held stable and employed about twice as many people as agriculture because of the employment gains that came with the meatpacking industry.

A population increase in some counties came from expanded employment in transportation, communication, and public utilities, which collectively increased 9.5 percent. The finance, insurance, and real estate areas also experienced a 26.8 percent employment gain in the metropolitan areas. Sioux Falls developed as a major center for business credit employment, particularly regarding the issuing of credit cards. South Dakota lured this business by forgoing ceilings on interest rates and corporate income taxes, ensuring low hourly wage rates, advertising a favorable time zone, and hailing a workforce that could provide employees who spoke English clearly and accurately over the phone. Telemarketing businesses also increased, particularly in Omaha.[12]

During the 1990s, then, many of the nonmetropolitan counties in the Great Plains experienced population declines. In North Dakota, only six counties gained population (and four of them served as urban hubs), while 57 percent of Nebraska's nonmetropolitan counties lost population during the decade. Across the Great Plains, residents — usually the younger and better educated — left the region. Further population decline came from deaths, which caused one journalist to write in the late 1990s, "There is not a large demand for farm labor. So, people are leaving the Great Plains in one of two ways: They pack their bags and drive away or they die." Many others drifted to the towns and preferably to the cities in the region, such as Lubbock, Wichita, and Rapid City. As the working-age and work-ready people left the Great Plains, many who remained were too old, underskilled, or too uneducated to find employment, and this potential workforce did not attract employers or lead to new businesses. City officials across the region struggled to halt the economic decline and depopulation of the countryside. Yet the longer that residents lived in a community and the higher their income, the less likely they were to leave, while those in the age group from nineteen to forty proved the most likely to depart.[13]

Many Great Plains farmers and small-town residents chose to leave the rural plains for employment in the larger towns and cities. Encroaching urban development and escalating land prices, which meant higher property taxes, also encouraged them to go. The plains area below the Front Range in Colorado provides an example. The urban areas on the western fringe of the plains from Colorado Springs to Boulder experienced a rapid and large population increase, with a corresponding loss of nearby farmland in eastern Colorado.

After the late 1970s, however, the decline in agricultural land along the Front Range resulted from counties purchasing land for open-space programs and the development of a recreational horse market and "horse properties." Population decrease and the loss of agricultural land did not mean a decline in the economic "health" of this portion of the Great Plains. Indeed, during the late twentieth century, the rural population of eastern

Colorado was relatively stable, while the urban areas continued to increase in population. Moreover, although farm and ranch employment declined in rural eastern Colorado after 1950, jobs in the agricultural, retail, and financial services (businesses that moved to the larger communities from the smaller, rural towns) increased in the urban counties.

In addition, after 1950, corn production increased 1,000 percent, wheat 200 percent, and hay 100 percent in the plains of eastern Colorado. Seventy percent of the corn and hay production came from irrigated lands where improved plant varieties, more fertilizer, better tillage techniques, and the increased use of herbicides and pesticides contributed to greater production. As a result, while rangeland and cropland acreage declined because of urban sprawl, irrigated acreage expanded and crop production increased, which sustained farm incomes through most of the late twentieth century. As a result, agricultural employment declined the least in urban areas because of the increase in farm service jobs. The overall decline in farmland and the intensification of farming on the remaining agricultural lands indicated a persistence of successful agriculture that prevented a mass exodus from this subregion of the Great Plains.[14]

The paradox of population decrease in the open country of the Great Plains while the population of the cities and towns increased also can be seen in West Texas. In a fifty-six-county area from the Permian Basin in the South to the panhandle border to the north, only 8 percent of the state's population spread across 21.6 percent of the land. In the late 1970s, more than half of the region's 999,200 people called Lubbock, Amarillo, Midland, Odessa, and a few other cities their home. The remainder of the population lived sparsely scattered across the open countryside, giving the southern plains the appearance of being a big empty region. At the same time, because of irrigation from groundwater, the South Plains became the richest agricultural region in Texas, including eight of the top ten agricultural counties. During the 1970s, South Plains farmers produced 61 percent of the state's cotton, 50 percent of the grain sorghum, and 61 percent of the state's wheat, all based on irrigation from the Ogallala Aquifer, proving too that the region was not collapsing.[15]

Similarly, a study of family structure and socioeconomic viability in 281 Great Plains counties in the highly productive irrigated area overlying the Ogallala Aquifer indicated that the farm economy remained economically strong and socially stable. In the agriculturally based counties that experienced extensive population declines, those entities often had higher employment and income rates, lower poverty rates, and more married couples than counties that had become dependent on nonfarm industries and service-based employment. Although many farm communities experienced population declines during the last half of the twentieth century while communities that became dependent on manufacturing grew in population, farm men and women in the study area generally were married, their fertility rates were higher, and their unions were less likely to end in divorce than those among urban residents. Median annual family income averaged about $25,000 for both areas, and the employment of women averaged about 48 percent in these counties. Approximately 20 percent of the population lived in poverty in the service counties, while about 17 percent lived in poverty in the agricultural counties. Moreover, nearly 75 percent of adult males held employment in the agricultural counties compared to about 62 percent in the service-based counties. Overall, then, the agriculturally based counties adjusted better to population loss than did the counties that gained population, service industries, and manufacturing. The agricultural counties had similar average annual incomes compared to the manufacturing and service-based counties, as well as higher employment and lower poverty rates.[16]

Although the population of the Great Plains remained mobile, usually moving from rural to urban areas during the late twentieth century, the region also experienced a growing international refugee population. Refugees, of course, differ from immigrants because they are involuntary newcomers. Between July 1, 1983, and June 30, 2000, approximately 147,772 refugees settled in the Great Plains; this is about 9 percent of the refugees who settled in the United States during that period. Compared to the number of refugees who settled in California, Florida, and New York, this number is small, because refugees tend to settle in areas with large population bases that support refugee organizations. Texas attracted the most refugees of the Great Plains states, but those newcomers were not necessarily relocated to the plains area. Colorado ranked second and Kansas third, while Montana and Wyoming attracted the fewest refugees during that period. In terms of per capita population, the leading states for the relocation of refugees were North Dakota, South Dakota, and Nebraska, with Texas ranking fourth. More important demographically than the number of refugees who have relocated to the Great Plains was their country of origin: the refugees primarily came from Vietnam, the former USSR, and Yugoslavia.

The refugee mix in the Great Plains, however, is more complex than total numbers might suggest. Cubans, for example, constituted approximately 49 percent of the refugees in New Mexico, Pacific Rim refugees represented 85 percent of the refugees in Oklahoma, and Afghanis made up 23 percent of the refugees in Wyoming. Nearly all refugees who relocated to Nebraska lived in Lincoln (91 percent) or Omaha (9 percent). Lincoln, as the capital city, had the state agencies responsible for resettling the refugees, and a multiethnic enclave (without self-imposed ethnic divisions) developed for businesses, which resulted in an economic boost to the community.[17]

In 1990, Nebraska, Kansas, Colorado, and Texas marketed more than 70 percent of the 23 million cattle fattened in the thirteen major feedlot states. Kansas, Nebraska, and Texas also ranked first, second, and third, respectively, in the slaughter and packing of beef. In southwestern Kansas, the beef packing plants near Garden City, Liberal, and Dodge City formed the industry's "Golden Triangle," with the slaughter rate at more than 24,000 head per day, six days a week. There, Iowa Beef Processors and Monfort employed 4,200 workers. The Garden City–area packers drew on the cattle that fattened in more than one hundred feedlots, where 13,000 head in each lot fed on alfalfa, grain sorghum, and corn that had been irrigated by center-pivot sprinklers that drew from the Ogallala Aquifer. Smaller beef packing plants, such as IBP in Lexington, Nebraska, employed 2,100 workers, who processed as many as 4,000 cattle daily.[18]

In the Texas Panhandle and South Plains, cattle feeding boomed, expanding from 221,000 head in 1966 to 1,168,000 in 1974. IBP arrived the following year. In 1980, producers fed 4,891,000 head; the number of cattle "finished" (that is, fed to the desired weight for slaughter) increased to approximately 7 million annually by the middle of the decade. At that time, the Amarillo Cattle Auction alone sold 624,409 head and generated $236 million, which boosted income for cattle raisers and encouraged bank lending. The cattle-feeding business created jobs for feedlot workers, truck drivers, veterinarians, and agricultural supply stores.[19]

Garden City, Kansas, with a population of 24,097 (75 percent of the residents in Finney County) and having no other town within about twenty-five miles to compete, became the primary trade, service, and banking center for southwestern Kansas. The beef packers stimulated the economy of Garden City; thirty-nine new retail stores as well as seventeen new eating and drinking establishments and four new motels opened there between 1980 and 1990. Although more than 4,000 men and women made up the workforce, most held low-paying jobs. In 1990, entry-level wages averaged $6.00 per hour at Monfort and $6.40 at IBP, with annual incomes ranging from $15,500 to $22,000, which kept workers near or below the poverty line. In Nebraska, IBP paid slightly higher wages that averaged $9.05 per hour in 1990. Meatpacking wages ensured poverty and attracted only the working poor, particularly immigrants, minorities, and women, with jobs that did not require training. Women increasingly took the low-paying jobs to boost family income. At the IBP plant in Garden City, women constituted 20 percent of the workforce in 1984 and 26 percent of the workforce in 1992. Without union protection, the low-paid, dangerous jobs in the meatpacking plants did not attract native-born whites who could find jobs elsewhere. Without earning and purchasing power, the meatpacking workers could not improve their standard of living.[20]

Through the 1990s, meatpacking was not only low-paying work but also the most dangerous occupation in the Great Plains, but workers could not qualify for health insurance until they had worked for six months. If they opted for insurance, the companies, such as IBP, deducted $300 per month from their paychecks, leaving them little for daily needs. With one doctor for every 1,897 people in Garden City and Finney County, Kansas, in the mid-1990s, health care remained insufficient, particularly for the working poor. With workman's compensation costing the meat packers only $1.47 per $100 in sales during the mid-1980s and only 5 percent of earnings in the mid-1990s, they had little economic incentive to improve working conditions. As a result, injuries, poverty, and high turnover rates characterized the meatpacking industry. Other beef packing towns, such as Lexington, Nebraska, confronted similar problems. There, the turnover rate at IBP averaged 250 percent (12 percent per month) during the early 1990s. In addition, the large-scale packers forced out the small-scale packers and feedlots and reduced cattle prices, thereby creating a powerful oligopoly in the Great Plains.[21]

During the 1990s, hog production on an industrial scale also spread to the Great Plains, where state environmental regulations proved lax or nonexistent. In 1992, producers in Texas County, Oklahoma, marketed only 31,274 hogs, but in 1996, large-scale hog farms, called confinements (often financed by outside corporations and investors), produced 2 million hogs. Water and air pollution became serious problems. A nearby packing plant in Guymon processed 1,000 hogs per hour and 2 million head per year and created the same employment and social problems that characterized the beef packing industry and towns.

Pork production increased approximately 900 percent in the Oklahoma Panhandle. Seven of the fifteen major hog producers in the nation, such as the Seaboard Corporation, drew on the hogs fattened on local feed crops that had been watered by the Ogallala Aquifer. The sparse population had little political voice to complain about the stench that drifted for miles on the prevailing winds, and the availability of migrant workers and good rail and highway transportation to national and international markets enticed more packers into the area. In 1998, however, the state legislature responded to growing public opposition to these large hog confinement facilities and enacted new licensing and waste-disposal regulations, but the hog-related environmental problems did not end with the century.[22]

Thus, even as the meatpacking industry created thousands of jobs by moving to the intersection of cattle, hogs, feed, water, and transportation and by drawing a cheap workforce to the region, the meatpacking jobs contributed to the rapid expansion of poverty rather than prosperity in the Great Plains. Meatpacking jobs did not require a skill, education, or command of English. Overall, the meatpacking towns primarily attracted unskilled Latino workers who accepted the dangerous jobs that local residents rejected. Language barriers and uncertain legal status perpetuated this underclass of the working poor. The service industries that sprang up nearby to meet a host of daily needs provided additional low-paid, hourly jobs that proved little better than those in the packing plants. Workers in the packing plants and related services did not have opportunities for upward mobility and increased purchasing power that would enhance their standard of living. They remained voiceless and vulnerable workers inextricably linked by poverty who lived in desperation in one of the most productive agricultural regions on earth.

In 1990, agriculture employed only 6.6 percent of the workforce (a 12.7 percent decline since 1980), and manufacturing employed nearly twice as many workers as agriculture, even exceeding the employment of agriculture-related workers in the nonmetropolitan counties. Manufacturers sought dependable, efficient, and cheap nonunion labor, the meatpacking industry being a case in point. With an estimated 125 jobs created for every 100 meatpacking positions, the multiplier effect boosted some local economies despite its foundation on low-wage, unskilled, poorly educated, immigrant, and refugee labor. Community leaders often sought this economic boost but struggled with the social problems that came with it.[23]

In many respects, the association of oil and the Permian Basin, that vast area below the Texas Panhandle and part of southeastern New Mexico, seemed symbiotic. Beginning in the 1920s, it had been a region of giant oil and natural gas fields. It was the largest area in the lower forty-eight states for the production of oil (constituting some 12 percent of daily production in the United States) by the mid-twentieth century, giving the southern plains wealth and a culture of roughnecks, wildcatters, and geologists who influenced the world from drilling platforms and air-conditioned offices in Midland, Levelland, and Odessa. Between 1980 and 2000, however, an oversupply of natural gas kept prices flat while crude oil prices fluctuated wildly, ranging from $30.71 per barrel in 1981 to $10.80 per barrel in 1998 before increasing to more than $30.00 per barrel in early 2000. By the late 1990s, the major oil companies had begun responding to this price vola- tility by selling out and focusing on more-lucrative production overseas. Some companies expanded production by acquiring other companies, such as the acquisition of Gulf by Chevron and Getty by Texaco, rather than by exploration for new oil pools. Regional offices closed, thousands of jobs disappeared, and oil company workers moved away or found other jobs in the area. Although many independent oil companies or producers purchased leases and other assets from the major oil companies, they did not create enough jobs to replace those lost, nor did they have the capital to invest in research and exploration. Many of the upper-level positions with the major oil companies had salaries ranging from $75,000 to $100,000 annually. When these jobs disappeared, the local economy felt the loss.

At the same time, the smaller oil companies continued to produce oil and make a profit on lands acquired from the major oil companies by operating on the principle that "their garbage is our gold". "harvesting" or "gleaning" oil from the leases acquired from the major companies that had been by- passed or had reserves or pools too small for the majors to pursue drilling. By operating with low overhead and state-of-the-art seismic and drilling technology, the independent companies maintained viable oil-producing operations. Yet well-drilling crews and servicing companies largely dis- appeared, and these workers and service companies no longer substantially contributed to the economy of the southern Great Plains. Moreover, the restructuring of the industry along with high capitalization costs and a lack of workers and well service providers meant that the economy of the Perm- ian Basin changed dramatically and perhaps permanently.[24]

As the oil industry collapsed, Hispanics became the predominant work- ers in the oil fields, constituting approximately 90 percent of the workforce by 2000, in part because the work was hard, undependable, and paid low wages (often about the per-hour wages of Wal-Mart employees). At the same time, when oil-field and oil-company workers moved away, the eco- nomic multiplier effect decimated the cities and towns in the region. Tax revenues declined and local businesses lost customers. Midland County, Texas, lost 1,809 residents between 1998 and 2000; this out-migration caused the local school district to lose 600 students. In the once-thriving towns of Midland and Odessa, the trades, service industries, and local gov- ernment each employed more people than the oil industry. By the end of the twentieth century, the big oil companies essentially had left the Permian Basin. Knowledgeable observers did not expect them to return.

Others, however, expressed more optimism about the viability of the oil industry in the Oklahoma Panhandle, where new oil and gas wells had begun producing during the 1970s and 1980s. Beaver, Texas, and Cimarron counties pumped the most oil and produced the most natural gas, the latter of which reached customers in Nebraska, Iowa, Minnesota, and South Dakota by pipeline. By the end of the twentieth century, these wells had declined, but pumping remained profitable.[25]

As the oil industry declined, regional trading centers and county seats provided jobs that attracted workers from several hundred miles away. Community health-care workers, for example, often drove long distances to work each day. Some rented apartments in the towns that were regional medical centers. To work a forty-hour week in as few days as possible, they went with little rest on nearly consecutive shifts before returning home for a few days off. Although this lifestyle proved grueling, these workers and others like them were grateful for their jobs. Moreover, beginning in 1940, employment in government jobs (including schools) exceeded employment in manufacturing. In some counties, government entities employ more than half of the labor force.[26]

In the northern Great Plains, major oil discoveries occurred in Montana's Williston Basin during the 1950s. Billings soon became the home for oil companies and refineries. People and money flowed into the city, giving Billings the appearance of an oil boomtown in Oklahoma or Texas. Natural gas production accompanied oil production, but coal mining became the greatest economic boost to western North Dakota, eastern Montana, and northeastern Wyoming during the late twentieth century. Most of this coal lay shallow beneath the surface, which made strip-mining easy. Most of the coal was lignite, which is low in sulfur and therefore less of an air pollutant than other grades but also produces a low heat.[27]

In 1968, Montana Power began stripping coal near Colstrip, and the Peabody Coal Company also began shipping coal from the area to electric utility companies in Minnesota. The energy crisis of the 1970s stimulated more strip-mining and the leasing of lands from the Northern Cheyennes and Crows and ranchers, both groups of whom needed money. By the mid-1970s, coal from the Montana plains was rolling eastward in railroad cars bound for electricity-generating power plants in Chicago and Detroit. As coal production increased, environmental groups aggressively launched anti-strip-mining campaigns, and the Indians challenged coal leases negotiated by the Bureau of Indian Affairs that denied them fair royalty payments for the extraction of coal on tribal lands. Both animosity and coal mining continued at the end of the twentieth century, partly because many people favored employment and income despite the damage to the land from strip-mining, and coal companies paid taxes, which enhanced county income — but, some argued, not enough. Fear of environmental damage and air pollution caused the state legislature to enact a tough environmental protection law in 1971.[28]

Strip-mining also brought social problems to the coal towns. Gillette, Wyoming, for example, grew from a population of 3,580 in 1960 to 19,646 by 2000, which strained city services in a town that could not at first afford sewer and water systems, paved roads, or adequate schools. In 1974, one journalist reported, "It is a raw jumble of rutted streets and sprawling junkyards, red mud and dust, dirty trucks, crowded bars, added billboards and sagging utility lines, and block after block of house trailers, squatting in the dirt like a nest of giant grubs. Gillette looks and feels as if the whole town is on the wrong side of the tracks." One resident reflected, "This is starting to look like a good town to be from — a long way from." But with coal companies paying farmers and ranchers a million dollars for their land, the takers quickly stepped forward. Most of Gillette's physical problems could be solved with money and planning. During the late twentieth century, Gillette was sending heavily loaded coal cars eastward to waiting power plants, and the coal companies of the northern Great Plains professed responsible environmental practices. Yet tensions, animosity, and distrust remained between merchants, miners, and residents as well as the coal companies, all torn between the need for jobs, profits, and the land.[29]

Overall, outside investors and corporations financed cattle feedlots, hog confinement facilities, mining, and oil and natural gas extraction, among other businesses in the Great Plains. Land and regional businesses often were bought by outside corporations, and their identity, existence, or ties to local communities were lost. With corporate offices beyond the region and an outflow of profits, the economy remained colonial.

Despite the importance of the meatpacking, oil, and other industries, such as coal mining, the federal government influenced the economy of the Great Plains through spending and taxation to a greater degree than for the nation as a whole. In some Great Plains states, federal spending contributed more than 25 percent of the economy. Federal spending for farm programs remained particularly important for the nonmetropolitan counties, but that contribution was relatively insignificant compared to all federal spending in the region. Social Security payments represented a

By the late twentieth century, coal mining had become an important extractive
industry in the Great Plains. Coal mines in North Dakota, Montana, and Wyoming
fueled electric power plants in major cities to the east. The resulting environmental
damage caused fears that the land would be irreparably ruined and polluted, but the
need for jobs often overrode those concerns. The removal of the "overburden" of
soil to reach the coal at this strip mine in North Dakota contrasts sharply with the
undisturbed grassland beyond.

major federal expenditure in and influence on the economy of the Great
Plains. Hospitals were often the major employer in many communities,
and the federal Medicare program enabled these facilities to remain in
business.

In the late 1990s, the federal government spent $1.4 trillion on various
programs in the fifty states. The ten Great Plains states received about $174
billion of those federal funds, which translated into per capita spending
ranging from a low of $4,544 in Texas to a high of $7,192 in New Mexico.
Six Great Plains states had a per capita income above the national average of $5,133 for federal expenditures. Nationwide, the per capita income
from federal spending as a percentage of federal spending tallied 20.3 percent. In Montana, New Mexico, North Dakota, Oklahoma, South Dakota,
and Wyoming, federal expenditures ranged from 24.4 percent of personal
income in Wyoming to 37.3 percent in New Mexico. Clearly, these six
Great Plains states were more dependent on the federal government for
spending and income than were the states of other regions. The other four

Great Plains states depended on federal spending for personal income only slightly less than the national average, ranging from 18.7 percent in Colorado to 20.1 percent in Kansas.

In addition to Social Security, Medicare, and Medicaid, the federal contribution to personal income came from food stamps, veterans' benefits, and unemployment insurance, as well as student loans, grants to state and local governments, aid to families with dependent children, and economic development programs, along with assistance for airport and highway construction projects. Federal agencies also purchased goods and services and paid civilian and military salaries and wages, as well as supported agricultural programs and research. Only Texas fell below the national average for the receipt of federal salaries and wages, while Oklahoma ranked above the national average for direct federal payments to individuals. Montana, New Mexico, North and South Dakota, and Wyoming ranked above the national per capita average for the receipt of grants and loans to state and local governments, while Colorado, New Mexico, and Texas ranked above the national per capita average for spending on the procurement of goods and services, although the data included Texas in its entirety and not just the region of the Great Plains. In this category, however, the per capita federal spending in New Mexico ranked more than three times the national average. Only Colorado, Kansas, Nebraska, and Texas paid more in per capita taxes to the federal government than these states received in federal spending, but those tax payments were nearly equaled by the federal monies received.

In 1996, a study of 478 Great Plains counties identified only 40 as metropolitan, with an estimated population of 6.5 million, 61 percent of the region's population. In these counties, federal expenditures also exceeded the per capita average nationwide. In the mid-1990s, the national per capita expenditure of federal funds for metro and nonmetropolitan counties averaged $4,973, but in the Great Plains the average totaled $5,447, with the difference between metro and nonmetro federal expenditures averaging only $59 more for metro counties. Nationwide, the difference was $543. In the metro counties of the Great Plains, the federal contribution to salaries and wages totaled 20 percent, compared to 9 percent in the nonmetro counties, primarily because of the location of federal regional and district offices and nearby military bases, such as those near Lubbock, Omaha, Rapid City, and Grand Forks. In contrast, the nonmetropolitan counties received more federal funds paid directly to individuals, primarily because of the larger number of elderly who received Social Security and Medicare payments and farmers who drew income from the agricultural programs.

Nationwide, 49.9 percent of the direct federal payments to individuals involved retirement and disability insurance programs. In Nebraska and South Dakota, however, those payments averaged 55.8 percent and 53.9 percent, respectively. The poverty rate for Nebraska and South Dakota was 10.5 percent and 15.4 percent, respectively, in 1997, with the rural counties slightly higher.

In Nebraska and South Dakota, then (two typical farm states in the Great Plains), the per capita federal payments to individuals considerably exceeded the per capita expenditure for farm programs. Direct federal payments to Nebraska and South Dakota metropolitan counties were $3,231 and $3,214, respectively, while farm program payments per capita contributed $794 in Nebraska and $1,018 in South Dakota. Overall, per capita government payments to individuals and from farm programs contributed 22.6 cents and 21.2 cents of every dollar of personal income in Nebraska and South Dakota, respectively. In the nonmetropolitan counties, the federal per capita contribution was 9.6 and 10.2 cents from every dollar of personal income, the difference primarily due to the absence of agricultural program payments. Moreover, as counties lost population and became more rural, the total per capita federal payments increased.

Overall, then, federal spending per capita was higher in the Great Plains than the national average. The region essentially received more federal money than it paid in taxes; in some plains states, federal spending contributed more than 25 percent to the economy. Direct payments to individuals were substantially larger than per capita payments for farm programs. By the late twentieth century, the people of the Great Plains had become dependent on the federal government for a significant portion of their personal income and for the per capita income of the region as a whole. Ironically, while the people of the Great Plains often were considered politically conservative, independent, self-reliant, and suspicious of government, they were substantially dependent on the federal government for their income and standard of living. While they often complained about federal regulations, taxes, and infringement on their freedom of action, they were more dependent on the federal government than were the people in any other region in the country.[30]

During the late twentieth century, Great Plains farmers professed the axiom that bigger was better. Residents in the small towns that dotted the countryside, however, believed that smaller was getting smaller. Young people often left the towns and usually the region. The elderly stayed. Only the churchyard cemeteries seemed to grow. Roger Johnson, North Dakota's commissioner of agriculture succinctly assessed the situation: "Our countryside is just emptying out."[31]

Yet empty space did not mean economic collapse. Although the agricultural and small-town population declined, the urban areas developed economies that no longer primarily depended on agriculture. Various service and light manufacturing industries met the needs of residents, most of whom did not have farm or rural backgrounds. Although the population of the Great Plains declined significantly, particularly in rural areas during the last half of the twentieth century, the majority of its residents lived in cities from San Antonio to Bismarck. Farm consolidation and the restructuring of agriculture with the establishment of feedlots, packing plants, and hog confinement facilities reduced the number of farmers and the businesses that served them, such as cotton gins, feed mills, and branch-line railroads, but even so, agriculture remained productive and generated income from commodity sales and government programs (although for fewer people than in the past).

Still, by 1990, businesses in many small towns often had been reduced to a beauty salon that had replaced or absorbed the barbershop, an automobile repair shop, and a convenience store. If the town expanded to or along a highway, a Dairy Queen frequently served as the main place to eat out. Residents purchased their clothing, groceries, and medicines and conducted their banking in the county seats or larger trade centers. Farm consolidation and improved transportation had reduced the number of customers that previously supported these businesses on main street. Country roads that had led to town had been superseded by state and federal highways that led to interstate highways, which in turn enabled people to travel faster over longer distances to meet their shopping needs. Economic diversity supported by transportation had a multiplier effect. Although county seat towns still attracted customers to grocery stores, churches, and automobile sales and services, Great Plains men and women became long-distance shoppers who willingly drove several hours and several hundred miles for shopping choices and favorable prices, particularly for clothing, household appliances, and various special services, such as entertainment at movie theaters. As a result, a cycle of growth in the cities and decline in the countryside became reinforcing.[32]

The keys to economic development and sustainability during the late twentieth century depended on transportation. Access to markets by residents and manufacturers and suppliers became essential. The towns bypassed by an interstate highway, like those bypassed by a railroad during the nineteenth century, struggled economically. Major federal and state highways could alleviate some of the isolation and uncompetitive geographical positions of towns that were not positioned along an interstate, but they still remained at a disadvantage. Interstate cities became focal points for trade and services. The cities along an interstate that offered health care, higher education, and good selections of retail stores grew and drew customers and businesses. These towns became multicounty trade centers and suppliers of goods to their regional base. Smaller satellite communities also prospered within these trade areas by providing some services, but on a lesser scale, with linkages to suppliers in the major trade and service centers. The once-booming railroad towns became geographical relics of the past. Towns with fewer than 2,500 residents were destined for further decline unless they served as bedroom communities to the cities or metropolitan counties. By the late twentieth century, many Great Plains men and women had become commuters. They took distant jobs but preferred to remain in their small towns. For them the Great Plains provided a comforting sense of place.[33]

During the late twentieth century, then, the residents of the Great Plains paradoxically remained isolated and mobile. They were a people who depended on trucks to ship goods into the towns and carry products, often but not always agricultural, out. Their cars remained necessities, because public transportation usually did not exist outside the major cities. Although some residents still worried about the traffic when they drove to county seats to shop for various goods and services, they thought little about driving a hundred miles for dinner at a favorite restaurant. Space became only a matter of time.

The people of the Great Plains, who primarily were Christian in religion, also practiced a devout secular faith in technology. They might pray to God for resolution of their problems in hope of results, but they expected technology to solve their difficulties. And if technology created more problems (such as the contamination of drinking water with chemical fertilizers, herbicides, and pesticides) or depleted the Ogallala for irrigation, other technologies would surely solve those problems. With a mentalité of an earlier age, the men and women of the Great Plains expected progress by the late twentieth century as much as their predecessors had a century earlier. They particularly considered economic setbacks as mere bumps in the road.

Yet small towns became havens for the poor, immigrants, and the unskilled who did not have the resources or desire to leave the communities that for some had been their family homes all of their lives. They willingly accepted a low standard of living and diminished services. Despite the growth of the metropolitan areas in the Great Plains, the towns of Lubbock, Rapid City, and Bismarck, among others, had little chance of becoming new Dallas–Fort Worths, Kansas Cities, or Denvers given the decline of agriculture, mining, and the oil industry. Even as some island communities in the region of the Ogallala Aquifer and Platte River valley grew in population and economic development, many of those residents preferred the standard of living and lifestyle that their rural oases provided.[34]

At the end of the twentieth century, young adults, disproportionally women and primarily from agriculturally dependent counties, left the Great Plains for better economic and social opportunities beyond the region. The population increase of the 1990s primarily came in urban gains. Some North Dakotans, trying to be optimistic, responded in a less than welcoming market-oriented fashion, saying, "40 Below Keeps the Riff Raff Out." No matter whether the people of the Great Plains were optimistic or discouraged about the future, the urban counties became increasingly urban and the rural counties increasingly rural with no change in sight. By the end of the twentieth century, the population of the Great Plains had become primarily urban and the region essentially empty.[35]

CHAPTER EIGHT

The Politics of Race and Agriculture

Despite the population loss in the rural Great Plains during the late twentieth century, in-migration increased in some areas, and it changed the economic, social, and political dynamics of the region. Immigrant labor became essential for the economic success of the newly established meatpacking plants. The meat packers recruited workers from Mexico and Asia, as well as Latinos from Texas and California. Latinos and Asians soon dominated that workforce, and they earned wages ranging from $7 to $10 per hour, for an annual income of about $15,500 to $22,000, just enough to keep them on the cusp of poverty, while challenging educational, health-care, and welfare services beyond organizational and financial means of support. Language barriers, particularly in the public schools (where few teachers spoke Spanish), and racial hostility in the towns presented problems and prevented community-wide adaptation to this rapid population change. The small meatpacking towns, like others, had been socially, culturally, and ethnically homogeneous. The rapid arrival of Latino and other immigrant workers and their families brought a latent racism to the social surface that had long-term implications. By the turn of the twenty-first century, cultural heterogeneity had not replaced cultural homogeneity in the immigrant-based meatpacking towns across the Great Plains.[1]

In Nebraska, the Latino population increased from 36,969 in 1990 to 94,425 a decade later, mostly because of immigration, including 30,452 foreign-born Mexicans. Lexington became the first town with more than half of its population classified as Latino in 2000, earning it the pejorative sobriquet of "Mexington." During that decade, the Latino population skyrocketed from about 400 to approximately 4,000, while the town increased from 6,600 to more than 10,000 (a 52 percent increase), primarily because of Latino immigration. Schuyler, Nebraska, had a population of 4,720, and 70 percent of the employees at the Excel beef packing plant there were Latino. In Madison, a town of 2,309 people, Latinos constituted 65 percent of the Iowa Beef Processors (IBP) workforce. In Lexington, housing prices increased about 21.7 percent during the decade, which ended the precipitous decline in home values from an average of $45,198 in 1980 to $27,723 in 1990 before recovering to $33,751 by the end of the decade. At IBP and related food industries, where most of the immigrants found employment, wages rose 15.6 percent (from $13,944 to $16,116) during the decade, and the unemployment rate held steady at about 3 percent, primarily because of employment opportunities at the meatpacking plant.[2]

The growth of ethnic enclaves based, in part, on affordable housing, together with white flight, fueled segregation in the communities with large Latino populations, such as Lexington, Lincoln, and Omaha. Non-Latino white and Latino sections of town developed. One Schuyler resident remarked that "there are 'white' bars and 'Hispanic' bars, 'white' stores and 'Hispanic' stores, separate masses. . . . There is some integration among the kids, in sports and the classrooms, but not as far as community goes." Some residents in the packing towns sought mutual accommodation, but most expected the Latinos to "integrate themselves." The language barrier usually kept people apart, and non-Latino whites expected the immigrants to learn English. Ten-hour shifts, six days a week at the dangerous and physically demanding meatpacking plants, however, left little energy or will for the immigrants to attend classes and learn a new language.

At the same time, middle-income and college-educated Latinos experienced less segregation than those with low income and little education. As the population in the meatpacking towns soared, white flight occurred among those who could not make the ethnic and social adjustments in daily living. The immigrants diversified the towns with new businesses that catered to Latino needs, such as restaurants, grocery stores or markets, and clothing stores. Latino jobs and incomes, however, did not always benefit local retailers because Latinos, like residents across the Great Plains, preferred to drive to larger towns to shop (preferably at a Wal-Mart) and because the immigrants sent substantial portions of their income to family in their native countries. Non-Latino parents who had financial resources and racial biases often placed their children in parochial rather than public schools. A lack of affordable housing quickly became a problem, and slumlords preyed on the immigrants. Long-time local residents argued that multi-Latino generations lived in single-family homes for cultural or economic reasons, thereby decreasing property values and stifling home construction.

Some residents in the packing towns had sufficient education to understand the relationship between increased crime rates and an expanding population, particularly of young males. Others attributed increased social transgressions (from driving without a license to violent crime) as indicative of the ignorance or proclivity of Latinos. One contemporary observed that after the Latinos arrived, "The jail is always full." Cultural differences resurrected long-held ethnic prejudices not seen since the worst days of white animosity against African Americans in parts of the region decades earlier.[3]

In many respects, Nebraska epitomized the rapid increase of the Latino population in the Great Plains during the 1990s. By the end of the twentieth century, the Latino population had increased more than 155 percent during the decade, thereby minimizing the loss of the state's overall non-Latino population. Still, Nebraska's population increased only 8.4 percent. Oklahoma experienced a 108 percent and Kansas a 101 percent increase in the Latino population during that decade. The rapid growth of the Latino population in these and other Great Plains states resulted from in-migration and a high birth rate. Although Latinos remained an underprivileged minority with relatively weak social, economic, and political power, their rapid gain in numbers made the Great Plains unique not only because the Latino population was young but also because the white population was aging and its numbers declining, in part because of out-migration of the young, particularly from rural areas. In the 1990s, the Latino population exceeded the African American population in the Cornhusker State.[4]

The 1990s, then, became the Latino decade for the Great Plains, resulting from unprecedented immigration by those who sought employment and a better life for themselves and their families. Latinos of Mexican heritage constituted most of this population increase, although Puerto Ricans, Central and South Americans, and Cubans (the latter of whom primarily settled in New Mexico) added increasing diversity to Latino culture in the region. Most Latinos usually migrated to the Great Plains for economic reasons, while Cubans tended to immigrate for political reasons. Mexican Americans, Mexicans, and Latinos from Central America frequently took jobs in the meatpacking plants and the construction and service industries, where rudimentary English-language skills and limited education did not exclude those who wanted to work. At the same time, the rapid growth of the Latino population caused local governments and school districts to improve roads, trash collection, and sewage and water services as well as provide bilingual teachers and Spanish-speaking police officers. Yet while Latinos occupied the lower end of the economic ladder, primarily because employers saw them as cheap, replaceable labor, they did not use welfare and other social services as much as other groups in the region did. At the end of the twentieth century, however, they epitomized the working poor in the Great Plains.[5]

During the 1990s, because of prejudices based on ethnicity and class, local whites seldom welcomed Latinos. As a result, communities with large Latino populations became segregated based on ethnicity and wealth. Chain migration sustained these ethnic enclaves. White flight also increased in rural areas because of anti-Latino, anti-immigrant, and anti-farmworker prejudices. As Latino neighborhoods grew, community resources lagged, which prompted charges of discrimination and racism by both Latinos and whites. No matter where the Latinos worked or their income, whites considered them merely migrant and seasonal farmworkers who contributed little to the area other than social and economic problems. The high turnover among Latinos at the meatpacking plants because of injury, illness, and parsimonious health-care benefits, as well as low wages and few opportunities for advancement, caused great mobility. These problems reinforced the perception that Latinos were transients even though the meatpacking workers often remained and found better-paying jobs in the area. Although few local whites sought employment in meatpacking, and while Latino workers spent their earnings on housing, food, and basic services in their communities, whites tended to take their money almost as an entitlement but not in gratitude.[6]

At the same time, white flight can be attributed more to the exodus of better-educated young whites who found better employment and social opportunities in the cities of the Great Plains or beyond the region than to Latino immigration, and it contributed to substantial economic and social decline of the communities that experienced such losses. Still, some communities worked to accommodate, even embrace, the Latino immigrants and the cultural diversity that they brought to the region, including the opening of small businesses and the sound of Tejano music over local Spanish-language radio stations. When the twentieth century ended, however, whites still tended to react to Latinos rather than proactively work with them to solve mutual problems and pursue new, culturally linked opportunities.[7]

The Latino immigration to the Great Plains during the 1990s, then, influenced both urban and rural areas. As Latinos sought work in the meat and poultry processing plants, particularly in Kansas and Nebraska, the competition of a global economy encouraged employers to deskill jobs, speed production lines, institute continuous shifts, and foil labor unions by encouraging high turnover rates for workers. Fiscally conservative local and state governments assisted these businesses and found little reason to provide adequate social safety nets in preference of a continuous supply of low-wage, minority, and immigrant workers. Meatpacking and government officials were assisted by the Immigration Act of 1965 and the Immigration Reform and Control Act of 1986, which legalized 2.9 million illegal Latino immigrants and encouraged family reunion, mobility, and residence in the United States. Protected by this legislation, Latinos often exercised their new freedoms by migrating to the Great Pains in search of work. Once there, they showed little desire to leave. A recession in California also made the Great Plains states more attractive to Latinos. As a result, Latinos usually constituted between 50 percent and 90 percent of the workforce in the meat processing plants. Employers used family and friends to recruit workers and provided rudimentary training, which reduced, if not eliminated, recruitment and training costs for these businesses. At the same time, the turnover rate averaged more than 100 percent annually.

Even as the meat-processing industries pulled immigrants from Mexico and Central America, poor economic conditions in these areas pushed Latinos northward in search of a better life in the Great Plains. At the same time, many Great Plains communities worked hard to lure companies with large payrolls that would attract workers and revitalize the local economy — even save a declining and dying community. Nebraska was the most dependent of the Great Plains states on the meatpacking industry, with 15 percent of the state's jobs in this industry. Kansas ranked second, with 7.4 percent of its jobs in meatpacking. Only 40 percent of the largest meatpacking plants in Kansas were unionized, while about 19 percent of the largest meatpackers were unionized in Nebraska.[8]

While the Latino population flocked to the towns with meatpacking plants, cultural and economic divisions segregated the Latinos from whites and created tensions between the newcomers and the old-timers in the Latino community. This new immigration showed that cultural diversity is complex, because longtime Latino residents of Omaha, for example, only guardedly accepted the newcomers. They had achieved some socioeconomic success and upward mobility. They tended to live in nicer homes, drove newer automobiles that were in better condition, and sent their children to school, including college. Moreover, they spoke English as a means of assimilation, and many longtime Latino residents, who tended to be older than the newcomers, worried that the arrivals would adversely affect their socioeconomic gains in the community. Different generational, immigration, and class differences, then, caused some misgivings about the benefits of the Latino decade for them. Mexican American residents became increasingly concerned about status degradation, and they felt the need to prove to local whites that they were American born, spoke English, and had integrated into white society, while younger Mexican Americans worried about being labeled as gang members. Moreover, middle-class and elderly Mexican Americans feared that the new wave of Latino immigrants, largely from Mexico, would relegate them to the prior second-class status from which they had worked hard to escape.[9]

Yet, until the 1990s, small-town residents in the Great Plains (outside of Texas and New Mexico) had little firsthand experience with Latinos, immigrants, and nonwhites. Garden City, Kansas, the largest of the meatpacking towns, quickly became not only the fastest-growing city, with a large Latino population (43 percent of the total), but also the most culturally diverse, with more than 3,000 Vietnamese immigrants. Social and educational services soon proved inadequate. The great Latino influx was the first population gain for some counties in the region since the 1930s, when many Anglo-Americans returned home. The Latino migration within and immigration to the Great Plains reaffirmed that the people of the region moved quickly in response to economic opportunities. The meat packers, while providing employment opportunities, however, periodically reduced hours or closed plants, depending on market prices and demand, thereby adversely affecting local economies and social services, particularly food banks. The workers competed for scarce housing and often lived in mobile homes, colloquially called trailer houses, beyond the city limits. Still, the new immigrants earned money in the meatpacking communities by taking jobs that few locals wanted, and they spent it on housing and new businesses and paid taxes, thereby revitalizing and giving life to otherwise dying towns.[10]

In 1970, the Nixon administration gave new life to Indian self-determination and economic development. Outside corporations could receive low-interest federal loans if they would establish a business and manage it temporarily while Indians trained for its management. The Assiniboine and Sioux tribal councils at the Fort Peck Reservation in northeastern Montana took advantage of this opportunity. In November 1968, they had organized the Fort Peck Tribal Industries and incorporated under Montana law. The

Small Business Administration provided financing and the Office of Economic Opportunity job training to bring the Dynalecton Corporation to the reservation for the reconditioning of Air Force M1/M2 carbines.

Still, inadequate funding, job training, planning, and administration hindered economic development on the reservations. Moreover, the Red Power movement of the 1970s made many corporations hesitant to use government programs to expand onto the reservations. White executive boards became increasingly threatened by the new assertiveness of tribal governments for participation in and control of the economic development of the reservations. Budget cuts during the Reagan administration curtailed further economic development, and many programs of the Department of Health, Education, and Welfare, Department of Labor, and Commerce Department were eliminated. Because most reservation enterprises produced goods for the federal government, budget reductions meant reduced or canceled contracts. Private markets could not provide alternative sales or absorb the economic loss of the reservation enterprises. Throughout the late twentieth century, inadequate capital, job training, and technical assistance, as well as professional management expertise, still prevented substantive economic development on the reservations. Too few jobs and too little pay ensured the continuation of poverty.[11]

In the summer of 1968, the American Indian Movement (AIM) became a militant voice of protest that drew attention to Indian problems and grievances for the next decade before dissolving because of internal fighting and federal opposition. The leadership and membership of AIM primarily came from urban areas beyond the Great Plains, and it was younger and more progressive than the tribal leaders on the reservations, even though they too were divided into conservative and progressive camps. Essentially, AIM developed as an Indian rights association that intended to monitor the treatment of urban Indians by law enforcement agencies. In the Great Plains, most whites considered it a violent, radical Indian organization.

On February 27, 1973, after a native protest group called the Trail of Broken Treaties occupied and ransacked BIA offices in Washington, D.C., AIM leaders, including Russell Means (Oglala) and Dennis Banks (Ojibwa), arrived at Wounded Knee, South Dakota, where they joined traditional Oglalas (mostly full-bloods) who sought to replace the mixed-blood tribal chairman, Richard Wilson, whose strong-armed, dictatorial administration had brought fear, corruption, and violence to the Oglala community. They intended to protest the way that Wilson and the Pine Ridge Council conducted tribal affairs, referring to him as a puppet of the BIA. The protesters announced that they no longer accepted the Oglala constitution and proclaimed a sovereign Oglala Sioux Nation. In addition, they planned to make Wounded Knee a symbol of past and present transgressions by the federal government and used the news media to champion their programmatic demands for reform, including the respect of Indian treaty rights by the federal government, especially the treaty of 1868. AIM intended to use Wounded Knee to air Indian grievances and educate the public about Indian problems, particularly the state of economic and social destitution on the reservations, and to pressure federal authorities to address their grievances.[12]

When AIM leaders met with several conservative full-bloods who opposed Wilson, BIA police, Wilson supporters, FBI agents, and units of the National Guard prevented them from leaving Wounded Knee and threatened to arrest them because they had violated tribal self-determination and threatened tribal sovereignty. Means, Banks, and several AIM members then barricaded themselves in the local trading post. Quickly the standoff at Wounded Knee received national coverage on daily television news broadcasts, and the symbolism of armed, federal authorities surrounding Indians at Wounded Knee drew considerable attention to their plight and demands that the BIA improve its support for the Indians. Before the siege ended after seventy-one days, federal officials had shot and killed two Indians, and many on both sides had been injured by sporadic gunfire. On May 8, 1973, AIM members withdrew under a truce, but they had brought substantial attention to the social, economic, and political conditions at Wounded Knee and the Pine Ridge Reservation, for which they and many observers held the BIA responsible. Wilson and his "goon squad," however, continued to rule the community, and the public soon lost interest in the plight of the Oglalas and the other reservation Indians.

Many Indians condemned the violence at Wounded Knee and attributed it to young, urban Indians who had not experienced reservation life. One Pine Ridge resident and AIM activist remembered, "After all was said and done things became worse for the long-suffering people of the reservation. The media packed up and left as did the occupiers. The people were left to clean up the mess." In the minds of the traditionalists, however, the damage was more than physical. Holly Wilson, an AIM member and Wilson's daughter, remembered, "Because of the violent actions of a few, a backlash of hate and anger came down on the Indian people left behind in the wake of the takeover. . . . Legal cases the Oglala Sioux should have won in court suddenly went against them. Funds vital to the survival of the Lakota people were slashed and cut by a Congress bent on revenge."[13]

Yet the siege at Wounded Knee publicized the destitution of many reser-

vation Indians and their desire for a greater voice in the formulation and ex-
ecution of Indian policy and contributed to increasing self-determination.
Wounded Knee helped create a sense of Indian identity and pride, and it
played a major role in Indian demands that their views be heard, considered, and acted upon. The Indians would no longer accept treatment as
victims. Thereafter, they demanded control of their own affairs. As a result,
by the end of the late twentieth century, the Indians had gained a greater
voice in determining their future than at any time since their military
defeat and forced relocation on the reservations during the late nineteenth
century.[14]

Although the federal government backed down on its formal policy
of termination, it still sought to reduce expenditures, in part by ending
BIA support for boarding and day schools. The BIA wanted to close those
schools and force Indian children to attend public schools, often to the
chagrin of local school officials and white taxpayers and parents. The
BIA had pursued this policy since the early twentieth century. In 1956,
no federal Indian schools operated in Nebraska or Wyoming. Many off-
reservation boarding schools, such as Chilocco in Oklahoma, closed during the 1970s for want of students and the attraction of better educational
facilities in the nearby public schools. Indian full-bloods or those considered more than half-blood had greater educational difficulties than did
mixed-bloods, whose English and acculturation proved more conducive
to learning in the public schools. At the same time, Indian communities
sought increased federal and state support for their public schools. During
the late twentieth century, most Indian children attended public schools.
Yet education on the reservations remained inadequate despite improved
funding and management.[15]

While the Indians in the Great Plains struggled to provide an adequate
education for their children, they made some progress in improving access
to institutions of higher education. The Lakotas established reservation-
based colleges on the Pine Ridge and Rosebud reservations in South Dakota. They also established several community colleges in North and South
Dakota and Montana. By 1988, only two post-secondary BIA schools remained — Haskell Indian Nations University (formerly Haskell Junior College in Lawrence, Kansas) and the Southwest Indian Polytechnic Institute
in Albuquerque. The reservation-based schools provided a second chance
for many tribal adults to gain an education. These schools also educated
Indian students who became teachers, lawyers, and other professionals,
some of whom remained after the completion of their studies and worked
to improve reservation life. In Oklahoma, one Indian leader spoke for all

Native Americans in saying that "education is one of the ingredients toward self-determination."[16]

In 1975, demands for Indian self-determination were met, in part, with passage of the Indian Self-Determination and Education Assistance Act. Some observers hailed this act as the most important legislation since the Indian Reorganization Act of 1934 because it required the secretary of the interior and the secretary of health, education, and welfare to contract with any tribal government that requested federal program assistance and services. It also recognized the right of Indians to participate in the planning and direction of all federally funded programs for Indian children in the public schools and provided other educational benefits. The tribes would plan and administer those programs, thereby eliminating the paternalism of the federal government. Yet increased dependency on the BIA resulted because reservation bureaucracies did not have the resources, experience, or training to administer needed federal programs. Reservation bureaucracies eventually grew to administer the programs and, by so doing, often became the largest employer on the reservations. During the Reagan years, however, the tribes fought government efforts to eliminate Indian education as a "trust responsibility" and opposed plans to transfer the financial and administrative responsibility for Indian education on the reservations to the states, which they considered the "deadliest enemies" of the Indians. When the twentieth century ended, the Indians maintained their right to self-determination in education based on strong legal support.[17]

Yet setbacks often superseded small gains. At the Kickapoo Reservation, like others in the Great Plains, the Indians suffered from chronic poverty, endemic unemployment, inadequate education, and major health and social problems. The Kickapoos in Northern Kansas had a life expectancy of fifty years. To overcome these problems, the Kickapoos attempted to use the Indian Self-Determination and Education Assistance Act to pursue federal grants, or as one tribal member said, "hunt the federal buffalo." At first, the Kickapoos succeeded. Between 1976 and 1981, they received grants from the Department of Housing and Urban Development (HUD), the Economic Development Administration (EDA), and the Department of Commerce that enabled them to build a community center, library, and shopping center that included a grocery store, cafe, and gas station as well as a Laundromat, day-care center, and housing. A water treatment facility followed, along with a print shop and the creation of the Kickapoo Construction Company. They also repurchased 2,400 acres and began a tribal farming and ranch operation with a BIA loan. In 1981, the Kickapoos established their own contract school for grades K–12, although most of the funding to support it came from the BIA. The tribal budget rose from $30,000 to $1.7 million.

During the 1980s, however, the Reagan administration reduced federal spending, and the budget cuts caused the termination of programs, jobs, and services. In August 1980, 142 Kickapoos worked on the reservation, but only 16 remained by January 1982. During that time, the unemployment rate increased from 34 percent to 93 percent, and the tribal budget decreased by two-thirds. Pleas to the BIA for help did not bring needed funding for programmatic support, including education. Thus, the Indian Self-Determination and Education Act actually made the tribes more dependent on the federal government because it authorized the creation of a multitude of Indian assistance programs that would be Indian directed but federally financed. When the money largely disappeared, the Indians, such as the Kickapoos, were left with expensive programs that they could not fund. By taking federal funds to help determine their own future, they became increasingly dependent on the whims of the executive and legislative branches of the federal government for the monetary lifeline that would sustain them. Although the Indian Self-Determination and Education Act remained, federal funding ebbed and flowed during the remainder of the twentieth century and reminded the Great Plains tribes that what the federal government gave, it could also take away.[18]

Other tribal enterprises proved more economically viable and reliable. In 1987, Turtle Mountain Chippewas in North Dakota established a data-entry firm that employed 875 people nationwide, and it had an annual payroll of $18 million. As a minority-owned business, it successfully competed for government contracts, giving further proof that self-reliance did not require termination. Still, isolation, a poorly educated workforce, and the inability of white managers and supervisors to work with people whose cultural values remained different plagued efforts to establish businesses, manufacturing, and industry on the reservations. Moreover, the reservations usually lacked the capital to finance the development of oil, gas, and mineral resources, and the allotment pattern so checkerboarded the reservations that the establishment of extractive industries proved difficult. Moreover, tribal economic interests sometimes did not harmonize with Indian individual and family interests.[19]

Hunger and inadequate nutrition also remained daily problems. Tribal food programs became increasingly important as the food stamp program declined after passage of the Personal Responsibility and Work Opportunity Reconciliation Act in 1996, which required welfare clients to work a certain number of hours in order to receive assistance. Opportunities for work on the Northern Cheyenne Reservation remained severely limited, and the law essentially created greater hardship rather than forced the Indians to learn skills and achieve permanent employment and become economically independent. Most of the reservation employment involved public-sector jobs at schools, hospitals, social services, and government agencies. These Cheyennes often were removed from the food stamp assistance program if they did not find jobs, which at best were temporary and usually nonexistent. Similar situations existed on the other reservations in the Great Plains. Instead of ending welfare, the legislation contributed to the need for it, but the federal government absolved itself of any responsibility for the increasing suffering and want that were evident on the Indian reservations. The twenty-first century did not promise immediate relief from this government-compounded problem.[20]

At the same time, many Indians moved back to the reservations because of jobs in gaming enterprises and casinos, which some have called "the new buffalo." Yet Indian gaming often did not return great earnings, because many reservations were too isolated to draw large numbers of gamblers. Others proved successful. In 1993, a casino opened on the Standing Rock Reservation in South Dakota; it became the biggest employer in the county by providing 376 jobs. By the turn of the twenty-first century, it had expanded six times. Most tribal governments operated the casinos and redistributed the profits for community benefit based on the regulations of the Indian Gaming Regulatory Act (IGRA) of 1988. Yet many Indian casinos confronted difficulties. In 1996, the casino at Pine Ridge earned only $1 million, which had little economic effect on the community, where unemployment remained at 75 percent. Even so, the establishment of casinos on the reservations became a form of Indian self-sufficiency.[21]

Indian gaming became particularly successful and profitable in Oklahoma, where the state legislature limited it to small-scale and less profitable games of chance. In Oklahoma, casinos could only offer bingo, pull-tab, and electronic versions of these and other games. The stakes and winnings were smaller than from gambling with dice, cards, and slot machines, but such gaming facilities still provided needed jobs and local revenue. At the end of the twentieth century, twenty-three tribes owned and operated fifty-five gaming facilities in Oklahoma. Most of this development occurred during the 1990s. By the turn of the twenty-first century, these gaming activities were earning an estimated $208 million, employing 3,857 people (about the same number as employed in home construction and the petroleum and coal industries), purchasing $73 million in goods and services from Oklahoma and other businesses, and paying $43 million in wages and salaries. Tribal governments received approximately $83 million from gaming revenue and paid an estimated $500,000 in state unemployment taxes.

The Indian Gaming Regulatory Act required tribal governments to regulate Class II gaming with oversight by the federal government's National Indian Gaming Commission (NIGC). The IGRA also required the use of gaming profits to improve the tribal welfare. The tribes used their gaming income for health, law enforcement, and educational programs. Some projects included the Seneca-Cayugas' tribal day-care center and the Miamis' public library. The Choctaws and Creeks used gaming revenues to help build hospitals. Tribal groups also used gambling revenues as matching funds for federal grants. Without gaming revenues, many such projects would have been impossible to achieve, and gaming revenues became a significant portion of the tribal budgets. Moreover, Indian gaming benefited the state's economy by an estimated $329 million for goods and services from the multiplier effect of tribal expenditures and the employment of 13,240 people in service industry positions, as well as more than $23 million in new tax revenues from those jobs. Because thirty-six of the fifty-five gaming enterprises were located in economically depressed areas, gaming enterprises proved essential for Oklahoma's tribal people.[22]

Indian casinos, however, caused new problems, because Indians as well as whites gambled in those enterprises. Like white patrons, Indian gamblers often lost their money in pursuit of more money. One Omaha woman observed, "People are flocking to the gambling halls, not to have fun, but to get money to survive." Another Omaha noted, "Indian gaming would be okay if it took money from the White man, but it also affects Indians without money." Casinos provided jobs and revenue for community projects, but these tribal enterprises took money from whites and Indians alike, often to the detriment of those who had little. Moreover, tribal groups with casinos soon began contesting jurisdictional and regulatory claims of state governments as legislatures attempted to capitalize economically on the gaming revenue of the reservation casinos.[23]

Despite tribal and government efforts to improve the economy of the reservations, many Indians chose to leave the reservations for the cities. During the late twentieth century, large Indian populations lived in Oklahoma City, Dallas–Fort Worth, Denver, and Albuquerque. Many smaller cities also gained Indian residents. Cultural adaptation remained an ongoing struggle for many, and urban Indians did not have access to BIA programs and support unless they lived close enough to a reservation that they remained socially, culturally, and economically affiliated with the tribe.[24]

During the late 1990s, Texas led the Great Plains states with the most native businesses, with 15,668 firms, followed by Oklahoma with 15,066. Most of these native-owned businesses operated in urban areas, with Tulsa having 3,822 Indian firms and Oklahoma City, 3,295 enterprises. These urban environments provided greater entrepreneurial and economic opportunities than did the reservations. Moreover, Indian culture often impeded the development of Indian-owned businesses because the accumulation of monetary wealth had not been a traditional objective. Instead, the Indians had privileged generosity, redistribution, and egalitarianism, and tribal governments favored the collective development and ownership of enterprises rather than the establishment of privately owned businesses. The native cultures in the Great Plains, then, often did not consider private enterprise a primary goal.[25]

Although the Bureau of Indian Affairs remained the major federal agency that dealt with Indian affairs, particularly in relation to the federal trust relationship regarding land, natural resources, economic development, housing, and health care, other federal agencies, such as the Department of Housing and Urban Development and the Indian Health Service, also helped the federal government fulfill its trust responsibilities. A variety of other federal programs, such as Social Security and food stamps, provided additional assistance. In 1996, however, passage of the Personal Responsibility and Work Opportunity Reconciliation Act, commonly called the welfare reform act, cut and consolidated some programs such as food stamps, school lunches, and aid to women, infants, and children. These welfare-related reductions seriously reduced cash income and exacerbated poverty on the reservations. Some Indians such as those at Fort Belknap criticized these cuts as a form of termination of the government's trust responsibilities and retribution for their advocacy of greater self determination. These federal budgetary cuts by various agencies did, however, cause a reaffirmation and strengthening of kin-based support networks and relationships, particularly among women.[26]

At the same time, tribal governments sought economic development and contended that Indian sovereignty was not possible without economic independence and the end of their reliance on government programs and funding. Moreover, tribal leaders made the business decisions for their tribe, thereby blending political and economic leadership, which remained a management model that was not characteristic of mainstream political and economic life. The result was a collective capitalism that the leaders used to enhance sovereignty and improve the tribal standard of living through economic development. Collective capitalism theoretically did not encourage class development based on wealth or diminish tribal social and cultural values.

Some Great Plains tribes such as the Northern Cheyennes joined this collective capitalism with a strong environmental awareness. During the 1970s, for example, the Northern Cheyennes considered the lease of their lands for strip-mining as not only the alienation of their land but also a matter that would contribute to the loss of their social identity and religious beliefs.[27]

The Northern Cheyenne Reservation is located along the Tongue and Rosebud rivers in southeastern Montana, and it comprises approximately 447,000 acres, of which the tribe owns 262,000 acres. The reservation provided a home for approximately four thousand Cheyennes. Between 1966 and 1973, the BIA and the tribal council leased the reservation to several national and multinational corporations for the extraction of coal. The Cheyennes received $.175 per ton, which totaled $2.25 million for the leases. Upon learning about the leases, many Northern Cheyennes opposed the agreements, complaining about the environmental damage despite the economic gain for the tribe. They organized the Northern Cheyenne Landowner's Association and, aided by federal law, pressured the tribal council to terminate the leases not only for environmental reasons but also for matters of law that protected them from outside exploitation. They also wanted to assume full responsibility for the management of mineral exploitation on the reservation. In 1988, Congress voided the leases because the coal gasification plants proposed for the area violated the Clean Air Act. The Northern Cheyennes also fought the Pegasus Gold Corporation, which opened a mining operation in 1979 that used cyanide for the extracting process. In 1996, tribal environmental groups and the Fort Belknap Community Council ultimately forced the company to pay $32.2 million in fines for pollution on the reservation, and they blocked further expansion.[28]

The efforts of the BIA to support economic development (usually agriculture, mineral extraction, or manufacturing) to integrate the reservation economies into the national economy struggled because of inadequate financial support, low educational achievements, and differing attitudes about concepts of time and work. Corporate capitalism and tribal cultures clashed in the semisovereign world of the reservations. Moreover, government offers of cheap, nonunion labor and no taxes failed to lure business development to any appreciable degree. Isolation and an inadequate workforce presented problems that most businesses did not want to confront. When businesses were established, outside, not Indian, control prevailed. Moreover, tribal governments did not have sufficient capital to establish businesses, and manufacturing jobs paid only the minimum wage, required regular work schedules, and frequently necessitated relocations on the reservation even while they provided only temporary employment.[29]

Through the late 1990s, a growing national energy crisis made the tribal lands of the Great Plains increasingly attractive for coal, oil, gas, and uranium mining, and corporations pressured tribal governments for cheap leases on Indian lands in Montana and North Dakota that contained deep coal deposits. Mining promised quick monetary income for tribal benefit, but the resulting degradation of the land, particularly from strip-mining, gave many tribes pause. The conservatives usually opposed such economic development because it not only damaged the land but also disrupted their traditional culture and brought more whites to the reservations. The more progressive tribal leaders, often mixed-bloods, favored development to improve the tribal standard of living from royalty income. These tribal leaders believed that they could have income and control. One Northern Cheyenne, however, spoke for many when he urged caution, saying, "Coal has been under the Cheyenne reservation for a long time, and it can stay there until we know the best thing to do." One Crow clearly affirmed this view in saying, "I'm for coal development, but I'm for control."

The tribal groups that favored natural resource development entered the twenty-first century with plans to develop zoning and land-use regulations as well as severance tax structures to protect the land and the tribe while enhancing revenue. Some tribal groups such as the Crows and Northern Cheyennes also sought the renegotiation of leasing contracts that clearly took advantage of previous leaders who had lacked the education and experience to deal with the mining companies. Although the BIA still must approve leases for the extraction of natural resources, the Indians demand an active role in those negotiations. At Fort Peck in Montana, the tribal government financed the drilling of their own oil and gas wells with tribal funds. When the century ended, however, the Great Plains tribes still expressed great distrust of the BIA regarding the exploitation of natural resources on the reservations, and the development of energy resources continued to foster tribal factionalism. They also adamantly defended their treaty rights on the reservations, although tribal jurisdiction over land owned by whites within the reservation boundaries regarding such matters as state highways, county roads, and representation on school boards often required litigation for solutions. The future remained contentious and uncertain.[30]

In 1977, a new farmers' organization, the American Agriculture Movement (AAM), emerged in the Great Plains. Organized by large-scale wheat farmers and farm-related business owners with headquarters in Springfield, Colorado, the AAM protested against a political system that did not provide economic relief after the federal government had urged them to increase production. They faced inflation and high interest rates, which increased their operating costs. The AAM intended to organize local chapters similar to the American Farm Bureau Federation and to establish state and national offices to lobby for economic change in agriculture. Harkening back to the past, AAM leadership planned a farm strike during which they would neither sell food and fiber nor plant or purchase goods and services until the federal government guaranteed 100 percent parity prices in new agricultural legislation. Naively, they believed that the family farm was the critical link in the national economy, that a strike would force the federal government to act, and that the AAM would educate the American public about the significance of the family farm. If the government did not meet their demands, they were certain that the family farm would soon succumb to large-scale corporate agriculture. This free-flowing organization did not charge dues, maintain membership rolls, formally elect officers, or provide rules. Anyone could speak at an AAM rally, provided he or she supported the goals of the organization.[31]

By December 1977, the AAM had organized 1,100 locals in forty states, according to its leaders. Using the tactics of the many college students who had participated in the civil rights movement and anti–Vietnam War demonstrations, they demonstrated in their local communities with a tractor parade, dubbed a "tractorcade," and carried signs that proclaimed "Hell No, We Won't Grow." Quickly, the AAM captured the attention of the local and national press as well as television stations and networks. One supporter said, "We may be stupid but at least we're smart enough not to buy TV time." The AAM also used peer pressure and intimidation to force other farmers to support the movement. AAM rallies were designed to show anger, activism, and unity as well as resolve and the possibility of violence if the federal government did not meet its demands.[32]

After Congress rejected the demands of the AAM, the organization planned to demonstrate in Washington, D.C., to pressure Congress to approve favorable agricultural legislation that would help improve their income. In January 1978, some three thousand farmers paraded their tractors in Washington, D.C., and met with congressional leaders. Congress responded with a moratorium on foreclosures by the Farmers Home Administration, which replaced the Farm Security Administration in 1946, and provided an 11 percent increase in price-support payments. AAM leaders, however, contended that they had been betrayed and that they would reduce planting by 10 percent, but the rank and file failed to respond. The agricultural strike, such as it was, had virtually no effect on the production of food and fiber across the nation.

The failure of the AAM to hold a major farm strike and gain 100 percent parity prices caused the leadership to place a new emphasis on militant protest. In January 1979, the tractorcade returned to Washington, D.C., but only radicals remained in the organization. Although considerably fewer participants demonstrated compared to the previous year, they did not do so peacefully. AAM farmers used their tractors to block traffic, drove over government lawns, released goats on the capitol grounds, and threw tomatoes at Secretary of Agriculture Bob Bergland. Eventually, the police confined their activities to the mall area.[33]

Congress and the USDA remained unreceptive to their demands for 100 percent parity prices, and the newspapers and television reports portrayed AAM farmers as belligerent and threatening. Instead of gaining public support, these farmers alienated it. By June, an estimated 60 percent to 90 percent of the AAM locals had disbanded, and only twenty-eight states claimed even minimal activity. Although the AAM planned to establish an office in Washington, D.C., hire a lobbyist, and formally organize the movement, and the organization called for another tractorcade in February 1980, these efforts disintegrated.[34]

The AAM was similar to other agricultural movements in which farmers joined an organization that offered a specific plan or quick fix for an immediate problem. The AAM identified the enemies of farmers and used dramatic efforts to gain public attention and attempt to achieve its goals. It glorified the family farm and criticized the federal government, the public, and other agricultural organizations such as the Farm Bureau for not understanding the problems of family farmers and forsaking them for the preferences of agribusiness and industrial and urban America. In the end, the public grew tired of the AAM's radical activities and pronouncements When the AAM no longer made the news, the movement essentially died. Its most ardent members continued to feel excluded from the political system, and they dreamed of resurrecting the movement. Without the support of most Great Plains farmers and the major agricultural organizations, however, the AAM was relegated to history, if not oblivion.[35]

The decline of agriculture's political influence, as measured by the inability of the AAM to marshal enough support by Great Plains farmers to change agricultural policy, also can be seen in Kansas. In 1993, a federal court ruled that the selection of the Kansas State Board of Agriculture required election rather than appointment by a select group of farmers.

The board also appointed the state secretary of agriculture. The court determined that the board's electoral process violated the one-person, one-vote mandate of the Fourteenth Amendment. Members of the state legislature then provided for the election of the secretary with authorization to appoint the board members. Urbanites preferred this reform because the state board of agriculture and the secretary of agriculture touched every aspect of their daily lives by regulating food purity, water quality, and the use of pesticides, particularly atrazine, a possible cancer-causing chemical that had begun to appear in drinking water and could not be removed by standard water purification systems. When the state board of agriculture ignored public complaints and only recommended that farmers voluntarily limit their applications of atrazine, environmental groups challenged the constitutionality of the board's selection process. Farmers and their organizations also objected to the court's ruling because it gave urbanites too much political power to determine agricultural matters, and the state attorney general contended that all Kansans were represented in the making of agricultural and environmental policies because the legislature made the laws and the state board of agriculture and the secretary of agriculture merely enforced them.[36]

Near the end of the twentieth century, a flash of radicalism reminiscent of the agrarian revolt a century earlier also burned hot enough for some to ask, "What's the matter with Kansas?" The flare-up began in May 1992, when the state legislature approved a new school financing formula that adversely affected many counties in southwestern Kansas. The law set a tax rate of 32 mills, that is, $32 in taxes for every $1,000 of assessed property valuation. It also capped tax support at $3,600 per student. Many counties in southwestern Kansas, however, collected higher taxes and provided more than $5,000 per student. The new state law required all tax collections that exceeded the $3,600-per-student limit to be returned to the state for disbursement to counties that fell below that target. The problem became more inflammatory when residents of southwestern Kansas learned that many big companies in Topeka and Wichita had been granted tax exemptions in excess of $1 billion. As one Morton County Commissioner put it, "The problem is the state telling us what we can and cannot do." A resident of Stevens County agreed, saying, "The only time anymore that we hear from Topeka is when they want more money." Residents and school officials in southwestern Kansas believed that the new school finance formula would require the dismissal of teachers, a reduction in course offerings, and the closing of local schools. Residents also opposed their loss of spending control for their schools and, by implication, state micromanagement of their lives and the loss of their liberty. The legislature in Topeka far to the east, in their view, clearly did not understand their needs or represent them. The solution seemed clear: secession.[37]

In southwestern Kansas, rich agricultural lands (often irrigated), cattle, and natural gas provided a large tax base that permitted local officials to fund schools, pave roads, and construct community buildings from a low tax levy for individuals. News of the new state tax levy formula brought immediate criticism and signs that read "To Hell With Topeka, Let's Secede" along Highway 50 in Lakin. Town hall meetings in Kearny, Stevens, and Morton counties held advisory elections on secession, with strong voter support favoring it. Soon coalitions of businesspeople, local politicians, farmers, county commissioners, and proschool and antitax residents began calling for the creation of the fifty-first state of "West Kansas," which one Stevens County resident thought could be a "fair-sized little state," about the size of South Carolina.[38]

Many residents in southwestern Kansas believed that the State of Kansas was trying to take control of their local institutions. Historically isolated by geography and transportation from eastern Kansas, where the state legislature met and where most of the population resided, and living in an area that provided a comfortable and often booming economy, over time they had developed a sense of economic and political independence that required deference, not oppression. Moreover, the region primarily had been settled by migrants from the Upper South during the late nineteenth century and by Mexicans during the 1920s. The descendants of both groups had cultural attachments and political proclivities that looked elsewhere and not to Topeka for leadership. They often turned west to Denver for their newspapers and television stations and shopped in Amarillo, both of which had closer proximity than Topeka and the rest of eastern Kansas. They also believed that people in the eastern part of the state looked down on them as uneducated and unsophisticated rubes and that only taxes gave commonality between eastern and western Kansas. For them, Kansas had seceded from them. The last time the residents in this area got so excited, six people were shot dead fighting over the location of the county seat for Stevens County.

The state attorney general reminded the people of southwestern Kansas that secession was unconstitutional. Local residents, however, met through the summer to express their grievances and plan a constitutional convention for September 11; this convention would be in Ulysses, some 370 miles from Topeka. Although delegations from only seven counties met in convention, they approved the creation of a new state of West Kansas, with the pheasant as the state bird and the yucca plant as the state flower. Then they sent a list of grievances to the governor. The delegates also drafted a rough constitution, which permitted secession, and then proposed secession from the State of Kansas.

Although the state legislators, except those from southwestern Kansas, laughed at the secessionists, the threat to withhold all school and other tax money from the state proved no joking matter, and the attorney general quickly informed them that he would oust any local officials who retained tax revenues. The secessionists countered by paying their taxes under protest, a legal action in Kansas that put their money in an escrow account and beyond the use of the state. Locally based large companies, such as Colorado Interstate Gas, also paid their taxes under protest. The secessionists then pledged to boycott (that is, deny their business to) all counties where state senators and representatives had voted for the new tax law. This threatened boycott stung the regional trade centers of Garden City and Dodge City, whose representatives had voted for the new school financing levy.

Much of the emotional reaction to the new school financing formula stemmed from a sense of community identity among the people of southwestern Kansas, and the local school was central to that identity. They feared that school consolidations would result from the new legislation. One Morton County resident put the matter succinctly, saying, "I'm in a little dinky town out here — population 500 — and if the school closes, the town closes. It's all over." Moreover, if schools could be consolidated, counties also could be collapsed and merged for economic and administrative efficiency. Those who looked ahead recommended the merger of counties in eastern Kansas to help save money. When, in December 1994, the state Supreme Court held the school tax law constitutional, the secessionist movement died away and the residents of southwestern Kansas learned to live with the new school financing formula. But their loss of voice, power, and freedom to make their own decisions and run their own affairs remained bitter and, if nothing else, serves as a reminder that radicalism in the Great Plains has emerged for many reasons that outsiders do not consider viable but which remain locally important and part of the region's history.[39]

Despite outbreaks of radicalism, the Great Plains states shared a political tradition in which twice as many people considered themselves conservatives as liberals. Women voters tended to support female candidates, and most states did not confront major racial or ethnic divisions, because the population remained overwhelmingly white. Great political diversity existed, however, in Texas and New Mexico, where Latino and African

American voters had low incomes and allegiance to the Democratic Party. In 1990, women cast 54 percent of the Democratic vote and 49 percent of the Republican vote. Democratic candidates for governor usually received more votes from party conservatives than from liberals. In contrast, Republican candidates usually received about 40 percent of their votes from ideological conservatives. Democratic gubernatorial candidates also organized coalitions that were more ideologically diverse than did Republican candidates.[40]

Throughout the late twentieth century, politics in the Great Plains remained conservative and sometimes ideological, particularly for members of the Republican Party. In the southern Great Plains, this conservatism within the Republican Party developed from an aversion to centralization in the federal government, loyalty to local communities, and shared standards and values that voters did not necessarily see existing beyond their region. The region also experienced high voter registration and participation in the electoral process, regular church attendance, and organizational and volunteer work in local communities. Essentially, voters in the southern plains, like most across the Great Plains, were Protestant and patriotic and believed in the sacred trilogy of family, capitalism, and democracy: in a word, conservatism. Many of these conservatives found a political home in the Republican Party. Still, conservatism was not limited to one party, and the Democratic Parties in Oklahoma and Kansas had many conservative members. Small-town laissez-faire capitalism and an aversion to strong, regulatory central government, with an understanding that some governmental social services were necessary for the general welfare at the county, state, and federal levels, provided a philosophical foundation for political views and solidarity across most of the region, particularly the southern plains.

The increasing number of Latino, Catholic residents had greater political affinity with the Democratic Party, which had a better record on civil rights, voter registration, and a commitment to addressing social problems through government actions or programs than did the Republican Party. As the cities and towns became more culturally and racially heterogeneous, particularly with the increase of the Latino population, the voter base became less agricultural and rural and more blue collar, wage earning, and urban, as well as less white, which meant that a new politics of race had emerged at least on the southern plains by the end of the twentieth century. Political observers expected Democrats to become less socially conservative as this new population prospered, contributed time and money to political campaigns, and voiced its opinion about matters of affirmative action,

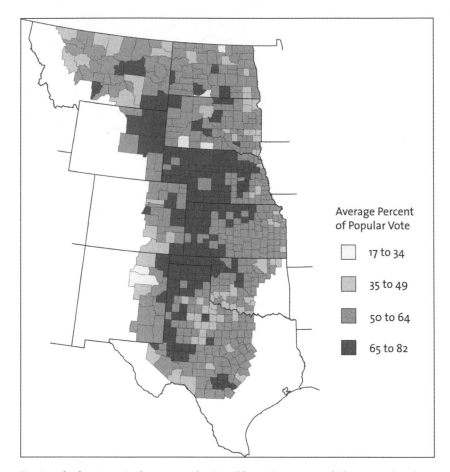

Average Percent
of Popular Vote

☐ 17 to 34

▨ 35 to 49

▨ 50 to 64

■ 65 to 82

During the late twentieth century, the Republican Party expanded its appeal and influence into Oklahoma and Texas from its traditional stronghold in the central and northern Great Plains. Great Plains voters have a reputation for supporting conservative fiscal policies, but they have aggressively sought federal funding essential for social programs. They have also considered federal agricultural programs to be matters of entitlement. This map shows the Republican vote in presidential elections from 1980 to 2000.

school boundaries, congressional districts, voting precincts, immigration restrictions, and the criminal justice system, and voted. Some political observers believed that the political identity of the southern Great Plains in particular soon would be epitomized by urban, Catholic, working-class voters.[41]

Still, these political generalizations require some qualifications. Latinos in New Mexico and Texas have been among the most vocal in demanding their civil rights and in their support of liberal issues. In the cities, such as Dallas and Denver, Latinos crafted a new politics of constituency — a voting bloc that favored candidates in either party so long as they supported Latino issues or agendas. Moreover, the political interests of these Latinos were transnational, particularly through relatives who immigrated to their towns or the region. The politics of immigration regulation became increasingly important to Latino voters as the issue intensified in the national political debate during the late twentieth century. Both the Republican and the Democratic Party began to vie for Latino support, particularly the Republican Party when its leaders recognized that the more affluent and educated Latinos were not particularly interested in criticizing the American political system because of the economic and social ramifications. Both parties had begun practicing the politics of recognition and inclusion for Latinos.[42]

The rapidly increasing Latino population had, by the late twentieth century, begun to create its own political power base in some areas of the Great Plains, especially in urban locales. Several individuals of Mexican descent were elected to city commissions, which reflected growing political strength in numbers, while local businesses made efforts to hire bilingual employees to accommodate new customers and demonstrate sensitivity to multiculturalism while avoiding antidiscrimination lawsuits. Moreover, Mexican American employees understood American culture, and some whites considered them agents of assimilation for non–American born Latino immigrants. At the same time, the potential for increased, if not dominant, Latino political power, particularly in the towns and cities, depended on increasing the naturalization, registration, and voter turnout, while leaders and voters negotiated the mire of illegal immigration, undocumented workers, and a growing new nativism in some portions of the plains.[43]

During the 1996 presidential election, Latinos cast 85 percent of their vote for Democrat Bill Clinton in Colorado, although he did not carry the state. In New Mexico and Texas, 65 percent and 75 percent of the Latino vote, respectively, went to Clinton, and that vote proved essential for his win in New Mexico. In many respects, because of differences in the party platforms by the end of the twentieth century, Latino voters had gravitated to the Democratic Party, and the Republican Party made little effort to include them. As a result, the Latino vote promised increased opportunity for the Democratic Party.[44]

Native American politics in the Great Plains, as in the Far West, centered on the insistence of the Indians to their unquestioned right of tribal sovereignty, treaty rights, cultural retention, and self-determination. In the Great Plains, Indian political power had been hindered by low voter registration and turnout. In the 1996 senatorial election in South Dakota, however, an intensive drive to register voters on the nine reservations enabled Indians to become important swing votes in the election of Tim Johnson, a Democratic member of the U.S. House of Representatives, when he contested the senatorial seat of Republican Larry Pressler. These Indian voters considered Johnson friendly to Indian issues and the conservative Pressler unsympathetic to their needs and concerns.[45]

Above all, the Indians insisted on the right of self-determination. Along with that belief was their contention that treaties with the federal government were the highest law of the land for them. Treaty rights recognized the territorial integrity of reservations and political rights that distinguished Indians from other Americans. Cultural retention also remained a major political issue that the Great Plains Indians insisted on having respected. The matters of preserving traditional languages, customs, arts, and spiritual beliefs were areas that could not be questioned by the larger society or body politic. Even so, the federal government remained a pervasive force on the reservations regarding educational, economic, and social services. Throughout the late twentieth century, then, the Indians in the Great Plains lived with a political legacy created during the New Deal and secured with the Indian activist movement of the 1960s and 1970s. Despite tribal diversity, their political demands for tribal sovereignty, treaty rights, self-determination, and cultural retention remained inviolate.[46]

In relation to national politics, political continuity prevailed. The Great Plains remained solidly Republican in the presidential elections from 1964 to 2000. In 1964, only Texas and Wyoming went Democratic, and the Republican voting tradition held thereafter until 1992, when Colorado, Montana, and New Mexico supported Democratic candidate Bill Clinton. In 1996, only New Mexico supported him again, and the Democrats held the state by a close vote (47.9 percent Democrat to 47.8 percent Republican). With the exception of voting for Lyndon Jonson in 1964, the ten Great Plains states essentially supported Republicans on the presidential tickets. Collectively, Great Plains voters were conservatives, but they also supported moderate candidates and social programs in congressional and statehouse campaigns if the goal helped conserve federal social services and agricultural programs. A few liberals remained, but they could not marshal significant political strength to topple conservative Republican presidential candidates; nevertheless, they occasionally achieved some success at the statehouse level. With few electoral votes, the Great Plains states seemed unimportant in national politics to outside observers.[47]

Most Great Plains counties continued to lose population at the turn of the twenty-first century, which some observers called "Manifest Destiny in Reverse." Nevertheless, urban areas often gained residents, and with the exception of North Dakota, state populations on the whole also grew. The environment of the Great Plains still presented challenges, and the geography still imposed relative isolation. Agriculture remained basic to the region's economy (for both good and ill), followed by regional manufacturing such as the aircraft industry in Wichita. Urban sprawl became a new reality for some cities, such as Oklahoma City and Tulsa, while Amarillo, Lincoln, and Lubbock, among others, expanded in population. Many cities and regional trade centers such as Bismarck, Fargo, and North Platte remained tied to the farm economy, and the meatpacking towns still hailed as rural boomtowns, with all the benefits and problems that such status implied. All Great Plains states sought the tourist trade. Conservatism often meant saving federal government programs to protect state taxpayers, while Republican moderates were often considered liberals and conservative Democrats the equivalent of Republicans because they generally rejected the national party platform on social issues. In the absence of being able to put families on 160 acres of highly profitable farmland, some critics suggested selling much of the region to the federal government, essentially expanding the national grasslands to the region as a whole, or much of it. By the time the twentieth century ended, considerable economic, social, and political change had occurred. Only the environment remained essentially the same, although some would deny that, given the evidence of global warming. Whether the twenty-first century dawned bright with promise or dim with despair depended on the perspective of those who took the long view back toward the turn of the twentieth century.[48]

Epilogue

"How far can you see out there?" he asked. "As far as your eye will let you," replied the Kansan. "I don't think I'd like that," said the easterner. Another remarked, "Colorado is a beautiful state, the western part. The east is nothing." South Dakota writer Kathleen Norris puts this sense of space and emptiness differently, writing that "it's hard to pay attention when there's so much of nothing to take in, so much open land that evokes in many people a panicked desire to get through it as quickly as possible." Wright Morris similarly wrote, "The men call it God's country — but the women asked, who else wants it." Dan O'Brien affirms that feeling, writing that when you travel west and reach the Missouri River, "it all goes to hell." Then, "When you get the feeling that the whole world can see you but no one is watching, you have come to the grasslands of North America." But there is a more admiring perspective on the region. N. Scott Momaday wrote, "At the slightest elevation you can see to the end of the world. To look upon that landscape in the early morning with the sun at your back is to lose the sense of proportion. Your imagination comes to life, and this you think is where Creation was begun." Many people like living in the Great Plains, and while standing beneath a blue sky that stretches from horizon to horizon as the wind runs through the cottonwood trees accompanied by the sound of falling water, they easily can believe that Copernicus got it wrong.[1]

It is the sense of space that impresses (often negatively) those who see the Great Plains for the first time. But some embrace it, as did Willa Cather. In *My Ántonia*, she chiseled in words a passage that would mark the litera-

242

ture of the plains for all time and give expression to the same feelings that many settlers had recorded in their diaries and letters sent from across the Great Plains during the late nineteenth century. Cather wrote, "There was nothing but land. . . . I had the feeling that the world was left behind, that we had got over the edge of it, and were outside of man's jurisdiction." Her character Jim Burden remembered, "As I looked about me, I felt that the grass was the country, as the water is the sea. . . . And, there was so much motion in it; the whole country seemed somehow, to be running." Seventy-five years later, Kathleen Norris affirmed the persistent image of the land as the sea, writing that "few appreciate the harsh beauty of a land that rolls like the ocean floor." Norris called the Great Plains "the great void at the heart of North America," and "a vast ocean of prairie." It is the land, often associated with the sea, which links the literature of the Great Plains across generations of writers.[2]

The land as the sea, as a garden, and as a desert are the most persistent symbols of the Great Plains in contemporary writing. No matter the description or narrative about it, twentieth-century writers focused on the manner in which men and women came to terms with the land. Their writing is clear, with an economy of words that reflects the directness of the Great Plains on the mind and eye and the people themselves; as literary scholar Diane Quantic writes, "Great Plains fiction is a web of connections of land, society, myth, and reality."[3]

The land shaped the writing of O. E. Rölvaag, Mari Sandoz, Frederick Manfred, Larry McMurtry, and others whose characters were hardened by it. Hamlin Garland created a vivid story of suffering men, women, and children in the Great Plains. In *Main Traveled Roads* (1891), he presented his characters as victims of the environment and capitalism. As men and women settled the land, they often reaped want and despair. The literature of the Great Plains is often grim and lonely, centered on the land, and bound by struggle and endurance, the stories of lives governed by the environment and geography. Sandoz called the Great Plains a "hard-land country." Larry McMurtry said as much but with more edge. He spoke of the Texas Panhandle, but his words apply to the Great Plains when he called it "pitiless" and "a land so powerful that it is all but impossible to live on it pleasantly." Still, the literature of the plains cannot escape the sky, because, as McMurtry wrote, "the sky determines so much." Norris poses the axiom that Great Plains people know never to turn their backs on it. Under the vastness of the sky, plains men and women are a "wind bullied people." The literature of the Great Plains, then, dwells on isolation and remoteness, with no illusion that the good times are mostly gone. It also is a literature that accepts the Great Plains for what it is, thereby giving truth to fiction. It is a stoic literature that conveys pride, perhaps beaten, but resilient, often a literature of "unredeemed dreams."[4]

Great Plains writers have emphasized the way the land transforms people for good and ill, usually beaten by the environment, work, and isolation, as exemplified by Rölvaag's *Giants in the Earth* (1927) and Sandoz's *Old Jules* (1935) for defeat, or with lives bettered by their relationship to the land, as in Cather's *My Ántonia* (1918) and John Ise's *Sod and Stubble* (1936). Essentially, this literature emphasizes the intersection of land and people, often portraying the dark side of the Great Plains with symbol, metaphor, and mythic false promise.[5]

The literature of the plains has been a regional literature, and writers who focus on the region today, usually academics, essentially reach small, specialty audiences. It is even hard to find many Great Plains authors in bookstores. No contemporary writer has produced a major book about the human condition set in a city of the Great Plains, although most of these writers, including Cather, lived there. Rather, the land remains the great crucible for ideas, and the literature that comes from it remains regional, unable to gain a national, general audience to absorb the emotional experience of the Great Plains.[6]

Kathleen Norris, who has written much about life in the region during the late twentieth century, likewise conveys the sense of persistence of the people against an unforgiving environment. She has a melancholy optimism, within which hope is as natural as breathing prairie wind. Norris writes about a wary people who live in a culture "where outsiders are treated with an uneasy mix of hospitality and rejection." For her, the Great Plains is not the "Great Desolation" of Rölvaag or the "American Outback" of *Newsweek*. She and other Great Plains writers have accepted that life will be better as a secular faith. How could they not, for those men and women of the plains who, as Norris writes, see resurgence in the February dusk where "instead of darkness at five in the afternoon; already hope is stirring at the edges of the day"?

In many ways, being associated with the Great Plains makes people self-conscious with a feeling of inferiority, in part because coastal people often consider the region socially and culturally wanting and the people poorly educated and insignificant. In some circles, being from the South is more acceptable than being from the Great Plains. Certainly, the Great Plains has its own cultural identity, which scholars have labored to understand. It is a distinctive region where those who go away and later return somehow feel that they are outsiders. What Norris says of South Dakota applies to the

Great Plains — that those who live there enjoy "a privileged and endangered way of life, one that, ironically, only the poor may be able to afford."

The residents of the Great Plains are a conservative people often living in small towns where life was better in the past and progress means a return to an age when the trains not only ran on time but ran at all. Change comes hard to small towns where economic realities dictate it, but it is made more difficult because plains men and women too often believe the axiom that "an expert is someone who's fifty miles from home." Norris warns plains people that disconnecting from change does not recapture the past, "[i]t loses the future." Equally important is the risk posed by the pervasive attitude toward change in the Great Plains, as summed up by Norris: "Change means failure; it is a contaminant brought in by the outside elements." In addition, politically, socially, and culturally (but not economically, particularly in relation to agriculture and energy resources), the Great Plains did not seem to matter much to most Americans outside of the region by the late twentieth century.[7]

Great Plains visual artists, like the writers, have emphasized the land from which the environment created a God-fearing, stern people, best exemplified by John Stewart Curry's *Baptism in Kansas* and *Tornado Over Kansas* and his controversial murals in the Kansas statehouse. Alexander Hogue, who painted the wind-eroded southern Great Plains during the Dust Bowl, dealt with a torn, drifted, and scorched land that led to the failure of a people. Hogue's paintings brought considerable criticism from southern plains residents who believed that they could still gain control of the environment and restore the land to its past bounty for their own purposes.[8]

The literature and art of the Great Plains show what the region was, is, and can be. Only through the region's literature, paintings, photography, music, and other art forms can its history be fully understood. With understanding comes recognition of the special qualities of the Great Plains, its distinctiveness where the common cultural denominator is paradox — a land harsh and gentle, violent and peaceful, bountiful and desolate, urban and rural.[9]

So, when potential tourists ask, "What is there to see?" The answer is "Not much" or, perhaps better, "Nothing but land and sky" or "A hard country." Tourists like to see things and do something, and the Great Plains does not meet the desires of most tourists, who are just passing through, headed for another destination. Mostly it is "quick stop tourism" along the interstate highways, in a word, "transient" tourism. Only a few natural places provide destinations for tourists: the Black Hills and Mount Rushmore in South Dakota, Devils Tower in Wyoming, and Carlsbad Caverns in New Mexico, to name a few. Overall, tourism relied mostly on the myth of the Old West. The Little Bighorn Battlefield National Monument in Montana, the Cowboy Hall of Fame and Western Heritage Center in Oklahoma City, and the Alamo in Texas remained perennially popular. Historic cow towns, army posts, and eccentricities of the area drew some travelers from afar. The Great Plains, however, provided more recreational sites for locals than destinations for tourists. Plains men and women who wanted to get away might enjoy local lakes and campsites during the year, although many made the pilgrimage to Mount Rushmore as much from a sense of duty as from curiosity. But all of the states boasted (not always accurately) about tourism opportunities, dreaming about the multiplier effect of the gasoline tax, food sales, and hotel accommodations. The outsiders or locals who appreciated the natural and sometimes spectacular beauty of the land were the real tourists.[10]

The Dakota Badlands provides an example. The Badlands, covering portions of North and South Dakota, is an austere region carved by a half-million years of wind and water erosion that left a vast graveyard of fossils. In the nineteenth century, not everyone appreciated the geological formation. In 1864, General Alfred Sully called it "hell with the fires burned out." Early in the twentieth century, a photographer complained, "There was no background. Nothing but earth and sky and a blinding sunlight." When referring to the Badlands, many people used the adjective *desolate*, alluding to a sense of loss. Consequently, efforts in 1909 to create a Badlands national park failed. Not until 1939 did the Badlands gain federal protection and then only as a national monument, because federal officials did not believe that the area had the scenic beauty required for a national park.

Highway construction during 1940s and 1950s brought some tourists to the Badlands, but perhaps fearful of the empty, desolate land, they tended to stay in their cars and did not linger. In 1951, though, one observer advised that travelers could break the monotony of South Dakota by driving through the Badlands, which, like the Black Hills, were a regional oddity. In 1978, aided by the environmental movement and the baby boom generation, many of whom wanted to commune with nature, the Badlands finally gained designation as a national park. Travel guides lauded the Badlands for its "strange and wild beauty" and as scenic in its "uncompromising savagery." By the end of the twentieth century, the Badlands had become a place for physical and spiritual renewal. In the southern plains, only Palo Duro Canyon and the canyonlands in West Texas compared, and many would argue that these sites had more natural beauty than the

Tourism has been limited in the Great Plains, but Mount Rushmore became one of the most popular tourist attractions in the region. Begun in 1927 and dedicated in 1941, the sculpture is shown as it neared completion.

Badlands. In between, tourist attractions remained few, problematic, and arguable.[11]

The farm and ranch counties of the Great Plains continued to weather and wither away during the late twentieth century. Fewer men and women could make an acceptable living from the land, and farms consolidated and declined in number while their size expanded. The small towns dwindled as well, victims of the rural exodus and the corresponding want of customers. The population aged with the flight of the young for greener pastures in Lubbock, North Platte, Bismarck, and cities beyond. When they left for jobs or college, they had no intention of going back. True to their word, most did not return. As the young departed and the old remained, biology inexorably eroded the population, the economy, and the farm and rural community. With most farm families producing two children, half of whom were likely to be females, and with women still not considered true farmers in this gender-ordered world, the demographic pool for the replenishment of farmers nearly dried up, because not all young men wanted to farm. Consequently, the farm family and the farm could not always be maintained or continued. Moreover, unless a man inherited a farm or married into it, he had virtually no hope of becoming a successful farmer, and even if he did have the opportunity, the odds were against him. Human reproduction, sophisticated and expensive technology, and the need for extensive lands set the parameters for agriculture in the Great Plains.[12]

This is not to say that agriculture had become unimportant, because it still drove the economy of the region with a host of multiplier effects. One of the great transformations in agriculture occurred with the shift of the cattle feeding industry to the Great Plains. During the 1940s, the feedlot industry began to shift from the midwestern Corn Belt states of Illinois, Iowa, and Minnesota to the Great Plains of Colorado, Kansas, and Nebraska. In the central and southern plains, the Ogallala Aquifer increasingly provided water for the irrigation of feed crops that permitted farmers to raise corn where that crop would have been impossible without it. Cattle raisers soon developed feedlots to maximize their investment with close proximity to feed and stocker cattle. The packing plants arrived soon thereafter to provide a nearby market, which helped reduce transportation costs. The nexus of feed grains, water, stocker cattle, transportation, and the economies of scale that encouraged the development of large-scale packing plants indicated that this aspect of the feeder cattle industry would remain prominent into the twenty-first century.[13]

At the same time, the number of feedlots declined while production remained essentially unchanged. As the feedlots became concentrated in the central and southern Great Plains, the financing often came from investors outside of agriculture. And as the feedlots drew the packinghouses, Latinos and Southeast Asians arrived to take the hard, dangerous, and necessary jobs that kept the packinghouses going and these workers employed, providing them with hope for a better life. When the twentieth century ended, Great Plains agriculture remained based on wheat, corn, cotton, and cattle. The depletion of the Ogallala Aquifer, however, remained a potential problem that could cause a return to dryland farming.[14]

Still, by the end of the twentieth century, tens of thousands of farm families and agricultural workers who had cut wheat, stacked bales, stripped cotton, and fed cattle had departed, never to return. They left the countryside and small towns for the cities of the region or someplace beyond. No one could say whether their lives were worse for leaving the land, but a certainty remained (especially among those who had not been farmers or lived in the small towns) that an agricultural and rural life was morally superior to life in the cities and that this way of life merited saving for the good of the nation. Few such moral sojourners and public intellectuals took time to reflect that such an assumption implied that those residents of the Great Plains who lived in urban areas were less moral and less familiar with the meaning of independence, truth, and democracy than were country people.

When railroad expansion ended in the plains by 1920, town building also terminated. Automobiles, paved roads, and interstate highways enabled people to live far beyond the city limits yet reach their employment and needed services quickly and conveniently, helped decrease isolation, and in time brought the demise of many small towns as consumers sought more choices and better prices in the county seats and growing regional trade centers. Steadily, rural residents moved to the larger towns for better employment opportunities and a higher standard of living. Oil, gas, and coal deposits created some regional towns such as Midland, Texas, Hugoton, Kansas, and Gillette, Wyoming, but the Great Plains had too few people and the markets were too distant to support large-scale, urban-based manufacturing. The rim cities prospered because they provided services for a large geographical area, but they did not depend on the interior for markets. Some small towns, however, became commuter suburbs for county seats and regional trade centers. The economically viable small towns depended on the extraction of agricultural or mineral products for shipment elsewhere. As the population of the larger towns and cities expanded, the proportion of people living in urban areas increased over those residing in the countryside. The towns and cities became magnets, increasingly independent of the agricultural economy, and provided a focal or contact point for isolated individuals spread across the vastness of the Great Plains.[15]

World War II stimulated the growth of many cities through the war industries that provided jobs. In 1940, the largest cities began to sprawl in the southern and central Great Plains, led by Denver, Dallas, San Antonio, Omaha, Oklahoma City, Fort Worth, Tulsa, Wichita, and Lincoln. Between 1940 and 1950, Oklahoma became an urban state with 51 percent of the population living in cities. During that same period, New Mexico's urban population rose to 50 percent of the state's total, while Colorado's urban population increased to 63 percent and Nebraska's city population to 47 percent of the state total. Even South Dakota's urban population increased to 33 percent and North Dakota's to 27 percent of the total count. In 1990, Dallas–Fort Worth, Denver, San Antonio, Oklahoma City, Tulsa, Omaha, Albuquerque, and Wichita led the Great Plains states in urban population.[16]

Many Great Plains cities became regional distribution centers and markets for local, often high-tech, products, and Dallas, Denver, Tulsa, Oklahoma City, and Omaha expanded rapidly as wholesaling metropolitan areas. The low-population northern plains states could not compete, because they lacked the critical mass of preexisting manufacturing and industry on which to build, as well as workers, capital, and technical resources. By the 1970s, corporations had increasingly begun to locate their headquarters in Tulsa, Dallas, Denver, Wichita, and San Antonio. In these cities, information-based companies reshaped the urban landscape and created "transactional cities" where information, financial networks, and political and economic decision making intersected to meet business needs on a global scale. During the late twentieth century, San Antonio claimed international importance as a center for biotechnology, business telecommunications, Latin American finance, and tourism. In the northern Great Plains, only Grand Forks, North Dakota, achieved distinction for a well-educated population that had the potential to attract high-technology industries, because more than 20 percent of its population aged twenty-five or over had completed at least four years of college.[17]

During the 1960s, the increasing African American and Hispanic populations began changing the political demography of many cities. The needs of these voters often diverged from the white majority. They made small gains in representation on city councils and became members of policy-making bodies, but these groups remained slighted and ignored by municipal governments regarding services from paved streets to health care. San Antonio proved a model of neglect for the underprivileged and, along with Dallas, Lubbock, and Wichita Falls, remained among the most rigidly segregated cities in Texas. The politics of gender also changed slowly, but women became increasingly politically active. In 1971, Patience Latting became mayor of Oklahoma City. By the end of the twentieth century, women had been elected mayor in a host of cities and towns, including Dallas, Fort Worth, and San Antonio. Many new urban residents did not have ties to the old power structure, and Great Plains cities did not have powerful political machines or strong party ties. Politicians also began moving to the center and supported economic development and minority interests to a greater extent than before.[18]

The Hispanic or Latino population also steadily moved northward from the southern Great Plains. In 1980, Dallas and Denver had more than fifty thousand residents with Spanish surnames. Omaha, Nebraska, Casper, Wyoming, and Garden City, Kansas, among other smaller cities, also grew in Hispanic population. Mexican restaurants soon provided the most common ethnic food in the region, and grocery stores and other businesses catered to this new population. Cities with nearby military bases and large universities, such as Fargo, as well as smaller urban areas, such as Topeka, also attracted Asian immigrants, particularly refugees from Indochina.

By 1990, Dallas and San Antonio had become international cities, while Denver, Oklahoma City, and others remained dependent on regional or national connections. Dallas served as an international business city with an excellent airport and interstate highway system and an educated workforce that enabled telecommunications, regional banks, and business services to reach a wide market across Texas, Oklahoma, and Arkansas. International businesses considered Dallas as an entrepôt to American markets. In 1990, foreign corporations and banks employed approximately thirty-five thousand workers, making Dallas an important city for international finance.[19]

In the Great Plains, three major metropolitan hinterlands — Denver, Dallas–Fort Worth, and Kansas City — dominated the region. They provided banking, retail, medical, and other services as well as economic, social, and cultural networks that affected everyday life far into the region. Minneapolis–St. Paul provided the same services for the northern Great Plains. Kansas City influenced the economy of Wichita, and Dallas–Fort Worth that of Oklahoma City. Denver's influence reached Casper, Douglas, and Buffalo, Wyoming, particularly by Interstate 25. During the late twentieth century, business activity for Montana, Nebraska, South Dakota, and North Dakota depended on linkages to Omaha and regional cities such as Lincoln, Bismarck, and Billings for retailing, wholesaling, transportation, manufacturing, and other services necessary to sustain communities where success meant the absence of decline. At the same time, these cities drew upon a labor force that might commute a hundred miles for employment, thereby giving these urban areas considerable economic reach.

At the end of the twentieth century, the cities of the Great Plains provided the major economic, educational, social, and cultural opportunities for the region. Individual freedom far removed from the social constraints of small-town life gave vitality to the cities of the plains. Social inequities remained, but a broadening of the political base due to ethnic changes and politics driven by technocrats who often were more administrators than politicians, as well as the added complexity of issues, voting power, and interests in the suburbs, created a tension between identity and interest-group politics.[20]

During the late twentieth century, each Great Plains state had its own political culture, and several generalizations apply about politics in the region. After World War II, the Great Plains followed the national postwar trend to the right, then stabilized with a middle-of-the road conservatism, although an occasional liberal, such as George McGovern from South Dakota and Congressman Carl Albert from Oklahoma, reached Congress. But Great Plains conservatives, such as Bob Dole from Kansas, often had reputations for pragmatism rather than for being party ideologues. Often they were elected to Congress because of identity politics (that is, voter identification with them) rather than because of party affiliation. The defeat of Senator Tom Daschle by John Thune in 2002 is an example of voters no longer identifying with an elected leader or deciding that they like another better, not necessarily for ideological political reasons. Economics rather than party often shaped political loyalties. Plains men and women generally opposed federal centralization, and their congressional representatives toed that line, with the exception of aggressively gaining federal funding for necessary social, highway, educational, and farm programs.

Oklahoma's Senator Robert Kerr (1948–63) is a case in point. He used his popularity to win election and his political influence to benefit his family's Kerr-McGee oil company while gaining millions of federal dollars for various development programs in Oklahoma. In New Mexico, the Democratic Party remained strong with its traditional Hispanic influence, but newly arrived federal employees and military men and women often voted Republican. Montanans elected progressive Democrat Mike Mansfield to the U.S. Senate but voted in conservative Republican governors at home. In Wyoming, the conservative miners and farmers had no qualms about sending liberals Joseph O'Mahoney and Gale McGee to the U.S. Senate. Republican conservatism crept into, then dominated, politics in Texas, with election victories from the governorship to the U.S. Senate. In general, Republican conservatism ranged from moderate to right wing, while

Democratic conservatism tended to be less right of center. On the state level, Great Plains voters expected legislators to practice fiscal conservatism by reducing spending and taxes. Additionally, interest-group rather than identity politics prevailed; for example, the conservative Wyoming Stock Growers Association generally controlled statehouse business. Nebraskans seemingly grew fond of rotating Republican and Democratic governors, with their shared conservative views providing political continuity. In Kansas, Democratic governors in the staunchly Republican state usually proved sufficiently conservative to pass as Republicans.[21]

The rapidly changing demographics of the countryside after World War II diminished party strength while enhancing interest-group influence in the state legislatures. In 1940, more than 58 percent of the Kansas population lived in rural areas, but this figure had declined to less than 25 percent by the mid 1980s. The wholesale and retail trades, not agriculture, constituted the largest component of the state's economy. Agricultural interest groups remained strong, but they primarily worked to influence policy at the national level because farm programs emanated from Congress. Kansas City, Topeka, and Wichita formed the points of the triangle within which most of the people lived. Kansas, like the other Great Plains states, did not have an interventionist, activist state government regarding economic and social affairs. Although the Republican Party dominated state electoral politics and government, party differences did not prevent conservative Democrats from gaining the governor's office. Urban Democrats often joined suburban Republicans in opposing rural issues. The most progressive politicians were often Republicans from suburban Kansas City, while the most successful statewide Democratic politicians were more conservative than their Republican opponents. Kansas government was weak because the state legislature met for only ninety days each year, making state legislators part-time public servants. As a result, they were constituent- rather than party-oriented and independent even though the parties gave some definition to public issues. Consequently, interest groups such as insurance, health care, business/industry, and education associations, as well as public utilities, played a major role in shaping public policy. Policy making was pluralistic with no one interest group or party dominating the political agenda.[22]

During the late twentieth century, then, Kansas remained Republican in national political orientation, but on the state level, candidate-centered electioneering in which issues were more important than party gave the conservative Democrats many opportunities. Kansas, like the other Great Plains states, did not have the economic, cultural, and racial diversity that

often creates two-party politics, and right-to-work laws hindered the unionization of workers who often support the Democratic Party. The Republican Party remained strong in all urban areas except Wyandotte County
(Kansas City). Most Kansans considered themselves moderates, and few
conservatives or liberals placed themselves on the far right or left of the
political spectrum. Kansas had a reputation for sending fiscally conservative Republicans to Congress, with the understanding that they would work
hard for government dollars. Kansans were strong supporters of expensive
federal programs, from defense spending to Social Security to farm subsidies. In Kansas, political values still reflected a strain of populism because
voters expected the federal government to be responsible for the general
welfare, a concept that is often trumped by interest-group politics. Personal
rather than party identification often carried elections, and Democrats
skillfully capitalized on Republican factionalism. Indeed, the differences
between eastern suburban Republicans and western rural Republicans
were noticeable over taxes on the oil and gas industry, the formula for state
aid to the public schools (which involved the redistribution of wealth), and
moral issues such as abortion. Moreover, nearly as many voters considered themselves independents as Republicans, and about one-third of the
independents considered themselves liberals. Kansans were comfortable
electing Republican presidents and senators and Democratic governors
and state legislators. The Republican Party did not have a lock on Kansas
voters when the century ended.[23]

Nebraska likewise was a strong interest-group state because the population was homogeneous in its social, economic, and political outlook.
Nebraskans had few reasons for disagreements, and they cared little for
political issues and conflicts. Political parties remained weak, the legislature was elected on a nonpartisan ballot, and interest groups controlled
public policy. Nebraska also had a reputation for sending independent and
liberal politicians to Congress, including George Norris, who served in
the U.S. House (1909–13) as a Republican and in the Senate (1913–43) as
first a Republican, then an independent; Democratic senator Bob Kerrey
(1989–2001); and moderate Republican senator Chuck Hagel (1997–2009).
Yet because Nebraskans took little interest in state government, they were
resistant to change, and they took the conservative position that state expenditures should be minimal. The state legislature and interest groups
(such as banking and insurance companies, local governments, and education groups) usually resolved public policy issues. Interest groups linked
state legislators with constituents. Nebraska, then, supported the status
quo, which gave interest groups a strong voice among legislators.[24]

In North Dakota, the legislature privileged agriculture and rural issues. The state's economy remained extractive, based on grain, livestock, coal, oil, and gas, which were mostly exported and controlled by outside corporations. North Dakota politicians had little money and maintained a "root cellar" mentality (that is, they were reluctant to spend for the improvement of public services, preferring to save their resources). The fusion of the Nonpartisan League with the Democratic Party in 1956 created a viable second party, although most North Dakotans considered themselves independents by the late twentieth century. With the state legislature meeting only once every two years for about eighty days, interest groups provided essential, technical information to help shape public policy. The Farm Bureau, Farmers Union, North Dakota Sunflower Growers Association, and Agricultural Coalition served as strong interest groups that developed tax, revenue sharing, and cooperative associational policies. The North Dakota Education Association also served as a strong interest group, along with the North Dakota Petroleum Council and the Lignite Council, the latter representing the mining and energy companies (such as Basin Electric, which operated the Great Plains Gasification plant), with both groups providing technical information to help legislators develop energy and environmental policy. The state legislature, however, showed remarkable independence from these interest groups.[25]

In Oklahoma, education, labor, newspapers, and local officials ranked as the most influential interest groups. In 1947, John Gunther wrote in *Inside U.S.A.* that Oklahoma teachers were "sophisticated politically and highly vocal." They remained so at the end of the twentieth century and skillfully competed for support, often at the expense of social welfare programs. Agriculture, oil, and the Baptist church as interest groups declined in, but did not concede, influence, which made Oklahoma a strong interest-group state. These groups also worked to influence public policy in Washington, D.C. Group demands superseded state and party needs.[26]

Moderately conservative South Dakota had little political dissension during the late twentieth century. Like Nebraska, South Dakota had a homogeneous population. Sharp political conflict rarely occurred even between whites and Native Americans. As a rural state with limited wealth, South Dakota politicians exercised a "drought mentality" that implied a reluctance to tax and spend, preferring fiscal conservatism over a liberal approach to providing expansive social services. Politicians and interest groups necessarily functioned within the parameters of fiscal conservatism that existed as matters of both law (deficit financing was illegal) and philosophy (don't spend what you don't have). Moderate conservatism was opposed by moderate liberalism. While South Dakota liberals addressed social justice, education, labor, and environmental issues, they always did so within the state's limited revenue base (low population and industrial development for tax purposes) and with the belief that limited government was the best government.[27]

In South Dakota, moderate conservatives favored the Republican Party in state politics, while the Democrats were major players in congressional politics, in which identity politics rather than interest-group politics provided the greatest rewards. Democratic senators George McGovern and Tom Daschle, for example, gained federal programs for the state, and South Dakotans considered them to be politicians who could deliver federal funding. South Dakota also used the initiative and referendum to "do" or "undo" popular or unpopular legislation and thereby keep state legislators in check. South Dakotans believed in direct democracy, and voters used it frequently. One environmental group, for example, used the initiative to prevent a conservative, business-oriented legislature from approving the location of a nuclear waste dump in the state. Periodically, voters also used the threat of a referendum to prevent unwanted legislative action, such as the deregulation of Bell Telephone, at least for a while. With the legislature elected for two-year terms from districts with small populations, "cracker barrel" (that is, local issues) politics based on personalities often became more important than issues and party.

Lacking strong party doctrine, chambers of commerce, businesses, and health care associations ranked among the major interest groups in South Dakota. Agricultural groups proved less politically effective, with specialized commodity groups more focused on Congress than on statehouse politics. The state legislature also reflected rural taxpayers' desires to keep property taxes low. Consequently, the South Dakota Education Association was less effective than its counterparts in other Great Plains states. Labor groups also had little political influence, in part because of an absence of manufacturing and union jobs and right-to-work legislation. Conservative, well-organized, and solidly financed interest groups successfully used non-threatening tactics to influence public policy in South Dakota.[28]

The Great Plains states that constituted a portion of the Mountain West exhibited some of the same weak party and legislature characteristics of the other Great Plains states. There, interest groups lobbied for specific policies that benefited their members, not necessarily the general welfare. There, too, absentee ownership of mineral deposits continued to foster a colonial relationship with outside corporations and investors. Weak political parties also contributed to the rise of interest-group politics. In Montana, Anaconda Copper, Montana Power, and the Northern Pacific and Great Northern railroads had strong interest-group representation in the state legislature, while oil, gas, timber, and cattle interests dominated in New Mexico. In Wyoming, strong interest-group power emanated from the Wyoming Stock Growers Association, oil and gas interests, the Wyoming Farm Bureau, and the Wyoming Education Association.[29]

In Montana, personal style remained more important than party affiliation for politicians, once again proving the power of identity politics. Political parties lacked discipline because the open primary enabled a large number of voters to consider themselves independents whose split-ticket voting contributed to divided party control in the state legislature. In the plains area, the Republican Party benefited from the Montana Stock Growers Association, which ranked among the most prestigious and influential agricultural organizations in the state, and it provided coalition leadership for other agricultural groups, collectively known as the Montana Agriculture Political Action Committee. The Montana Plains Resources Council became a major organization for environmentalists and ranchers who opposed the construction of coal-fired power plants at Colstrip and slurry pipelines for transporting coal to urban areas. Montanans used coalitions to support the status quo and defeat change rather than to achieve reform, with mining, livestock, timber, and agricultural interests prevailing.[30]

New Mexico, with its racially plural and fast-growing population, remained sparsely populated and relatively poor in the plains area, where ranching and oil interests prevailed among Baptists and Democrats who leaned toward the Republican Party when federal policies annoyed them. Political parties remained weak at the state level because single-issue groups in urban areas dominated the legislature. The legislature also was nonprofessional, meeting only ninety days during a two-year biennium. Interest groups easily influenced public policy with business, oil, and gas dominating because of their organizational and lobbying skills. In Albuquerque and Las Cruces, women's and environmental groups also waged successful interest-group politics. Political parties remained weaker than interest groups.[31]

In Wyoming, voters favored conservatism and individualism while distrusting the federal government, in part because about 48 percent of the state was federal or public land. The political philosophy was libertarian. Wyoming's voters were fiscal conservatives but opposed governmental regulation of abortion and prayer in the public schools. Society remained socially and ethnically homogeneous. The combination of conservatism, racial and ethnic homogeneity, and individualism made the state a Republican bastion without political clout on the national level, given its low population for representation. The Wyoming Stock Growers Association remained the most important interest group in the state. Ranchers opposed the encroachment of the mining industry and demanded the protection of their water rights. Congressional delegates aggressively supported federal policies beneficial to oil and gas development. Constituent demands, however, superseded interest-group demands. Business and environmental groups counterbalanced each other in a libertarian environment where voters were suspicious of the federal government, organized labor, and big business.[32]

Interest-group influence proved the weakest in Colorado, where the Republican Party controlled the political agenda, but there, too, the Colorado Cattlemen's Association, chambers of commerce, Farmers Union, and League of Women Voters exercised demonstrable political influence. In Colorado, the Denver suburbs and the eastern plains provided a solid base for the Republican Party, while the Democratic Party became strong in the city. The "centrists" who supported urban growth, water and energy development, and modest financial support for social services controlled state government. Conservative ranchers and office holders were replaced by young, well-educated, business-oriented, suburbanite Republicans, but the Democratic Party proved competitive for congressional offices when the identity of politicians mattered most, such as the election of liberal Democratic senator Gary Hart (1975–87) and liberal Democratic congresswoman Patricia Schroeder (1973–97). This also indicated differences in voting district characteristics. In Colorado, the legislature was more amateurish than professional, and it met for only a few weeks each year. As a result, the members usually favored the conservative status quo, not innovative policy. Colorado's conservative legislators tended to focus on issues of business and government regulations rather than social causes. Interest groups provided the necessary information for legislative decision making because the legislators had little staff support.[33]

During the late twentieth century, the Republican Party gained considerable strength in the southern Great Plains because many traditional Democrats no longer supported the social issues of the national party platform. In the central and northern Great Plains, the Republican Party ruled the statehouses. Overall, the residents of the Great Plains distrusted the federal government but demanded farm programs, aid for the elderly, and various social programs that they could not finance or administer.

Christianity predominated as the major religion of the Great Plains, with the Southern Baptists the largest denomination south of Kansas. Methodism prevailed in the central plains, while the Lutherans had great appeal in the northern plains. Religious preferences are complex in the region because they have been formed as much by ethnicity as by theology. Roman Catholicism remained predominant in New Mexico, where Spanish heritage influenced religious practices among Hispanics. The church also served as a major institution for cultural and social support. The Volga Germans practiced Catholicism, but Germans and Scandinavians often favored Protestantism. Judaism and Islam expanded slowly. Native American religious practices remained traditional through the practice of ceremonies and dances along with the adoption of some aspects of Christianity. Some Indian worshipers used the hallucinogenic peyote in the rituals of the Native American Church. Evangelicalism and the cult of the individual prospered in varying degrees, primarily in the southern plains. Evangelical, Pentecostal, and mainstream Protestant beliefs fostered a diverse, complex mix of religious practices in the Great Plains. Theologically, Great Plains men and women lived in an Old Testament world where reality was often harsh and unforgiving, but they prayed with hope and expectation to a New Testament God.

At the end of the twentieth century, problems born of racism, poverty, and unemployment plagued many urban areas, while the cities and towns strove to improve employment, health care, and educational opportunities. Rural areas suffered demographic and economic decline. Residing in a land where they were powerless before the environment and unable to control it, plains men and women lived carefully because persistence, no matter the outcome, meant to conquer. Fatalism did not reflect failure but instead manifested a sense of endurance with resignation, in a land where both good and bad were still largely attributed to the will of God.

The Great Plains remained a "next year" country, a region that never quite measured up to expectations, although cities such Dallas, San Antonio, and Denver proved the exception to the rule and became major entities in the global economy and world affairs while smaller cities such as Omaha, Wichita, and Sioux Falls offered comparatively vibrant economic and social lures. Many residents could agree with an observer who remarked on Thanksgiving Day in 1915, "We should be thankful . . . that we are still living to try it again." This sentiment expressed as much optimism as disappointment. At the end of the twentieth century, the Great Plains still offered men and women opportunity and hope for a better life. For some, opportunity lay in the packing towns. Others found it in the cities where outside corporations, service industries, and light manufacturing provided jobs. Farming had changed dramatically, but those who had the capital, land, and skill could enjoy a productive life. Fewer farmers did not mean that the Great Plains was the lesser for it. The depopulation or changing population of rural areas was not necessarily bad, because it indicated the traditional, historical process of adjustment of plains men and women to their environment, something they had done since they first came to the plains. During the twentieth century, some chose to stay while others chose to leave, but for those who stayed by choice and even for many who could not, the Great Plains became their sense of place, the land where they belonged.[34]

Next year people in a next year country — the Big Empty.

Notes

Preface

1. Great Plains Committee, *The Future of the Great Plains: Report of the Great Plains Committee* (Washington, D.C.: Government Printing Office, 1936).

2. For an engaging literary study of the above ideas, see Lou Halsell Rodenberger, Laura Butler, and Jacquelin Kolosov, eds., *Writing the Wind: An Anthology of Texas Women Writers* (Lubbock: Texas Tech University Press, 2005).

3. Willa Sibert Cather, *My Ántonia* (Boston: Houghton Mifflin, 1918), 8.

Chapter 1. The Age of Optimism

1. Elwyn B. Robinson, *History of North Dakota* (Lincoln: University of Nebraska Press, 1966), 236; Katherine Harris, *Long Vistas: Women and Families on Colorado Homesteads* (Niwot: University Press of Colorado, 1993), 58–59; Paula M. Nelson, *After the West Was Won: Homesteaders and Town-Builders in Western South Dakota, 1900–1917* (Iowa City: University of Iowa Press, 1986), xiv.

2. Nelson, *After the West Was Won*, xv, 17–19; Herbert S. Schell, "Widening Horizons at the Turn of the Century: The Last Dakota Land Boom," *South Dakota History* 12 (Summer–Fall 1982): 101.

3. Steven R. Kinsella, *900 Miles from Nowhere: Voices from the Homestead Frontier* (St. Paul: Minnesota Historical Society Press, 2006), 30–32; Nelson, *After the West Was Won*, 17, 20, 22–23.

4. Kenny L. Brown, "Building a Life: Culture, Society and Leisure in the Cherokee Outlet," *Chronicles of Oklahoma* 71 (Summer 1993): 193–97.

5. Thomas A. Britten, "Changing Land Use in Carson County: A Microcosm of the Panhandle Experience," *Panhandle-Plains Historical Review* 66 (1993): 57.

6. Paul H. Carlson, *Amarillo: The Story of a Western Town* (Lubbock: Texas Tech University Press, 2006), 54, 60.

7. Carlson, *Amarillo*, 61–64, 74, 80–81; J. Evetts Haley, *The XIT Ranch of Texas and the Early Days of the Llano Estacado* (Norman: University of Oklahoma Press, 1982), 214–26.

8. Carlson, *Amarillo*, 74–77.

9. Nelson, *After the West Was Won*, 27–28; Kinsella, *900 Miles from Nowhere*, 69.

10. Kinsella, *900 Miles from Nowhere*, 32, 123, 178–79; H. Elaine Lindgren, *Land in Her Own Name: Women as Homesteaders in North Dakota* (Norman: University of Oklahoma Press, 1996), vi, viii, 111–24, 207.

11. Lindgren, *Land in Her Own Name*, 214–15; see also Glenda Riley, *The Female Frontier: A Comparative View of Women on the Prairie and the Plains* (Lawrence: University Press of Kansas, 1988).

12. Lindgren, *Land in Her Own Name*, 22–24, 273; Harris, *Long Vistas*, 20, 24, 61, 62, 142; Sheryll Patterson-Black, "Women Homesteaders on the Great Plains Frontier," *Frontiers: A Journal of Women's Studies* 1 (Spring 1976): 68, 72; Riley, *Female Frontier*, 133.

13. Lindgren, *Land in Her Own Name*, xiii, 2–4; Harris, *Long Vistas*, 21, 161.

14. Lindgren, *Land in Her Own Name*, 15, 19–23, 205–6, 238.

15. Harris, *Long Vistas*, 2–3, 161–62.

16. Mary Wilma M. Hargreaves, *Dry Farming in the Northern Great Plains, 1900–1925* (Cambridge, Mass.: Harvard University Press, 1957), 88–89.

17. *Proceedings of the Fourth Annual Session of the Dry Farming Congress: Held at Billings, Montana, October 26, 27, 28, 1909* (Billings: Billings Chamber of Commerce, 1909), 20.

18. Paul W. Gates, "Homesteading in the High Plains," *Agricultural History* 51 (January 1977): 122; Kinsella, *900 Miles from Nowhere*, 11.

19. Greg Hall, *Harvest Wobblies: The Industrial Workers of the World and Agricultural Laborers in the American West, 1905–1930* (Corvallis: Oregon State University Press, 2001), 10–24.

20. Nigel Anthony Sellars, *Oil, Wheat and Wobblies: The Industrial Workers of the World in Oklahoma, 1905–1930* (Norman: University of Oklahoma Press, 1998), 16–17; Hall, *Harvest Wobblies*, 75–77.

21. Sellars, *Oil, Wheat and Wobblies*, 5–13, 20–21, 25–26, 31–33.

22. *Clay Center (Kan.) Dispatch*, January 3, 1901.

23. Gilbert C. Fite, *Peter Norbeck: Prairie Statesman* (Columbia: University of Missouri Press, 1948; repr., Pierre: South Dakota State Historical Society Press, 2005), 31.

24. Herbert S. Schell, *History of South Dakota* (Lincoln: University of Nebraska Press, 1975; repr., Pierre: South Dakota State Historical Society Press, 2004), 259.

25. Fite, *Peter Norbeck*, 28–31; Steven L. Pratt, "The Origins of the Initiative and Referendum in South Dakota: The Political Context," *Great Plains Quarterly* 12 (Summer 1992): 181, 190–91; Kenneth E. Hendrickson Jr., "The Populist Era: Richard Franklin Pettigrew, Andrew E. Lee, and Coe I. Crawford," in *South Dakota Leaders: From Pierre Chouteau, Jr., to Oscar Howe*, ed. Herbert T. Hoover and Larry J. Zimmerman (Vermillion: University of South Dakota Press, 1989), 202.

26. Richard Lowitt, *George W. Norris: The Making of a Progressive, 1861–1912* (New York: Syracuse University Press, 1963), 152, 166–88, 201, 248; Richard Lowitt, *George W. Norris: The Persistence of a Progressive, 1913–1933* (Urbana: University of Illinois Press, 1971), 197–216.

27. Michael P. Malone and Richard B. Roeder, *Montana: A History of Two Centuries* (Seattle: University of Washington Press, 1976), 196–97.

28. Robert W. Richmond, *Kansas: A Land of Contrasts* (St. Charles, Mo.: Forum Press, 1974), 190–92.

29. Wilda M. Smith, "A Half Century of Struggle: Gaining Woman Suffrage in Kansas," *Kansas History* 4 (Summer 1981): 75–76, 81, 91, 93–95.

30. Norma Smith, *Jeannette Rankin: America's Conscience* (Helena: Montana Historical Society Press, 2002), 75–79; Robinson, *History of North Dakota*, 259; Burton W. Folson, "Tinkers, Tipplers, and Traitors: Ethnicity and Democratic Reform in Nebraska during the Progressive Era," *Pacific Historical Review* 50, no. 1 (1981): 53–56; Schell, *History of South Dakota*, 260–62; Riley, *Female Frontier*, 191–92.

31. Richmond, *Kansas*, 193.

32. Robinson, *History of North Dakota*, 256.

33. Patrick G. O'Brien, "Prohibition and the Kansas Progressive Example," *Great Plains Quarterly* 7 (Fall 1987): 219, 221, 223, 225, 227, 229; Robinson, *History of North Dakota*, 258; see also Robert Bader Smith, *Prohibition in Kansas: A History* (Lawrence: University Press of Kansas, 1986).

34. Jim Bissett, *Agrarian Socialism in America: Marx, Jefferson, and Jesus in the Oklahoma Countryside, 1904–1920* (Norman: University of Oklahoma Press, 1999), 28–38.

35. John Thompson, *Closing the Frontier: Radical Response in Oklahoma, 1889–1923* (Norman: University of Oklahoma Press, 1986), 100–101, 104–5, 113.

36. James R. Scales and Danney Goble, *Oklahoma Politics: A History* (Norman: University of Oklahoma Press, 1982), 63, 76; Thompson, *Closing the Frontier*, 128, 130; W. David Baird and Danney Goble, *The Story of Oklahoma* (Norman: University of Oklahoma Press, 1994), 346.

37. Scales and Goble, *Oklahoma Politics*, 68; Bissett, *Agrarian Socialism in America*, 68.

38. Bissett, *Agrarian Socialism in America*, 66–70, 108–9, 126–29, 137–41.

39. Carlos G. Bates and Roy G. Pierce, *Forestation of the Sand Hills of Nebraska and Kansas*, Bulletin 121 (Washington, D.C.: U.S. Department of Agriculture, Forest Service, 1913), 8–9, 11; Raymond J. Poole, "Fifty Years on the Nebraska National Forest," *Nebraska History* 34 (September 1953): 143; John Clark Hunt, "The Forest that Men Made, Part II," *American Forests* 71 (December 1965): 34.

40. B. E. Fernow, *What Is Forestry?* Bulletin 5 (Washington, D.C.: U.S. Department of Agriculture, Forest Service, 1891), 34–35.

41. Bates and Pierce, *Forestation of the Sand Hills*, 20; Poole, "Fifty Years," 145.

42. John Clark Hunt, "The Forest that Men Made, Part I," *American Forests* 71 (November 1965): 46; Poole, "Fifty Years," 145–46.

43. Bates and Pierce, *Forestation of the Sand Hills*, 19.

44. Bates and Pierce, *Forestation of the Sand Hills*, 22; Poole, "Fifty Years," 148–49.

45. Addison E. Sheldon, "Silver Anniversary of the Nebraska National Forest," *Journal of Forestry* 25 (December 1927): 1021; Poole, "Fifty Years," 157–59; Bates and Pierce, *Forestation of the Sand Hills*, 22–23; Seward D. Smith, "Forestation a Success in the Sand Hills of Nebraska," *Proceedings of the Society of American Foresters* (Washington, D.C.: Judd and Detwiler, 1914), 389–90.

46. Bates and Pierce, *Forestation of the Sand Hills*, 8, 18–19.

47. Bates and Pierce, *Forestation of the Sand Hills*, 22; Smith, "Forestation a Success," 388.

48. Hunt, "Forest that Men Made, Part II," 34; Smith, "Forestation a Success," 389, 394; J. Higgins, "Facts and Figures Regarding the Nebraska Planting Project," *Journal of Forestry* 25 (December 1927): 1027, 1029.

49. Willis Conner Sorensen, "The Kansas National Forest, 1905–1915," *Kansas Historical Quarterly* 35 (Winter 1969): 388–89; Brian Allen Drake, "Waving 'A Bough of Challenge': Forestry on the Kansas Grasslands, 1865–1915," *Great Plains Quarterly* 23 (Winter 2003): 30.

50. Bates and Pierce, *Forestation of the Sand Hills*, 19; R. S. Kellogg, *Forest Planting in Western Kansas*, Circular 161 (Washington, D.C.: U.S. Department of Agriculture, Forest Service, March 2, 1909), 10, 50; Sorensen, "Kansas National Forest," 389–90.

51. Bates and Pierce, *Forestation of the Sand Hills*, 22, 38; Drake, "Waving 'A Bough of Challenge,'" 30.

52. Sorensen, "Kansas National Forest," 392.

53. Sorensen, "Kansas National Forest," 390; Bates and Pierce, *Forestation of the Sand Hills*, 38.

54. Sorensen, "Kansas National Forest," 389–90, 393–94; Bates and Pierce, *Forestation of the Sand Hills*, 24, 38.

55. *Ellis County News* (Hays, Kan.), January 6 and 13, 1900; Mary Hurlbut Cordier, *School Women of the Prairies and Plains: Personal Narratives from Iowa, Kansas, and Nebraska, 1860s–1920s* (Albuquerque: University of New Mexico Press, 1992), 245–70; Mary W. M. Hargreaves, "Rural Education on the Northern Plains Frontier," *Journal of the West* 18 (Winter 1979): 27.

56. Carlson, *Amarillo*, 82–83; Francis W. Schruben, *Wea Creek to Eldorado: Oil in Kansas, 1860–1920* (Columbia: University of Missouri Press, 1972), 37–68, 137, 140.

57. James R. Shortridge, *Cities on the Plains: The Evolution of Urban Kansas* (Lawrence: University Press of Kansas, 2004), 193–95, 197; Schruben, *Wea Creek to Eldorado*, 37–68.

58. Roger M. Olien and Diana Davids Olien, *Oil Booms: Social Change in Five Texas Towns* (Lincoln: University of Nebraska Press, 1982), 8.

59. Glenn W. Miller and Jimmy Skaggs, eds., *Metropolitan Wichita: Past, Present, and Future* (Lawrence: Regents Press of Kansas, 1978), 23; *Historical Statistics of the United States*, vol. 1, part A, *Population* (Cambridge: Cambridge University Press, 2006), 1-129, 1-132; Carl Abbott, *The Metropolitan Frontier: Cities in the Modern American West* (Tucson: University of Arizona Press, 1993), xvii–xviii; Walter Nugent, *Into the West: The Story of Its People* (New York: Knopf, 1999), 133; Lawrence H. Larsen, Barbara J. Cottrell, Harl A. Dalstrom, and Kay Calamé Dalstrom, *Upstream Metropolis: An Urban Biography of Omaha and Council Bluffs* (Lincoln: University of Nebraska Press, 2007), 174–76, 181, 186, 205–11.

60. John C. Hudson, "The Plains Country Town," in *The Great Plains: Environment and Culture*, ed. Brian W. Blouet and Frederick C. Luebke (Lincoln: University of Nebraska Press, 1979), 99–118; Nelson, *After the West Was Won*, 86; Lawrence H. Larsen and Roger T. Johnson, "Obstacles to Urbanization on the Northern Great Plains of the United States," *North Dakota History* 50 (Summer 1983): 14–22.

61. Nugent, *Into the West*, 134, 138, 149–51.

62. *Congressional Quarterly's Guide to U.S. Elections*, 2d ed. (Washington, D.C.: Congressional Quarterly, 1985), 345–49.

63. Nathan Meyer, "The Election of 1916 in Kansas," *Kansas Historical Quarterly* 35 (Spring 1969): 50–51, 53, 56–57; *Congressional Quarterly's Guide*, 463, 468, 474, 476, 478–79, 482–83, 486.

Chapter 2. The Ethnic and Racial Divide

1. Walter Nugent, *Into the West: The Story of Its People* (New York: Knopf, 1999), 198–208. The term *Hispanic* refers to all people who are descendents of Spanish or Spanish-speaking people. It is dependent more on history and geography than ethnicity because Hispanics can be of any race. Until the mid-1960s, the most numerous Hispanics were of Mexican origin. Others included Tejanos (as Mexican Americans in Texas have long been called). With the increase of immigrants from Central America during the late twentieth century, the word *Latino* became the most commonly used term. Here I use the term *Mexicanos* to include people of Mexican American and Mexican descent and *Hispanic* when referring to people of Spanish descent in New Mexico. I use the term *Anglo* for all non-Hispanic whites. The term *Hispanic* primarily refers to people living in New Mexico who were descendants of Spanish people with little or no mestizo heritage. During the 1920s, Hispanics preferred the identifying term of *Spanish American*, which had cultural and racial connotations. This term predominated until the 1960s, when lower-class Spanish Americans became referred to as Mexicans. This terminology is further complicated because Hispanics usually call themselves Spanish Americans when speaking English and Mexicanos when conversing in Spanish, but *Mexicanos* does not mean Mexican. The term *Hispanic* is vague, and it is complicated with multiple meanings. For a detailed study of this terminology, see Terrance Haverluk, "The Changing Geography of U.S. Hispanics, 1850–1900," *Journal of Geography* 96 (May–June 1977): 134–45; and Richard L. Nostrand, *The Hispanic Homeland* (Norman: University of Oklahoma Press, 1992).

2. David Montejano, *Anglos and Mexicans in the Making of Texas, 1836–1986* (Austin: University of Texas Press, 1987), 183, 185, 187; Jorge Iber and Arnoldo De León, *Hispanics in the American West* (Santa Barbara, Calif.: ABC Clio, 2006), 164.

3. Montejano, *Anglos and Mexicans*, 189, 193–94; Iber and De León, *Hispanics in the American West*, 166–67; Michael M. Smith, "Beyond the Borderlands: Mexican Labor in the Central Great Plains, 1900–1930," *Great Plains Quarterly* 1 (Fall 1981): 239–40.

4. Sarah Deutsch, *No Separate Refuge: Culture, Class and Gender on an Anglo-Hispanic Frontier in the American Southwest, 1880–1940* (New York: Oxford University Press, 1987), 82–106.

5. Deutsch, *No Separate Refuge*, 129–30, 141.

6. Deutsch, *No Separate Refuge*, 31–32, 36–49, 126; William Wyckoff, *Creating Colorado: The Making of a Western American Landscape, 1860–1940* (New Haven, Conn.: Yale University Press, 1999), 186, 215; Iber and De León, *Hispanics in the American West*, 168, 175–76, 181, 189.

7. Smith, "Beyond the Borderlands," 239–40.

8. Smith, "Beyond the Borderlands," 241, 244.

9. Carl Abbott, "Plural Society in Colorado: Ethnic Relations in the Twentieth Century," *Phylon* 39, no. 3 (1978): 252; Antonio Rios-Bustamante, "Wyoming's Mexican Hispanic History," *Annals of Wyoming* 73 (Spring 2001): 6.

10. Michael de la Garza, "The Lynching of Juan Gonzalez," *Nebraska History* 85 (Spring 2004): 24–37.

11. Iber and De León, *Hispanics in the American West*, 189–97.

12. Janet E. Schulte, "'Proving Up and Moving Up': Jewish Homesteading Activity in North Dakota, 1900–1920," *Great Plains Quarterly* 10 (Fall 1990): 231–32, 234, 237–42; R. Douglas Hurt, "Miller and Lux, Rachael Calof, Nannie Alderson and the Settlement of the Agricultural Frontier," in *Western Lives: A Biographical History of the American West*, ed. Richard W. Etulain (Albuquerque: University of New Mexico Press, 2004), 229–54.

13. Hal Rothman, "'Same Horse, New Wagon': Tradition and Assimilation among the Jews of Wichita, 1865–1930," *Great Plains Quarterly* 15 (Spring 1995): 85–96, 98–100.

14. Nicholas P. Cioloto, "From Agriculturists to Entrepreneurs: Economic Success and Mobility among Albuquerque's Italian Immigrants, 1900–1930," *New Mexico Historical Review* 74 (January 1999): 3–27.

15. Daniel C. Fitzgerald, "'We Are All in This Together': Immigrants in the Oil and Mining Towns of Southern Kansas, 1890–1920," *Kansas History* 10 (Spring 1987): 22–24.

16. David G. Loconto, "Discrimination against and Adaptation of Italians to the Coal Counties of Oklahoma," *Great Plains Quarterly* 24 (Fall 2004): 251–54.

17. Fitzgerald, "We Are All," 25, 27–28.

18. James R. Shortridge, "Culture Areas in the Central and Northern Great Plains," *Great Plains Quarterly* 8 (Fall 1988): 210–12.

19. Don Hodgson, "The Other Germans in Wyoming," *Annals of Wyoming* 63, no. 4 (1991): 145–46; Gordon L. Iseminger, "The McIntosh County German Russians: The First Fifty Years," *North Dakota History* 51 (Summer 1988): 4–23; Elwyn B. Robinson, *History of North Dakota* (Lincoln: University of Nebraska Press, 1966), 282–87.

20. Timothy J. Kloberdanz, "'Unsere Un' Die Andre': In-Group Affiliation among the Volga Germans of Russia and the Great Plains," *Plains Anthropologist* 31 (1986): 289–90; Carol K. Coburn, "Ethnicity, Religion, and Gender: The Women of Block, Kansas, 1868–1940," *Great Plains Quarterly* 8 (Fall 1988): 229–30; see also Carol K. Coburn, *Life at Four Corners: Religion, Gender, and Education in a German-Lutheran Community, 1868–1945* (Lawrence: University Press of Kansas, 1992); and D. Aidan McQuillan, *Prevailing over Time: Ethnic Adjustment on the Kansas Prairies, 1875–1925* (Lincoln: University of Nebraska Press, 1990).

21. Wilson J. Warren, *Tied to the Great Packing Machine: The Midwest and Meat Packing* (Iowa City: University of Iowa Press, 2007), 50–56.

22. Lowell L. Blaisdell, "Anatomy of an Oklahoma Lynching: Bryan County, August 12–13, 1911," *Chronicles of Oklahoma* 79 (Fall 2001): 300–303, 308.

23. Linda Williams Reese, *Women of Oklahoma, 1890–1920* (Norman: University of Oklahoma Press, 1997), 153–55, 160–61, 178–79.

24. Nugent, *Into the West*, 211; Moya B. Hansen, "'Trying to Be a Black Woman!': Jobs in Denver, 1900–1970," in *African American Women Confront the West, 1600–*

2000, ed. Quintard Taylor and Shirley Ann Wilson Moore (Norman: University of Oklahoma Press, 2003), 208–11; Lawrence H. Larsen, Barbara J. Cottrell, Harl A. Dalstrom, and Kay Calamé Dalstrom, *Upstream Metropolis: An Urban Biography of Omaha and Council Bluff* (Lincoln: University of Nebraska Press, 2007), 205, 216–17.

25. Clayton D. Laurie, "The U.S. Army and the Omaha Race Riot of 1919," *Nebraska History* 72 (Winter 1991): 137; Clare V. McKenna Jr., "Seeds of Destruction: Homicide, Race, and Justice in Omaha, 1880–1920," *Journal of American Ethnic History* 14, no. 1 (1994): 67–68, 80, 85.

26. Orville D. Menard, "Tom Dennison, the *Omaha Bee*, and the 1919 Omaha Race Riot," *Nebraska History* 68 (Winter 1987): 152, 159–60, 162, 164; Larsen et al., *Upstream Metropolis*, 219–26.

27. R. Halliburton Jr., "The Tulsa Race War of 1921," *Journal of Black Studies* 2, no. 3 (1972): 333–34, 341–43, 345–50, 354–55; see also Scott Ellsworth, *Death in a Promised Land* (Baton Rouge: Louisiana State University Press, 1982).

28. Beth Crabb, "May 1930: Whiteman's Justice for a Black Man's Crime," *Journal of Negro History* 75, nos. 1–2 (1990): 29–30, 38.

29. Charles C. Alexander, *The Ku Klux Klan in the Southwest* (Lexington: University of Kentucky Press, 1965), 1–11, 14, 19, 21.

30. David M. Chalmers, *Hooded Americanism: The History of the Ku Klux Klan* (Durham, N.C.: Duke University Press, 1987), 40–43; Rosaland Benjet, "The Ku Klux Klan and the Jewish Community of Dallas, 1921–1923," *Southern Jewish History* 6 (2003): 137–38.

31. Chalmers, *Hooded Americanism*, 3, 39, 12, 45, 47, 299.

32. Sheldon Neuringer, "Governor Walton's War on the Ku Klux Klan: An Episode in Oklahoma History," *Chronicles of Oklahoma* 45 (Summer 1967): 153–55, 162–66; Chalmers, *Hooded Americanism*, 49–52; Alexander, *Ku Klux Klan*, 60; Michael M. Jessup, "Consorting with Blood and Violence: The Decline of the Oklahoma Ku Klux Klan," *Chronicles of Oklahoma* 78 (Fall 2000): 297, 304.

33. Neuringer, "Governor Walton's War," 176.

34. Alexander, *Ku Klux Klan*, 2, 46, 240; Neuringer, "Governor Walton's War," 178; Jessup, "Consorting with Blood and Violence," 306–7; Chalmers, *Hooded Americanism*, 52–55, 299.

35. William Sloan, "Kansas Battles the Invisible Empire: The Legal Ouster of the KKK from Kansas, 1922–1927," *Kansas Historical Quarterly* 40 (Autumn 1974): 393–98; Chalmers, *Hooded Americanism*, 143–44.

36. Chalmers, *Hooded Americanism*, 143–48.

37. Michael W. Schuyler, "The Ku Klux Klan in Nebraska, 1920–1930," *Nebraska History* 66 (Fall 1985): 234–42, 244–45, 248, 250, 252–53.

38. Gerald Lynn Marriner, "Klan Politics in Colorado," *Journal of the West* 15 (January 1976): 77; Chalmers, *Hooded Americanism*, 126–32.

39. Marriner, "Klan Politics in Colorado," 76–79, 81, 88–94, 96, 98; Chalmers, *Hooded Americanism*, 133, 163.

40. Catherine McNicol Stock, *Main Street in Crisis: The Great Depression and the Old Middle Class on the Northern Plains* (Chapel Hill: University of North Carolina Press, 1992), 66; Charles Rambow, "The Ku Klux Klan in the 1920s: A Concentration on the Black Hills," *South Dakota History* 4 (Fall 1984): 71, 74, 81; William L.

Harwood, "The Ku Klux Klan in Grand Forks, North Dakota," *South Dakota History* 1 (Fall 1971): 306.

41. Harwood, "Ku Klux Klan," 301–2, 311–13, 322, 334, 335; Chalmers, *Hooded Americanism*, 219–21, 223–24.

42. Alexander, *Ku Klux Klan*, 252.

43. Clyde Ellis, *To Change Them Forever: Indian Education at the Rainy Mountain Boarding School, 1893–1920* (Norman: University of Oklahoma Press, 1996), xiii–xvi, 20; K. Tsianina Lomawaima, *They Called It Prairie Light: The Story of Chilocco Indian School, 1898–1933* (Norman: University of Oklahoma Press, 1994), 1, 17–18.

44. Ellis, *To Change Them Forever*, 27, 47–49, 70–74, 136.

45. Ellis, *To Change Them Forever*, 144–45, 148; Lomawaima, *They Called It Prairie Light*, 13, 82–84; Scott Riney, *The Rapid City Indian School, 1898–1933* (Norman: University of Oklahoma Press, 1999), 219; Brenda J. Child, *Boarding School Seasons: American Families, 1900–1940* (Lincoln: University of Nebraska Press, 1998); Peter Iverson, *We Are Still Here: American Indians in the Twentieth Century* (Wheeling, Ill.: Harlan Davidson, 1998), 22.

46. Ellis, *To Change Them Forever*, 178, 182, 187–88.

47. Ellis, *To Change Them Forever*, 195–96; Frederick E. Hoxie, *A Final Promise: The Campaign to Assimilate the Indians, 1880–1920* (Lincoln: University of Nebraska Press, 1984), 237–44; Frederick E. Hoxie, "From Prison to Homeland: The Cheyenne River Reservation before World War I," *South Dakota History* 10 (Winter 1979): 134; Riney, *Rapid City Indian School*, 216.

48. David Wallace Adams, *Education for Extinction: American Indians and the Boarding School Experience, 1875–1928* (Lawrence: University Press of Kansas, 1995), 336; Iverson, *We Are Still Here*, 25.

49. Sally J. McBeth, "Indian Boarding Schools and Ethnic Identity: An Example from the South Plains Tribes of Oklahoma," *Plains Anthropologist* 28, no. 100 (1983): 124.

50. McBeth, "Indian Boarding Schools," 125; Adams, *Education for Extinction*, 308–10, 336–37.

51. Thomas G. Andrews, "Turning the Tables on Assimilation: Oglala Lakotas and the Pine Ridge Day Schools, 1889–1920s," *Western Historical Quarterly* 33 (Winter 2002): 407, 412, 415, 417, 420–21, 427–29.

52. R. Douglas Hurt, *Indian Agriculture in America: Prehistory to the Present* (Lawrence: University Press of Kansas, 1987), 143–73.

53. Janet A. McDonnell, *The Dispossession of the American Indians, 1887–1934* (Bloomington: Indiana University Press, 1991), 87–92; Iverson, *We Are Still Here*, 33–34.

54. Paul C. Rosier, *Rebirth of the Blackfeet Nation, 1912–1954* (Lincoln: University of Nebraska Press, 2001), 13–53.

55. Donald L. Fixico, *The Invasion of Indian Country in the Twentieth Century: American Capitalism and Tribal Natural Resources* (Niwot: University Press of Colorado, 1998), 27–49.

56. Tom Holm, *The Great Confusion in Indian Affairs: Native Americans and Whites in the Progressive Era* (Austin: University of Texas Press, 2005), 34–36.

57. John Troutman, "The Citizenship of Dance: Politics of Music among the Lakotas, 1900–1924," in *Beyond Red Power: American Indian Politics and Activism*

since 1900, ed. Daniel M. Cobb and Loretta Fowler (Santa Fe, N.Mex.: School for Advanced Research, 2007), 93–104.

58. Iverson, *We Are Still Here*, 74–76; Donald L. Parman, *Indians and the American West in the Twentieth Century* (Bloomington: Indiana University Press, 1994), 83–87; Vine Deloria Jr. and Clifford N. Lytle, *American Indians, American Justice* (Austin: University of Texas Press, 1983), 12–13.

59. Michael Phillips, *White Metropolis: Race, Ethnicity, and Religion in Dallas* (Austin: University of Texas Press, 2006), 57–76.

Chapter 3. The Age of Uncertainty

1. Frederick C. Luebke, *Bonds of Loyalty: German Americans and World War I* (DeKalb: Northern Illinois University Press, 1974), 50–51, 84, 104, 106, 111; Carl Wittke, *German Americans and the World War (With Special Emphasis on Ohio's German Language Press* (Columbus: Ohio State Archaeological and Historical Society, 1936), 145.

2. Luebke, *Bonds of Loyalty*, 226, 234, 237, 247; Lyle W. Dorsett, "The Ordeal of Colorado's Germans during World War I," *Colorado Magazine* 51, no. 4 (1974): 279; Robert N. Manley, "The Nebraska State Council of Defense: Loyalty Programs and Politics during World War I" (Ph.D. diss., University of Nebraska, Lincoln, 1959), 9; Darrell R. Sawyer, "Anti-German Sentiment in South Dakota during World War I," *South Dakota Historical Collections* 38 (1976); 490–91.

3. Manley, "Nebraska State Council," 5; Jack W. Rodgers, "The Foreign Language Issue in Nebraska, 1918–1923," *Nebraska History* 39 (March 1958): 4–6.

4. Luebke, *Bonds of Loyalty*, 238; Manley, "Nebraska State Council," 39, 111, 114, 168–70, 251.

5. Manley, "Nebraska State Council," 59, 81–83.

6. Dorsett, "Ordeal of Colorado's Germans," 281, 283, 285–87.

7. Dorsett, "Ordeal of Colorado's Germans," 289; Manley, "Nebraska State Council," 34–35; Rodgers, "Foreign Language Issue," 2.

8. Rex C. Myers, "An American Immigrant Heritage: South Dakota's Foreign Born in the Era of Assimilation," *South Dakota History* 19 (Summer 1989): 148; Sawyer, "Anti-German Sentiment," 456–57, 470–73, 486.

9. Luebke, *Bonds of Loyalty*, 253–55, 278–79; Dorsett, "Ordeal of Colorado's Germans," 291; Manley, "Nebraska State Council," 132.

10. Luebke, *Bonds of Loyalty*, 252, 281–82; Wittke, *German Americans*, 147; H. C. Peterson and Gilbert C. Fite, *Opponents of War, 1917–1918* (Madison: University of Wisconsin Press, 1957), 196; Manley, "Nebraska State Council," 59, 81–83; Burton W. Folson, "'Tinkers, Tipplers, and Traitors': Ethnicity and Democratic Reform in Nebraska during the Progressive Era," *Pacific Historical Review* 50, no. 1 (1981): 74.

11. Luebke, *Bonds of Loyalty*, 236–37; Myers, "American Immigrant Heritage," 137, 142–43.

12. Arlyn John Parish, *Kansas Mennonites during World War I*, Fort Hays Studies, n.s., History Series no. 4 (Hays: Fort Hays Kansas State College, 1968), 7, 10–11, 15, 20–21, 25–26, 29–31, 33–34, 37–42, 48–50.

13. James C. Juhnke, "Mob Violence and Kansas Mennonites in 1918," *Kansas Historical Quarterly* 43 (Autumn 1977): 335, 337–40, 344–46.

14. Juhnke, "Mob Violence," 345.

15. Juhnke, "Mob Violence," 344, 347–49; Luebke, Bonds of Loyalty, 314, 322–23.

16. Luebke, Bonds of Loyalty, 277; Sawyer, "Anti-German Sentiment," 473.

17. Luebke, Bonds of Loyalty, 312.

18. J. Milton Cooper Jr., Pivotal Decades: The United States, 1900–1920 (New York: W. W. Norton, 1990), 322–30; Robert K. Murray, Red Scare: A Study of National Hysteria, 1919–1920 (New York: McGraw-Hill, 1955), 3–17, 30.

19. Craig Miner, Kansas: The History of the Sunflower State, 1854–2000 (Lawrence: University Press of Kansas, 2008), 242, 245; Nigel Anthony Sellars, Oil, Wheat and Wobblies: The Industrial Workers of the World in Oklahoma, 1905–1930 (Norman: University of Oklahoma Press, 1998), 114, 119; Michael P. Malone and Richard B. Roeder, Montana: A History of Two Centuries (Seattle: University of Washington Press, 1976), 207–15; Patrick Renshaw, The Wobblies: The Story of Syndicalism in the United States (Garden City, N.Y.: Doubleday, 1967), 162–94; Murray, Red Scare, 30, 217.

20. Murray, Red Scare, 233–34, 240.

21. Larry Remele, "Power to the People: The Nonpartisan League," in The North Dakota Political Tradition, ed. Thomas W. Howard (Ames: Iowa State University Press, 1981), 66–73; Dale Baum, "The New Day in North Dakota: The Nonpartisan League and the Politics of Negative Revolution," North Dakota History 40 (Spring 1973): 9.

22. Baum, "New Day in North Dakota," 9–10.

23. Samuel P. Huntington, "The Election Tactics of the Nonpartisan League," Missouri Valley Historical Review 36 (March 1950): 618–19, 629; see also Robert L. Morlan, Political Prairie Fire: The Nonpartisan League, 1915–1922 (St. Paul: Minnesota Historical Society Press, 1985).

24. Remele, "Power to the People," 74–81; Baum, "New Day in North Dakota," 11.

25. Remele, "Power to the People," 81–88; Baum, "New Day in North Dakota," 16.

26. Douglas Bakken, "NPL in Nebraska, 1917–1920," North Dakota History 39 (Spring 1972): 28–31; Robert N. Manley, "The Nebraska State Council of Defense and the Non-Partisan League, 1917–1918," Nebraska History 43 (December 1962): 229–52.

27. Bruce L. Larson, "Kansas and the Nonpartisan League: The Response to the Affair at Great Bend," Kansas Historical Quarterly 34 (Spring 1968): 51–55, 62–63, 70–71.

28. Gilbert C. Fite, "Peter Norbeck and the Defeat of the Non-Partisan League in South Dakota," Mississippi Valley Historical Review 33 (September 1946): 218–25; see also Gilbert C. Fite, Peter Norbeck: Prairie Statesman (Columbia: University of Missouri Press, 1948; repr., Pierre: South Dakota State Historical Society Press, 2005); and Larry Remele, "An Experiment in State Sponsored Economy: Peter Norbeck and William Henry McMaster," in South Dakota Political Leaders, ed. Herbert T. Hoover and Larry J. Zimmerman (Vermillion: University of South Dakota Press, 1989), 207–19.

29. Gilbert C. Fite, "The Nonpartisan League in Oklahoma," Chronicles of Oklahoma 24 (Summer 1946): 147–49, 151–53, 155–57.

30. Frederick C. Luebke, "Political Response to Agricultural Depression in Nebraska, 1922," Nebraska History 47 (March 1966): 17–18; Paul H. Carlson, Amarillo: The Story of a Western Town (Lubbock: Texas Tech University Press, 2006), 81; Malone and Roeder, Montana, 217–18; John L. Shover, "The Farm Holiday Movement in

Nebraska," *Nebraska History* 43 (March 1962): 53–78; Elwyn B. Robinson, *History of North Dakota* (Lincoln: University of Nebraska Press, 1966), 377; Herbert S. Schell, *History of South Dakota* (Lincoln: University of Nebraska Press, 1975; repr., Pierre: South Dakota State Historical Society Press, 2004), 283–84; see also John L. Shover, *Cornbelt Rebellion: The Farmers' Holiday Association* (Urbana: University of Illinois Press, 1965).

31. Van L. Perkins, *Crisis in Agriculture: The Agricultural Adjustment Administration and the New Deal* (Berkeley: University of California Press, 1969), 10–13; Janet M. Neugebauer, *Plains Farmer: The Diary of William DeLoach* (College Station: Texas A&M University Press, 1991), 136; Robinson, *History of North Dakota*, 374.

32. Shover, *Cornbelt Rebellion*, 44–45, 47–48, 72.

33. Catherine McNicol Stock, *Rural Radicals: Righteous Rage in the American Grain* (Ithaca, N.Y.: Cornell University Press, 1996), 138–39.

34. John E. Miller, "Restrained, Respectable Radicals: The South Dakota Farm Holiday," *Agricultural History* 59 (July 1985): 429–47.

35. Larry Remele, "The North Dakota Farm Strike of 1932," *North Dakota History* 41 (Fall 1974): 6, 8, 10–13, 15–16, 18.

36. Shover, *Cornbelt Rebellion*, 82–83; Schell, *History of South Dakota*, 287–88; Miller, "Restrained, Respectable Radicals," 429–47.

37. Stock, *Rural Radicals*, 141.

38. R. Douglas Hurt, *The Dust Bowl: An Agricultural and Social History* (Chicago: Nelson-Hall, 1981), 23–29.

39. Carlson, *Amarillo*, 90; Daniel Yergin, *The Prize: The Epic Quest for Oil, Money, and Power* (New York: Simon and Schuster, 1993), 223; Michael P. Malone and Richard W. Etulain, *The American West: A Twentieth Century History* (Lincoln: University of Nebraska Press, 1989), 34–36; see also Diana Davids Hinton and Roger M. Olien, *Oil in Texas: The Gusher Age, 1895–1945* (Austin: University of Texas Press, 2002), 136–66.

40. Norma Crockett, "Crime on the Petroleum Frontier: Borger, Texas, in the Late 1920s," *Panhandle-Plains Historical Review* 64 (1991): 53–65.

41. Thomas A. Britten, "Changing Land Uses in Carson County: A Microcosm of the Panhandle Experience," *Panhandle-Plains Historical Review* 66 (1993): 62–63; Miner, *Kansas*, 268.

42. Walter Nugent, *Into the West: The Story of Its People* (New York: Knopf, 1999), 198.

43. Roger M. Olien and Diana Davids Olien, *Oil Booms: Social Change in Five Texas Towns* (Lincoln: University of Nebraska Press, 1982), 30–31, 88–89, 93, 109.

44. Remele, "Experiment in State Sponsored Economy," 110, 113–15, 123.

45. Nugent, *Into the West*, 197; Carlson, *Amarillo*, 91; John Carter, "Land Marks on Paper," *Nebraska History* 86 (Winter 2005): 133.

46. Lawrence L. Graves, ed., *A History of Lubbock* (Lubbock: West Texas Museum Association, 1962), 421, 425; Robinson, *History of North Dakota*, 395; *Historical Statistics of the United States*, vol. 1, part A, *Population* (Cambridge: Cambridge University Press, 2006), 1-129, 1-132.

47. Remele, "Experiment in State Sponsored Economy," 216–17; Robinson, *History of North Dakota*, 371, 390; Schell, *History of South Dakota*, 276.

48. Malone and Roeder, *Montana*, 222, 224.

49. Richard M. Scammon and Alice V. McGillivray, *America Votes, 17: A Handbook of Contemporary American Election Statistics* (Washington, D.C.: Congressional Quarterly, 1987), 6–13.

Chapter 4. The Anxious Years

1. Donald Worster, *The Dust Bowl: The Southern Plains in the 1930s* (New York: Oxford University Press, 1979), 89–94, 106–7, 151; Pamela Riney-Kehrberg, *Rooted in Dust: Surviving Drought and Depression in Southwestern Kansas* (Lawrence: University Press of Kansas, 1994), 5; R. Douglas Hurt, *The Dust Bowl: An Agricultural and Social History* (Chicago: Nelson-Hall, 1981), 23–27, 29; Paul Bonnifield, *The Dust Bowl: Men, Dirt, and Depression* (Albuquerque: University of New Mexico Press, 1979), 31–60; Geoff Cunfer, *On the Great Plains: Agriculture and Environment* (College Station: Texas A&M University Press, 2005), 143–63; Craig Miner, *Next Year Country: Dust to Dust in Western Kansas, 1890–1940* (Lawrence: University Press of Kansas, 2006), 235–89.

2. Worster, *Dust Bowl*, 13–14; Hurt, *Dust Bowl*, 33–34.

3. Hurt, *Dust Bowl*, 34–46; Worster, *Dust Bowl*, 17–18; Bonnifield, *Dust Bowl*, 63.

4. Hurt, *Dust Bowl*, 49–53; Worster, *Dust Bowl*, 20–21; Bonnifield, *Dust Bowl*, 74.

5. Hurt, *Dust Bowl*, 37–38; Riney-Kehrberg, *Rooted in Dust*, 28–34.

6. Hurt, *Dust Bowl*, 3, 97–98; Worster, *Dust Bowl*, 28, 54, 57–61.

7. Catherine McNicol Stock, *Main Street in Crisis: The Great Depression and the Old Middle Class on the Northern Plains* (Chapel Hill: University of North Carolina Press, 1992), 18, 25, 39; Paula M. Nelson, *The Prairie Winnows Out Its Own: The West River Country of South Dakota in the Years of Depression and Dust* (Iowa City: University of Iowa Press, 1996), 188; Elwyn B. Robinson, *History of North Dakota* (Lincoln: University of Nebraska Press, 1966), 401; D. Gerome Tweton, "The New Deal, the Great Plains, and the People," *Panhandle-Plains Historical Review* 67 (1994): 7; Riney-Kehrberg, *Rooted in Dust*, 40–42, 140–49, 166; see also Peter Fearon, *Kansas in the Great Depression: Work, Relief, the Dole, and Rehabilitation* (Columbia: University of Missouri Press, 2007).

8. Worster, *Dust Bowl*, 49; Riney-Kehrberg, *Rooted in Dust*, 38; Alfred M. Landon, interview with the author, July 16, 1978.

9. Nelson, *Prairie Winnows Out Its Own*, 119, 123, 132, 147; Robinson, *History of North Dakota*, 398–99.

10. David B. Danbom, *Going It Alone: Fargo Grapples with the Great Depression* (St. Paul: Minnesota Historical Society Press, 2005), 16–27, 31–34, 65–66; Riney-Kehrberg, *Rooted in Dust*, 70; Paul H. Carlson, *Amarillo: The Story of a Western Town* (Lubbock: Texas Tech University Press, 2006), 121.

11. Julia Kirk Blackwelder, *Women of the Depression: Caste and Culture in San Antonio, 1929–1939* (College Station: Texas A&M University Press, 1984), 7–8, 78, 80–81, 85, 91, 112, 120, 173.

12. Danbom, *Going It Alone*, 86–89; Stock, *Main Street in Crisis*, 33; Carlson, *Amarillo*, 132; Riney-Kehrberg, *Rooted in Dust*, 80; Blackwelder, *Women of the Depression*, 110.

13. Robinson, *History of North Dakota*, 407; Nelson, *Prairie Winnows Out Its Own*, 157; Danbom, *Going It Alone*, 82–83, 94.

14. Danbom, *Going It Alone*, 101.

15. Danbom, *Going It Alone*, 111, 129–30; Riney-Kehrberg, *Rooted in Dust*, 67.

16. Danbom, *Going It Alone*, 144, 158–59, 161; Carlson, *Amarillo*, 121–22.

17. Riney-Kehrberg, *Rooted in Dust*, 105; Hurt, *Dust Bowl*, 91.

18. Hurt, *Dust Bowl*, 92; Nelson, *Prairie Winnows Out Its Own*, 188.

19. R. Douglas Hurt, "Prices, Payments, and Production: Kansas Wheat Farmers and the Agricultural Adjustment Administration, 1933–1939," *Kansas History* 23 (Spring–Summer 2000): 80, 83.

20. Herbert S. Schell, *History of South Dakota* (Lincoln: University of Nebraska Press, 1975; repr., Pierre: South Dakota State Historical Society Press, 2004), 289; Hurt, *Dust Bowl*, 103–9; Worster, *Dust Bowl*, 113–14.

21. Hurt, *Dust Bowl*, 94–95.

22. Hurt, *Dust Bowl*, 99, 101; Worster, *Dust Bowl*, 40; Riney-Kehrberg, *Rooted in Dust*, 105–6; Stock, *Main Street in Crisis*, 38; Schell, *History of South Dakota*, 290, 292.

23. E. N. Munns and J. H. Stoeckler, "How Are the Great Plains Shelterbelts," *Journal of Forestry* 44 (April 1946): 237; Wilmon H. Droze, *Trees, Prairies, and People: A History of Tree Planting in the Plains States* (Denton: Texas Woman's University, 1977), 61, 71.

24. Munns and Stoeckler, "How Are," 237; Droze, *Trees, Prairies, and People*, 63–64.

25. Hurt, *Dust Bowl*, 125, H. H. Chapman, "The Shelterbelt Tree Planting Project," *Journal of Forestry* 32 (November 1934): 801; Royal S. Kellogg, "The Shelterbelt Scheme," *Journal of Forestry* 32 (December 1934): 977; Thomas R. Wessel, "Roosevelt and the Great Plains Shelterbelt," *Great Plains Journal* 8 (Spring 1969): 58; Droze, *Trees, Prairies, and People*, 97.

26. Droze, *Trees, Prairies, and People*, 74; Wessel, "Roosevelt," 58–59; *Report of the Chief of the Forest Service, 1934* (Washington, D.C.: U.S. Department of Agriculture, 1934), 6.

27. Droze, *Trees, Prairies, and People*, 74.

28. *Amarillo Globe*, July 22 and December 28, 1934; Raphael Zon, "Shelterbelts – Futile Dream or Workable Plan," *Science* 81 (April 26, 1935): 394.

29. Droze, *Trees, Prairies, and People*, 86, 96, 98–100; *Amarillo Globe*, July 22, 1934.

30. *Report of the Chief of the Forest Service, 1936* (Washington, D.C.: U.S. Department of Agriculture, 1936), 41; Droze, *Trees, Prairies, and People*, 102–4.

31. Droze, *Trees, Prairies, and People*, 115.

32. Droze, *Trees, Prairies, and People*, 151, 195, 197–98; *Report of the Chief of the Forest Service, 1937* (Washington, D.C.: U.S. Department of Agriculture, 1937), 29; Wessel, "Roosevelt," 58–59, 61; *Report of the Chief of the Forest Service, 1939* (Washington, D.C.: U.S. Department of Agriculture, 1939), 27; Edgar B. Nixon, *Franklin D. Roosevelt and Conservation, 1911–45*, vol. 1 (Washington, D.C.: Government Printing Office, 1957), 335; John N. Ballantyne, "The Prairie States Shelterbelt Project" (master's thesis, Yale University, 1949), 6.

33. *Report of the Chief of the Forest Service, 1936,* 42.

34. James B. Lang, "The Shelterbelt Project in the Southern Great Plains, 1934–1970: A Geographic Appraisal" (master's thesis, University of Oklahoma, 1970), 99.

35. Lang, "Shelterbelt Project," 114; Charles A. Scott, "The Plains Shelterbelt Project," in *Report of the Kansas State Board of Agriculture for the Quarter Ending March 1935* (Topeka: Kansas State Board of Agriculture, 1935), 47.

36. Scott, "Plains Shelterbelt Project," 48–50.

37. T. Russell Reitz, "Farm Forestry in Kansas," in *Thirty-first Biennial Report of the Kansas State Board of Agriculture, 1937–38* (Topeka: Kansas State Board of Agriculture, 1938), 60; Vera Carney Alden, "A History of the Shelterbelt Project in Kansas" (master's thesis, Kansas State College, 1949), 28–29.

38. *Amarillo Globe,* March 19, 1935; *Dodge City Daily Globe,* June 20, 1935; *Report of the Chief of the Forest Service, 1937,* 29; *Report of the Chief of the Forest Service, 1936,* 42; Lang, "Shelterbelt Project," 39.

39. Ballantyne, "Prairie States Shelterbelt Project," 12; Droze, *Trees, Prairies, and People,* 210–13; Wessel, "Roosevelt," 63.

40. *Report of the Chief of the Forest Service, 1942* (Washington, D.C.: U.S. Department of Agriculture, 1942), 22; Munns and Stoeckler, "How Are," 239; Droze, *Trees, Prairies, and People,* 222–23.

41. Droze, *Trees, Prairies, and People,* 225–27.

42. Cunfer, *On the Great Plains,* 193–210; R. Douglas Hurt, "The National Grasslands: Origin and Development in the Dust Bowl," *Agricultural History* 59 (April 1985): 246–59; Hurt, *Dust Bowl,* 116–18; R. Douglas Hurt, "Gaining Control of the Environment: The Morton County Land Utilization Project in the Kansas Dust Bowl," *Kansas History* 19 (Summer 1986): 140–53; R. Douglas Hurt, "Federal Land Reclamation in the Dust Bowl," *Great Plains Quarterly* 6 (Spring 1986): 94–106.

43. Vine Deloria Jr. and Clifford M. Lytle, *American Indians, American Justice* (Austin: University of Texas Press, 1983), 13; R. Douglas Hurt, *Indian Agriculture in America: Prehistory to the Present* (Lawrence: University Press of Kansas, 1987), 175.

44. Hurt, *Indian Agriculture in America,* 174–76; Francis Paul Prucha, *The Great Father: The United States and the American Indians,* vol. 2 (Lincoln: University of Nebraska Press, 1984), 945; Robert Bromert, "The Sioux and the Indian CCC," in *The Sioux in South Dakota: A Twentieth-Century Reader,* ed. Richmond L. Clow (Pierre: South Dakota State Historical Society Press, 2007), 10, 104–5.

45. Kenneth R. Philip, *John Collier's Crusade for Indian Reform, 1920–1954* (Tucson: University of Arizona Press, 1981), 121; Hurt, *Indian Agriculture in America,* 176.

46. Philip, *John Collier's Crusade,* 121; Bromert, "Sioux and the Indian CCC," 107, 114.

47. Prucha, *Great Father,* 947.

48. Prucha, *Great Father,* 951; Hurt, *Indian Agriculture in America,* 177.

49. Hurt, *Indian Agriculture in America,* 177.

50. Deloria and Lytle, *American Indians, American Justice,* 14; Prucha, *Great Father,* 957–58; Philip, *John Collier's Crusade,* 141–43; Hurt, *Indian Agriculture in America,* 178.

51. Vine Deloria Jr., *Behind the Trail of Broken Treaties: An Indian Declaration of Independence* (Austin: University of Texas Press, 1985), 196–98; Hurt, *Indian Agriculture in America,* 178.

52. Prucha, *Great Father*, 956, 963; Philip, *John Collier's Crusade*, 158–59; Hurt, *Indian Agriculture in America*, 179.

53. Prucha, *Great Father*, 958–59, 964–65, 970–73; Philip, *John Collier's Crusade*, 146–54, 163, 195; Deloria, *Behind the Trail*, 201; Hurt, *Indian Agriculture in America*, 179.

54. Richmond L. Clow, "Tribal Populations in Transition: Sioux Reservations and Federal Policy, 1935–1965," in *The Sioux in South Dakota: A Twentieth-Century Reader*, ed. Richmond L. Clow (Pierre: South Dakota State Historical Society Press, 2007), 183–84; Philip, *John Collier's Crusade*, 138–40, 148.

55. Philip, *John Collier's Crusade*, 166; Paul C. Rosier, "'The Real Indians, Who Constitute the Real Tribe': Class, Ethnicity, and IRA Politics on the Blackfeet Reservation," *Journal of American Ethnic History* 18 (Summer 1999): 9–14.

56. Deloria, *Behind the Trail*, 187, 195; Prucha, *Great Father*, 967–68; Deloria and Lytle, *American Indians, American Justice*, 15, 101–2; Philip, *John Collier's Crusade*, 186.

57. Prucha, *Great Father*, 963, 994, 996, 1010; Deloria, *Behind the Trail*, 100.

58. Thomas Biolsi, *Organizing the Lakota: The Political Economy of the New Deal on the Pine Ridge and Rosebud Reservations* (Tucson: University of Arizona Press, 1992), 114; Clow, "Tribal Populations in Transition," 188.

59. Joane Nagel, *American Indian Ethnic Renewal: Red Power and the Resurgence of Identity and Culture* (New York: Oxford University Press, 1997), 114–17; Prucha, *Great Father*, 1013.

60. Stock, *Main Street in Crisis*, 112; Richard M. Scammon and Alice V. McGillivray, *America Votes, 17: A Handbook of Contemporary American Election Statistics* (Washington, D.C.: Congressional Quarterly, 1987), 17.

61. Stock, *Main Street in Crisis*, 10, 18–25; Richard Lowitt and Maurice Beasley, ed., *One Third of a Nation: Lorena Hickok Reports on the Great Depression* (Urbana: University of Illinois Press, 1981), 56, 83, 334–35.

62. Stock, *Main Street in Crisis*, 90, 101–2, 107, 110.

63. Paula M. Nelson, "Traveling the Hope Highway: An Intellectual History of the West River Country of South Dakota," in *Centennial West: Essays on the Northern Tier States*, ed. William E. Lang (Seattle: University of Washington Press, 1991), 256–57; Ruby Winona Adams, "Social Behavior in a Drought-Stricken Panhandle Community" (master's thesis, University of Texas, Austin, 1939), 177.

64. Stock, *Main Street in Crisis*, 32, 38; Nelson, *Prairie Winnows Out Its Own*, 189.

Chapter 5. The Age of Certainty

1. Robert James Leonard, "The Nye Committee: Legislating against War," *North Dakota History* 41 (Fall 1974): 21–24.

2. Thomas A. Bailey, *A Diplomatic History of the American People* (Englewood Cliffs, N.J.: Prentice-Hall, 1980), 701–2; Stephen E. Ambrose, *Rise to Globalism: American Foreign Policy since 1938* (New York: Penguin, 1988), 26.

3. Neis Erikson, "Prairie Pacifist: Senator Lynn J. Frazier and America's Global Mission, 1927–1940," *North Dakota History* 52 (Fall 1985): 27–29; Homer E. Socolof-

sky, *Arthur Capper: Publisher, Politician and Philanthropist* (Lawrence: University of Kansas Press, 1962), 175–76, 180.

4. R. Douglas Hurt, *The Great Plains during World War II* (Lincoln: University of Nebraska Press, 2008), 15–20; *Congressional Record* 85, pt. 1 (October 12, 1939): 311–12.

5. Hurt, *Great Plains*, 19–20.

6. John W. Partin, "The Dilemma of 'a Good, Very Good Man': Capper and Non-interventionism, 1936–1941," *Kansas History* 2 (Summer 1979): 94; Philip A. Grant, "The Kansas Congressional Delegation and the Lend-Lease Act of 1941," *Kansas History* 14 (Summer 1991): 73–75, 78; Donald E. Spitzer, "Senators in Conflict," *Montana: The Magazine of Western History* 23 (Spring 1973): 27; T. A. Larson, *Wyoming's War Years, 1941–1945* (Laramie: University of Wyoming, 1954; repr., Cheyenne: Wyoming Historical Foundation, 1993), 2; Hurt, *Great Plains*, 23–25.

7. Alan M. Winkler, *Home Front U.S.A.: America during World War II*, 2d ed. (Wheeling, Ill.: Harlan Davidson, 2000), 8; Richard Pollenberg, *War and Society: The United States, 1941–1945* (Westport, Conn.: Greenwood, 1972), 11; Harold G. Vatter, *The U.S. Economy in World War II* (New York: Columbia University Press, 1985), 11; Hurt, *Great Plains*, 32–60.

8. Tracy Lyn Wit, "The Social and Economic Impact of World War II Munitions Manufacture on Grand Island, Nebraska," *Nebraska History* 71 (Fall 1990): 151, 153; Todd L. Peterson, "Kearney, Nebraska, and the Kearney Army Airfield in World War II," *Nebraska History* 72 (Fall 1991): 118–26; Peter Fearon, "Ploughshares into Airplanes: Manufacturing Industries and Workers in Kansas during World War II," *Kansas History* 22 (Winter 1999–2000): 300–301; R. Alton Lee, *Farmers vs. Wage Earners: Organized Labor in Kansas, 1860–1960* (Lawrence: University Press of Kansas, 2005), 212–48.

9. Susan M. Hartmann, *The Home Front and Beyond: American Women in the 1940s* (Boston: Twayne, 1982), 21; Karen Anderson, *Wartime Women: Sex Roles, Family Relations, and the Status of Women during World War II* (Westport, Conn.: Greenwood, 1981), 4; Susan L. Allen, "Preparing Women for the National Crisis," *Chronicles of Oklahoma* 69 (Winter 1991–92): 393; Wit, "Social and Economic Impact," 155–56; Hurt, *Great Plains*, 61.

10. Hartmann, *Home Front and Beyond*, 54; Winkler, *Home Front U.S.A.*, 55–56; Michael C. C. Adams, *The Best War Ever: America and World War II* (Baltimore, Md.: Johns Hopkins University Press, 1994), 123; William L. O'Neill, *A Democracy at War: America's Fight at Home and Abroad in World War II* (New York: Free Press, 1993), 242; Hurt, *Great Plains*, 61–62.

11. Hurt, *Great Plains*, 62–66; Richard Marcias, "'We All Had a Cause': Kansas City's Bomber Plant, 1941–1945," *Kansas History* 28 (Winter 2005–6): 253, 255; Fearon, "Ploughshares into Airplanes," 38–39; Judith R. Johnson, "Uncle Sam Wanted Them Too! Women Aircraft Workers in Wichita during World War II," *Kansas History* 17 (Spring 1994): 38–49.

12. Leila J. Rupp, *Mobilizing Women for War: German and American Propaganda, 1939–1945* (Princeton: Princeton University Press, 1978), 61; Johnson, "Uncle Sam Wanted Them Too," 40–41; Hurt, *Great Plains*, 68.

13. Hurt, *Great Plains*, 106–7.

14. George A. Larson, "Nebraska's World War II Bomber Plant: The Glenn L.

Martin–Nebraska Company," *Nebraska History* 74 (Spring 1993): 39–41, 45–48; Hurt, *Great Plains*, 78.

15. John W. Jefferies, *Wartime America: The World War II Home Front* (Chicago: Ivan Dee, 1996), 100–101; David M. Kennedy, *Freedom from Fear: The American People in Depression and War, 1929–1945* (New York: Oxford University Press, 1999), 777; Adams, *Best War Ever*, 70, 123–24, 144; D'Ann Campbell, *Women at War with America: Private Lives in a Patriotic Era* (Cambridge, Mass.: Harvard University Press, 1984), 216, 237; Hurt, *Great Plains*, 79–85.

16. Hartmann, *Home Front and Beyond*, 15, 78–80, 93–95, 214; Doris Weatherford, *American Women and World War II* (New York: Facts on File, 1990), 48–49, 119, 152, 195; Jefferies, *Wartime America*, 96; Winkler, *Home Front U.S.A.*, 58; Anderson, *Wartime Women*, 173, 175, 178; Hurt, *Great Plains*, 84–85.

17. William J. Furdell, "The Great Falls Home Front during World War II," *Montana: The Magazine of Western History* 48 (Winter 1998): 68; Stephen J. Leonard, "Denver at War: The Home Front in World War II," *Colorado Heritage* no. 4 (1987): 36; Hurt, *Great Plains*, 89–98.

18. Hurt, *Great Plains*, 93–97.

19. Michael Cassity, "'In a Narrow Grave': World War II and the Subjugation of Wyoming," *Wyoming Historical Journal* 68, no. 2 (1996): 6; Hurt, *Great Plains*, 121, 125–30.

20. Amy Bentley, *Eating for Victory: Food Rationing and the Politics of Domesticity* (Urbana: University of Illinois Press, 1998), 15–17, 33, 86, 93, 102, 198; Hurt, *Great Plains*, 130–44.

21. Hurt, *Great Plains*, 118–19.

22. Larson, "Nebraska's World War II," 32–34; Hurt, *Great Plains*, 112–15; Jerold Simmons, "Public Leadership in a World War II Boom Town: Bellevue, Nebraska," *Nebraska History* 65 (Winter 1984): 485–88, 491–93, 495–96; Jacqueline McGlade, "The Zoning of Fort Crook: Urban Expansion vs. County Home Rule," *Nebraska History* 64 (Spring 1983): 21–23, 28, 32; Patrick G. O'Brien, "Kansas at War: The Home Front, 1941–1945," *Kansas History* 17 (Spring 1994): 18.

23. Richard R. Lingeman, *Don't You Know There's a War On? The Home Front, 1941–1945* (New York: Putnam, 1970), 247; Furdell, "Great Falls Home Front," 72.

24 Hurt, *Great Plains*, 400.

25. Joseph V. Metzgar, "Guns and Butter: Albuquerque Hispanics, 1940–1975," *New Mexico Historical Review* 56 (April 1981): 117–18, 121; Hurt, *Great Plains*, 215–22; Arnoldo De León, *Mexican Americans in Texas: A Brief History* (Wheeling, Ill.: Harlan Davidson, 1999). A metropolitan area is imprecise in definition. I use the term to mean a county containing a city having a population of at least 50,000 along with surrounding counties that are socially and economically integrated with the core county. Although most Mexican Americans remained unskilled or semiskilled workers, a middle class composed of craftsmen, sales clerks, and professionals also grew. During the 1970s, this Mexican American middle class popularized the term *Hispanic* to embrace all people who had cultural roots in Latin America. This more expansive term appealed to businesses that wanted to target a wider range of customers. The term also enabled Mexican Americans to emphasize their preferred racial categorization of white. Not until the late twentieth century would *Hispanic* essentially be replaced by the term *Latino/a*, largely by academics and later the public to strengthen the emphasis on cultural ties rather than racial or national antecedents.

26. Dennis N. Mihelich, "The Lincoln Urban League: The Travail of Depression and War," *Nebraska History* 70 (Winter 1989): 303–16; Dennis N. Mihelich, "World War II and the Transformation of the Omaha Urban League," *Nebraska History* 60 (Fall 1979): 401–23.

27. Rusty L. Monhollon and Kristen Tegtmeier Oertel, "From Brown to Brown: A Century of Struggle for Equality in Kansas," *Kansas History* 27 (Spring–Summer 2004): 117, 124, 126–27; Mary L. Dudziak, "The Limits of Good Faith: Desegregation in Topeka, Kansas, 1950–1956," *Law and History Review* 5 (Autumn 1987): 353; Richard W. Byrd, "Interracial Cooperation in the Decade of Conflict: The Denton (Texas) Christian Women's Inter-racial Fellowship," *Oral History Review* 19, nos. 1–2 (1991): 38; Ron Waters, "The Great Plains Sit-In Movement, 1958–60," *Great Plains Quarterly* 16 (Spring 1986): 85–94.

28. Gretchen Casal Eick, *Dissent in Wichita: The Civil Rights Movement in the Midwest, 1954–72* (Urbana: University of Illinois Press, 2001), 1–9, 22, 24, 45, 75–82, 120, 172, 194, 219.

29. Carl R. Graves, "The Right to Be Served: Oklahoma City's Lunch Counter Sit-Ins, 1958–1964," *Chronicles of Oklahoma* 59 (Summer 1981): 152–57, 161–62; Eick, *Dissent in Wichita*, 9–10.

30. Monhollon and Oertel, "From Brown to Brown," 131, 133; Dudziak, "Limits of Good Faith," 352, 367–70; Jean Van Delinder, "Early Civil Rights in Topeka, Kansas, Prior to the 1954 *Brown* Case," *Great Plains Quarterly* 21 (Winter 2001): 46, 58; Robert Beatty and Mark A. Petersen, "Covert Discrimination: Topeka Before and After Brown," *Kansas History* 27 (Autumn 2004): 148.

31. Dudziak, "Limits of Good Faith," 372, 387–89; Beatty and Petersen, "Covert Discrimination," 159, 163. The NAACP filed suit against the Topeka Board of Education on February 28, 1951.

32. Beatty and Petersen, "Covert Discrimination," 152, 154.

33. D. Keith Lough, "'Hoorah for Integration!': The Adoption of the 1955 Better Schools Amendment," *Chronicles of Oklahoma* 85 (Summer 2007): 162, 169.

34. Michelle Celarier, "A Study of Public Opinion on Desegregation in Oklahoma Higher Education," *Chronicles of Oklahoma* 47 (Autumn 1969): 268–69, 271–72.

35. Alfred H. Kelly and Winfred H. Harbison, *The American Constitution: Its Origins and Development*, 3d ed. (New York: W. W. Norton, 1963), 932; Celarier, "Study of Public Opinion," 275, 279, 280–81.

36. Kristy Feldhausen Giles, "A Century of Black Towns in Oklahoma," *Gilcrease Journal* 15, no. 1 (2007): 61–62.

37. Rusty L. Monhollon, "Race, Rights and the Politics of Desegregation in Lawrence, Kansas, 1960," *Kansas History* 20 (Autumn 1997): 140–42, 144–45, 151–54, 156, 158–59; Rusty L. Monhollon, *This Is America? The Sixties in Lawrence, Kansas* (New York: Palgrave, 2004), 46–47, 53, 61.

38. R. Douglas Hurt, *Indian Agriculture in America: Prehistory to the Present* (Lawrence: University Press of Kansas, 1987), 194, 201–3.

39. Francis Paul Prucha, *The Great Father: The United States Government and the American Indians*, vol. 2 (Lincoln: University of Nebraska Press, 1984), 1013–14; Larry Burt, *Tribalism in Crisis: Federal Indian Policy, 1953–1961* (Albuquerque: University of New Mexico Press, 1982), 30.

40. Hurt, *Indian Agriculture in America*, 198–99; Burt, *Tribalism in Crisis*, 20–26.

41. Prucha, *Great Father*, 1028–30, 1041–43; Hurt, *Indian Agriculture in America*, 199.

42. Prucha, *Great Father*, 1044; Peter Iverson, *We Are Still Here: American Indians in the Twentieth Century* (Wheeling, Ill.: Harlan Davidson, 1998), 121, 129–30; Elizabeth S. Grobsmith and Beth R. Ritter, "The Ponca Tribe of Nebraska: The Process of Restoration of a Federally Terminated Tribe," *Human Organization* 51 (Spring 1992): 1–16; Burt, *Tribalism in Crisis*, 81; Steven C. Schulte, "Wyoming Politicians and the Shaping of United States Indian Policy, 1945 to 1980," *Wyoming Annals* 63 (Fall 1994): 48–65.

43. Beth R. Ritter, "The Politics of Retribalization: The Northern Ponca Case," *Great Plains Research* 4 (August 1994): 246–47; Prucha, *Great Father*, 1044; Iverson, *We Are Still Here*, 121, 129–30; Grobsmith and Ritter, "Ponca Tribe of Nebraska," 1–16.

44. Ritter, "Politics of Retribalization," 248–49.

45. Burt, *Tribalism in Crisis*, 126; Prucha, *Great Father*, 1056–58; Hurt, *Indian Agriculture in America*, 200.

46. Prucha, *Great Father*, 1058–59; Hurt, *Indian Agriculture in America*, 200.

47. Iverson, *We Are Still Here*, 136.

48. Larry Burt, "Western Tribes and Balance Sheets: Business Development Programs in the 1960s and 1970s," *Western Historical Quarterly* 23 (November 1992): 483–88.

49. Prucha, *Great Father*, 1099–1100, 1111–12, 1115.

50. Richard M. Scammon and Alice V. McGillivray, *America Votes, 17: A Handbook of Contemporary American Election Statistics* (Washington, D.C.: Congressional Quarterly, 1987), 17, 19, 21, 23, 25, 27; Ricky Floyd Dobbs, "Continuities in American Anti-Catholicism: The Texas *Baptist Standard* and the Coming of the 1960 Election," *Baptist History and Heritage* 42, no. 1 (2007): 87, 90–91.

51. Jeff Roche, "Identity and Conservative Politics in the Southern Plains," in *The Future of the Southern Plains*, ed. Sherry L. Smith (Norman: University of Oklahoma Press in cooperation with the William P. Clements Center for Southwest Studies, Southern Methodist University, 2003), 169–70, 179–89.

52. James E. Sherow and Homer E. Socolofsky, "Kansas and Water: Survival in the Heartland," in *Politics in the Postwar American West*, ed. Richard Lowitt (Norman: University of Oklahoma Press, 1995), 106–8, 112–15.

53. William C. Pratt, "Employee Offensive in Nebraska Politics, 1946–1949," in Lowitt, *Politics in the Postwar West*, 142, 145–46; David B. Danbom, "A Part of the Nation and Apart from the Nation: North Dakota Politics since 1945," in Lowitt, *Politics in the Postwar West*, 174–80.

54. Danbom, "Part of the Nation," 180, 182–83.

55. Danney Goble, "'The More Things Change . . .': Oklahoma since 1945," in Smith, *Future of the Southern Plains*, 186–90, 195–96, 199–201; see also Matthew G. McCoy, "Dark Spot on the Sunbelt: Economic Stagnation and Political Corruption in 1950s Oklahoma," *Chronicles of Oklahoma* 85 (Summer 2007): 176–97.

56. Herbert T. Hoover and Steven C. Emery, "South Dakota Governance since 1945," in Smith, *Future of the Southern Plains*, 221–24, 229.

57. Robert H. Watrel and Erin Hogan Fouberg, "Presidential Voting Regions of the Northern Great Plains: No Need for an East Dakota and West Dakota," *Great Plains Research* 10 (Spring 2000): 189–213.

58. Phil Roberts and Peggy Bieber-Roberts, "'Politics Is Personal': Postwar Wyoming Politics and the Media," in Lowitt, *Politics in the Postwar West*, 306–7.

59. David Emmons, "The Price of 'Freedom': Montana in the Late and Post Anaconda Era," in Lowitt, *Politics in the Postwar West*, 121–22, 126–27, 131.

60. Herbert S. Schell, *History of South Dakota* (Lincoln: University of Nebraska Press, 1975; repr., Pierre: South Dakota Historical Society Press), 320–21; R. Alton Lee, "'New Dealers, Fair Dealers, Misdealers, and Hiss Dealers': Karl Mundt and the Internal Security Act of 1950," *South Dakota History* 10 (Fall 1980): 277, 279.

61. Lee, "New Dealers, Fair Dealers," 288–89; Schell, *History of South Dakota*, 321; R. Alton Lee, "McCarthyism at the University of South Dakota," *South Dakota History* 19 (Fall 1989): 426–27, 429.

62. Lee, "McCarthyism," 434; personal experience of the author.

63. Paul H. Carlson, *Amarillo: The Story of a Western Town* (Lubbock: Texas Tech University Press, 2006), 160–67, 180; Lawrence H. Larsen, Barbara J. Cottrell, Harl A. Dalstrom, and Kay Calamé Dalstrom, *Upstream Metropolis: An Urban Biography of Omaha and Council Bluffs* (Lincoln: University of Nebraska Press, 2007), 272, 418; Elwyn B. Robinson, *History of North Dakota* (Lincoln: University of Nebraska Press, 1966), 442; Schell, *History of South Dakota*, 326.

64. Schell, *History of South Dakota*, 326–27; Michael P. Malone and Richard B. Roeder, *Montana: A History of Two Centuries* (Seattle: University of Washington Press, 1976), 288.

65. Larsen et al., *Upstream Metropolis*, 61, 64–65, 68.

66. Schell, *History of South Dakota*, 341–43, 346–47, 370.

67. R. Douglas Hurt, *American Agriculture: A Brief History*, rev. ed. (West Lafayette, Ind.: Purdue University Press, 2003); see also Douglas Helms, "Conserving the Great Plains: The Soil Conservation Service in the Great Plains," *Agricultural History* 64 (Spring 1990): 58–73.

68. Walter Nugent, *Into the West: The Story of Its People* (New York: Knopf, 1999), 297–300, 302, 332; Roger M. Olien and Diana Davids Olien, *Oil Booms: Social Change in Five Texas Towns* (Lincoln: University of Nebraska Press, 1982), 166.

69. Susan B. Carter, ed., *Historical Statistics of the United States: Earliest Times to the Present*, vol. 1, part A, Millennial Edition (Cambridge: Cambridge University Press, 2006), 129, 130, 132, 135, 316; Metzgar, "Guns and Butter," 122, 125, 129–30, 133; Carl Abbott, *The Metropolitan Frontier: Cities in the Modern American West* (Tucson: University of Arizona Press, 1993), xiii, 26.

70. Larsen et al., *Upstream Metropolis*, 33, 36–37, 42–43, 45, 48–49.

71. Personal observation of the author.

Chapter 6. The Perils of Agriculture

1. R. Douglas Hurt, *The Great Plains during World War II* (Lincoln: University of Nebraska Press, 2008), 150–53, 157–63, 193, 199, 203, 207–8.

2. Wayne D. Rasmussen, *A History of the Emergency Farm Labor Supply Program, 1943–47*, Agriculture Monograph no. 13 (Washington, D.C.: U.S. Department of Agriculture, Bureau of Agricultural Economics, 1951), 20–21, 26–27, 36, 201–3, 208, 214; Robert C. Jones, *Mexican Workers in the United States: The Mexico–United*

States Manpower Recruiting Program and Its Operation (Washington, D.C.: Pan American Union, Division of Labor and Social Information, 1945), 1–26; M. Scruggs Otey, "The Bracero Program under the Farm Security Administration, 1942–1943," *Labor History* 4 (Spring 1962): 149–62; William L. Hewitt, "Mexican Workers in Wyoming during World War II: Necessity, Discrimination and Protest," *Annals of Wyoming* 54 (Fall 1982): 26–27.

3. Hurt, *Great Plains*, 224–33.

4. Hurt, *Great Plains*, 173.

5. Bradley H. Baltensperger, "Larger and Fewer Farms: Patterns and Abuses of Farm Enlargement on the Central Great Plains, 1930–1978," *Journal of Historical Geography* 19, no. 3 (1993): 300–301.

6. R. Douglas Hurt, *The Dust Bowl: An Agricultural and Social History* (Chicago: Nelson-Hall, 1981), 141–44, 149–50; Leslie Hewes, "The Great Plains One Hundred Years after Major John Wesley Powell," in *Images of the Great Plains: The Role of Human Nature in Settlement*, ed. Brian W. Blouet and Merlin P. Lawson (Lincoln: University of Nebraska Press, 1975), 208.

7. R. Douglas Hurt, *American Agriculture: A Brief History*, rev. ed. (West Lafayette, Ind.: Purdue University Press, 2003), 339, 341–43.

8. Jere Lee Gilles and Michael Dalecki, "Rural Well-Being and Agricultural Change in Two Farming Regions," *Rural Sociology* 53, no. 1 (1988): 52; Gilbert C. Fite, "The Transformation of South Dakota Agriculture: The Effects of Mechanization, 1939–1964," *South Dakota History* 19 (Fall 1989): 291.

9. Thomas D. Isern, "Custom Combining in North Dakota," *North Dakota History* 49 (Spring 1982): 4–11; see also Thomas D. Isern, *Custom Combining on the Great Plains* (Norman: University of Oklahoma Press, 1981).

10. Harry G. Sitler and Melvin D. Skold, "Analysis of Change in the Agrarian Sector of the Great Plains," *Rocky Mountain Social Science Journal* 5, no. 2 (1968): 42; Fite, "Transformation of South Dakota Agriculture," 295.

11. Bradley H. Baltensperger, "Farm Consolidation in the Northern and Central States of the Great Plains," *Great Plains Quarterly* 7 (Fall 1987): 257.

12. Elwyn B. Robinson, *History of North Dakota* (Lincoln: University of Nebraska Press, 1966), 444–46; Baltensperger, "Larger and Fewer Farms," 300–301; Fite, "Transformation of South Dakota Agriculture," 299, 301–3, 305; Herbert S. Schell, *History of South Dakota* (Lincoln: University of Nebraska Press, 1975; repr., Pierre: South Dakota Historical Society Press, 2004), 323.

13. Jon Lauck, "The Corporate Farming Debate in the Post–World War II Midwest," *Great Plains Quarterly* 18 (Spring 1998): 140–43, 146, 149.

14. Steve H. Murdock, Don E. Albrecht, Rita R. Hamm, F. Larry Leistritz, and Arlen G. Leholm, "The Farm Crisis in the Great Plains: Implications for Theory and Policy Development," *Rural Sociology* 51, no. 4 (1986): 406, 415–16, 425.

15. Richard W. Rathge, "Women's Contribution to the Family Farm," *Great Plains Quarterly* 9 (Winter 1989): 41, 45.

16. Robinson, *History of North Dakota*, 449–50; Hurt, *American Agriculture*, 344.

17. Baltensperger, "Farm Consolidation," 259–60, 263–64; Baltensperger, "Larger and Fewer Farms," 299–313.

18. Robert Kelley Schneiders, *Unruly River: Two Centuries of Change along the*

Missouri (Lawrence: University Press of Kansas, 1999), 166–70; Michael L. Lawson, *Dammed Indians: The Pick-Sloan Plan and the Missouri River Sioux, 1944–1980* (Norman: University of Oklahoma Press, 1982), 9–10.

19. Mark W. T. Harvey, "North Dakota, the Northern Great Plains, and the Missouri Valley Authority," *North Dakota History* 59 (Summer 1992): 29; Schneiders, *Unruly River*, 166–67, 170–72; Schell, *History of South Dakota*, 324.

20. Harvey, "North Dakota," 31; Schneiders, *Unruly River*, 173; John Ferrell, "Developing the Missouri: South Dakota and the Pick-Sloan Plan," *South Dakota History* 19 (Fall 1989): 309–10.

21. Schneiders, *Unruly River*, 172–74; *Denver Post*, November 17, 1944; Ferrell, "Developing the Missouri," 311.

22. Harvey, "North Dakota," 29, 32.

23. Ferrell, "Developing the Missouri," 314; Schneiders, *Unruly River*, 173, 178–79; Lawson, *Dammed Indians*, 17–20.

24. *Denver Post*, November 17, 1944; Harvey, "North Dakota," 34–38.

25. Lawson, *Dammed Indians*, 18; Harvey, "North Dakota," 38.

26. John R. Ferrell, "Missouri Basin Land and Water Control Controversies, 1933–1951," in *Agricultural Legacies: Essays in Honor of Gilbert C. Fite*, ed. R. Alton Lee (Vermillion: University of South Dakota Press, 1986), 127–28; Ferrell, "Developing the Missouri," 314.

27. Robert Kelly Schneiders, "Flooding the Missouri River Valley: The Politics of Dam Site Selection and Design," *Great Plains Quarterly* 17 (Fall 1997): 244; Ferrell, "Developing the Missouri," 314.

28. Schneiders, *Unruly River*, 179–80; Lawson, *Dammed Indians*, 30, 45; Ferrell, "Developing the Missouri," 316.

29. Lawson, *Dammed Indians*, 20, 27, 29, 56.

30. Schneiders, *Unruly River*, 88–91, 196, 199–200; Ferrell, "Missouri Basin," 129–33; Lawson, *Dammed Indians*, 112, 115.

31. Peter Carrels, *Uphill against Water: The Great Dakota Water War* (Lincoln: University of Nebraska Press, 1999); Ferrell, "Developing the Missouri," 331.

32. Lawson, *Dammed Indians*, xi–xii, 29, 199–200.

33. Donald E. Green, *Land of the Underground Rain: Irrigation on the Texas High Plains, 1910–1970* (Austin: University of Texas Press, 1973); John Opie, *Ogallala: Water for a Dry Land* (Lincoln: University of Nebraska Press, 1993), 122–60. For the development of irrigation in the Arkansas River valley, see James Earl Sherow, *Watering the Valley: Development along the High Plains Arkansas River, 1870–1950* (Lawrence: University Press of Kansas, 1990).

34. R. Douglas Hurt, "Irrigation in the Kansas Plains since 1930," *Red River Valley Historical Review* 4 (Fall 1979): 65–66.

35. Opie, *Ogallala*, 137–39, 146, 158.

36. David E. Kromm and Stephen E. White, "The High Plains Ogallala Region," in *Groundwater Exploitation in the High Plains*, ed. David E. Kromm and Stephen E. White (Lawrence: University Press of Kansas, 1992), 15–16; Hurt, "Irrigation in the Kansas Plains," 69; Geoff Cunfer, *On the Great Plains: Agriculture and Environment* (College Station: Texas A&M University Press, 2005), 199–200.

37. Green, *Land of the Underground Rain*, 146–47, 150, 153, 158–59, 162–63, 230.

38. Green, *Land of the Underground Rain*, 201–04; Opie, *Ogallala*, 153.

39. David E. Kromm and Stephen E. White, "Groundwater Problems," in Kromm and White, *Groundwater Exploitation*, 54; Sam S. Kepfield, "The 'Liquid Gold' Rush: Groundwater Irrigation and Law in Nebraska, 1900–1993," *Great Plains Quarterly* 13 (Fall 1993): 237–50.

40. Hurt, "Irrigation in the Kansas Plains," 69.

41. Kromm and White, "High Plains Ogallala Region," 15, 20–24; Kromm and White, "Groundwater Problems," 46–49, 54; Opie, *Ogallala*, 118.

42. David E. Kromm and Stephen E. White, "Future Prospects," in Kromm and White, *Groundwater Exploitation*, 229; David J. Carlson, "High Plains–Ogallala Aquifer Study," in *Proceedings of the Great Plains Agricultural Council, June 6–9, 1983* (Lincoln, Nebr.: Great Plains Agricultural Council), 15.

43. Timothy L. Amsden, "Progress and Problems in Developing and Implementing a Groundwater Protection Strategy," in *Proceedings of the Great Plains Agricultural Council, 1987* (Lincoln, Nebr.: Great Plains Agricultural Council), 92.

44. J. F. Power, L. N. Mielke, J. W. Doran, and W. W. Wilhelm, "Chemical, Physical, and Microbial Changes in Tilled Soils," in *Proceedings of the Great Plains Agricultural Council, 1984* (Lincoln, Nebr.: Great Plains Agricultural Council), 157; C. R. Fenster, "Potential and Problems of Ecofarming in Drier Environments," in *Proceedings of the Great Plains Agricultural Council, 1982* (Lincoln, Nebr.: Great Plains Agricultural Council), 56; Dale H. Vanderholm, "Development of Farming Systems to Reduce Adverse Effects on the Environment," in *Proceedings of the Great Plains Agricultural Council, 1989* (Lincoln, Nebr.: Great Plains Agricultural Council), 85.

45. Myron D. Johnsrud, "An Overview of Environmental Issues and Great Plains Agriculture," in *Proceedings of the Great Plains Agricultural Council, 1989*, 1–6; Amsden, "Progress and Problems," 94.

46. Thomas L. Dobbs, "Economic Considerations in Evaluating Alternative Agricultural Practices," in *Proceedings of the Great Plains Agricultural Council, 1989*, 109.

47. Kromm and White, "Groundwater Problems," 61; Opie, *Ogallala*, 293–96.

Chapter 7. The Inevitability of Change

1. Charlene R. Nickels and Frederick A. Day, "Depopulation of the Rural Great Plains Counties of Texas," *Great Plains Research* 7 (Fall 1997): 228, 230–31, 236, 239.

2. David E. Kromm and Stephen E. White, "The High Plains Ogallala Region," in *Groundwater Exploitation in the High Plains*, ed. David E. Kromm and Stephen E. White (Lawrence: University Press of Kansas, 1992), 10–14, 17.

3. Stephen E. White, "Ogallala Oases: Water Use, Population Redistribution, and Policy Implications in the High Plains of Western Kansas, 1980–1990," *Annals of the Association of American Geographers* 84 (March 1994): 31–33, 36, 38.

4. White, "Ogallala Oases," 42–43; Jeffrey M. Peterson and Daniel J. Bernarso, "High Plains Regional Aquifer Study Revisited: A 20-Year Retrospective for Western Kansas," *Great Plains Research* 13 (Fall 2003): 184–85, 188–89.

5. Mark A. Drummond, "Regional Dynamics of Grassland Change in the Western Great Plains," *Great Plains Research* 17 (Fall 2007): 135.

6. Donald E. Albrecht and Steven H. Murdock, "Natural Resource Availability and Social Change," *Sociological Inquiry* 56, no. 3 (1986): 384; Drummond, "Regional Dynamics," 140–42.

7. Kromm and White, "High Plains Ogallala Region," 8–11.

8. Craig Miner, *Kansas: The History of the Sunflower State, 1854–2000* (Lawrence: University Press of Kansas, 2002), 405; Susan Hautaniemi Leonard and Myron P. Gutmann, "Isolated Elderly in the U.S. Great Plains: The Roles of Environment and Demography in Creating a Vulnerable Population," *Annales de Démographie Historique*, no. 2 (2005): 82; James R. Shortridge, "A Cry for Help: KansasFreeland.com," *Geographical Review* 94, no. 4 (2004): 530–40.

9. Leonard and Gutmann, "Isolated Elderly," 84–85, 88; Miner, *Kansas*, 405.

10. Max Lu, "Homesteading Redux: New Community Initiatives to Reverse Rural Depopulation in the Great Plains," *Journal of the West* 46 (Winter 2007): 75.

11. Don E. Albrecht, "The Renewal of Population Loss in the Nonmetropolitan Great Plains," *Rural Sociology* 58 (Summer 1993): 233–34, 238–44.

12. Richard E. Lonsdale and J. Clark Archer, "Changing Employment Patterns on the Northern and Central Great Plains," *Great Plains Research* 5 (February 1995): 47–48, 53, 55, 57, 61–62; see also F. Larry Leistritz, Sam Cordes, and Randall S. Sell, "Characteristics of In-Migration to the Northern Great Plains: Survey Results from Nebraska and North Dakota," *Great Plains Research* 11 (Fall 2001): 275-99.

13. *Des Moines (Iowa) Register*, July 31, 1998; James R. Shortridge, *Cities on the Plains: The Evolution of Urban Kansas* (Lawrence: University Press of Kansas, 2004), 377–80; Rebecca Vogt, John C. Allen, and Sam Cordes, "Relationship between Community Satisfaction and Migration Intentions of Rural Nebraskans," *Great Plains Research* 13 (Spring 2003): 63–64, 69.

14. William J. Parton, "Sustainability and Historical Land-Use Change in the Great Plains: The Case of Eastern Colorado," *Great Plains Research* 13 (Spring 2003): 97–98, 111–13, 115, 117, 120.

15. Richard Mason, "A Handful of Farmers: The South Plains, Politics, and Water," *West Texas Historical Association Year Book* 60 (1984): 19–20, 30.

16. Don E. Albrecht, "The Industrial Transformation of Farm Communities: Implications for Family Structure and Socioeconomic Conditions," *Rural Sociology* 63 (March 1998): 51.

17. John Gaber, Sharon Gaber, and Jeff Vincent, "An Analysis of Refugee Resettlement Patterns in the Great Plains," *Great Plains Research* 14 (Fall 2004): 167, 172–79, 182.

18. Lourdes Gouveia and Donald D. Stull, "Dances with Cows: Beefpacking's Impact on Garden City, Kansas, and Lexington, Nebraska," in *Any Way You Cut It: Meat Processing and Small-Town America*, ed. Donald D. Stull, Michael J. Broadway, and David Griffith (Lawrence: University Press of Kansas, 1995), 85–86.

19. Paul H. Carlson, *Amarillo: The Story of a Western Town* (Lubbock: Texas Tech University Press, 2006), 186–88.

20. Gouveia and Stull, "Dances with Cows," 87–90, 92, 98, 103; Lonsdale and Archer, "Changing Employment Patterns," 55, 57; Wilson J. Warren, *Tied to the Great Packing Machine: The Midwest and Meat Packing* (Iowa City: University of Iowa Press, 2007), 67, 107.

21. Gouveia and Stull, "Dances with Cows," 92, 98.

22. Richard Lowitt, *American Outback: The Oklahoma Panhandle in the Twentieth Century* (Lubbock: Texas Tech University Press, 2006), 99–102.

23. Gouveia and Stull, "Dances with Cows," 92–103; Lonsdale and Archer, "Changing Employment Patterns," 53, 57–58, 66, 93.

24. Diana Davids Olien, "Exploitationists and Depletionists: Petroleum in the Future of the Southern Great Plains," in *The Future of the Southern Plains*, ed. Sherry L. Smith (Norman: University of Oklahoma Press in cooperation with the William P. Clements Center for Southwest Studies, Southern Methodist University, 2003), 152–56, 163.

25. Olien, "Exploitationists and Depletionists," 156, 159–60, 162–65; Lowitt, *American Outback*, 87–88.

26. Carlson, *Amarillo*, 208; personal observations of the author; Leonard and Gutmann, "Isolated Elderly," 89.

27. Michael P. Malone and Richard B. Roeder, *Montana: A History of Two Centuries* (Seattle: University of Washington Press, 1976), 257–58; K. Ross Toole, *The Rape of the Great Plains: Northwest America, Cattle and Coal* (Boston: Little, Brown, 1976), 13–15, 18–19.

28. Malone and Roeder, *Montana*, 259–60; Toole, *Rape of the Great Plains*, 45–49, 87.

29. Toole, *Rape of the Great Plains*, 95–96.

30. Sam Cordes and Evert Van der Sluis, "The Contemporary Role of the Federal Government in the Great Plains Economy: A Comprehensive Examination of Federal Spending and Related Fiscal Activities," *Great Plains Research* 11 (Fall 2001): 301–25.

31. *Ames (Iowa) Tribune*, March 7, 1998.

32. Brian L. Schulz, "Where Is Main Street? The Commercial Landscape of Four Oklahoma Small Towns," *Chronicles of Oklahoma* 7 (Spring 1993): 95–97, 101–2.

33. Shortridge, *Cities on the Plains*, 377–80, 433.

34. Kromm and White, "High Plains Ogallala Region," 10–14.

35. *Ames (Iowa) Tribune*, March 7, 1998; Leonard and Gutmann, "Isolated Elderly," 91; Katherine J. Curtis White, "Population Change and Farm Dependence: Temporal and Spatial Variation in the U.S. Great Plains, 1900–2000," *Demography* 45 (May 2008): 384–85; for women's views of life in the Great Plains, see Cary W. deWit, "Women's Sense of Place on the American High Plains," *Great Plains Quarterly* 21 (Winter 2001): 29–44.

Chapter 8. The Politics of Race and Agriculture

1. James Potter, Rodrigo Cantarero, X. Winson Yan, Steve Larrick, and Blanca Ramirez-Salazar, "A Case Study of the Impact of Population Influx on a Small Community in Nebraska," *Great Plains Research* 14 (Fall 2004): 220–21, 230; Rochelle L. Dalla, Francisco Villarruel, and Sherman C. Cramer, "Examining Strengths and Challenges of Rapid Rural Immigration," *Great Plains Research* 14 (Fall 2004): 233–34.

2. Dalla, Villarruel, and Cramer, "Examining Strengths and Challenges," 235; Örn Bodvarsson and Hendrik Van den Berg, "The Impact of Immigration on a Local

Economy: The Case of Dawson County, Nebraska," *Great Plains Research* 13 (Fall 2003): 291–93, 299, 301; Ana-María Wahl, Steven E. Gunkel, and Bennie Shobe Jr., "Becoming Neighbors or Remaining Strangers? Latinos and Residential Segregation in the Heartland," *Great Plains Research* 15 (Fall 2005): 299, 305–6, 308, 312–13, 324.

3. Dalla, Villarruel, and Cramer, "Examining Strengths and Challenges," 240–41, 237–39; Potter et al., "Case Study," 221, 225; Bodvarsson and Van den Berg, "Impact of Immigration," 301.

4. Miguel A. Carranza, Gustavo Carlo, and Maria Rosario T. de Guzman, "The Role of Research Scholarship in Enhancing the Quality of Life for Latinos on the Great Plains," *Great Plains Research* 10 (Fall 2000): 410–11; Lourdes Gouveia and Rogelio Saenz, "Global Forces and Latino Population Growth in the Midwest: A Regional and Subregional Analysis," *Great Plains Research* 10 (Fall 2000): 320, 323; Dalla, Villarruel, and Cramer, "Examining Strengths and Challenges," 232.

5. Gouveia, "Global Forces," 307; Robert P. Moreno, Lawrence P. Hernandez, Jennifer D. Schroeder, and Ani Yazedjian, "Rethinking Human Services for Latinos in the Plains: New Paradigms and Recommendations for Practice," *Great Plains Research* 10 (Fall 2000): 389; Refugio I. Rochín, "Latinos on the Great Plains: An Overview," *Great Plains Research* 10 (Fall 2000): 244, 245–46.

6. Evelyn Ravuri, "Changes in Asian and Hispanic Population in the Cities of the Great Plains, 1990–2000," *Great Plains Research* 13 (Spring 2003): 87; Rochín, "Latinos on the Great Plains," 246–48.

7. Rochín, "Latinos on the Great Plains," 249–50.

8. Ravuri, "Changes," 80; Gouveia, "Global Forces," 308–12; Ana-María Wahl, Steven E. Gunkel, and Thomas W. Sanchez, "Death and Disability in the Heartland: Corporate (Mis)Conduct, Regulatory Responses, and the Plight of Latino Workers in the Meatpacking Industry," *Great Plains Research* 10 (Fall 2000): 335.

9. D. A. Lopez, "Attitudes of Selected Latino Oldtimers toward Newcomers: A Photo Elicitation Study," *Great Plains Research* 10 (Fall 2000): 253, 271–72; Tomás R. Jiménez, "Weighing the Costs and Benefits of Mexican Immigration: The Mexican-American Perspective," *Social Science Quarterly* 88 (September 2007): 604, 607–9.

10. David E. Kromm and Stephen F. White, ed., "Ground Water Problems," in *Ground Water Exploitation in the High Plains*, ed. David E. Kromm and Stephen E. White (Lawrence: University Press of Kansas, 1992), 54, 56; Wilson J. Warren, *Tied to the Great Packing Machine: The Midwest and Meat Packing* (Iowa City: University of Iowa Press, 2007), 68; Bodvarsson and Van den Berg, "Impact of Immigration," 306–7.

11. Jeff Corntassel and Richard C. Witmer, *Forced Federalism: Contemporary Challenges to Indigenous Nationhood* (Norman: University of Oklahoma Press, 2008), 14; Larry Burt, "Western Tribes and Balance Sheets: Business Development Programs in the 1960s and 1970s," *Western Historical Quarterly* 23 (November 1992): 489–90, 493–95.

12. Joane Nagel, *American Indian Ethnic Renewal: Red Power and the Resurgence of Indian Identity and Culture* (New York: Oxford University Press, 1997), 166–68, 171–72; Francis Paul Prucha, *The Great Father: The United States Government and the Indians*, vol. 2 (Lincoln: University of Nebraska Press, 1984), 1119; Tom Holm, "The Crisis in Tribal Government," in *American Indian Policy in the Twentieth Century*, ed.

Vine Deloria Jr. (Norman: University of Oklahoma Press, 1985), 138. See also Vine Deloria Jr., *Behind the Trail of Broken Treaties: An Indian Declaration of Independence* (Austin: University of Texas Press, 1985), 85–111; Floyd A. O'Neil, June K. Lyman, and Susan McKay, eds., *Wounded Knee, 1973: A Personal Account by Stanley David Lyman* (Lincoln: University of Nebraska Press, 1991); and Akim D. Reinhart, *Ruling Pine Ridge: Oglala Lakota Politics from the IRA to Wounded Knee* (Lubbock: Texas Tech University Press, 2007).

13. Holm, "Crisis in Tribal Government," 139; Peter Iverson, *We Are Still Here: American Indians in the Twentieth Century* (Wheeling, Ill.: Harlan Davidson, 1998), 148–54; Nagel, *American Indian Ethnic Renewal,* 172–73.

14. Nagel, *American Indian Ethnic Renewal,* 140, 173; Prucha, *Great Father,* 1085–86, 1120.

15. Prucha, *Great Father,* 1065–67; Iverson, *We Are Still Here,* 159–60, 164; Margaret Connell Szasz, "Listening to the Native Voice: American Indian Schooling in the Twentieth Century," *Montana: The Magazine of Western History* 39 (Summer 1989): 44.

16. Iverson, *We Are Still Here,* 162, 164; Szasz, "Listening to the Native Voice," 44, 51–52.

17. Corntassel and Witmer, *Forced Federalism,* 14; Donald D. Stull, Jerry A. Schultz, and Ken Cadue Sr. "Rights without Resources: The Rise and Fall of the Kansas Kickapoo," *American Indian Culture and Research Journal* 10, no. 2 (1986): 43–44.

18. Stull, Schultz, and Cadue, "Rights without Resources," 46–49, 55, 57.

19. Iverson, *We Are Still Here,* 197, 203.

20. Erin Feinauer Whiting, Carol Ward, Rita Hiwalker Villa, and Judith Davis, "How Does the New TANF Work Requirement 'Work' in Rural Minority Communities? A Case of the Northern Cheyennes," *American Indian Culture and Research Journal* 29, no. 4 (2005): 95–120; Carol Ward, "The Importance of Context in Explaining Human Capital Formation and Labor Force Participation of American Indians in Rosebud County, Montana," *Rural Sociology* 63 (September 1998): 455, 468–69, 477.

21. *New York Times,* May 5 and 27, 2001; Duane Champagne, "Tribal Capitalism and Native Capitalists: Multiple Pathways of Native Economy," in *American Indian Culture and Economic Development in the Twentieth Century,* ed. Brian Hosmer and Colleen O'Neill (Boulder: University of Colorado Press, 2004), 322–23; Iverson, *We Are Still Here,* 192.

22. Kenneth W. Grant, Katherine A. Spilde, and Jonathan B. Taylor, "Social and Economic Consequences of Indian Gaming in Oklahoma," *American Indian Culture and Research Journal* 28, no. 2 (2004): 97–129.

23. Douglas A. Abbott, "Strengths and Stresses of Omaha Indian Families Living on the Reservation," *Great Plains Research* 10 (Spring 2000): 159; Corntassel and Witmer, *Forced Federalism,* 117, 135.

24. Prucha, *Great Father,* 1192, 1194–97.

25. Champagne, "Tribal Capitalism and Native Capitalism," 319–21.

26. Tressa Berman, "'All We Needed Was Our Gardens': Women's Work and Welfare Reform in the Reservation Economy," in Hosmer and O'Neill, *Native Pathways,* 135–36, 139, 150–51.

27. Champagne, "Tribal Capitalism and Native Capitalism," 322, 325–26.
28. Gregory R. Campbell, "Northern Cheyenne Ethnicity, Religion, and Coal Energy Development," *Plains Anthropologist* 32, no. 118 (1987): 378–79, 382–84; Zoltán Grossman, "Cowboy and Indian Alliances in the Northern Plains," *Agricultural History* 77 (Spring 2003): 359–61, 364–65.
29. Burt, "Western Tribes and Balance Sheets," 476, 478–79; David L. Vinge, "Cultural Values and Economic Development: U.S. Indian Reservations," *Social Science Journal* 19, no. 3 (1982): 88.
30. Donald L. Fixico, "The Demand for Natural Resources on Reservations: American Capitalism and Tribal Natural Resources," in *The Invasion of Indian Country in the Twentieth Century: American Capitalism and Tribal Natural Resources*, ed. Donald L. Fixico (Niwot: University Press of Colorado, 1998), 143–51, 153, 155; Herbert T. Hoover and Steven C. Emry, "South Dakota Governance since 1945," in *Politics in the Postwar American West*, ed. Richard Lowitt (Norman: University of Oklahoma Press, 1995), 231–38; see also James J. Lopach, Margery Hunter Brown, and Richmond L. Clow, *Tribal Government Today: Politics on Montana Reservations* (Boulder, Colo.: Westview Press, 1990).
31. William P. Browne and John Dinse, "The Emergence of the American Agriculture Movement, 1977–1979," *Great Plains Quarterly* 5 (Fall 1985): 221–23; William P. Browne, "Mobilizing and Activating Group Demands: The American Agriculture Movement," *Social Science Quarterly* 64 (March 1983): 22–23; R. Douglas Hurt, *American Agriculture: A Brief History*, rev. ed. (West Lafayette, Ind.: Purdue University Press, 2003), 369; Gilbert C. Fite, *American Farmers: The New Minority* (Bloomington: Indiana University Press, 1981), 207–10.
32. Browne, "Mobilizing and Activating Group Demands," 25–26, 28; Hurt, *American Agriculture*, 369–70; Fite, *American Farmers*, 210–17.
33. Browne, "Mobilizing and Activating Group Demands," 30; Hurt, *American Agriculture*, 370.
34. Browne and Dinse, "Emergence," 227; Hurt, *American Agriculture*, 370.
35. Browne and Dinse, "Emergence," 227–28; R. Douglas Hurt, "Agricultural Politics in the Twentieth-Century American West," in *The Political Culture of the New West*, ed. Jeff Roche (Lawrence: University Press of Kansas, 2008), 51, 65–66.
36. *Des Moines Register*, January 31, 1993.
37. *Ames (Iowa) Daily Tribune*, December 14, 1992; Peter J. McCormick, "The 1992 Secession Movement in Southwest Kansas," *Great Plains Quarterly* 15 (Fall 1995): 247, 254–56; Craig Miner, *Kansas: The History of the Sunflower State, 1854–2000* (Lawrence: University Press of Kansas, 2002), 394; see also Thomas Frank, *What's the Matter with Kansas? How Conservatives Won the Heart of America* (New York: Henry Holt, 2004).
38. McCormick, "1992 Secession Movement," 247–48; *Ames (Iowa) Daily Tribune*, December 14, 1992.
39. McCormick, "1992 Secession Movement," 249, 251–52, 256.
40. Thomas M. Carsey, "Gubernatorial Electoral Coalitions in the Great Plains," *Great Plains Research* 7 (Spring 1997): 50–51, 58–60, 64, 66.
41. Jeff Roche, "Identity and Conservative Politics on the Southern Plains," in *The Future of the Southern Plains*, ed. Sherry L. Smith (Norman: University of Oklahoma

Press in cooperation with the William P. Clements Center for Southwest Studies, Southern Methodist University, 2003), 169–98.

42. Ignacio M. García, "Latinos in the Politics of the West," in Roche, *Political Culture*, 183–87.

43. Jiménez, "Weighing the Costs and Benefits," 610–12; García, "Latinos," 189.

44. Maurilio E. Vigil, "Hispanics and the 1996 Presidential Election," *Latino Studies Journal* 9 (Winter 1998): 56, 58, 59.

45. Corntassel and Witmer, *Forced Federalism*, 98–100.

46. Bradley Glenn Shreve, "The Evolution of Modern American Indian Politics," in Roche, *Political Culture*, 196, 213.

47. Richard M. Scammon, Alice McGillivray, and Rhodes Cook, *America Votes, 24: A Handbook of Contemporary American Election Statistics* (Washington, D.C.: Congressional Quarterly, 2004), 1–33; see also David B. Danbom, "A Part of the Nation and Apart from the Nation: North Dakota Politics since 1945," in Lowitt, *Politics in the Postwar*, 174–84; and Herbert T. Hoover and Steven C. Emry, "South Dakota Governance since 1945," in Lowitt, *Politics in the Postwar*, 221–38.

48. Amanda Rees, ed., *The Great Plains Region* (Westport, Conn.: Greenwood Press, 2004), 93–95; Dan L. Flores, *The Natural West: Environmental History in the Great Plains and Rocky Mountains* (Norman: University of Oklahoma Press, 2001).

Epilogue

1. Personal recollections of the author; Kathleen Norris, *Dakota: A Spiritual Geography* (New York: Ticknor and Fields, 1993), 151; Wright Morris, *God's Country and My People* (New York: Harper and Row, 1968); Dan O'Brien, *In the Center of the Nation* (New York: Atlantic Monthly Press, 1991), 3; N. Scott Momaday, *House Made of Dawn* (New York: Harper and Row, 1966), 127–28. The identity and distinctiveness of the Great Plains is complex, and while it is the result of environmental and human causation, extensive analysis would require this study to depart far from its purpose. Anyone pursuing this subject will do well to consult the following sources: Howard F. Stein and Robert F. Hall, eds., *The Culture of Oklahoma* (Norman: University of Oklahoma Press, 1993); James H. Madison, ed., *Heartland: Comparative Histories of the Midwestern States* (Bloomington: Indiana University Press, 1988): Robert Bader Smith, *Hayseeds, Moralizers, and Methodists: The Twentieth-Century Image of Kansas* (Lawrence: University Press of Kansas, 1988); Joe Carr and Alan Munde, *Prairie Nights to Neon Lights: The Story of Country Music in West Texas* (Lubbock: Texas Tech University Press, 1995); John Gunther, *Inside U.S.A.* (New York: Curtis Publishing, 1947); and *American Panorama: Portraits of 50 States by Distinguished Authors* (Garden City, N.Y.: Doubleday, 1960). See also James R. Shortridge, "The Expectations of Others: Struggles toward a Sense of Place in the Northern Great Plains," in *Many Wests: Place, Culture, and Regional Identity*, ed. David M. Wrobel and Michael C. Steiner (Lawrence: University Press of Kansas, 1997), 114–35; Bert Wallach, "The Telltale Southern Plains," in Wrobel and Steiner, *Many Wests*, 141–55; Richard W. Etulain, *Re-imagining the Modern American West: A Century of Fiction, History, and Art* (Tucson: University of Arizona Press, 1996); and Carol Fairbanks, *Prairie Women:*

Images in American and Canadian Fiction (New Haven, Conn.: Yale University Press, 1986). For an excellent collection of contemporary writing about the Texas plains, see Lou Halsell Rodenberger, Laura Payne Butler, and Jacqueline Kolosov, eds., *Writing on the Wind: An Anthology of West Texas Women Writers* (Lubbock: Texas Tech University Press, 2005). For an introduction to film, music, and literature, see David J. Wishart, ed., *The Encyclopedia of the Great Plains* (Lincoln: University of Nebraska Press, 2004).

2. Willa Sibert Cather, *My Ántonia* (Boston: Houghton Mifflin, 1918), 8, 16; Norris, *Dakota*, 153.

3. Diane Dufva Quantic, *The Nature of Place: A Study of Great Plains Fiction* (Lincoln: University of Nebraska Press, 1995), 158, 169; Larry Woiwode, *Beyond the Bedroom Wall* (New York: Farrar, Straus, and Giroux, 1975); Morris, *God's Country and My People*.

4. Howard Lamar, "Image and Counterimage: The Regional Artist and the Great Plains Landscape," in *The Big Empty: Essays on Western Landscape as Narratives*, ed. Leonard Engle (Albuquerque: University of New Mexico Press, 1994), 78; Mari Sandoz, *Old Jules* (Boston: Little, Brown, 1935), 424; Larry McMurtry, *In a Narrow Grave: Essays on Texas* (New York: Simon and Schuster, 1968), 17–18; Norris, *Dakota*, 13, 39, 120; Larry McMurtry, *The Last Picture Show* (New York: Dial Press, 1966).

5. McMurtry, *In a Narrow Grave*, 120, 173; Rodenberger, Butler, and Kolosov, *Writing on the Wind*; Quantic, *Nature of Place*, 9, 28, 59, 83–87.

6. Norris, *Dakota*, 87; Guy Reynolds, "Willa Cather's Case: Region and Reputation," in *Regionalism and the Humanities*, ed. Timothy R. Mahoney and Wendy Katz (Lincoln: University of Nebraska Press, 2008), 79–94; McMurtry, *In a Narrow Grave*, 54, 137.

7. Norris, *Dakota*, 6–7, 25, 35, 55, 64, 84, 108, 165, 169.

8. Lamar, "Image and Counterimage," 80–81; R. Douglas Hurt, *The Dust Bowl: An Agricultural and Social History* (Chicago: Nelson-Hall, 1981), 63; Donald Worster, *The Dust Bowl: The Southern Plains in the 1930s* (New York: Oxford University Press, 1979), 32–33.

9. Lamar, "Image and Counterimage," 88; Donald Bartlett Doe, "The Great Plains: The Land in the History of Nebraska Art," in *Art and Artists in Nebraska*, ed. Norman A. Geske (Lincoln: Center for Great Plains Studies and Sheldon Art Gallery, 1983), 136–41.

10. Norris, *Dakota*, 155, 157; Karen J. DeBres, "Cowtowns or Cathedral Precincts? Two Models for Contemporary Urban Tourism," *Arena* 26 (1994): 57–67; John Jakle, *The Tourist: Travel in Twentieth-Century North America* (Lincoln: University of Nebraska Press, 1985); Walter Nugent, *Into the West: The Story of Its People* (New York: Knopf, 1999), 348.

11. Elise L. Broach, "Angles, Architecture, and Erosion: The Dakota Badlands as a Cultural Symbol," *North Dakota History* 59 (Winter 1992): 2–15; Dan Flores, *Caprock Canyonlands: Journeys into the Heart of the Southern Plains* (Austin: University of Texas Press, 1990).

12. Nugent, *Into the West*, 338–39, 371.

13. L. R. Corah, "ASAS Centennial Paper: Development of a Corn-Based Beef Industry," *Journal of Animal Science* 86 (December 2008): 3635–36; John Opie, *Ogallala: Water for a Dry Land* (Lincoln: University of Nebraska Press, 1993), 151–55;

Garry L. Nall, "The Cattle Feeding Industry on the Texas High Plains," in *Southwestern Agriculture: Pre-Columbian to Modern*, ed. Henry C. Dethloff and Irvin R. May (College Station: Texas A&M University Press, 1982), 106–15.

14. James Mintert, "Beef Feedlot Industry," *Veterinary Clinics Food Animal Practice* 19, no. 2 (2003): 388–89, 394; T. W. Perry, "Feedlot Fattening in North America," in *Beef Cattle Production*, ed. Robert Jarrige and C. Béranger (Amsterdam: Elsevier, 1992), 289–90, 304.

15. Carl Abbott, *The Metropolitan Frontier: Cities in the Modern American West* (Tucson: University of Arizona Press, 1993), xiii, xv, 128–29.

16. Carl Abbott, *How Cities Won the West: Four Centuries of Urban Change in Western North America* (Albuquerque: University of New Mexico Press, 2008), 178; Abbott, *Metropolitan Frontier*, xviii.

17. Abbott, *Metropolitan Frontier*, 72–74, 76, 81.

18. David Montejano, "The Demise of 'Jim Crow' for Texas Mexicans, 1940–1970," *Aztlán* 16, nos. 1–2 (1987): 59–60; Abbott, *Metropolitan Frontier*, 104–5, 111, 117.

19. Abbott, *Metropolitan Frontier*, 83–87, 92, 96; Abbott, *How Cities Won the West*, 183–84, 281 82.

20. Abbott, *Metropolitan Frontier*, 154–55, 169, 197.

21. Michael P. Malone and Richard W. Etulain, *The American West: A Twentieth-Century History* (Lincoln: University of Nebraska Press, 1989), 266–67, 273–77, 280, 290–92.

22. Allan J. Cigler and Dwight Kiel, "Kansas: Representation in Transition," in *Interest Group Politics in the Midwestern States*, ed. Ronald J. Hrebenar and Clive S. Thomas (Ames: Iowa State University Press, 1993), 95–97, 99, 114–15.

23. Allan Cigler and Brudett Loomis, "Kansas: Two-Party Competition in a One-Party State," in *Party Realignment and State Politics*, ed. Maureen Moakley (Columbus: Ohio State University Press, 1992), 163–66, 168–69, 171, 174.

24. John C. Comer, "Nebraska: Almost Heaven," in Hrebenar and Thomas, *Interest Group Politics in the Midwestern States*, 192–95, 210–11, 213–14.

25. Theodore B. Pedeliski, "North Dakota: Constituency Coupling in a Moderate Political Culture," in Hrebenar and Thomas, *Interest Group Politics in the Midwestern States*, 216–19, 221–25.

26. John Gunther, *Inside U.S.A.* (New York: Curtis Publishing, 1947), 881; Robert F. England and David R. Morgan, "Oklahoma: Group Power in Transition," in Hrebenar and Thomas, *Interest Group Politics in the Midwestern States*, 278–81; Abbott, *How Cities Won the West*, 190.

27. Bradley Glenn Shreve, "The Evolution of Modern American Indian Politics," in *The Political Culture of the New West*, ed. Jeff Roche (Lawrence: University Press of Kansas, 2008), 195–218; Robert E. Burns and Herbert E. Cheever Jr., "South Dakota: Conflict and Cooperation among Conservatives," in Hrebenar and Thomas, *Interest Group Politics in the Midwestern States*, 286–87.

28. Burns and Cheever, "South Dakota," 288–91, 296–97, 300, 303.

29. Ronald J. Hrebenar, "Interest Group Politics in the American West: A Comparative Perception," in *Interest Group Politics in the American West*, ed. Ronald J. Hrebenar and Clive S. Thomas (Salt Lake City: University of Utah Press, 1987), 6–7, 9–10.

30. Thomas Payne, "Montana: From Copper Fiefdom to Pluralist Polity," in Hre-

benar and Thomas, *Interest Group Politics in the American West*, 75–76, 78–79, 83–84; Michael P. Malone and Richard B. Roeder, *Montana: A History of Two Centuries* (Seattle: University of Washington Press, 1976), 292–94, 296.

31. Jose Garcia with Clive S. Thomas, "New Mexico: Traditional Interests in a Traditional State," in Hrebenar and Thomas, *Interest Group Politics in the American West*, 93–94, 96, 98–99, 101.

32. Janet M. Clark and B. Oliver Walter, "Wyoming: Populists versus Lobbyists," in Hrebenar and Thomas, *Interest Group Politics in the American West*, 133–36, 140–41.

33. John P. McIver and Walter J. Stone, "Stability and Change in Colorado Politics," in Moakley, *Party Realignment and State Politics*, 56–73; Paul Brace and John A. Stranger, "Colorado: PACs, Political Candidates, and Conservatism," in Hrebenar and Thomas, *Interest Group Politics in the American West*, 49, 51, 55, 57; Abbott, *How Cities Won the West*, 188–89.

34. Paula M. Nelson, *After the West Was Won: Homesteaders and Town-Builders in Western South Dakota, 1900–1917* (Iowa City: University of Iowa Press, 1986), 175.

Selected Bibliography

Abbott, Carl. *How Cities Won the West: Four Centuries of Urban Change in Western North America*. Albuquerque: University of New Mexico Press, 2008.

———. *The Metropolitan Frontier: Cities in the Modern American West*. Tucson: University of Arizona Press, 1993.

Abbott, Douglas A. "Strengths and Stresses of Omaha Indian Families Living on the Reservation." *Great Plains Research* 10 (Spring 2000): 145–68.

Adams, David Wallace. *Education for Extinction: American Indians and the Boarding School Experience, 1875–1928*. Lawrence: University Press of Kansas, 1995.

Albrecht, Don E. "The Industrial Transformation of Farm Communities: Implications for Family Structure and Socioeconomic Conditions." *Rural Sociology* 63 (March 1998): 51–64.

———. "The Renewal of Population Loss in the Nonmetropolitan Great Plains." *Rural Sociology* 58 (Summer 1993): 233–46.

Alexander, Charles C. *The Ku Klux Klan in the Southwest*. Lexington: University of Kentucky Press, 1965.

Andrews, Thomas C. "Turning the Tables on Assimilation: Oglala Lakotas and the Pine Ridge Day Schools, 1889–1920s." *Western Historical Quarterly* 33 (Winter 2002): 407–32.

Backwelder, Julia Kirk. *Women of the Depression: Caste and Culture in San Antonio, 1929–1939*. College Station: Texas A&M University Press, 1984.

Bakken, Douglas. "NPL in Nebraska, 1917–1920." *North Dakota History* 39 (Spring 1972): 26–31.

Baltensperger, Bradley H. "Farm Consolidation in the Northern and Central States of the Great Plains." *Great Plains Quarterly* 7 (Fall 1987): 256–65.

———. "Larger and Fewer Farms: Patterns and Abuses of Farm Enlargement on the Central Great Plains, 1930–1978." *Journal of Historical Geography* 19, no. 3 (1993): 299–313.

Baum, Dale. "The New Day in North Dakota: The Nonpartisan League and the Politics of Negative Revolution." *North Dakota History* 40 (Spring 1973): 5–19.

Beatty, Robert, and Mark A. Petersen. "Covert Discrimination: Topeka Before and After Brown." *Kansas History* 27 (Autumn 2004): 146–63.

Benjet, Rosaland. "The Ku Klux Klan and the Jewish Community of Dallas, 1921–1923." *Southern Jewish History* 6 (2003): 133–62.

Berman, Tressa. "'All We Needed Was Our Gardens': Women's Work and Welfare Reform in the Reservation Economy." In *Native Pathways: American Indian Culture and Economic Development in the Twentieth Century*, edited by Brian Hosmer and Colleen O'Neill, 133–55. Boulder: University Press of Colorado, 2004.

Biolsi, Thomas. *Organizing the Lakota: The Political Economy of the New Deal on the Pine Ridge and Rosebud Reservations*. Tucson: University of Arizona Press, 1992.

Bissett, Jim. *Agrarian Socialism in America: Marx, Jefferson, and Jesus in the Oklahoma Countryside, 1904–1920*. Norman: University of Oklahoma Press, 1999.

Blaisdell, Lowell L. "Anatomy of an Oklahoma Lynching: Bryan County, August 12–13, 1911." *Chronicles of Oklahoma* 79 (Fall 2001): 298–313.

Blouet, Brian W., and Frederick C. Luebke, eds. *The Great Plains: Environment and Culture*. Lincoln: University of Nebraska Press, 1979.

Bodvarsson, Örn, and Hendrik Van den Berg. "The Impact of Immigration on a Local Economy: The Case of Dawson County, Nebraska." *Great Plains Research* 13 (Fall 2003): 291–309.

Bonnifield, Paul. *The Dust Bowl: Men, Dirt, and Depression*. Albuquerque: University of New Mexico Press, 1979.

Broach, Elise L. "Angles, Architecture, and Erosion: The Dakota Badlands as a Cultural Symbol." *North Dakota History* 59 (Winter 1992): 2–15.

Browne, William P. "Mobilizing and Activating Group Demands: The American Agriculture Movement." *Social Science Quarterly* 64 (March 1983): 19–34.

Browne, William P., and John Dinse. "The Emergence of the American Agriculture Movement, 1977–1979." *Great Plains Quarterly* 5 (Fall 1985): 221–35.

Burt, Larry W. *Tribalism in Crisis: Federal Indian Policy, 1953–1961*. Albuquerque: University of New Mexico Press, 1982.

———. "Western Tribes and Balance Sheets: Business Development Programs in the 1960s and 1970s." *Western Historical Quarterly* 23 (November 1992): 476–95.

Campbell, Gregory R. "Northern Cheyenne Ethnicity, Religion, and Coal Energy Development." *Plains Anthropologist* 32, no. 118 (1987): 378–88.

Carlson, Paul H. *Amarillo: The Story of a Western Town*. Lubbock: Texas Tech University Press, 2006.

Carranza, Miguel A., Gustavo Carlo, and Maria Rosario T. de Guzman. "The Role of Research Scholarship in Enhancing the Quality of Life for Latinos on the Great Plains." *Great Plains Research* 10 (Fall 2000): 409–21.

Carrels, Peter. *Uphill against Water: The Great Dakota Water War*. Lincoln: University of Nebraska Press, 1999.

Carsey, Thomas M. "Gubernatorial Electoral Coalitions in the Great Plains." *Great Plains Research* 7 (Spring 1997): 41–70.

Celarier, Michelle. "A Study of Public Opinion on Desegregation in Oklahoma Higher Education." *Chronicles of Oklahoma* 47 (Autumn 1969): 268–81.

Chalmers, David M. *Hooded Americanism: The History of the Ku Klux Klan*. Durham, N.C.: Duke University Press, 1987.

Champagne, Duane. "Tribal Capitalism and Native Capitalists: Multiple Pathways of Native Economy." In *American Indian Culture and Economic Development in the Twentieth Century*, edited by Brian Hosmer and Colleen O'Neill, 308–329. Boulder: University of Colorado Press, 2004.

Child, Brenda J. *Boarding School Seasons: American Families, 1900–1940*. Lincoln: University of Nebraska Press, 1998.

Cioloto, Nicholas P. "From Agriculturists to Entrepreneurs: Economic Success and Mobility among Albuquerque's Italian Immigrants, 1900–1930." *New Mexico Historical Review* 74 (January 1999): 3–27.

Clow, Richmond L., ed. *The Sioux in South Dakota: A Twentieth-Century Reader*. Pierre: South Dakota Historical Society Press, 2007.

Cobb, Daniel M., and Loretta Fowler. *Beyond Red Power: American Indian Politics and Activism since 1900*. Santa Fe, N.Mex.: School for Advanced Research, 2007.

Coburn, Carol K. *Life at Four Corners: Religion, Gender and Education in a German-Lutheran Community, 1868–1945*. Lawrence: University Press of Kansas, 1992.

Cordes, Sam, and Evert Van der Sluis. "The Contemporary Role of the Federal Government in the Great Plains Economy: A Comprehensive Examination of Federal Spending and Related Fiscal Activities." *Great Plains Research* 11 (Fall 2001): 301–25.

Cordier, Mary Hurlbut. *School Women of the Prairies and Plains: Personal Narratives from Iowa, Kansas, and Nebraska, 1860s–1920s*. Albuquerque: University of New Mexico Press, 1992.

Cornnassel, Jeff, and Richard C. Witmer. *Forced Federalism: Contemporary Challenges to Indigenous Nationhood*. Norman: University of Oklahoma Press, 2008.

Crabb, Beth. "May 1930: Whiteman's Justice for a Black Man's Crime." *Journal of Negro History* 75, nos. 1–2 (1990): 29–40.

Crockett, Norma. "Crime on the Petroleum Frontier: Borger, Texas, in the Late 1920s." *Panhandle-Plains Historical Review* 64 (1991): 53–65.

Cunfer, Geoff. *On the Great Plains: Agriculture and Environment*. College Station: Texas A&M University Press, 2005.

Dalla, Rochelle L., Francisco Villarruel, and Sherman C. Cramer. "Examining Strengths and Challenges of Rapid Rural Immigration." *Great Plains Research* 14 (Fall 2004): 231–51.

Danbom, David B. *Going It Alone: Fargo Grapples with the Great Depression*. St. Paul: Minnesota Historical Society Press, 2005.

De León, Arnoldo. *Mexican Americans in Texas: A Brief History*. Wheeling, Ill.: Harlan Davidson, 1999.

Delinder, Jean Van. "Early Civil Rights in Topeka, Kansas, Prior to the 1954 *Brown* Case." *Great Plains Quarterly* 21 (Winter 2001): 45–61.

Deloria, Vine, Jr. *Behind the Trail of Broken Treaties: An Indian Declaration of Independence*. Austin: University of Texas Press, 1985.

Deloria, Vine, Jr., and Clifford N. Lytle. *American Indians, American Justice*. Austin: University of Texas Press, 1983.

Deutsch, Sarah. *No Separate Refuge: Culture, Class and Gender on an Anglo-Hispanic Frontier in the American Southwest, 1880–1940*. New York: Oxford University Press, 1987.

deWit, Cary W. "Women's Sense of Place on the American High Plains." *Great Plains Quarterly* 21 (Winter 2001): 29–44.

Drake, Brian Allen. "Waving 'A Bough of Challenge': Forestry on the Kansas Grasslands, 1865–1915." *Great Plains Quarterly* 23 (Winter 2003): 19–34.

Droze, Wilmon H. *Trees, Prairies, and People: A History of Tree Planting in the Plains States.* Denton: Texas Woman's University, 1977.

Drummond, Mark A. "Regional Dynamics of Grassland Change in the Western Great Plains." *Great Plains Research* 17 (Fall 2007): 133–44.

Dudziak, Mary L. "The Limits of Good Faith: Desegregation in Topeka, Kansas, 1950–1956." *Law and History Review* 5 (Autumn 1987): 351–91.

Eick, Gretchen Casal. *Dissent in Wichita: The Civil Rights Movement in the Midwest, 1954–72.* Urbana: University of Illinois Press, 2001.

Ellis, Clyde. *To Change Them Forever: Indian Education at the Rainy Mountain Boarding School, 1893–1920.* Norman: University of Oklahoma Press, 1996.

Ellsworth, Scott. *Death in a Promised Land: The Tulsa Race Riot of 1921.* Baton Rouge: Louisiana State University Press, 1982.

Etulain, Richard W. *Re-imagining the Modern American West: A Century of Fiction, History, and Art.* Tucson: University of Arizona Press, 1996.

Fearon, Peter. *Kansas in the Great Depression: Work, Relief, the Dole, and Rehabilitation.* Columbia: University of Missouri Press, 2007.

———. "Ploughshares into Airplanes: Manufacturing Industry and Workers during World War II." *Kansas History* 22 (Winter 1999–2000): 298–314.

Ferrell, John. "Developing the Missouri: South Dakota and the Pick-Sloan Plan." *South Dakota History* 19 (Fall 1989): 306–41.

———. "Missouri Basin Land and Water Control Controversies, 1933–1951." In *Agricultural Legacies: Essays in Honor of Gilbert C. Fite,* edited by R. Alton Lee, 118–42. Vermillion: University of South Dakota Press, 1986.

Fite, Gilbert C. *American Farmers: The New Minority.* Bloomington: Indiana University Press, 1981.

———. "The Nonpartisan League in Oklahoma." *Chronicles of Oklahoma* 24 (Summer 1946): 146–57.

———. *Peter Norbeck: Prairie Statesman.* Columbia: University of Missouri Press, 1948. Reprint, Pierre: South Dakota State Historical Society Press, 2005.

———. "Peter Norbeck and the Defeat of the Non-Partisan League in South Dakota." *Mississippi Valley Historical Review* 33 (September 1946): 218–25.

———. "The Transformation of South Dakota Agriculture: The Effects of Mechanization, 1939–1964." *South Dakota History* 19 (Fall 1989): 279–305.

Fitzgerald, Daniel C. "'We Are All in This Together': Immigrants in the Oil and Mining Towns of Southern Kansas, 1890–1920." *Kansas History* 10 (Spring 1987): 17–28.

Fixico, Donald L. *The Invasion of Indian Country in the Twentieth Century: American Capitalism and Tribal Natural Resources.* Niwot: University Press of Colorado, 1998.

Flores, Dan L. *Caprock Canyonlands: Journeys into the Heart of the Southern Great Plains.* Austin: University of Texas Press, 1990.

———. *The Natural West: Environmental History in the Great Plains and Rocky Mountains.* Norman: University of Oklahoma Press, 2001.

Foley, Neil. *The White Scourge: Mexicans, Blacks and Poor Whites in Texas Cotton Culture.* Berkeley: University of California Press, 1997.

Folson, Burton W. "'Tinkers, Tipplers, and Traitors': Ethnicity and Democratic Reform in Nebraska during the Progressive Era." *Pacific Historical Review* 50, no. 1 (1981): 53–75.

Frank, Thomas. *What's the Matter with Kansas? How Conservatives Won the Heart of America.* New York: Henry Holt, 2004.

Frazier, Ian. *The Great Plains.* New York: Farrar, Straus, Giroux, 1989.

Furdell, William J. "The Great Falls Home Front during World War II." *Montana: The Magazine of Western History* 48 (Winter 1998): 63-75.

Gaber, John, Sharon Gaber, and Jeff Vincent. "An Analysis of Refugee Resettlement Patterns in the Great Plains." *Great Plains Research* 14 (Fall 2004): 165–83.

Giles, Kristy Feldhausen. "A Century of Black Towns in Oklahoma." *Gilcrease Journal* 15, no. 1 (2007): 54–63.

Gilles, Jere Lee, and Michael Dalecki. "Rural Well-Being and Agricultural Change in Two Farming Regions." *Rural Sociology* 53, no. 1 (1988): 40–55.

Gouveia, Lourdes, and Rogelio Saenz. "Global Forces and Latino Population Growth in the Midwest: A Regional and Subregional Analysis." *Great Plains Research* 10 (Fall 2000): 305–28.

Gouveia, Lourdes, and Donald D. Stull. "Dances with Cows: Beefpacking's Impact on Garden City, Kansas, and Lexington, Nebraska." In *Any Way You Cut It: Meat Processing and Small-Town America,* edited by Donald D. Stull, Michael J. Broadway, and David Griffith, 85-107. Lawrence: University Press of Kansas, 1995.

Grant, Kenneth W., Katherine A Spilde, and Jonathan B. Taylor. "Social and Economic Consequences of Indian Gaming in Oklahoma." *American Indian Culture and Research Journal* 28, no. 2 (2004): 97-129.

Grant, Michael Johnston. *Down and Out on the Family Farm: Rural Rehabilitation in the Great Plains, 1929–1945.* Lincoln: University of Nebraska Press, 2002.

Grasrud, Bruce A., and Charles A. Braithwaite. *African Americans on the Great Plains: An Anthology.* Lincoln: University of Nebraska Press, 2009.

Graves, Carl R. "The Right to Be Served: Oklahoma City's Lunch Counter Sit-Ins, 1958-1964." *Chronicles of Oklahoma* 59 (Summer 1981): 152–66.

Graves, Lawrence L., ed. *A History of Lubbock.* Lubbock: West Texas Museum Association, 1962.

Great Plains Committee. *The Future of the Great Plains: Report of the Great Plains Committee.* Washington, D.C.: Government Printing Office, 1936.

Green, Donald E. *Land of the Underground Rain: Irrigation on the Texas High Plains, 1910–1970.* Austin: University of Texas Press, 1973.

Grobsmith, Elizabeth S., and Beth R. Ritter. "The Ponca Tribe of Nebraska: The Process of Restoration of a Federally Terminated Tribe." *Human Organization* 51 (Spring 1992): 1–16.

Grossman, Zoltán. "Cowboy and Indian Alliances in the Northern Plains." *Agricultural History* 77 (Spring 2003): 355–89.

———. "Unlikely Alliances: Treaty Conflicts and Environmental Cooperation between Native America and Rural White Communities." *American Indian Culture and Research Journal* 29, no. 4 (2005): 21–43.

Haley, J. Evetts. *The XIT Ranch of Texas and the Early Days of the Llano Estacado.* Norman: University of Oklahoma Press, 1982.

Hall, Greg. *Harvest Wobblies: The Industrial Workers of the World and Agricultural Laborers in the American West, 1905–1930.* Corvallis: Oregon State University Press, 2001.

Halliburton, R., Jr. "The Tulsa Race War of 1921." *Journal of Black Studies* 2, no. 3 (1972): 333–57.

Handy-Marchello, Barbara. *Women of the Northern Plains: Gender and Settlement on the Homestead Frontier, 1870–1930.* St. Paul: Minnesota Historical Society Press, 2005.

Hargreaves, Mary Wilma M. *Dry Farming in the Northern Great Plains, 1900–1925.* Cambridge: Harvard University Press, 1957.

———. *Dry Farming in the Northern Great Plains: Years of Readjustment, 1920–1990.* Lawrence: University Press of Kansas, 1993.

Harris, Katherine. *Long Vistas: Women and Families on Colorado Homesteads.* Niwot: University Press of Colorado, 1993.

Harvey, Mark W. T. "North Dakota, the Northern Great Plains, and the Missouri Valley Authority." *North Dakota History* 59 (Summer 1992): 28–39.

Harwood, William L. "The Ku Klux Klan in Grand Forks, North Dakota." *South Dakota History* 1 (Fall 1971): 301–35.

Helms, Douglas. "Conserving the Great Plains: The Soil Conservation Service in the Great Plains." *Agricultural History* 64 (Spring 1990): 58–73.

Hinton, Diana Davids, and Roger M. Olien. *Oil in Texas: The Gusher Age, 1895–1945.* Austin: University of Texas Press, 2002.

Holm, Tom. "The Crisis in Tribal Government." In *American Indian Policy in the Twentieth Century,* edited by Vine Deloria Jr., 135–54. Norman: University of Oklahoma Press, 1985.

———. *The Great Confusion in Indian Affairs: Native Americans and Whites in the Progressive Era.* Austin: University of Texas Press, 2005.

Hoover, Herbert T., and Larry J. Zimmerman. *South Dakota Leaders: From Pierre Chouteau, Jr., to Oscar Howe.* Vermillion: University of South Dakota Press, 1989.

Howard, Thomas W., ed. *The North Dakota Political Tradition.* Ames: Iowa State University Press, 1981.

Hoxie, Frederick E. *A Final Promise: The Campaign to Assimilate the Indians, 1880–1920.* Lincoln: University of Nebraska Press, 1984.

Hrebenar, Ronald J., and Clive S. Thomas, eds. *Interest Group Politics in the American West.* Salt Lake City: University of Utah Press, 1987.

———. *Interest Group Politics in the Midwestern States.* Ames: Iowa State University Press, 1993.

Hurt, R. Douglas. *American Agriculture: A Brief History.* Rev. ed. West Lafayette, Ind.: Purdue University Press, 2003.

———. *The Dust Bowl: An Agricultural and Social History.* Chicago: Nelson-Hall, 1981.

———. "Federal Land Reclamation in the Dust Bowl." *Great Plains Quarterly* 6 (Spring 1986): 94–106.

———. "Gaining Control of the Environment: The Morton County Land Utilization Project in the Kansas Dust Bowl." *Kansas History* 19 (Summer 1986): 140–53.

———. *The Great Plains during World War II.* Lincoln: University of Nebraska Press, 2008.

———. *Indian Agriculture in America: Prehistory to the Present.* Lawrence: University Press of Kansas, 1987.

———. "Irrigation in the Kansas Plains since 1930." *Red River Valley Historical Review* 4 (Fall 1979): 64–72.

———. "The National Grasslands: Origin and Development in the Dust Bowl." *Agricultural History* 59 (April 1985): 246–59.

———. "Prices, Payments, and Production: Kansas Wheat Farmers and the Agricultural Adjustment Administration, 1933–1939." *Kansas History* 23 (Spring-Summer 2000): 72–87.

Iber, Jorge, and Arnoldo De León. *Hispanics in the American West.* Santa Barbara, Calif.: ABC Clio, 2006.

Iseminger, Gordon L. "The McIntosh County German Russians: The First Fifty Years." *North Dakota History* 51 (Summer 1988): 4–23.

Isern, Thomas D. "Custom Combining in North Dakota." *North Dakota History* 49 (Spring 1982): 4–11.

———. *Custom Combining on the Great Plains.* Norman: University of Oklahoma Press, 1981.

Iverson, Peter. *Plains Indians of the Twentieth Century.* Norman: University of Oklahoma Press, 1986.

———. *We Are Still Here: American Indians in the Twentieth Century.* Wheeling, Ill.: Harlan Davidson, 1998.

Jessup, Michael M. "Consorting with Blood and Violence: The Decline of the Oklahoma Ku Klux Klan." *Chronicles of Oklahoma* 78 (Fall 2000): 296–315.

Jiménez, Tomás R. "Weighing the Costs and Benefits of Mexican Immigration: The Mexican-American Perspective." *Social Science Quarterly* 88 (September 2007): 599–618.

Juhnke, James C. "Mob Violence and Kansas Mennonites in 1918." *Kansas Historical Quarterly* 43 (Autumn 1977): 334–50.

Kepfield, Sam S. "The 'Liquid Gold' Rush: Groundwater Irrigation and Law in Nebraska, 1900–1993." *Great Plains Quarterly* 13 (Fall 1993): 237–50.

Kinsella, Steven R. *900 Miles from Nowhere: Voices from the Homestead Frontier.* St. Paul: Minnesota Historical Society Press, 2006.

Kraenzel, Carl Frederick. *The Great Plains in Transition.* Norman: University of Oklahoma Press, 1955.

Kromm, David E., and Stephen E. White, eds. *Groundwater Exploitation in the High Plains.* Lawrence: University Press of Kansas, 1992.

Larsen, Lawrence H., Barbara J. Cottrell, Harl A. Dalstrom, and Kay Calamé Dalstrom. *Upstream Metropolis: An Urban Biography of Omaha and Council Bluffs.* Lincoln: University of Nebraska Press, 2007.

Larsen, Lawrence H., and Roger T. Johnson. "Obstacles to Urbanization on the Northern Great Plains of the United States." *North Dakota History* 50 (Summer 1983): 14–22.

Larson, Bruce L. "Kansas and the Nonpartisan League: The Response to the Affair at Great Bend." *Kansas Historical Quarterly* 34 (Spring 1968): 51–71.

Lauck, Jon. *American Agriculture and the Problem of Monopoly: The Political Economy of Grain Belt Farming, 1953–1980.* Lincoln: University Press of Kansas, 2000.

———. "The Corporate Farming Debate in the Post–World War II Midwest." *Great Plains Quarterly* 18 (Spring 1998): 139–53.

———. *Daschle vs Thune: Anatomy of a High-Plains Senate Race.* Norman: University of Oklahoma Press, 2007.

Lawson, Michael L. *Dammed Indians: The Pick-Sloan Plan and the Missouri River Sioux, 1944–1980.* Norman: University of Oklahoma Press, 1982.

Lee, R. Alton. *Farmers vs. Wage Earners: Organized Labor in Kansas, 1860–1960.* Lawrence: University Press of Kansas, 2005.

———. "McCarthyism at the University of South Dakota." *South Dakota History* 19 (Fall 1989): 424–38.

———. "'New Dealers, Fair Dealers, Misdealers, and Hiss Dealers': Karl Mundt and the Internal Security Act of 1950." *South Dakota History* 10 (Fall 1980): 277–90.

Leistritz, F. Larry, Sam Cordes, and Randall S. Sell. "Characteristics of In-Migrants to the Northern Great Plains: Survey Results from Nebraska and North Dakota." *Great Plains Research* 11 (Fall 2001): 275–99.

Leonard, Stephen J. "Denver at War: The Home Front in World War II." *Colorado Heritage*, no. 4 (1987): 30–39.

Leonard, Susan Hautaniemi, and Myron P. Gutman. "Isolated Elderly in the U.S. Great Plains: The Roles of Environment and Demography in Creating a Vulnerable Population." *Annales de Démographie Historique*, no. 2 (2005): 81–108.

Lindgren, H. Elaine. *Land in Her Own Name: Women as Homesteaders in North Dakota.* Norman: University of Oklahoma Press, 1996.

Loconto, David G. "Discrimination against and Adaptation of Italians to the Coal Counties of Oklahoma." *Great Plains Quarterly* 24 (Fall 2004): 249–61.

Lomawaima, K. Tsianina. *They Called It Prairie Light: The Story of Chilocco Indian School, 1898–1933.* Norman: University of Oklahoma Press, 1994.

Longo, Peter J., and David W. Yoskowitz, eds. *Water on the Great Plains: Issues and Policies.* Lubbock: Texas Tech University Press, 2002.

Lonsdale, Richard E., and J. Clark Archer. "Changing Employment Patterns on the Northern and Central Great Plains." *Great Plains Research* 5 (February 1995): 47–70.

Lopach, James L., Margery Hunter Brown, and Richmond L. Clow. *Tribal Government Today: Politics on Montana Indian Reservations.* Boulder, Colo.: Westview Press, 1990.

Lough, D. Keith. "'Hoorah for Integration!': The Adoption of the 1955 Better Schools Amendment." *Chronicles of Oklahoma* 85 (2007): 158–75.

Lowitt, Richard. *American Outback: The Oklahoma Panhandle in the Twentieth Century.* Lubbock: Texas Tech University Press, 2006.

———, ed. *Politics in the Postwar American West.* Norman: University of Oklahoma Press, 1995.

Lowitt, Richard, and Maurice Beasley, eds. *One Third of a Nation: Lorena Hickok Reports on the Great Depression.* Urbana: University of Illinois Press, 1981.

Lu, Max. "Homesteading Redux: New Community Initiatives to Reverse Rural Depopulation in the Great Plains." *Journal of the West* 46 (Winter 2007): 74–80.

Luebke, Frederick C. *Bonds of Loyalty: German Americans and World War I.* DeKalb: Northern Illinois University Press, 1974.

———, ed. *Ethnicity on the Great Plains.* Lincoln: University of Nebraska Press, 1980.

———. "Political Response to Agricultural Depression in Nebraska, 1922." *Nebraska History* 47 (March 1966): 15–55.

Malone, Michael P., and Richard W. Etulain. *The American West: A Twentieth-Century History.* Lincoln: University of Nebraska Press, 1989.

Malone, Michael P., and Richard B. Roeder. *Montana: A History of Two Centuries.* Seattle: University of Washington Press, 1976.

Manley, Robert N. "The Nebraska State Council of Defense and the Non-Partisan League, 1917–1918." *Nebraska History* 43 (December 1962): 229–52.

Marriner, Gerald Lynn. "Klan Politics in Colorado." *Journal of the West* 15 (January 1976): 76–101.

Mason, Richard. "A Handful of Farmers: The South Plains, Politics, and Water." *West Texas Historical Association Year Book* 60 (1984): 19–34.

McBeth, Sally J. "Indian Boarding Schools and Ethnic Identity: An Example from the South Plains Tribes of Oklahoma." *Plains Anthropologist* 28, no. 100 (1983): 119–28.

McCormick, Peter J. "The 1992 Secession Movement in Southwest Kansas." *Great Plains Quarterly* 15 (Fall 1995): 247–58.

McDonnell, Janet A. *The Dispossession of the American Indians, 1887–1934*. Bloomington: Indiana University Press, 1991.

McKenna, Clare V., Jr. "Seeds of Destruction: Homicide, Race, and Justice in Omaha, 1880–1920." *Journal of American Ethnic History* 14, no. 1 (1994): 65–90.

McQuillan, D. Aidan. *Prevailing over Time: Ethnic Adjustment on the Kansas Prairies, 1875–1925*. Lincoln: University of Nebraska Press, 1990.

Metzgar, Joseph V. "Guns and Butter: Albuquerque Hispanics, 1940–1975." *New Mexico Historical Review* 56 (April 1981): 117–39.

Mihelich, Dennis N. "The Lincoln Urban League: The Travail of Depression and War." *Nebraska History* 70 (Winter 1989): 303–16.

———. "World War II and the Transformation of the Omaha Urban League." *Nebraska History* 60 (Fall 1979): 401–23.

Miller, Glenn W., and Jimmy Skaggs, eds. *Metropolitan Wichita: Past, Present, and Future*. Lawrence: Regents Press of Kansas, 1978.

Miller, John E. "Restrained, Respectable Radicals: The South Dakota Farm Holiday." *Agricultural History* 59 (July 1985): 429–47.

Miner, Craig. *Kansas: The History of the Sunflower State, 1854–2000*. Lawrence: University Press of Kansas, 2002.

———. *Next Year Country: Dust to Dust in Western Kansas, 1890–1940*. Lawrence: University Press of Kansas, 2006.

Moakley, Maureen, ed. *Party Realignment and State Politics*. Columbus: Ohio State University Press, 1992.

Monhollon, Rusty L. *This Is America? The Sixties in Lawrence, Kansas*. New York: Palgrave, 2004.

Monhollon, Rusty L., and Kristen Tegtmeier Oertel. "From Brown to Brown: A Century of Struggle for Equality in Kansas." *Kansas History* 27 (Spring–Summer 2004): 116–33.

Montejano, David. *Anglos and Mexicans in the Making of Texas, 1836–1986*. Austin: University of Texas Press, 1987.

———. "The Demise of 'Jim Crow' for Texas Mexicans, 1940–1970." *Aztlán* 16, nos. 1–2 (1987): 27–69.

Moreno, Robert P., Lawrence P. Hernandez, Jennifer D. Schroeder, and Ani Yazedjian. "Rethinking Human Services for Latinos in the Plains: New Paradigms and Recommendations for Practice." *Great Plains Research* 10 (Fall 2000): 387–407.

Morlan, Robert L. *Political Prairie Fire: The Nonpartisan League, 1915–1922*. Minneapolis: University of Minnesota Press, 1955. Reprint, St. Paul: Minnesota Historical Society Press, 1985.

Murdock, Steve H., Don E. Albrecht, Rita R. Hamm, F. Larry Leistritz, and Arlen G. Leholm. "The Farm Crisis in the Great Plains: Implications for Theory and Policy Development." *Rural Sociology* 51, no. 4 (1986): 406–35.

Murray, Robert K. *Red Scare: A Study of National Hysteria, 1919–1920.* New York: McGraw-Hill, 1955.

Nagel, Joane. *American Indian Ethnic Renewal: Red Power and the Resurgence of Identity and Culture.* New York: Oxford University Press, 1997.

Nelson, Paula M. *After the West Was Won: Homesteaders and Town-Builders in Western South Dakota, 1900–1917.* Iowa City: University of Iowa Press, 1986.

———. *The Prairie Winnows Out Its Own: The West River Country of South Dakota in the Years of Depression and Dust.* Iowa City: University of Iowa Press, 1996.

———. "Traveling the Hope Highway: An Intellectual History of the West River Country of South Dakota." In *Centennial West: Essays on the Northern Tier States,* edited by William E. Lang, 244–64. Seattle: University of Washington Press, 1991.

Neugebauer, Janet M. *Plains Farmer: The Diary of William DeLoach.* College Station: Texas A&M University Press, 1991.

Neuringer, Sheldon. "Governor Walton's War on the Ku Klux Klan: An Episode in Oklahoma History." *Chronicles of Oklahoma* 45 (Summer 1967): 153–79.

Nickels, Charlene R., and Frederick A. Day. "Depopulation of the Rural Great Plains Counties of Texas." *Great Plains Research* 7 (Fall 1997): 225–50.

Norris, Kathleen. *Dakota: A Spiritual Geography.* New York: Ticknor and Fields, 1993.

Nugent, Walter. *Into the West: The Story of Its People.* New York: Knopf, 1999.

Olien, Roger M., and Diana Davids Olien. *Oil Booms: Social Change in Five Texas Towns.* Lincoln: University of Nebraska Press, 1982.

O'Neil, Floyd A., June K. Lyman, and Susan McKay, eds. *Wounded Knee, 1973: A Personal Account by Stanley David Lyman.* Lincoln: University of Nebraska Press, 1991.

Opie, John. *Ogallala: Water for a Dry Land.* Lincoln: University of Nebraska Press, 1993.

Oyinlade, A. Olu. "Reverse Migration and Nonmetropolitan Employment in Four Great Plains States, 1970–1980." *Great Plains Research* 13 (Fall 2003): 253–70.

Parish, Arlyn John. *Kansas Mennonites during World War I.* Fort Hays Studies, n.s., History Series no. 4 (Hays: Fort Hays Kansas State College, 1968).

Parton, William J. "Sustainability and Historical Land-Use Change in the Great Plains: The Case of Eastern Colorado." *Great Plains Research* 13 (Spring 2003): 97–125.

Peirce, Neal R. *The Great Plains States: People in the Nine Great Plains States.* New York: W. W. Norton, 1973.

Perkins, Van L. *Crisis in Agriculture: The Agricultural Adjustment Administration and the New Deal.* Berkeley: University of California Press, 1969.

Peterson, Jeffrey M., and Daniel J. Bernarso. "High Plains Regional Aquifer Study Revisited: A 20-Year Retrospective for Western Kansas." *Great Plains Research* 13 (Fall 2003): 179–97.

Philip, Kenneth R. *John Collier's Crusade for Indian Reform, 1920–1954.* Tucson: University of Arizona Press, 1981.

Phillips, Michael. *White Metropolis: Race, Ethnicity, and Religion in Dallas.* Austin: University of Texas Press, 2006.

Piott, Steven L. "The Origins of the Initiative and Referendum in South Dakota: The Political Context." *Great Plains Quarterly* 12 (Summer 1992): 181–93.

Potter, James, Rodrigo Cantarero, X. Winson Yan, Steve Larrick, and Blanca Ramirez-Salazar. "A Case Study of the Impact of Population Influx on a Small Community in Nebraska." *Great Plains Research* 14 (Fall 2004): 219–30.

Prucha, Francis Paul. *The Great Father: The United States Government and the American Indians.* Vol. 2. Lincoln: University of Nebraska Press, 1984.

Quantic, Diane Dufva. *The Nature of Place: A Study of Great Plains Fiction.* Lincoln: University of Nebraska Press, 1995.

Rambow, Charles. "The Ku Klux Klan in the 1920s: A Concentration on the Black Hills." *South Dakota History* 4 (Fall 1984): 63–81.

Ravuri, Evelyn. "Changes in Asian and Hispanic Population in the Cities of the Great Plains, 1990–2000." *Great Plains Research* 13 (Spring 2003): 75–96.

Rees, Amanda, ed. *The Great Plains Region.* Westport, Conn.: Greenwood Press, 2004.

Reese, Linda Williams. *Women of Oklahoma, 1890–1920.* Norman: University of Oklahoma Press, 1997.

Reinhart, Akim D. *Ruling Pine Ridge: Oglala Lakota Politics from the IRA to Wounded Knee.* Lubbock: Texas Tech University Press, 2007.

Remele, Larry. "The North Dakota Farm Strike of 1932." *North Dakota History* 41 (Fall 1974): 4–19.

———. "Power to the People: The Nonpartisan League." In *The North Dakota Political Tradition,* edited by Thomas W. Howard, 66–73. Ames: Iowa State University Press, 1981.

Riley, Glenda. *The Female Frontier: A Comparative View of Women on the Prairie and the Plains.* Lawrence: University Press of Kansas, 1988.

Riney, Scott. *The Rapid City Indian School, 1898–1933.* Norman: University of Oklahoma Press, 1999.

Riney-Kehrberg, Pamela. *Rooted in Dust. Surviving Drought and Depression in Southwestern Kansas.* Lawrence: University Press of Kansas, 1994.

Rios-Bustamante, Antonio. "Wyoming's Mexican Hispanic History." *Annals of Wyoming* 73 (Spring 2001): 2–9.

Ritter, Beth R. "The Politics of Retribalization: The Northern Ponca Case." *Great Plains Research* 4 (August 1994): 237–55.

Robinson, Elwyn B. *History of North Dakota.* Lincoln: University of Nebraska Press, 1966.

Roche, Jeff, ed. *The Political Culture of the New West.* Lawrence: University Press of Kansas, 2008.

Rochín, Refugio I. "Latinos on the Great Plains: An Overview." *Great Plains Research* 10 (Fall 2000): 243–52.

Rodenberger, Lou Halsell, Laura Payne Butler, and Jacqueline Kolosov, eds. *Writing on the Wind: An Anthology of West Texas Women Writers.* Lubbock: Texas Tech University Press, 2005.

Rodgers, Jack W. "The Foreign Language Issue in Nebraska, 1918–1923." *Nebraska History* 39 (March 1958): 1–22.

Rosier, Paul C. "'The Real Indians, Who Constitute the Real Tribe': Class, Ethnicity, and IRA Politics on the Blackfeet Reservation." *Journal of American Ethnic History* 18 (Summer 1999): 3–39.

———. *Rebirth of the Blackfeet Nation, 1912–1954*. Lincoln: University of Nebraska Press, 2001.

Rothman, Hal. "'Same Horse, New Wagon': Tradition and Assimilation among the Jews of Wichita, 1865–1930." *Great Plains Quarterly* 15 (Spring 1995): 83–104.

Sawyer, Darrell R. "Anti-German Sentiment in South Dakota during World War I." *South Dakota Historical Collections* 38 (1976): 439–514.

Scales, James R., and Danney Goble. *Oklahoma Politics: A History*. Norman: University of Oklahoma Press, 1982.

Scammon, Richard M., and Alice V. McGillivray. *America Votes, 17: A Handbook of Contemporary Election Statistics*. Washington, D.C.: Congressional Quarterly, 1987.

Scammon, Richard M., Alice V. McGillivray, and Rhodes Cook. *America Votes, 24: A Handbook of Contemporary American Election Statistics*. Washington, D.C.: Congressional Quarterly, 2004.

Schell, Herbert S. *History of South Dakota*. Lincoln: University of Nebraska Press, 1975. Reprint, Pierre: South Dakota Historical Society Press, 2004.

———. "Widening Horizons at the Turn of the Century: The Last Dakota Land Boom." *South Dakota History* 12 (Summer–Fall 1982): 93–117.

Schlebecker, John T. *Cattle Raising on the Plains, 1900–1960*. Lincoln: University of Nebraska Press, 1963.

Schneiders, Robert Kelley. "Flooding the Missouri River Valley: The Politics of Dam Site Selection and Design." *Great Plains Quarterly* 17 (Fall 1997): 237–49.

———. *Unruly River: Two Centuries of Change along the Missouri*. Lawrence: University Press of Kansas, 1999.

Schruben, Francis W. *Wea Creek to Eldorado: Oil in Kansas, 1860–1920*. Columbia: University of Missouri Press, 1972.

Schulte, Janet E. "'Proving Up and Moving Up': Jewish Homesteading Activity in North Dakota, 1900–1920." *Great Plains Quarterly* 10 (Fall 1990): 228–44.

Schulz, Brian L. "Where Is Main Street? The Commercial Landscape of Four Oklahoma Small Towns." *Chronicles of Oklahoma* 7 (Spring 1993): 88–103.

Schuyler, Michael W. "The Ku Klux Klan in Nebraska, 1920–1930." *Nebraska History* 66 (Fall 1985): 234–56.

Sellars, Nigel Anthony. *Oil, Wheat and Wobblies: The Industrial Workers of the World in Oklahoma, 1905–1930*. Norman: University of Oklahoma Press, 1998.

Sherow, James Earl. *Watering the Valley: Development along the High Plains Arkansas River, 1870–1950*. Lawrence: University Press of Kansas, 1990.

Shortridge, James R. *Cities on the Plains: The Evolution of Urban Kansas*. Lawrence: University Press of Kansas, 2004.

———. "A Cry for Help: KansasFreeland.com." *Geographical Review* 94, no. 4 (2004): 530–40.

———. "Culture Areas in the Central and Northern Great Plains." *Great Plains Quarterly* 8 (Fall 1988): 206–21.

Shover, John L. *Cornbelt Rebellion: The Farmers' Holiday Association*. Urbana: University of Illinois Press, 1965.

Sitler, Harry G., and Melvin D. Skold. "Analysis of Change in the Agrarian Sector of the Great Plains." *Rocky Mountain Social Science Journal* 5, no. 2 (1968): 38–46.

Sloan, William. "Kansas Battles the Invisible Empire: The Legal Ouster of the KKK from Kansas, 1922–1927." *Kansas Historical Quarterly* 40 (Autumn 1974): 393–409.

Smith, Michael M. "Beyond the Borderlands: Mexican Labor in the Central Great Plains, 1900–1930." *Great Plains Quarterly* 1 (Fall 1981): 239–51.

Smith, Robert Bader. *Prohibition in Kansas: A History*. Lawrence: University Press of Kansas, 1986.

Smith, Sherry L., ed. *The Future of the Southern Plains*. Norman: University of Oklahoma Press in cooperation with the William P. Clements Center for Southwest Studies, Southern Methodist University, 2003.

Smith, Wilda M. "A Half Century of Struggle: Gaining Woman Suffrage in Kansas." *Kansas History* 4 (Summer 1981): 74–95.

Sorensen, Willis Conner. "The Kansas National Forest, 1905–1915." *Kansas Historical Quarterly* 35 (Winter 1969): 386–95.

Stock, Catherine McNicol. *Main Street in Crisis: The Great Depression and the Old Middle Class on the Northern Plains*. Chapel Hill: University of North Carolina Press, 1992.

— — . *Rural Radicals: Righteous Rage in the American Grain*. Ithaca, N.Y.: Cornell University Press, 1996.

Stull, Donald D., Michael J. Broadway, and David Griffith, eds. *Any Way You Cut It: Meat Processing and Small Town America*. Lawrence: University Press of Kansas, 1995.

Stull, Donald D., Jerry A. Schultz, and Ken Cadue Sr. "Rights without Resources: The Rise and Fall of the Kansas Kickapoo." *American Indian Culture and Research Journal* 10, no. 2 (1986): 41–59.

Szasz, Margaret Connell. "Listening to the Native Voice: American Indian Schooling in the Twentieth Century." *Montana: The Magazine of Western History* 39 (Summer 1989): 42–53.

Taylor, Quintard, and Shirley Ann Wilson, eds. *African American Women Confront the West, 1600–2000*. Norman: University of Oklahoma Press, 2003.

Thompson, John. *Closing the Frontier: Radical Response in Oklahoma, 1889–1923*. Norman: University of Oklahoma Press, 1986.

Toole, K. Ross. *The Rape of the Great Plains: Northwest America, Cattle and Coal*. Boston: Little, Brown, 1976.

Troutman, John. "The Citizenship of Dance: Politics of Music among the Lakotas, 1900–1924." In *Beyond Red Power: American Indian Politics and Activism since 1900*, edited by Daniel M. Cobb and Loretta Fowler, 93–104. Santa Fe, N.Mex.: School for Advanced Research, 2007.

Vigil, Maurilio E. "Hispanics and the 1996 Presidential Election." *Latino Studies Journal* 9 (Winter 1998): 43–61.

Vinge, David L. "Cultural Values and Economic Development: U.S. Indian Reservations." *Social Science Journal* 19, no. 3 (1982): 87–100.

Vogt, Rebecca, John C. Allen, and Sam Cordes. "Relationship between Community

Satisfaction and Migration Intentions of Rural Nebraskans." *Great Plains Research* 13 (Spring 2003): 63–74.

Wahl, Ana-María, Steven E. Gunkel, and Thomas W. Sanchez. "Death and Disability in the Heartland: Corporate (Mis)Conduct, Regulatory Responses, and the Plight of Latino Workers in the Meatpacking Industry." *Great Plains Research* 10 (Fall 2000): 329–57.

Wahl, Ana-María, Steven E. Gunkel, and Bennie Shobe Jr. "Becoming Neighbors or Remaining Strangers? Latinos and Residential Segregation in the Heartland." *Great Plains Research* 15 (Fall 2005): 297–327.

Walters, Ron. "The Great Plains Sit-In Movement, 1958–60." *Great Plains Quarterly* 16 (Spring 1986): 85–94.

Ward, Carol. "The Importance of Context in Explaining Human Capital Formation and Labor Force Participation of American Indians in Rosebud County, Montana." *Rural Sociology* 63 (September 1998): 451–80.

Warren, Wilson J. *Tied to the Great Packing Machine: The Midwest and Meat Packing.* Iowa City: University of Iowa Press, 2007.

Watrel, Robert H., and Erin Hogan Fouberg. "Presidential Voting Regions of the Northern Great Plains: No Need for an East Dakota and West Dakota." *Great Plains Research* 10 (Spring 2000): 189–213.

Wessel, Thomas R. *Agriculture in the Great Plains, 1876–1936.* Washington, D.C.: Agricultural History Society, 1977.

White, Katherine J. Curtis. "Population Change and Farm Dependence: Temporal and Spatial Variation in the U.S. Great Plains, 1900–2000." *Demography* 45 (May 2008): 363–86.

White, Stephen E. "Ogallala Oases: Water Use, Population Redistribution, and Policy Implications in the High Plains of Western Kansas, 1980–1990." *Annals of the Association of American Geographers* 84 (March 1994): 29–45.

Whiting, Erin Feinauer, Carol Ward, Rita Hiwalker Villa, and Judith Davis. "How Does the New TANF Work Requirement 'Work' in Rural Minority Communities? A Case of the Northern Cheyenne Nation." *American Indian Culture and Research Journal* 29, no. 4 (2005): 95–120.

Wilson, Paul E. *A Time to Lose: Representing Kansas in "Brown v. Board of Education."* Lawrence: University Press of Kansas, 1995.

Wishart, David J., ed. *The Encyclopedia of the Great Plains.* Lincoln: University of Nebraska Press, 2004.

Worster, Donald. *The Dust Bowl: The Southern Plains in the 1930s.* New York: Oxford University Press, 1979.

Wuthnow, Robert. "Depopulation and Rural Churches in Kansas, 1950–1980." *Great Plains Research* 15 (Spring 2005): 117–34.

Wyckoff, William. *Creating Colorado: The Making of a Western American Landscape, 1860–1940.* New Haven, Conn.: Yale University Press, 1999.

Illustration Credits

Map of the boundaries of the Great Plains. Reproduced from *The Encyclopedia of the Great Plains*, edited by David J. Wishart, by permission of the University of Nebraska Press. Copyright © 2004 by the Center for Great Plains Studies.

Map of versions of the Great Plains regional boundary. Reproduced from *The Encyclopedia of the Great Plains*, edited by David J. Wishart, by permission of the University of Nebraska Press. Copyright © 2004 by the Center for Great Plains Studies.

Tar-paper house located in Meade County, South Dakota. Photo courtesy of the State Archives of the South Dakota State Historical Society.

Meadows, South Dakota, preparing for Election Day on November 8, 1910. Photo courtesy of the State Archives of the South Dakota State Historical Society.

A Mexican section crew working for the Atchison, Topeka and Santa Fe Railway near Pauline, Kansas. Courtesy of Kansas State Historical Society.

Klansmen parading down Larimer Street in Denver. Courtesy of the Denver Public Library, Western History Collection.

Arthur C. Townley speaking to a large crowd at Crosby, North Dakota, circa 1920s. Courtesy of the State Historical Society of North Dakota, A2902.

Crowd of Farmers' Holiday sympathizers at an auction in Nebraska. Courtesy of the Nebraska State Historical Society, 7231.

Map of the Dust Bowl depicting the area of the most severe wind erosion. Courtesy of the United States Department of Agriculture.

A "black blizzard" that swept across southwestern Kansas in the 1930s. Courtesy of Kansas State Historical Society.

FERA public works street paving project, Omaha, 1935. Courtesy of the Nebraska State Historical Society, 43657.

FERA sewing center in Fairbury, Nebraska. Courtesy of the Nebraska State Historical Society, 43656.

Mansion Extension Area to the Oklahoma City Oil Field in 1937. Courtesy of the Research Division of the Oklahoma Historical Society.

Prairie States Forest Project, or Shelterbelt Project. Courtesy of the Nebraska State Historical Society, M78-1935.

Women workers on a bomber assembly line in Wichita, Kansas, during World War II. Courtesy of Kansas State Historical Society.

Sit-in demonstration at a Katz Drug Store in Oklahoma City in 1958. Courtesy of the Research Division of the Oklahoma Historical Society.

Map of the Ogallala Aquifer. Reproduced from *The Encyclopedia of the Great Plains*, edited by David J. Wishart, by permission of the University of Nebraska Press. Copyright © 2004 by the Center for Great Plains Studies.

Distinctive circular fields with large sprinklers in the region watered by the Ogallala Aquifer. Courtesy of Valmont Industries, Inc.

Strip mine in North Dakota. Courtesy of the State Historical Society of North Dakota, 10692–Box 12-48.

Map illustrating the Republican vote in presidential elections from 1980 to 2000. Reproduced from *The Encyclopedia of the Great Plains*, edited by David J. Wishart, by permission of the University of Nebraska Press. Copyright © 2004 by the Center for Great Plains Studies.

The sculpting of Mount Rushmore as it neared completion. Photo courtesy of the State Archives of the South Dakota State Historical Society.

Index

Aberdeen, South Dakota, 11, 102
Abilene, Texas, 108, 163, 195
African Americans: and agricultural labor, 42–43; and civil rights demonstrations, 139–42; and Great Depression, 97; and Ku Klux Klan, 47–56; and meatpacking, 42–44; in Nebraska, 44–45; in oil towns, 88; in Oklahoma, 43–44; and Omaha race riot, 45; and politics, 250; and population, 43, 44; and Republican Party, 20; and segregation, 139–45; and Tulsa race riot, 45–46; as voters, 236–37; and women, 44; and World War II, 138–39
Agricultural Adjustment Act, 101
Agricultural Adjustment Administration, 101–2
agricultural labor, 10–12; in Colorado, 34; in Kansas, 10; Mexicano, 33–34; in Nebraska, 10; in South Dakota, 10; during World War II, 169–72; in Wyoming, 34. See also Hispanics; Mexican Americans
agricultural technology, 8, 10, 175–76, 187, 191–92
agriculture: Agricultural Adjustment Act, 101; Agricultural Adjustment Administration, 101–2, 112; and Bankhead-Jones Farm Tenant Act, 103; cattle feeding, 191, 204; Conservation Reserve Program, 162; and custom cutters, 175–76; and dry farming, 8; and Emergency Livestock Purchase Program, 102; and farm consolidation, 176–78; and Farm Credit Administration, 103; and farm population decline, 177; farm prices, 79, 80, 96; and Indians, 59–60, 148–49; irrigation, 198; and labor, 169–72; during 1920s, 91; after 1950, 202–3; during 1980s, 178; and Resettlement Administration, 103, 112, and Soil Bank Program, 162–63; and Soil Conservation and Domestic Allotment Act, 102; and soil conservation since 1960, 193–94; and technology, 8–10, 175–76, 187, 191–92; in Texas Panhandle, 4; and women during World War II, 171–72; during World War II, 166–72
Albuquerque, New Mexico, 39 40, 163, 164, 250
Amarillo: airport, 88; businesses, 4; cattle shipping point, 3, 204; and Civil Works Administration, 97, 98; and Cold War, 161; migration to, 195; railroad center, 3; telephone service, 26–27; white population, 155; women, 4
American Agriculture Movement, 231–33
American Indian Movement, 222–23
American Society of Equity, 74
Arapahos, 61, 62, 121, 149
Asians: in meatpacking, 216

badlands, 246–47
bank failures, 79
Banks, Dennis, 222, 223
Bellevue, Nebraska, 135
Billings, Montana, 29, 34, 163, 208, 251
Bismarck, North Dakota, 149, 215, 248, 251
Blackfeet, 60–62, 120, 121
Black Hills, 44, 246
black towns, 44, 145–46
bonanza farms, 10
Borger, Texas, 86–87
braceros, 170–71
Brown v. Board of Education, 142–43
Burke Act, 60

Campbell, Hardy Webster, 8
Cather, Willa, xiv, 242–44
cattle feeding, 191, 204
Cheyenne, Wyoming, 29, 163, 164
Cheyenne River Reservation: and Civilian Conservation Corps Indian Division, 116; and Indian Reorganization Act, 120, 121; and Pick-Sloan Plan, 184, 185, 186
Cheyennes, 61, 62, 149
Chilocco Indian School, 56, 57, 58, 224
Choctaw, 149, 228
Civilian Conservation Corps, 98; and Indian Emergency Conservation Work, 116–17
coal industry, 163, 208–10, 249
Cold War, 159–62
Collier, John, 115, 117; and Indian Reorganization Act, 118–19, 121
Colorado: Dust Bowl origins, 85; and federal spending, 211; and German Russians, 42, 47; and Germans during World War I, 66–67; and Ku Klux Klan, 53–55; and Mexican American labor, 34; and Mexican population, 33; and Ogallala Aquifer, 188; Red Scare in, 73; and state politics, 258; and urban population increase, 25; Women's Committee of the State Council of Defense, 67. *See also* Denver, Colorado
Colstrip, Montana, 208
Comanches, 120, 121
Crow, 152, 208, 231
Crow Creek Reservation, 117, 120, 184, 185, 186
custom cutters, 175–76

Dallas: and corporate development, 164; and economic development, 164, 251; as international city, 251; population, 28, 44, 250; and segregation, 250; and World War II, 128, 136, 250
Daschle, Tom, 252, 256
Democratic Party, 30, 89, 90, 122, 153–55; and Latinos, 237; in 1950s, 157; in Oklahoma, 158; and Progressive Movement, 30; in South Dakota, 158; in Wyoming, 158. *See also* state politics
Denver, Colorado: African American population, 44; and corporate development, 250; and economic development, 164, 251; and growth, 250, 251; and population, 29, 250
Dismal River Forest Reserve, 23
Dodge City, Kansas, 163, 196, 204, 236
Dole, Robert (Bob), 252
dry farming, 8
dry farming congresses, 8–9
Dust Bowl, 91–96; origins, 85–86; and population loss, 94–96

education: Indian schools, 56–59, 224–25; one-room country schools, 27; and teachers' salaries, 27
El Dorado, Kansas, 27, 39, 41
Ellis, Kansas, 98
Ellis County, Kansas, 42, 69
Emergency Livestock Purchase Program, 102
Enlarged Homestead Act, 9–10

Fargo, North Dakota, 100, 164
Farm Bureau, 255, 257
Farm Credit Administration, 103
Farmers Educational and Cooperative Union, 17
Farmers' Holiday Association, 81–85
Farmers Union, 17–18, 80, 179, 182; in Colorado, 258; in North Dakota, 255; in Oklahoma, 18
Farm Security Administration, 103
Five Civilized Tribes, 120
forestry, 21–26. *See also* Shelterbelt Project
Fort Belknap Reservation, 120, 229
Fort Berthold Reservation, 185, 186
Fort Peck Reservation, 221, 231
Fort Worth: and growth, 250–51; population, 28, 250; and World War II, 128

Frazier, Lynn J., 75, 76, 125–27
Fremont, Nebraska, 51, 52

Garden City, Kansas, 26, 191, 196, 204–5, 221; and Dust Bowl, 93–94; as trade center, 236
Garden City Forest Reserve, 25, 26
Garnett, Kansas, 27, 40
German Russians, 41–42
Germans: and language instruction, 67; and Lutheran church, 66, 68; and newspapers, 65, 67; and violence, 68, 70; during World War I, 61–72. *See also* Mennonites
Gillette, Wyoming, 163, 209, 249
Glenn L. Martin Company, 131, 135
Grand Forks, North Dakota, 55, 211
Grand Island, Nebraska, 51, 128
Great Depression, 96–104; and federal expenditures in 1990s, 209–12; and federal programs, success of, 122–23; labor strikes, 100; and Latino women, 97
Great Plains: aging population of, 195, 198, 248; agriculture in 1920s, 78–80, 85–86; agriculture in 1930s, 85–86; bank failures, 79; cattle feeding, 204, 248; cities in 1920s, 89; conservative politics, 237; definition of, xi–xii; Dust Bowl origins, 85–86; and dust storms during 1950s, 173–74; economic development, 164, 165, 249–51, 259; and federal spending, 162, 209–12; Great Plains Committee, xi; image of, 243–45; and Latinos, 204–5; and meatpacking, 204–6; and Mennonites, 69–71; Mexican migration to, 32–33; mountain ranges in, xiii; national politics in 1920s, 69, 89–90; national politics 1964 to 2000, 240–41; Ogallala Aquifer, 248–49; out migration, 89, 248; political culture, 252–58; population, 1900 to 1920, 28, 30, 89; population, 1940 to 1970, 163; population decline, 195–96, 199, 200–201, 213, 241 260; population increase, 199; population increase in metropolitan counties, 200–201; population increase in Ogallala region, 196–98, 202–3; and presidential elections, 153–54, 238–40; refugees, 203–4; and religion, 258–59; and segregation, 25; social life,

27; in Texas Panhandle, 204; tourism, 245–47; urbanization, 249–50. *See also* women
Guymon, Oklahoma, 191, 205

Haskell Indian Nations University, 224
Hays, Kansas, 2, 26, 94
heirship lands, 60, 118, 148
Hispanics: definition of, 265n1; and Democratic Party, 252; and discrimination, 33, 37; and identity, 32, 35; and migration, 251; in New Mexico, 32; and oil industry, 207; and politics, 250–51; in Texas, 32, and World War II, 138. *See also* Latinos; Mexican Americans; Mexicanos; Mexicans
homesteaders: average age, 7; on Brulé Reservation, 2; in Colorado, 1, 6; Jewish, 38–39; and nationality, 6, 7; in New Mexico, 3; in North Dakota, 1, 5–7; in Oklahoma, 2–3; in South Dakota, 1–2, 4; success rates, 6, 7; in Texas, 3, 8; and women, 5–8; in Wyoming, 6
House Concurrent Resolution, 150, 153
Hutterites, 72. *See also* Mennonites

Independent Voters Association, 76
Indian Emergency Conservation Work, 116–17
Indian Gaming Regulatory Act, 227–28
Indian New Deal, 115–22
Indian Reorganization Act, 118–22
Indians: and agriculture, 59–60, 148–49; allotment policy, 117–18, 121; casinos, 227–28; dancing, 61–62; economic development, 152–53, 226–31; economic problems in 1970s, 222; and heirship lands, 60, 118, 148; and Indian Reorganization Act, 118–22; natural resources, 121, 208–9, 230–31; New Deal, 115–22; and oil, 61; pan identity, 57–58; per capita income, 122; and Pick-Sloan Plan, 184–86; and politics, 60–61, 158, 222–24, 239–40; schools, 56–57, 224–25; and termination, 149–52; urban population, 228; and Wheeler-Howard Act, 118–22
Indian Self-Determination and Education Assistance Act, 225–26
Industrial Workers of the World, 11, 12, 73

irrigation, 186–91. *See also* Ogallala Aquifer
Italians: in Albuquerque, 39–40, 41

Jewish Agriculturalists' Aid Society
    (JAAS), 38
Jews, 38, 39, 41

Kansas: agriculture during World War II,
    168–69; Dust Bowl, 85–86, 93–96; and
    federal spending, 209–12; forestry in,
    25–26; Germans in World War I, 64;
    irrigation, 187, 191–92; Italians in oil
    fields, 40; Jews in, 39; and the Ku Klux
    Klan, 49–51; meatpacking, 220; Men-
    nonites in, 70–71; Mexican population
    in, 33; and Nonpartisan League, 77;
    and Ogallala Aquifer, 188, 191–92; oil
    industry in, 27–28, 87; population loss
    1950–1990, 195, 199; and Progressive
    Movement, 14–15; and prohibition,
    17; and segregation, 139–40, 142–43,
    146–48; and Shelterbelt Project, 106,
    108–10; sit-in demonstrations, 139–40;
    state politics, 253–54; tax revolt,
    234–36; telephones, 26; urban popula-
    tion growth, 250; Volga Germans in,
    42; water politics; 155–56; women's
    suffrage, 14
Kansas City, Kansas, 36–37, 42–43, 253
Kansas National Forest, 25–26
Kickapoos, 225–26
Kinkaid Act, 9, 24
Kiowa-Comanche-Apache Reservation, 56
Kiowas, 61, 120, 121
Ku Klux Klan, 47–56

Lakotas, 61–62, 223, 224
Land Utilization Projects, 112–15
Langer, William, 75, 156, 162
Langston, Oklahoma, 44
Langston University, 44
Latinos: definition of, 265n1; and
    demographic change, 155, 221, 251;
    and Great Depression, 97; and im-
    migration to Great Plains, 204–5; and
    meatpacking, 191, 206, 216–20; in
    Omaha, 220–21; and politics, 237, 239;
    population increase, 216–19; social
    and economic influences of, 217–21
    and towns, 216–17, 220–22; as voters,
    236–37; women, 97. *See also* Hispanics;
    Mexican Americans

Lawrence, Kansas, 139, 146–48
Lawrence League for the Practice of
    Democracy, 146–47
League of Women Voters, 258
Lemke, William, 76
Lexington, Nebraska, 204, 205, 216–17
Liberal, Kansas, 196, 202, 204–5
Lincoln, Nebraska, 52, 106, 250, 251
literature, 242–45
Little Missouri Land Utilization Project,
    113–14
Loriks, Emil, 84–85
Lower Brulé Reservation, 116, 184, 185,
    186
Lubbock, Texas: and Cold War, 162;
    movement to, 195, 201, 248; popula-
    tion, 89, 155, 163, 215; and segregation,
    250

McGovern, George, 162, 177, 252, 256
Means, Russell, 222–23
meatpacking: and ethnicity, 37, 42–43;
    and Ogallala Aquifer, 191, 204–6; and
    race, 44–45
Mennonites, 69–71. *See also* Hutterites
Meriam Report, 63, 118
Mexican Americans, 32–34; and Great
    Depression, 97; and meatpacking, 37,
    191; and migration, 32–33; and segrega-
    tion, 137–39; and women, 34; during
    World War II, 137–38, 170–71; *See
    also* Hispanics; Latinos; Mexicanos;
    Mexicans
Mexicanos: and agricultural labor, 33–35,
    37; definition of, 265n1; and meat pack-
    ing, 37; and migration, 32–33; and oil
    industry, 35; and population, 36; and
    railroad labor, 35–36; *See also* Hispan-
    ics; Latinos; Mexican Americans;
    Mexicans
Mexicans: and agricultural labor, 32–35,
    37; and barrios, 33; and meat packing,
    37, 42; and migration, 33; and oil in-
    dustry, 33; and railroad labor. *See also*
    Hispanics; Latinos; Mexicanos
Midland, Texas: Mexican population, 88;
    as oil town, 86, 163, 207, 249; popula-
    tion, 207
Mills Land Utilization Project, 114
Missouri Valley Authority, 181–83
Montana: and bank failures, 79; coal
    industry, 163, 208; and federal spend-

ing, 211; German Russians in, 42; Germans during World War I, 68; and Mexican American agricultural labor, 34; oil industry, 208; and outmigration, 89; politics, 90, 158–59; population increase 1970–2000, 197; Progressive Movement in, 14; State Council of Defense, 69; state politics, 257

Montana Stock Growers Association, 257

Morton County, Kansas, 234; and Land Utilization Project, 112, 114–15

Mundt, Karl E., 159–62

Murray, James E., 151–52

Native Americans. *See* Indians

Nebraska: African Americans in, 44; agricultural labor in, 10; bank failures, 79; and Cold War, 161; and defense industries, 128, 130–31; Farmers' Holiday Association, 81–82; and federal spending, 211–12; forestry in, 21–25; and Germans during World War I, 64–66, 68; irrigation, 188; and isolationism, 126–27; Ku Klux Klan, 51–53; labor politics, 156; meatpacking, 205, 220; and Mexican labor, 37; national forest, 23–25; Nonpartisan League, 76–77; and Ogallala Aquifer, 188; population increase in 1990s, 218; population loss, 195, 199; Progressive Movement in, 16; and Shelterbelt Project, 106; during World War II, 128, 130–32, 167–70

Nebraska National Forest, 24–25

New Mexico: and federal spending, 210–11; Italians in, 39–40; and Ogallala Aquifer, 188, 192; oil industry, 86; state politics, 254, 257; urban population increase, 250; women, 40, 178

Niobrara Forest Reserve, 23

Nonpartisan League, 74–78, 255

Norbeck, Peter, 77

Norris, George, 13, 128, 254

Norris, Kathleen, 242–45

North Dakota: bank failures in, 79; coal industry, 163, 208; and Cold War, 161; dust storms, 96; and economic development, 164; Farmers' Holiday Association in, 82, 84; and federal spending, 210–11; German Russians in, 41–42; grasshoppers, 96; and Great Depression, 97, 98; Independent Voters Association, 76; and Ku Klux Klan,

55; Mexican labor in, 37; Nonpartisan League in, 74–77; and oil industry, 208; out-migration, 89; political conservatism, 157; politics for economic development, 157; politics in 1920s, 89; population loss, 195, 199; Progressive Movement in, 16; prohibition in, 17; Shelterbelt Project in, 106, 108, 110; and state politics, 255; urban population increase, 250

Northern Cheyennes, 208, 226–27, 230–31

Northern Pacific Railway, 2, 257

Northern Poncas, 150–51

North Platte, Nebraska, 24, 52

Norwegians, 17, 41, 76

Nye, Gerald P., 125–27, 180

Odessa, Texas, 86, 163, 202, 207

Ogallala Aquifer, 186–92; and meatpacking, 191; and population increase, 196; and refugees, 203–4; and social stability, 202–3

Oglalas, 59, 222–23

Oglala Sioux Nation, 223

oil industry, 206–8, 249; in Kansas, 27–28; in Oklahoma, 28; in Texas Panhandle, 28, 86–88, 163; and towns, 27–28, 86, 88, 163, 207, 249. *See also* Kansas; Oklahoma; North Dakota

Oklahoma: African Americans in, 43–44; African American voters in, 20; agriculture during World War II, 169; casinos, 227–28; election in 1920, 20; and Farmers Union, 18; farm tenancy in, 18–19; and federal spending, 210; and German Russians, 42; and Germans during World War I, 69; and hog confinements, 205–6; irrigation, 188; Italian coal miners in, 41; Ku Klux Klan in, 48–49; meatpacking, 205; and Mexican labor, 37; Nonpartisan League in, 78; and Ogallala Aquifer, 192, 198; oil industry, 27–28, 87, 88, 208; politics for economic development, 157; population, 28, 163, 195, 218, 250; Red Scare in, 73; and segregation, 139–42, 144–45; Shelterbelt Project in, 106, 108–10; sit-in demonstrations, 139–42; Socialist Party in, 18–20; state politics, 255; women in, 205–6

Oklahoma City: and Cold War, 161–62; and economic development, 251; and growth, 250; and World War II, 128–29

Oklahoma Indian Welfare Act, 120

Omaha: and Cold War, 161; and economic development; and ethnicity, 42, 259; and growth, 250, 259; and Latinos, 220–21, 28; and meatpacking, 42–43; population, 163; and race riot, 45; as railroad city, 28; Union League in, 138–39

O'Mahoney, Joseph C., 151, 252

Osages, 61

Palmer raids, 72–73

penny auctions, 82

Permian Basin, 86, 88, 202, 206–8. *See also* oil industry

Personal Responsibility and Work Opportunity Reconciliation Act, 226, 229

Pick-Sloan Plan, 179–86

Pierre, South Dakota, 3

Pine Ridge Council, 222–23

Pine Ridge Reservation, 149, 152, 223; and Civilian Conservation Corps Indian Division, 116–17; and Indian Reorganization Act, 121; schools, 59

Plemons Four Section Act (Texas), 3–4

politics: national, 89–90; 1900 to 1912, 30; in 1920, 69; 1932 to 1940, 122–23, 153; in 1960, 154; in 1996, 239, 240; state, 252–58

Prairie States Forestry Project, 11–12. *See also* Shelterbelt Project

presidential elections, 153, 154. *See also* politics

Progressive Movement, 12–17; in Kansas, 14; in Montana, 14; in Nebraska, 13; in North Dakota, 16; in South Dakota, 12–13; and suffrage, 12, 14–16

Public Works Administration, 100

railroads, 213, 249; and African Americans, 44; in Amarillo, 3; and dry farming, 8–9, 11; and Omaha, 28; and politics, 257; and settlers, 7, 35; and shipping, 29; significance of, 2–3; and T-towns, 29

Rainy Mountain Indian School, 56

Rankin, Jeannette, 15–16

Rapid City, South Dakota, 102, 201, 215

Red Scare, 72–73

refugees, 203–4

religion, 214, 258–59

Republican Party, 12, 30, 122, 153–55; and conservatism, 237; and Ku Klux Klan, 53–54; in Oklahoma, 157; and Progressive Movement, 12–13. *See also* politics

Rosebud Reservation, 116–17, 120, 121, 148, 152

Salina, Kansas, 134–35

San Antonio: and Cold War, 161; and corporate development, 250; and Great Depression, 97; as an international city, 251–52; population in, 28, 163, 250; segregation in, 137, 250

Sand Hills Reconnaissance Survey Team, 23

Sandoz, Marie, 243, 244

schools: country, 27; Indian, 56–59, 224–25. *See also* education

Sears Roebuck sale, 82

settlement, 1–4, 29–30. *See also* homesteaders

Shelterbelt Project, 104–12. *See also* Prairie States Forestry Project

Sioux: and conservation, 116–17; and Indian Reorganization Act, 120, 121; and schools, 59; and Wounded Knee, 222–24. *See also* Lakotas; Oglalas

Sioux Falls, South Dakota, 67, 83, 259

Sisseton Reservation, 117, 120

Socialist Party, 18–20

Soil Bank Program, 162–63

Soil Conservation, 192–94. *See also* Shelterbelt Project

Soil Conservation and Domestic Allotment Act, 102

Soil Conservation Service, 103, 113–14; and Shelterbelt Project, 11–12

South Dakota: agricultural labor in, 10, 171; bank failures, 79; and Cold War, 159–61; and drought, 123; dust storms, 96; Farmers' Holiday Association, 82–83; and federal spending, 210–12; and foreign born, 29; Germans during World War I, 67–68; and Great Depression, 98–99; Ku Klux Klan, 55; Nonpartisan League, 77–78; and Ogallala Aquifer, 188; politics for economic development, 158; politics in 1920s, 89; population, 89, 195, 199; Progres-

sive Movement in, 12, 16; and Rural
Electrification Administration, 159;
and Shelterbelt Project, 106, 108, 110;
state politics, 255–56; urban population
increase, 250; and women, 171; and
World War II, 168, 170
Southwest Indian Polytechnic Institute,
224
Standing Rock Reservation: and casino,
227; and conservation, 116–17; and
dancing, 62; and Indian Reorganization Act, 120, 121; and Pick-Sloan Plan,
185, 186

telephone service, 26–27
termination, 149–52, 224
Texas: agriculture during World War II,
169; and cattle feeding, 204; Cold War
in Panhandle, 161; and federal spending, 210–11; German Russians in, 42;
homesteading in Panhandle, 3; irrigation, 189; Ku Klux Klan in, 47–48;
Mexican Americans in, 32–34; migration to Panhandle, 195, and Ogallala
Aquifer, 188, 192, outmigration, 207;
Panhandle oil industry, 28, 86–88;
Panhandle population in 1910, 3; and
Shelterbelt Project, 106, 100, 110,
telephones, 26–27; urban population
growth, 195. *See also* individual cities
Thune, John, 252
Topeka, Kansas, 17, 142–43, 253
tourism, 245–47
Townley, Arthur C., 74, 76, 78
Trinidad, Colorado, 32, 34
Tulsa, Oklahoma: and corporate develop-
ment, 250; and growth, 250; oil town,
28; and population, 250; race riot,
45–46, 48

University of Kansas, 146
University of Nebraska, 68–69
University of Oklahoma: and segregation,
144–45
urban growth, 89; during World War II,
135, 136
Urban League, 138–39

Wheeler-Howard Act, 118–22
White, William Allen, 16, 50–51
Wichita, Kansas: and corporate development, 250; and economic development,
250; and growth, 136, 201, 250, 253,
259; Jews in, 38–39; population, 28,
250; and water, 156; and World War II,
128–31, 136
Wichita Falls, Texas, 106, 250
Williston Basin, 208
women: African American, 44, 97; and
agricultural labor, 171–72; in agriculture in 1980s, 178–79; in Amarillo, 4;
German Russian, 6; homesteaders,
5–8; Italian, 40, 97; and Ku Klux Klan,
52, 54; Latino, 97; in meatpacking,
205; Mexican American, 34, 88; and
oil industry, 88; in politics, 251; Scandinavian, 6; and suffrage, 12, 14–16; as
voters, 236; and Women's Land Army,
171, 172; and World War I, 67; and
World War II, 128–32, 137–38
Women's Land Army, 171–72
Works Progress Administration, 97, 98,
100, 111
World War I, 64–72
World War II: and agriculture, 166–72;
and defense industries, 127–32, 136;
and housing, 134–35; and isolationism,
125–27; rationing, 133–34, 136–37;
scrap drives, 132–33; and urbanization,
135. *See also* women
Wounded Knee, 222–24
Wyoming: coal industry, 163, 208–9; and
federal spending, 210–11; German
Russians in, 42; Mexican Americans
in, 34; and Mexican labor, 37; and
Ogallala Aquifer, 188; political conservatism, 158; population, 192, 197; and
state politics, 257–58
Wyoming Stock Growers Association, 253,
258

XIT Ranch, 4

Yankton Reservation, 117, 120, 185, 186
York, Nebraska, 51, 52

About the Author

R. Douglas Hurt is a professor and head of the Department of History at Purdue University. He is a Fellow of the Agricultural History Society. He has served as the president of the Agricultural History Society, as editor of *Agricultural History*, and as director of the Graduate Program in Agricultural History and Rural Studies at Iowa State University. He completed his Ph.D. with a specialty on the history of the Great Plains at Kansas State University. His books include *The Great Plains during World War II*; *The Indian Frontier, 1763–1846*; *The Ohio Frontier: Crucible of the Old Northwest, 1720–1830*; and *Agriculture and Slavery in Missouri's Little Dixie*.